for AQA

Psychology A Level Year 2

Revision Guide

Mike Cardwell

Rachel Moody

Changes to the AQA Psychology specification (Version 1.1) and support for these changes

AQA released Version 1.1 of their A Level Psychology specification in June 2019. Most of the changes are very minor. Please refer to the AQA website for more information.

To support you with these changes, we have updated some sections within the optional topic of Gender and made some changes to the optional topic of Forensic psychology, as outlined below.

4.3.3: Chapter 4 Gender: AQA has replaced 'Gender Identity Disorder' with 'Gender dysphoria' to reflect changes made to the DSM.

To support you with this change, we have amended the terminology throughout the book.

4.3.9: Chapter 10 Forensic psychology: The first bullet point in this section relating to problems in defining crime and ways of measuring crime has been removed from the specification. This means that students **will no longer be examined** on this.

To support you with this change, the content on Defining and measuring crime has been removed from the book. There is additional support for training yourself to be an examiner on p.226.

OXFORD
UNIVERSITY PRESS

OXFORD
UNIVERSITY PRESS

Great Clarendon Street, Oxford, OX2 6DP, United Kingdom

Oxford University Press is a department of the University of Oxford. It furthers the University's objective of excellence in research, scholarship, and education by publishing worldwide. Oxford is a registered trade mark of Oxford University Press in the UK and in certain other countries

First published in 2019

Revised impression published in 2020

British Library Cataloguing in Publication Data
Data available

ISBN 978-019-844488-6

10 9 8 7 6

Paper used in the production of this book is a natural, recyclable product made from wood grown in sustainable forests. The manufacturing process conforms to the environmental regulations of the country of origin.

Printed and bound by CPI Group (UK) Ltd, Croydon, CR0 4YY

Acknowledgements

Cover photo: Chris Cardwell

Artworks: Oscar at Kevin Jones Artists & QBS Learning

Photos: p31 (R): Skip Odonnell/iStockphoto; **p31 (L):** Skip Odonnell/iStockphoto; **p38:** TIMOTHY A. CLARY/AFP/Getty Images; **p153:** History and Art Collection/Alamy Stock Photo; **p154:** William Lovelace/Daily Express/Hulton Archive/Getty Images; **p165:** Professor Zimbardo; All other photos are from Shutterstock.

How to use this book

The Complete Companions for AQA Psychology Revision Guides offer you condensed versions of the bestselling Student Books by Mike Cardwell and Cara Flanagan along with the structured revision approach of Recap, Apply and Review to prepare you for exam success. Although this Revision Guide draws solely on the material in *The Complete Companions Year 2 Student Book*, it is a standalone resource and so will be invaluable for all students taking Paper 3 of the AQA A Level Psychology exam.

RECAP Each 'Recap' section provides you with easy-to-digest bullets for the AO1 (description) you need to know for the exam. The material is stripped down to make it straightforward to revise from without sacrificing the detail necessary for full marks. This makes it easier to reproduce in an exam. The AO3 (evaluation) material is also condensed down to the right amount necessary for elaborated discussion/evaluation points in the exam. We have split each AO3 point into Point, Elaboration/Evidence and Conclusion/Link back format that makes each point clearer and more focused.

APPLY These 'Apply it' sections give you some essential practice for the AO2 (application) questions for each topic area. On each topic spread we have provided you with a worked example of an application question relating to that topic as well as a second application question for you to try yourself. We also provide sample AO2 (research methods) questions in the context of each topic for you to try. You can then compare your own answers with the answers we have provided on pages 227–240. A unique feature of this book is the 'How do I answer… questions?'. We show you how to structure responses to all the most common forms of question you are likely to encounter in your exams.

REVIEW Throughout each chapter you can review and reflect on the work you have done, and find advice on how to further refresh your knowledge and prepare for your exams.

Issues/Debates
You will also find some 'Issues and Debates' points scattered through the book. You will find these examples useful when you take Paper 3 of the AQA A Level Psychology exam. Issues and Debates are also valuable for developing effective discussion points in essays in Paper 1 and Paper 2.

Contents

	RECAP	APPLY	REVIEW

RECAP   APPLY   REVIEW

Chapter 10 Forensic psychology

Chapter 11 Addiction

RECAP

AO1 Description

Content analysis

- **Content analysis** is an indirect form of observational study, analysing materials produced by people, e.g. books, films, photographs.
- The procedure involves:
  - > Deciding on a sample, e.g. TV ads over a one-week period.
  - > **Coding** the data using behavioural categories, e.g. men or women using household products.
  - > Recording the occurrences of each coding category.
- In a quantitative analysis, the instances of each coding category are tallied, and can then be represented using descriptive statistics and graphs.
- In a qualitative analysis, examples in each category are described.

Thematic analysis

- **Thematic analysis** is a type of qualitative content analysis, which summarises the data descriptively. It aims to identify underlying themes in the data, rather than spotting obvious words or phrases.
- Thematic analysis aims to allow themes to emerge from the data and maintain the participants' perspectives.
- The steps include:
  - > Read and reread the data transcripts (or watch and re-watch a video).
  - > Break the data into meaningful units.
  - > Assign a label or code to each unit.
  - > Combine codes into larger themes.
  - > Ensure that these emerging themes represent all of the data.

Sniffer dogs are trained to seek out particular chemical compounds – content analysis counts occurrences of particular words or categories.

AO3 Evaluation / Discussion

A strength of content analysis is its high ecological validity…

| It is based on observations produced by people in their real lives. | This includes newspapers, books, paintings, photos, films, and videos. | These communications can be current and relevant to a specific research question. |

Content analysis is replicable…

| Materials are often publicly available and can be accessed by another researcher. | This means that the observations can be tested for inter-rater reliability. | If several researchers identify similar themes or occurrences of coding categories, the findings are reliable. |

Content analysis oversimplifies the data…

| A criticism of content analysis is that it summarises rich qualitative data in a simplified form. This means that the data loses its detailed descriptive flavour. | In addition, the observer cannot be truly objective, and may impose meaning on people's behaviour because of preconceptions. | So the coding categories may lack validity, as they do not fully represent people's understanding of their own behaviour or creative output. |

Thematic analysis is very time-consuming and painstaking to carry out…

| This is because it involves examining and re-examining huge amounts of data, with themes emerging iteratively. | This enables the data to be summarised and conclusions to be drawn from qualitative data. | But it is not always suitable when researchers have limited time available. |

Issues/Debates
Idiographic or nomothetic approach to research. Thematic analysis is an example of the idiographic approach.

 **APPLY**

A02: An example

SCENARIO A researcher analysed children's TV programmes over a period of a week to see what kinds of programmes were available.

Explain how the researcher could have used content analysis to analyse the data he collected. **(4 marks)**

ANSWER The researcher could choose a children's channel to watch for the week. They could devise a list of categories for the programmes to be put into such as educational, comedy or cartoon. They could then watch some of each programme and use a tally chart to categorise it. This would be repeated for each programme that week.

A02: Three for you to try

1. A psychology student wants to investigate the potential gender stereotypes presented in Disney films.

   a. **Suggest three items that could be used as coding categories in this study. (3 marks)**

   b. **Explain how the student could carry out this quantitative content analysis. (4 marks)**

   c. **Identify one issue of reliability in this research and describe how you could deal with it. (3 marks)**

   d. **Identify one issue of validity in this research and describe how you could deal with it. (3 marks)**

   e. **Explain how qualitative data could be included in the analysis. (2 marks)**

2. **One piece of research carried out in the UK used content analysis to study some children's drawings, and found that children draw more complex pictures of Santa before Christmas than afterwards.**

In this study, what is the complexity of the picture of Santa? (Tick one box only.)

A The independent variable ☐

B The dependent variable ☐

C The coding category ☐

D The sample ☐

3. **Match up the terms with the explanations.**

1	Coding	A	Indirect observation involving counting occurrences of particular behaviours
2	Sampling	B	Counting up occurrences of each coding category
3	Tallying	C	A type of qualitative analysis which allows themes to emerge from the data
4	Quantitative content analysis	D	Labelling data according to categories or themes
5	Thematic analysis	E	Selecting the content which will be analysed

How do I answer... questions on content analysis and thematic analysis?

Q1: How would the researchers carry out a content analysis of the interview transcripts to explore parents' beliefs about their children's anxiety? **(4 marks)**

Q2: How would the researcher carry out a thematic analysis of the interview transcripts? **(2 marks)**

Be clear about the difference between these two methodologies.

For **Q1**, content analysis is a four-step process:

- Read the transcripts.
- Identify potential categories relating to the research aim (in this case, parents' beliefs about their children's anxiety).
- Suggest two or three categories, e.g. how anxiety affects their sleep, anxiety about exams, anxiety about relationships.

Read the transcripts again, tally the number of examples in each category.

Thematic analysis looks for emergent themes relating to a research question. Do **not** refer to predetermined categories, codes or themes, or talk about counting or tallying frequencies – this would be content analysis, not thematic analysis. So for **Q2**, you need to explain the process:

- Read the transcripts and mark up with codes to summarise themes.
- Review the transcripts and codes, look for emergent overall themes linked to the research aim (in this case, parents' beliefs about their children's anxiety).

REVIEW

You could be asked to design a study which uses content analysis or thematic analysis, or there could be a shorter question worth 2 or 4 marks asking about the process in relation to a specific piece of research. Remember to apply the general steps to the specific study. Four-mark questions on content analysis are fairly common: can you recite the four steps of content analysis? Can you expand our suggested answer on thematic analysis to a 4-mark answer? Keep practising until the steps trip off your tongue or pen.

Case studies

A01 Description

- **Case studies** are a detailed study of a single individual, institution or event.

- A variety of research techniques can be used to gather data, such as observations, interviews, and cognitive or personality tests.

- They provide a rich, detailed description of a person's life. Case studies can be longitudinal, following the individuals over time.

- Findings are presented in a qualitative way, being organised into themes, but can also include quantitative data like scores from tests.

Case studies make use of a variety of research methods.

- **Individuals:**

  > Henry Molaison (HM) – His hippocampus was removed to reduce epileptic seizures, resulting in an inability to form new memories.

  > Little Hans – Freud (1909) used him to illustrate the principles of psychoanalysis.

  > Phineas Gage – In 1848 he survived an iron rod passing through his brain, but suffered changes to his personality.

- **Events:**

  > The London riots (2011) were studied by Reicher and Stott, to re-examine explanations of 'mob' behaviour from a social psychological perspective.

  > Mass suicide of a cult group – Reverend Jim Jones was responsible for the deaths of 900 followers in the 1970s. This case study illustrates processes of conformity and obedience.

A03 Evaluation/Discussion

Case studies can be used to study very rare experiences...

		Issues/Debates Case studies are an idiographic approach to research
Some situations could not be generated experimentally, for practical or ethical reasons, but can be studied qualitatively using case studies.	The case study of David Reimer, a boy whose penis was accidentally removed and who was raised as a girl, is a fascinating example (see p.60).	In this way, it is possible to provide insight into the complex interactions of many factors in people's experience after horrific events like accidents or extreme deprivation.

However, case studies study unique individuals...

The subjects of case studies often have particular or unusual characteristics.	For example, HM had suffered epilepsy for many years as well as the brain damage caused by the removal of his hippocampus.	We don't know how different factors interacted to affect the individual's behaviour, so it is difficult to generalise from individual cases.

Ethical issues...

Confidentiality and informed consent must be carefully considered in case studies.	As many cases are unique, they may be easily identifiable, even when individuals are identified by initials or given false names. In addition, individuals such as HM may not have been able to give informed consent.	So researchers should take care not to reveal personal details that enable the person to be located.

We often lack data from before a particular event...

The interest in an individual often begins after an event, such as the brain damage to HM or Phineas Gage.	For example, we do not know how HM's epilepsy and previous drug treatments may have affected his brain prior to his surgery.	We cannot compare before and after, which makes it difficult to draw valid conclusions.

Issues/Debates Ethical implications: social sensitivity

APPLY

AO2: An example

SCENARIO Louise wishes to find out about the life of a 'typical' teenager in the UK, and asks for three volunteers at a youth club.

What research methods could Louise use to find out about these teenagers' lives? Suggest how she could obtain quantitative and qualitative data for a case study. **(8 marks)**

ANSWER **An extract showing how you could address the AO2 requirements of this question:** *Quantitative data could be collected by using closed questions such as 'How much time do you spend on Netflix?' or 'Rate these activities on a scale of 1-5' (with relevant activities such as dancing, sport, reading, homework and a Likert scale for their answers). Qualitative data could be collected by asking open questions in an interview or questionnaire, such as 'Describe how you spend a typical Sunday morning', or by asking them to make video diaries.*

AO2: Four for you to try

Louise (see **AO2: An example**) feels these particular teenagers may not be typical, as they were highly motivated and keen to get involved.

1. a. How could she carry out further research to explore whether her volunteers were representative of the population of UK teenagers? (3 marks)

David is interested in the European migrant crisis, and decides to research an informal migrant camp in Northern France. He wants to understand why people are hoping to come to the UK. He is considering whether to spend time with one family at the camp and gather qualitative data for a case study, or whether to focus on a larger scale view of the issue by using statistical data gathered by aid organisations and the French police. He hopes to publish a report in the local newspaper.

b. Give one advantage and one disadvantage of each research method. (4 marks + 4 marks)

HM was unable to form new memories after his surgery. This meant that when the researcher came to see him, even though she had visited many times before, he did not recognise her. He could not remember giving consent, although he was always compliant and happy to be contributing to research.

2. How could researchers deal with the issue of informed consent in a case like HM? (3 marks)

3. Which one of the following pieces of research is not a case study? (Tick one only.)

A Freud's description of Little Hans

B Research into the psychological effects of the collapse of the World Trade Towers in 2001

C The study of Little Albert by Watson and Rayner

D The memory experiments carried out on HM by Susanne Corkin.

How do I answer... questions about case studies?

Q1: Does this case study support the Multi-store model of memory? Explain your answer. **(4 marks)**

Q1 is an application question, and you have to briefly explain an aspect of the theory (Working Memory Model) and how it is supported, or not supported, by an aspect of the case study that has been described. Do this twice for 4 marks. (See our advice on **How do I answer… application questions?** on p.31, for example.)

Q2: Evaluate the use of case studies such as… in psychological research. **(5 marks)**

For **Q2**, you can offer some positive and negative evaluation about case studies, and any of the AO3 evaluation points on the opposite page would be relevant, including ethical considerations. For 5 marks you should explain one strength and one limitation in detail. The phrase 'such as… ' means you can link to the case study described in the question, but this is not essential.

Q3: Identify one ethical issue associated with this case study. Suggest how researchers could deal with this ethical issue. **(4 marks)**

In **Q3**, there would be 1 mark for naming a relevant ethical issue, and 3 marks for explaining how it could be dealt with. For example, 'Confidentiality: The details of the individual should be kept out of any publication so he cannot be identified. The researchers could keep him anonymous or just use initials.'

REVIEW

Look through the Year 1 Student Book and make a list of all the case studies you have encountered. How do they illustrate features of case studies? Which evaluation points are relevant to each of them?

Reliability

RECAP

AO1 Description

- **Reliability** is the consistency of measurements.
- Procedures should be standardised in any research study to improve reliability and replicability.

Reliability of observational techniques

- In quantitative observations, researchers record behaviour using behavioural categories.
- **To assess** reliability:
  - > Compare the data from two or more observers. This is the **inter-observer reliability**.
  - > Inter-observer (or inter-rater) reliability is calculated as a correlation coefficient between the two sets of scores from independent observers.
  - > 'Good' reliability is a correlation of +.80 or more, or a correlation which is significant at $p < 0.05$ (Pearson's *r* or Spearman's *rho*).
- **To improve** reliability:
  - > Behavioural categories should be operationalised carefully so they are less subjective.
  - > Observers can improve by practising or being trained in choosing categories.

Reliability of self-report techniques

- Self-report includes questionnaires and interviews.
- **To assess** reliability:
  - > **Test–retest reliability** is used to assess reliability of self-report measures, IQ tests, personality tests and other psychological tests.
  - > The test is repeated after a short interval such as a week, and scores for each person are compared. Test–retest reliability is also calculated as a correlation coefficient, a measure of the consistency of scores for each individual.
  - > **Inter-interviewer reliability** could also be calculated, in the same way as inter-observer reliability.
- **To improve reliability:**
  - > Rewrite ambiguous questions. If people can understand the same question in different ways, they may answer them differently the second time. So removing ambiguity improves reliability.

Reliability of experiments

- The dependent variable (DV) in an experiment may be measured using a rating scale or behavioural categories. Reliability is the consistency of the way the DV is measured. In these experiments reliability is assessed using inter-observer or test–retest methods, as above.
- **To improve reliability** in any experiment, procedures should be standardised. This ensures that participants follow exactly the same procedure as each other, and that other researchers can repeat the experiment.

Test–retest reliability

⚙ APPLY

AO2: An example

SCENARIO Sienna is planning to research the experiences of girls in a secondary school in Uganda, to find out how they manage homework and helping with tasks in the home such as cooking and caring for younger siblings. She wants to collect quantitative and qualitative data. She is writing a questionnaire to find out their experiences, and their views of the importance of homework and helping with domestic tasks.

a. *How could she test the reliability of the questionnaire?* **(3 marks)**

b. *Why would it matter if the reliability was low?* **(3 marks)**

c. *How could she improve the reliability of her questionnaire?* **(4 marks)**

ANSWER *a. By test–retest method. She could ask a few of the girls the same questions a second time, a week later, to see if their answers were consistent.*

b. If the reliability was low, the girls may not have really understood the questions or may not have felt able to be honest, so the results would also lack validity.

c. Sienna could write the questions in simple, clear English so they are not ambiguous. She could collect data by interviewing the girls rather than just giving them a questionnaire to complete, so that she can explain the questions or explore further to make sure the girls have understood.

AO2: Three for you to try ✏

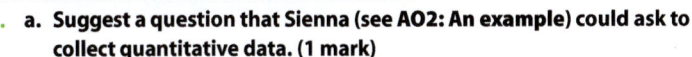

1. **a. Suggest a question that Sienna (see AO2: An example) could ask to collect quantitative data. (1 mark)**

   b. Write a question that would produce qualitative data for Sienna's study. (2 marks)

2. Two psychologists watched videos of politicians in a televised debate. They assessed body language, counting instances of aggressive posture and facial expressions (Behaviours A–E). The two observers' results for one politician are given below.

Behaviour	A	B	C	D	E
Observer 1	7	5	4	12	9
Observer 2	2	5	6	6	4

   a. From these results, why are the psychologists concerned about inter-observer reliability? (3 marks)

   b. How could they assess the inter-observer reliability more objectively? (2 marks)

   c. Suggest reasons why the behavioural observations may be unreliable. (4 marks)

   d. What could they do to improve the reliability of the coding of behaviour? (3 marks)

3. **Match up the terms with the explanations:**

1	Reliability	A	The extent of agreement between two researchers tallying behavioural categories
2	Inter-observer reliability		
3	Test–retest reliability	B	The correlation between the two sets of scores of the same participants taking the same test on two occasions
4	Inter-rater reliability		
5	Inter-interviewer reliability	C	Consistency of measurements
6	Replicability	D	Measured by comparing answers from the same person with two different interviewers
		E	Whether two researchers allocate the same scores to the same individuals' behaviour
		F	If a study is able to be repeated using the same procedure with different participants and yield the same results

🐾 How do I answer... questions about reliability in research?

As well as appearing in the Research methods section of Paper 2, questions on reliability could pop up in any section of the three papers. You could also be asked to consider issues of reliability in designing a study. As always, read the question carefully, and in this case, decide whether you are being asked how to **assess** or **improve** reliability.

Q1: What is meant by reliability? (1 mark)

Q1 is just a straightforward definition, so learn it.

Q2: Explain one way in which the researchers could check their data collection was reliable. (3 marks)

For **Q2**, you could explain inter-rater or test–retest reliability, depending on which is appropriate for the type of study in the question. Make sure you know how to explain each, and you are clear about the difference between them.

Q3: Using the data, explain why the psychologist is concerned about inter-rater reliability. (4 marks)

Q3 requires you to refer to data, and you must give a specific detailed explanation. For example, 'the observers should have similar tallies as they are looking at the same material/participant, but the tallies are different at every time interval and at some points there are large differences. This suggests one observer was not concentrating as well as the other, or they had not been properly trained in how to apply the behavioural categories'.

Q4: Suggest a suitable statistical test to check the inter-rater reliability of the two observers. Explain why this test is suitable. (3 marks)

Q4 asks you to choose a test. This will be Pearson's *r* or Spearman's *rho*, depending on whether the data is interval or ordinal level. Explain that the researcher is testing the correlation, and why it is interval/ordinal data.

Q5: What could she do to improve the inter-rater reliability? (4 marks)

For **Q5**, use the relevant AO1 points from the opposite page.

🔄 REVIEW

Pick three key studies from your A Level topics. Do you know how the researchers assessed the reliability of their measures? How might poor reliability be a problem for the findings of each study? How would this affect its support for the theory? How might the reliability be improved?

Validity

AO1 Description

- **Validity** refers to whether an observed effect is a genuine one.
- A test may be reliable (see previous spread) but lack validity if it does not actually measure the concept the researcher is aiming to measure.

Internal versus external validity

- **Internal validity** concerns whether the researcher is measuring what they intend to, or whether the findings are affected by other factors, such as:
  - > confounding variables
  - > investigator effects (behaviour of the investigator that affects the participants' performance in a study)
  - > demand characteristics
  - > social desirability bias
  - > poor operationalisation of the dependent variable or behavioural categories.
- **External validity** is how far the findings can be generalised outside the research setting, to other people (population validity), historical periods (historical or **temporal validity**) and settings (**ecological validity**).

Ecological validity

- In an experiment, the method used to measure the DV can be quite artificial, giving poor ecological validity. This could be a lab experiment, field experiment or natural experiment.
- We have to consider **mundane realism** – whether a study reflects real-world experiences – rather than just the location.
- For example, Godden and Baddeley (1975) carried out an experiment on context-dependent forgetting. Deep sea divers learnt word lists on land or underwater, then tried to recall the words on land or underwater. The situation was 'real life' but the task was very artificial, and the divers were aware they were being studied, so may not have behaved 'naturally'.
- **Demand characteristics** can affect ecological validity if participants are aware they are being studied, so alter their behaviour to look good (**social desirability bias**) or to fit what they think the researcher expects. This means they are not behaving as they would in real life.

Assessing and improving validity

- **Assessing validity**
  - > **Face validity** is an intuitive, common sense judgement of whether a self-report measure appears to measure what it claims to – do the questions seem to be related to the topic?
  - > **Concurrent validity** compares a new measure with an existing, validated one on the same topic. The same participants take both measures and scores are compared by correlation. 'Good' concurrent validity is a correlation of +.80 or more, or a correlation which is significant at $p<0.05$ (Pearson's r or Spearman's rho).
- **Improving validity**
  - > Face validity can be improved by replacing any irrelevant questions with new items more obviously related to the topic.
  - > Concurrent validity can also be improved by replacing items and checking whether the validity improves.
  - > Improving research design can deal with issues such as demand characteristics and investigator effects. For example, in a double blind design, neither the participants nor the researcher who interacts with them knows the true aims of the study.

APPLY

A02: An example

SCENARIO You have been asked to design an experiment to test whether annoying music affects children's performance in a smartphone game.

a. *Explain how* **two** *issues in the research design might affect the validity of your findings, and suggest how* **one** *of these issues could be overcome.* **(6 marks)**

ANSWER *Validity issues: if the children are aware they are being studied, it might make them try much harder than normal (demand characteristics). Whether the music is 'annoying' is subjective – some children may love it. This is an extraneous variable as the music may affect children differently depending on their reaction to it. To overcome this issue, a repeated measures design could be used, with all children playing a game with music or without, so that the effect of individual differences is controlled, and counterbalancing the orders would reduce the effect of order effects in this design.*

A02: Two for you to try

1. A sports psychologist has written a questionnaire to find out how people's beliefs about their sporting ability affects their participation in sport. She has found a previously published questionnaire about sporting preferences, and asks participants to complete this as well as her new questionnaire.

What is she testing? (Tick one box only.)

A Mundane realism ☐

B Ecological validity ☐

C Face validity ☐

D Concurrent validity ☐

2. A forensic psychologist uses cognitive tests and personality tests to assess young offenders and help to plan rehabilitation programmes for them. He is concerned that these tests may have some issues with validity, as they are relying on self-report data.

How could he ensure the validity of the tests? (3 marks)

How do I answer... questions on validity in research?

Q1: What is meant by internal validity and external validity? **(2 marks)**

Q1 just needs general definitions, learn them.

Q2: Briefly describe one way the psychologist could assess the validity of the data collected in this study. **(2 marks)**

For **Q2**, you could name a type for 1 mark, and very briefly explain the process for the second mark. This is likely to be face or concurrent validity, but, depending on the study, ecological validity or population validity could also be relevant.

Q3: How could the researchers have used a statistical test to establish the concurrent validity of the spatial reasoning test? **(4 marks)**

To answer **Q3**, you need to explain how two sets of results would be collected for the same group of people, from the new test and an existing one. The correlation of the results for the two tests would be tested with Spearman's *rho* (or Pearson's *r*). If the correlation is significant at $p < 0.05$ then the new test has good concurrent validity. Note that in this question it would not be sufficient to say 'a correlation over 0.8' as you are specifically asked about statistical testing.

REVIEW

Look through your Year 1 notes or Student Book. Find three different studies and assess their ecological validity by completing the table below. Decide how artificial the environment and the task were, and what confounding variables may have affected the findings.

Study (name and title or brief summary)	What environment was the study conducted in?	How was the DV measured?	Confounding variables: Were the participants aware their behaviour was being studied?	Overall, how high or low is the ecological validity of this study?
Godden and Baddeley (1975) deep-sea divers	On land and underwater – natural	Recall of word lists – artificial	Yes – demand characteristics?	Low

Features of science

RECAP

AO1 Description

Features of science

- Science is an evolving, systematic approach to creating knowledge, with five key features:

  > **Empirical methods** Empirical evidence is gained through direct observation or experiment. This means claims can be tested and use to make predictions.

  > **Objectivity** Objective data is collected systematically in controlled conditions, so it is not affected by the expectations of the researcher.

  > **Replicability** Procedures are carefully recorded, so that other scientists can replicate them with different groups of people to test their validity.

  > **Theory construction** Theories are explanations of observations and findings. Theories can emerge from observation or from hypothesis testing.

  > **Hypothesis testing** A good theory must be able to generate **testable hypotheses**. If the hypothesis is not supported by empirical evidence, the theory must be modified.

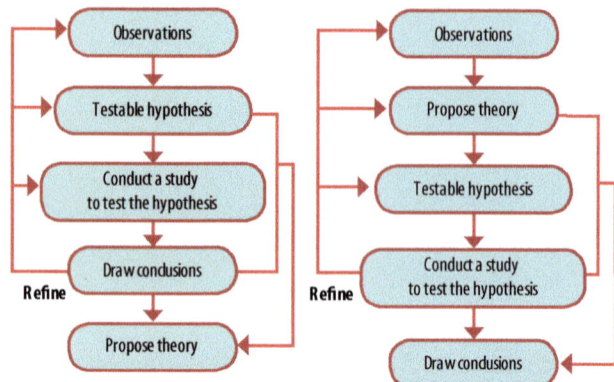

Inductive model (on the left) and deductive model (on the right)

Falsifiability

- Karl Popper (1934) argued that it is only possible to disconfirm a theory. He pointed out that however many confirmed sightings of white swans there are, we cannot conclude that all swans are white; the sighting of just one black swan will disprove this theory.

- Therefore, research tests the null hypothesis, e.g. 'not all swans are white'. If we are able to reject the null hypothesis (with reasonable certainty) we may accept the alternative hypothesis.

- A scientific theory must be falsifiable. Some approaches, such as Freudian psychoanalysis, can be criticised as lacking falsifiability.

Paradigms

- Thomas Kuhn (1962) proposed that scientific knowledge develops through revolutions, not the process of gradual change suggested by Popper's theory of falsification. Kuhn said that there are two main phases in science:

  > 'Normal science', in which existing theory remains dominant, while disconfirming evidence gradually accumulates.

  > Paradigm shift: a revolutionary overthrowing of existing theory and its replacement with a new set of assumptions and methods.

Just one black swan

AO3 Evaluation / Discussion

The empirical approach teaches us to question claims…

A good scientist is a sceptic, and always asks, 'where is the evidence?'	Good evidence should be directly observed or collected using controlled, objective methods.	*This means that we can reject pseudoscientific beliefs based on weak or subjective evidence.*

Kuhn's theory of paradigm shift…

Kuhn described scientific progress as more like a religious conversion than a systematic, logical process of hypothesis testing.	Therefore, according to Kuhn, science itself is socially constructed, through dialogue with other people, not just a logical process of evolving theory based on empirical evidence.	*This theory of paradigm shift is itself a paradigm shift from the previous way of understanding the scientific process.*

 **APPLY**

AO2: An example

SCENARIO Lauren is studying Psychology A Level. Her younger sister, Lucy, is taking GCSEs and choosing A Level courses. Lucy says, 'I don't like science but I think psychology sounds interesting because it's about people.' Lauren thinks she should explain to Lucy that psychology is based on scientific principles.

Help Lauren to identify three key features of psychology as a science that Lucy would encounter in A Level Psychology. **(3 marks)**

ANSWER *Psychology is based on empirical research – A Level Psychology involves learning evidence for and against each theory. Empirical data should be objective – A Level Psychology focuses on evaluating how objective the research is, or whether it is biased. Psychological theories are built on empirical evidence and tested scientifically by coming up with testable hypotheses – A Level Psychology includes practical research where you will come up with hypotheses based on existing theory, and test them using experiments or other research methods.*

AO2: Two for you to try

1. Rachel is a psychology teacher. She takes an online quiz which offers to identify whether her brain is male or female, based on answers to questions such as 'How do you feel about the idea of raising a family?' and 'Which of these movies would you choose to watch? *(Options: 'Star Wars,' 'The Twilight Saga,' 'Mean Girls,' 'Mad Max'.)* Her result is, 'Your brain is 72 per cent male – you like working systematically and taking the lead, and although you are able to empathise with others, you prefer to solve problems using logic rather than feelings.'

   Should Rachel take this seriously? Apply your knowledge of scientific processes to evaluate the conclusions of this quiz.

2. Karl Popper's contribution to the philosophy of science has led to empirical research being based on the principle of null hypothesis significance testing.

   What should the hypotheses be? (Tick one box only.)

   A Falsifiable ☐
   B Replicable ☐
   C Reliable ☐
   D Objective ☐

 How do I answer... questions about features of science?

These questions can appear in disguise, and in surprising sections of the A Level papers. For example, you could be asked why research places an emphasis on controlled experiments, or causal experiments, or how paradigm shift applies to a particular topic. You will need to be able to draw on your research methods knowledge and link it together. The AO1 material for these questions is on the opposite page.

Q1: Explain why it is important for scientific research to be replicated. **(4 marks)**

For **Q1**, use the 'Replicability' point and expand it by explaining about validity, generalisability, etc.

Q2: Referring to the study, explain why this research could be described as not being scientific. **(3 marks)**

Q2 requires you to apply the general points to a specific study. If you know the five key features of science in the AO1 points, you can use them as a mental checklist, or jot them down in a margin and check which are relevant. Explain explicitly how the piece of research fails to meet one or two of the features of science.

Q3: Outline two or more ways in which this study follows the process of scientific research. **(4 marks)**

Q3 is the opposite of **Q2**, and again a checklist of the five features would help you here.

REVIEW

Write one of the key features of science on each of five sticky notes. Then look through research you have studied to identify how these features apply, and stick the notes onto them.

Probability

 RECAP

AO1 Description

- A hypothesis must be falsifiable (see previous spread). In research, we seek to falsify the null hypothesis.
- If we are looking for a difference in the DV for two conditions of the IV in an experiment, the **null hypothesis** is 'there is no difference'. The **alternative hypothesis** is 'there is a difference'.
- Samples may have small differences due to random variation or 'chance'.
- Inferential statistical tests permit us to work out how probable it is that a pattern in research data could have arisen by chance (supporting the null hypothesis). Alternatively, the effect may represent a real difference/correlation in the populations from which the samples were drawn (supporting the alternative hypothesis).
- **Probability (p) levels** Psychologists generally use a p level of 5 per cent as the cut-off. This means there is a less than 5 per cent chance of the results occurring if the null hypothesis is true, given as $p<0.05$. So there is at least a 95 per cent chance that the effect observed in the sample is a real one in the population.

- In some studies, such as drug testing, researchers want to be more certain that effect is real. They may use a more stringent probability level of 1 per cent, given as $p<0.01$. This means there is less than 1 per cent chance of the results occurring when there is no real difference/correlation between the populations from which the samples are drawn.
- **Type I and Type II errors** The 5 per cent probability level gives a good compromise between Type I and Type II errors.
  > A Type I error is a false positive, in which the null hypothesis is rejected when it should have been accepted.
  > A Type II error is a false negative: the null hypothesis is accepted when it should have been rejected.

Issues/Debates
Nomothetic approach to research

'You're pregnant.' Type I error, false positive.

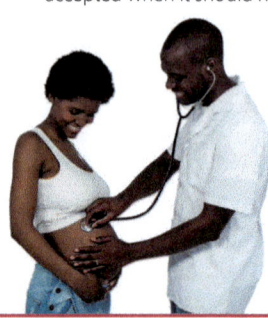

'You're not pregnant.' Type II error, false negative.

APPLY

AO2: An example

SCENARIO

A psychologist finds their results are significant at $p<0.05$.

Explain why the psychologist did not think they had made a Type 1 error in their study. **(3 marks)**

ANSWER

$p<0.05$ means that there is less than 0.05 chance that the effect has occurred by chance. So there is less than 5 per cent chance that they falsely rejected the null hypothesis (a Type I error), and they can be at least 95 per cent confident that they have not made a Type I error.

AO2: Two for you to try

1. **Write a null hypothesis and an alternative hypothesis for each of the following research aims. (2 marks each)**
   a. To see if cats or dogs are better at solving puzzles.
   b. To see if rats or lizards are more affectionate.
2. **Identify the null hypothesis and alternative hypothesis in these key studies from Year 1: (2 marks each)**
   a. Bandura – Bobo doll – imitation of violent behaviour (see Year 1 Student Book p.128)
   b. Asch – conformity to group norms (see Year 1 Student Book p.20)
   c. Harlow – attachment in monkeys (see Year 1 Student Book p.74)

How do I answer... questions about Type I and Type II errors?

Q1: Why did the researcher choose a significance level of $p<0.05$? **(1 mark)**

Q2: Why was a significance level of $p<0.01$ used for this study? **(1 mark)**

Q3: Explain why the researcher can be confident that they have not made a Type I error in this study. **(3 marks)**

There is a very particular requirement for these answers, which must be worded correctly. If you learn the answer to the **AO2: An example** on this page, this will give you a good answer for **Q3**. The answer to **Q1** and **Q2** are in the AO1 points on this page. Find them, and learn them word for word, and you'll be fine. Make sure to link your answer to the specific study if this is required by the question.

Statistical tests

 ## RECAP

AO1 Description

- Inferential statistics allow us to find out if results are significant using tables of critical values.

Selecting statistical tests

Design	Level of measurement		
	Nominal	**Ordinal**	**Interval**
Independent groups	Chi-squared test	Mann-Whitney U test	Unrelated t-test
Repeated measures	Sign test	Wilcoxon test	Related t-test
Correlational	–	Spearman's *rho*	Pearson's *r*

Parametric criteria

- Parametric tests (which use the mean and standard deviation to calculate the **test statistic**) are more powerful than non-parametric tests (which use ranked data). This means they can detect significance in some situations where non-parametric tests can't.
- They should only be used if certain criteria are met:
  > The **level of measurement** is interval or better.
  > The scores (or scores of the population they represent) are normally distributed, and not skewed.
  > The variances of the two samples are similar. This is not an issue with repeated measures design. For independent groups, the variance of one sample should not exceed four times the other. (Variance is the square of the standard deviation.)
  > See the Year 1/AS Student Book for explanations of levels of measurement, normal distribution, skew, standard deviation.

Using statistical tests

- Compare the **calculated value** of the test statistic with the **critical value** from the table of critical values.
- To find the critical value, you need to know:
  > **Significance** level (using $p<0.05$).
  > Kind of hypothesis: directional requires a **one-tailed test**, non-directional requires a **two-tailed test**.
  > Value of N, the number of participants, or the **degrees of freedom** (*df*).
- There is an instruction underneath the table stating how to compare the calculated value with the critical value.

APPLY

AO2: An example

SCENARIO While researching stress, you have collected data measuring students' salivary cortisol level before an exam, to see whether this relates to the number of hours of sleep they had the previous night.

Which statistical test should you use? Explain why this test would be appropriate. **(4 marks)**

ANSWER *Pearson's r. Both variables are interval data. The data is likely to be normally distributed, therefore parametric. We are looking for a correlation between two variables.*

AO2: One for you to try

A study is carried out asking A Level students about their main areas of concern. In one question, they are asked to select from five options.

Identify the level of measurement of data collected by this question. (Tick one box only.)

A	Nominal	☐	**C** Interval	☐
B	Ordinal	☐	**D** Ratio	☐

 ## How do I answer... questions about choosing a statistical test?

You could be asked to select a suitable statistical test in any section of any of the three A Level papers. Think carefully about the study that is described in the question and the type of data that will be collected. Remember there are three **Decisions** you need to make, and you can remember them with the 3 Ds:

- Are we testing a **Difference** or a correlation/association?
- Is the **Design** independent groups or repeated measures?
- What level of measurement is the **Data**?

These help you to choose the right test, and also give you the basis for your explanation of the reasons why you chose this test.

REVIEW

Make a table to identify the suitability of each of the eight statistical tests. The first row is completed for you. First use the summary table to help you, then try again and see how much you can complete from memory. Keep practising until you know all the characteristics relating to each test without effort.

TEST	Test statistic	Level of measurement	Parametric or non-parametric	Test of...	Design
Chi-squared	$x2$	Nominal	–	Association or difference	Independent
Sign test					

Non-parametric tests of difference

RECAP

AO1 Description

Wilcoxon test for related designs

- Reasons for choosing:
  - > The hypothesis states a difference.
  - > The two sets of data are related.
  - > The data are at least ordinal.
- If you are given the calculated value of T:
  - > Look at the data: is the difference in the predicted direction?
  - > Work out N = the number of participants minus any whose scores were the same in both conditions.
  - > Find critical value of T from table (see below).
  - > Compare calculated and critical values as instructed. (If the calculated value is equal to or less than the critical value, the result is significant.)
  - > Report the conclusion, e.g. 'As the calculated value is not significant ($p<0.05$, one-tailed, $N = 11$), we must accept the null hypothesis and conclude that there is no difference between…'

Mann-Whitney test for unrelated designs

- Reasons for choosing:
  - > The hypothesis states a difference.
  - > The two sets of data are unrelated.
  - > The data are at least ordinal.
- If you are given the calculated value of U:
  - > Is the difference in the right direction?
  - > N_A is the number of participants in one group, and N_B the number in the other group.
  - > Find critical value of U from table, where N_A and N_B intersect.
  - > Compare calculated and critical values.
  - > Report the conclusion.

The Wilcoxon test is used for related samples (repeated measures or matched pairs design) and the Mann-Whitney test is used for unrelated samples (independent groups design). To remember this: Mr and Mrs Wilcoxon are related by marriage. Mr Mann and Ms Whitney are unrelated.

APPLY

AO2: An example

SCENARIO Suzi compared the recall of concrete words (e.g. cat, fish, table, cloud) with abstract words (e.g. beauty, truth, calm, fear). She used the same participants in each condition, and measured how many words each participant remembered. There were 23 participants, most of whom remembered more concrete words than abstract words. Four participants remembered the same number in each condition.

a. *Write a directional hypothesis for this study.* **(2 marks)**

b. *Suzi analysed the results using a Wilcoxon test. Explain why this test is suitable.* **(3 marks)**

c. *The calculated value of T was 37. Use the table of critical values to decide if this is significant, and explain your decision.* **(3 marks)**

d. *What can Suzi conclude?* **(1 mark)**

Table of critical values for the Wilcoxon test

Level of significance for a one-tailed test	0.05	0.01
Level of significance for a two-tailed test	0.10	0.02
$N = 17$	41	34
18	47	40
19	53	46

Observed value of T must be EQUAL TO or LESS THAN the critical value in the table for significance to be shown.

ANSWER *a. People remember more concrete words than abstract words; b. The data is at least ordinal (numbers of words recalled), it is a test of difference (concrete or abstract words) and it is a related design (same participants in both conditions, repeated measures); c. Yes. The calculated value (37) is less than the critical value (53) ($N = 19$, $p<0.05$, one-tailed) so it is significant; d. The alternative hypothesis is supported – people remember more concrete words than abstract words.*

🐾 How do I answer... questions involving statistical testing?

You could be asked to interpret the findings of a statistical test, and decide whether the data is significant, in any section of any of the three papers, so be prepared.

Generally you will be given a test statistic and asked if it is significant, as in **AO2: An example** above. The table of critical values will always include the instruction for how to compare the calculated (observed) and critical (table) values of the test statistic, so look for this instruction. Write down the calculated value and the critical value in the same order to make sure you compare them the right way around. Turn it into a yes/no question:

Is the observed value of T EQUAL TO or LESS THAN the critical value in the table? If the answer is 'yes' then it is significant. If the answer is 'no', it is not significant. For our example, you write: Is 37 EQUAL TO or LESS THAN 53?

The answer is 'yes', so it is significant.

Note the different answers for part **c**, which is asking about significance, and part **d**, which asks for a conclusion.

Part **c** needs you to explain how you found the critical value and compared it with the calculated value. For part **d**, your conclusion must relate to the hypothesis. If the results were significant, the conclusion is exactly the same as the alternative hypothesis. If the results were not significant, the conclusion will match the null hypothesis because this was supported by the data.

Parametric tests of difference

 **RECAP**

A01 Description

Related *t*-test

- Reasons for choosing:
  - > The hypothesis states a difference.
  - > The two sets of data are related.
  - > The data are interval level and fit the parametric criteria (see p.17).
- If you are given the calculated value of *t*:
  - > Look at the data: is the result in the right direction?
  - > Find critical value of *t* from table, using $df = N - 1$. See p.17 for an explanation of how to use statistical tables.
  - > Compare calculated and critical values as instructed.
  - > Report the conclusion, e.g. 'As the calculated value ($t = 1.8$) is less than the critical value ($t = 1.812$) it is not significant ($p<0.05$, $df = 10$, one-tailed). So we must accept the null hypothesis and conclude that there is no difference between…'

Unrelated *t*-test

- Reasons for choosing:
  - > The hypothesis states a difference.
  - > The two sets of data are unrelated.
  - > The data are interval and fit the parametric criteria. (Variances can be assumed to be the same if participants were randomly assigned to conditions.)
- If you are given the calculated value of *t*:
  - > Is the difference in the right direction?
  - > Find critical value of *t* from the table. Use $df = N_A + N_B - 2$.
  - > Compare calculated and critical values of *t*.
  - > Report the conclusion.

 APPLY

A02: An example

SCENARIO Mr Smith, the new principal of Angel College, is considering changing the times of the college day after reading that teenagers' sleep patterns are different from adults'. He conducts a one-week trial to see whether academic performance improves when students are able to sleep in for longer, starting the day at 10am instead of 8.30am.

Design a study that Mr Smith could carry out. Explain how he would collect data, and state an operationalised hypothesis.

What experimental design is your study using? Which statistical test might be suitable to analyse the data from this study? Explain your choice. **(8 marks)**

ANSWER **An extract showing how you could address the AO2 requirements of this question:**

For example: give students tests in each subject after a week of normal working times, and after a week of later school days. IV = early or late. DV = test results. Hypothesis: students will achieve better test results after a week of starting school later than a normal week (10am instead of 8.30am). Repeated measures. Related t-test, because data is interval (test scores) and related, looking for a difference, and we assume it meets the parametric criterion of normal distribution. (This study could alternatively use an independent groups design, then you would use the unrelated t-test.)

A02: One for you to try

In a cognitive psychology experiment, participants are given word lists to memorise. One group is given words of one syllable, and the other group is given words of two syllables. They are tested to see how many words they accurately recall five minutes later.

Which statistical test would be suitable for this study? (Tick one box only.)

A Wilcoxon ☐ **C** Related *t*-test ☐

B Mann-Whitney ☐ **D** Unrelated *t*-test ☐

 How do I answer... questions with formulae?

You do not need to learn any formulae for A Level Psychology, except how to calculate a mean. But you could be asked to substitute numbers into a formula, such as $df = N_A + N_B - 2$, or even the formula for *t*. We think this is very unlikely to come up in an exam, but we want you to be prepared just in case. The formula is:

$$t = \frac{\Sigma d}{\sqrt{(N\Sigma d^2 - (\Sigma d)^2)/(N-1)}}$$

e.g. If the number of participants (*N*) was 10, $\Sigma d = 15$ and $\Sigma d^2 = 115$,

$$t = \frac{15}{\sqrt{(10 \times 115 - 15^2)/(10-1)}}$$

$$= \frac{15}{925/9}$$

$$= 0.146$$

Practise this calculation yourself, and see if you get the same answer.

Are you clear about the difference between Σd^2 and $(\Sigma d)^2$?

Σd^2 means 'add up all the values of d^2'

$(\Sigma d)^2$ means 'add up all the values of d, then square your answer'

 **REVIEW**

Look through past papers and practise as many of these questions as you can. Once you get into the flow, you will be able to answer them without anxiety and probably take less than the allotted 1 ¼ minutes per mark, so this will save you time for questions involving more planning and writing. We have included stats questions in each chapter of this Revision Guide too, so look out for them and keep practising.

Tests of correlation

RECAP

A01 Description

A non-parametric test: Spearman's *rho*

- Reasons for choosing:
  - > The hypothesis states a correlation between two variables.
  - > The two sets of data are related (pairs of scores from each person).
  - > The data are ordinal.
- If you are given the calculated value of *rho*:
  - > Is the correlation in the predicted direction? (The sign indicates a positive or negative correlation.)
  - > Find critical value of *rho* from the table.
  - > Compare calculated and critical values of *rho*, ignoring the sign.
  - > Report the conclusion, e.g. 'As the calculated value of *rho* (-0.58) is greater than the critical value (0.564), the correlation is significant ($p<0.05$, $N = 10$, one-tailed). This means the alternative hypothesis is supported: there is a negative correlation between… and….'

A parametric test: Pearson's *r*

- Reasons for choosing:
  - > The hypothesis states a correlation between two variables.
  - > The two sets of data are related (pairs of scores from each person).
  - > The data are interval and fit the parametric criteria.
- If you are given the calculated value of *r*:
  - > Is the correlation in the predicted direction? (The sign indicates a positive or negative correlation.)
  - > Find critical value of *r* from the table.
  - > Use $df = N - 2$.
  - > Compare calculated and critical values of *r*, ignoring the sign.
  - > Report the conclusion.

A correlation, but not significant?

- Sometimes there can be a moderate or strong correlation which turns out not to be significant. This can be caused by a small sample size.
- The conclusion would be 'There is not a significant correlation between…' You could suggest replicating the study with a larger sample.
- On the other hand, a correlation may be weak but still significant if a very large sample is tested.
- For example, see the stress study by Rahe *et al.* on p.196 of the Year 2 Student Book, which found a significant positive correlation between LCU scores and illness scores of +0.118 in a sample of 2664 men.

APPLY

A02: An example

SCENARIO **Calculate Spearman's *rho* for the following study:**

A comparison of self-report scores for attractiveness and happiness: $N = 19$, $rho = 0.438$.

Use the table of critical values to test the significance of these correlations, assuming there was previous research which indicated you could use a directional hypothesis, and choosing an appropriate level of significance.

Level of significance for a one-tailed test	0.05	0.01
19	.391	.460
20	.380	.460

Table of critical values for Spearman's *rho*

Observed value of *rho* must be EQUAL TO or GREATER THAN the critical value in this table for significance to be shown.

ANSWER *Significant at $p<0.05$ (critical value = 0.391) but not at $p<0.01$ (critical value = 0.460).*

A02: One for you to try

A group of students were investigating personality traits and film preferences. Fifty participants were asked to complete questionnaires which consisted of 10 items measuring the personality trait of 'openness to experience' and nine items rating their liking for different films, on a Likert scale. The scores for openness to experience and liking for sci-fi films had a correlation of 0.338.

a. **What can you conclude from these findings? (4 marks)**

b. **Why did the students choose this test of significance? (3 marks)**

 How do I answer... questions about correlation?

A researcher used standardised tests to measure children's intelligence and happiness, in a sample of 20 children. Analysis of the scores from the two tests gave a correlation coefficient of 0.310.

a. Write a hypothesis for this study. **(2 marks)**

b. What do these findings show about the relationship between intelligence and happiness? **(3 marks)**

c. This correlation is not significant at $p<0.05$. How could the researcher carry out further research to explore this correlation? **(1 mark)**

For **a**, the hypothesis must be in the form 'there is a (positive/ negative) relationship between…'.

Be careful to express it correctly, so it is not an experimental hypothesis (variable A affects variable B, OR there is a difference between condition A and condition B).

As you have not been told about previous research, it must be non-directional. So for this example, you would write 'There is a relationship between children's intelligence and happiness'.

For **b**, describe the **strength** and **direction** of the relationship: 'It is a weak positive correlation'. Then elaborate, using the names of the variables, 'so as happiness increases, intelligence also increases'.

The problem could be sample size, as 0.310 would have been significant with a larger sample, so for **c** you could suggest that the researcher could collect data from more children.

Chi-squared test (X^2)

A01 Description

Chi-squared test

- Reasons for choosing:
  - The hypothesis states a difference OR an association.
  - The data in each cell are independent: no item can appear in more than one cell of the contingency table.
  - The data are nominal.
- The chi-squared (X^2) test is one of the few that can deal with nominal (category) data. It tests differences between frequencies in different categories. These can also be expressed as an association between variables.
- Contingency table: The data is displayed in a table showing frequencies in each category.
  - A 2×2 contingency table has two conditions of each variable, e.g.:

	Left-handed	Right-handed	Totals
Left eye dominant	12	3	15
Right eye dominant	32	3	35
Totals	44	6	50

- There can be any number of rows and columns. A 3×2 contingency table would have three rows and two columns; three conditions of one variable, and two of the other.
- If you are given the calculated value of X^2:
  - Find critical value of X^2, using df = (number of rows − 1) × (number of columns − 1).
  - Compare calculated and critical values of X^2.
  - Report the conclusion.
  - For example, 'As the calculated value of X^2 (1.31) is less than the critical value (3.84), there is no association between handedness and eye dominance ($p<0.05$, $df = 1$).'

Level of significance for a one-tailed test	0.10	0.05	0.025	0.01
Level of significance for a two-tailed test	0.20	0.10	0.05	0.02
df = 1				
1	1.64	2.71	3.84	5.41
2	3.22	4.60	5.99	7.82

Observed value of X^2 must be EQUAL TO or GREATER THAN the critical value in this table for significance to be shown.

 APPLY

A02: An example

SCENARIO Jana has researched men's and women's coffee preferences. She thinks that more females drink latte or cappuccino, and more males drink Americano or espresso.

a. **Explain why a chi-squared test would be appropriate for this data. (3 marks)**

b. **Write a suitable directional hypothesis for this research. (2 marks)**

ANSWER *a. The data is nominal, with eight categories: two genders and four coffee types. Jana is looking for an association between gender and coffee preference. The data is independent, which means that each person only appears in one cell.*

b. More males prefer espresso or Americano, and more females prefer latte or cappuccino.

A02: One for you to try

A doctor's surgery sent out a feedback survey to patients who had received three types of treatment for mild depression: a self-help programme, computerised CBT, and a physical activity programme (involving three exercise classes per week). They asked the patients, 'Do you feel better now than you did before treatment, or not?' Out of 40 patients who had used the self-help programme, 24 felt better now. All but one patient who used computerised CBT (a total of 24) felt better, and half of the 16 patients who took part in the exercise classes felt better.

a. **Draw a contingency table of these results. (3 marks)**

b. **Write a suitable non-directional hypothesis for this study. (3 marks)**

c. **Degrees of freedom (df) are calculated using the formula: $df = (r−1) \times (c−1)$ (r = number of rows, c = number of columns). How many degrees of freedom (df) are there in this data? (2 marks)**

d. **The chi-squared statistic for this data was calculated to be 12.24. Use the table of critical values (above) for chi-squared to test the significance of the data, and give a conclusion to this study. (4 marks)**

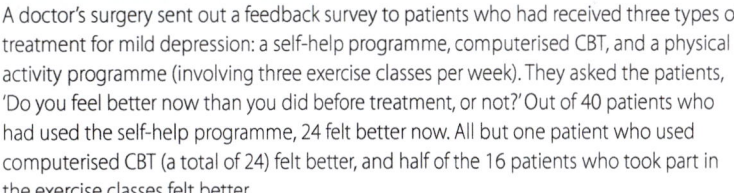 How do I answer... questions about chi-squared?

Remember that related data (repeated measures, usually before-and-after treatment of some kind) would be tested with the sign test (see Year 1 Student Book p.218).

Be careful how you express a hypothesis for nominal independent data. You shouldn't talk about 'relationship' or 'correlation' between variables; the correct word is 'association'. Alternatively, you can hypothesise a difference.

Remember to fully operationalise your variables: this means stating all the categories (the row and column titles in the contingency table).

Reporting investigations

A01 Description

- Research studies are written up in a standard format for publication in peer-reviewed academic journals.

- See section on peer review in Year 1 Student Book, p.220.

Sections of a journal article:

- Abstract: A summary of the entire study in 150–200 words.

  > A single sentence of each section: aims, hypothesis, procedure, sample, results and conclusions, including implications. It enables the reader to get a quick overview of the study and decide whether to read more detail.

- Introduction: This sets the context for the current research by reviewing previous research in the area, explaining the reasons for the current study.

  > This is like a funnel, starting broadly and narrowing down to focus on the aims and research hypothesis of the current research.

- Method: This should contain enough information for another researcher to replicate the study. Design, sampling and procedural decisions should be justified and explained. Ethical issues may also be mentioned, as well as how they were dealt with. This generally contains four sections:

  > Design: e.g. 'repeated measures' or 'covert observation'.

  > Participants: sampling methods, numbers and demographic details.

  > Materials: how they were made or sourced.

  > Procedure: including standardised instructions, environment, order of events.

- Results: This section includes:

  > Descriptive statistics, including tables and graphs.

  > Inferential statistics.

  > In qualitative research, categories and themes are described along with examples from each.

- Discussion: Here the researcher interprets the study and considers implications for future research and real-world applications. This section can include:

  > Summary of the findings, with some explanation of what the results show.

  > Relationship to previous research.

  > Methodological criticisms and suggestions for improvement.

  > Implications for theory and applications.

- References: All articles or books mentioned in the report are referenced in a standard format. This is usually:

  > Surname, Initials, other authors' names (date in brackets), title of article or book, etc…

- The references are listed alphabetically by surname of first author (see examples on p.69 and p.185).

APPLY

A02: An example

 *A researcher has conducted an experiment, and is writing it up for publication. Briefly describe the usual sections of a published journal article.* **(4 marks)**

 *The article begins with an abstract, which is a summary of the entire paper. Then the introduction, which explains previous research in the area and the reason for this research, including the hypotheses. The Method section includes details of research design (in this case an experiment, but also explaining how the participants were organised into conditions), participants (sampling, demographics, etc.), materials and procedure. It should have enough detail for someone to be able to replicate the study. Then the Results section has descriptive and inferential statistics. Finally, the Discussion section where the researcher should talk about the conclusions, and any implications and applications of the research.*

A02: Two for you to try

1. **Organise the journal article sections into their usual order.**

   A   References

   B   Results

   C   Introduction

   D   Abstract

   E   Design

   F   Procedure

   G   Discussion

   H   Participants

   J   Materials

2. **Write an abstract for the Stanford Prison Experiment carried out by Zimbardo and colleagues (Haney et al., 1973). Use one sentence for each section (Abstract, Introduction, Method, Results, Discussion) and a maximum of 150 words. (6 marks)**

How do I answer... questions about reporting investigations?

You could be asked to present information in the form it would appear in a journal article. Just stick to the instructions in the question, but express it in the form that it would appear in the published article, so you are writing as the researcher. You can use 'I' or 'we', but a more formal article would express the findings without this.

> **Q1:** The researchers wish to send their findings to a scientific journal for publication. Write a suitable results section for this study. You should include:
>
> - A summary table of the findings.
> - A graphical display of the findings.
> - Results of the inferential statistical test. **(9 marks)**

For **Q1**, follow the bullet points in order, as this makes it easier for the examiner to find what they're looking for. Start with the summary table, which will include measures of central tendency (mean or median) and dispersion (standard deviation or range), NOT the raw data for participants.

There will be marks allocated for each of the bullet points in a question like this, so take care to address them thoroughly. For example, if you are sketching a bar chart, you must label axes with general labels as well as labelling the separate bars or using a key. You should draw the bars the correct heights (roughly) and you should include a scale on your y-axis and a title.

Informal reporting would say 'We tested the data using Wilcoxon…' whereas a formal style of reporting would be: 'The table below shows the findings of this study…' and 'The data was tested using Wilcoxon test as it was a repeated measures design using ordinal level data and a test of differences was required.' It doesn't matter which style you choose, but remember to justify your choice of statistical test, and explain how you know whether you know the results are significant or not. The Results section doesn't include an actual conclusion (relating back to the hypothesis) as this would go at the start of the Discussion section.

> **Q2:** What types of information would the researcher include in the 'Design' section of the scientific paper for this study when she is preparing it for publication? **(3 marks)**

Q2 is more generic, but you must apply it to the particular study. So consider: is it an experiment or something else? If it is an experiment, which experimental design has been used? If it is something else, such as an observation, how was it organised? Overt or covert? How many observers, and were they observing the same participants or different ones?

REVIEW

Writing abstracts is a very good discipline, and excellent practice for summarising research concisely. Practise this for all of the key studies in the specification as you revise. The rule is, no more than one sentence for each section, and a maximum of 150 words:

Introduction (aims)

Method: Design

Materials

Participants

Procedure

Results

Discussion: Conclusion

Relationship to previous research

Evaluation

Applications and implications

Gender in psychology: Gender bias

RECAP

A01 Description

- **Alpha bias** occurs when a theory assumes that there is a real and enduring difference between males and females.

- There is a tendency to exaggerate the differences between men and women and therefore devalue one gender.

- For example, Freud's theories reflected the culture in which he lived, where men were more powerful and typically more educated. Consequently, Freud's theory of psychoanalysis viewed femininity as a form of failed masculinity and it exaggerated the differences between men and women – an alpha bias.

- **Beta bias** occurs when a theory ignores or minimises the differences between males and females.

- For example, biological psychologists examining the fight-or-flight response typically conduct research using male animals. However, recent research shows that females produce a 'tend-and-befriend' response at times of stress (Taylor *et al.*, 2000). This beta-biased approach meant that female behaviour went undiscovered and that the stress response was not fully understood in women until recently.

- Psychology is a male-dominated subject and, historically, almost all psychologists were men. Consequently, many psychological theories represent a male point of view, which is known as **androcentrism**.

- The aim of psychology is to produce theories that have **universality** and apply to all people.

Females and males may have different perspectives.

A03 Evaluation / Discussion

Feminist psychology aims to redress gender bias…

Feminist psychology agrees that there are real biologically based sex differences, but socially determined stereotypes make a far greater contribution to perceived differences.	A prerequisite to any social change must be a revision of our 'facts' about gender that perpetuate our beliefs about women.	So feminist psychology seeks to understand behaviour in terms of social processes and thus find a way to greater equality.

Research methods can be biased…

It may not be that males and females are different, but that the methods used to test or observe them are biased.	For example, Rosenthal (1966) found that male experimenters are more pleasant, friendly and encouraging to female participants than to male participants. The result was that the male participants appeared to perform less well on the tasks assigned.	This means that there are serious issues with the way data is collected, which creates a false picture of male-female differences.

Avoiding beta bias…

On the one hand, the beta bias promotes equal treatment and has allowed women greater access to a range of opportunities.	However, it also draws attention away from important differences, for example the biological demands of pregnancy and childbirth.	Therefore, according to Hare-Mustin and Marecek (1988), we should avoid beta bias to ensure that notable differences are taken into consideration.

Gender-biased assumptions in theories…

For example, Darwin's theory of sexual selection portrays women as choosy when it comes to mate selection.	However, these views were rooted in Victorian ideas about gender roles, and have recently been challenged. Evidence suggests that women are equally competitive and aggressive when the need arises.	This highlights the importance of challenging gender research, to ensure that research portrays a valid picture of women.

 **APPLY**

AO2: An example

SCENARIO In a report for the World Health Organization, Astbury (2001, p.2) wrote: 'Even when presenting with identical symptoms, women are more likely to be diagnosed as depressed than men and less likely to be diagnosed as having problems with alcohol.'

What kind of gender bias could these responses by professionals represent? Suggest two reasons why gender bias may not be a complete explanation. **(3 marks)**

ANSWER *It is possible that alpha bias is responsible for stereotyping women as more susceptible to depression compared to men and seeing men as more prone than women to alcohol problems. Diagnosis is, however, complicated by the greater tendency of women to seek professional help for depression and for more men to seek help for alcohol problems. There may also be an element of self-stereotyping in that men and women are possibly more likely to acknowledge problems that seem fitting for their gender.*

AO2: Research methods

A researcher wants to find out whether staying at home as full-time caregivers affects the psychological health of parents of young children, and whether there is a difference for men and women.

a. **How could the researchers select a sample for this study? (3 marks)**
b. **Suggest one way gender bias could affect their sample, and how the researchers could deal with this. (3 marks)**

AO2: One for you to try

Asch's (1951) experiment examining conformity used a sample of 50 male college students from three different American colleges.

Explain how Asch's research was gender biased. (4 marks)

Solomon Asch, 1907–1996

 How do I answer... selection (multiple choice) questions?

> Which **one** of the following is a possible consequence of beta gender bias in research? **(1 mark)**
>
> A   Differences between men and women may be exaggerated.
>
> B   Theories may be based on men's and women's experiences.
>
> C   Research findings may be applied equally to men and women, despite actual differences between men and women.
>
> D   Theories may apply to all people, and include a recognition of differences.

Usually these questions require you to pick out the **one** statement that is correct, matches or defines a concept or idea. They may also (on occasion) ask you to pick out the **one** statement that is *incorrect* or does *not* match or define a concept or idea.

Although these are generally worth only 1 mark, getting them correct is still important because that 1 mark can be the difference between one grade and another. So, some general advice on answering these:

• Read the question very carefully. Is it asking you to pick the statement that matches (as here) or the 'odd one out' that doesn't match?

• Make life easier by crossing out any that are obviously *not* going to be the correct answer given the specific demands of the question.

Applying this to the question above we cross out **A** because that is describing *alpha bias, not beta bias*. We can also cross out **B** because that is describing a universal theory which recognises differences between men and women, and so does **D**. That just leaves **C**, which is the right answer!

 **REVIEW**

Issues such as gender bias and cultural bias can be applied to many of the studies you have learned during the course. You could go through your notes or this Revision Guide and highlight each time gender bias is mentioned as an AO3 evaluation point. Can you identify whether it is alpha or beta bias? Sometimes there can be alpha and beta bias in the same research or theory, but you need to be able to explain your decision. For example, Kohlberg's research into stages of moral development was beta biased as he researched males and applied his findings to females. However, when he tested women he found they were less developed according to his stages, so this became alpha bias. Make sure you can explain why, using the definitions of alpha and beta bias.

Culture in psychology: Cultural bias

 **RECAP**

A01 Description

- **Cultural bias** is the tendency to judge all people in terms of your own cultural assumptions.
- An **alpha bias** is when a theory assumes that there are real and enduring differences between cultural groups.
- For example, assuming that people from individualistic cultures are less conformist.
- A **beta bias** is when a theory ignores or minimises cultural differences, by assuming that all people are the same.
- For example, using Western intelligence (IQ) tests in other cultures gives biased results.

- **Ethnocentrism** is judging behaviour from your own cultural point of view and seeing your own beliefs, customs and behaviours as 'normal'.
- This is alpha bias, as other cultures' norms are devalued compared to the norms of the dominant culture.
- **Cultural relativism** is the idea that we should study behaviour in the context of the culture in which it originates. However, cultural relativism can lead to an alpha bias. For example, Mead's (1935) research concluded that there were significant gender differences due to culture, when in fact there weren't.

A03 Evaluation / Discussion

Indigenous psychologies can counter ethnocentricity…

Indigenous psychologies – the development of different groups of theories in different countries.

For example, Afrocentrism is a movement whose central proposition is that all black people have their roots in Africa and that psychological theories concerning such people must, therefore, be African-centred and express African values.

It suggests that the values and culture of Europeans at worst devalue non-European people, and at best are irrelevant to the life and culture of people of African descent.

The emic–etic distinction…

An 'emic' approach emphasises the uniqueness of every culture by focusing on culturally specific phenomena. The problem with such approaches is that the findings tend to be significant only to the understanding of behaviour within that culture.

On the other hand, an 'etic' approach can use indigenous researchers in each cultural setting to find universal behaviours. For example, Buss's (1989) study of mate preference used local researchers in 37 countries.

This kind of approach allows researchers to investigate universal behaviour, while avoiding cultural bias.

Bias in research methods…

Smith and Bond (1998) surveyed a European textbook on social psychology and found that 66 per cent of the studies were American, 32 per cent European and 2 per cent from the rest of the world.

In addition, Henrich *et al.* (2010) calculated that a randomly selected American student was 4000 times more likely to be a participant in a psychology study than a non-Westerner.

This suggests that psychological research is severely unrepresentative and can be improved by using samples from different cultural groups.

Culturally biased research helps to create or reinforce stereotypes…

The US Army used an IQ test before WWI which was culturally biased.

The test showed that African Americans were at the bottom of the scale in terms of IQ.

The data from this test had a profound effect on the attitudes held by Americans towards other groups of people, highlighting the danger of culturally biased research.

Most research participants are from Western, Educated, Industrialised, Rich, Democratic backgrounds.

APPLY

AO2: An example

SCENARIO The US Army IQ test. Here are some items from the test:

1. Washington is to Adams as first is to…

2. Crisco is a: patent medicine, disinfectant, toothpaste, food product?

3. What items are missing in these pictures?

(Answers: 1. Second, because Washington was the first US president and Adams was the second.

2. It is a food product. 3. A ball is missing from the man's right hand, and the tennis net is missing.)

Explain why these questions might be considered 'ethnocentric'. **(3 marks)**

ANSWER *Ethnocentrism refers to using one's own ethnic or cultural group as a basis for judging other groups. These three questions assess knowledge that would only be familiar to American citizens. For example, Washington and Adams are US presidents, therefore it would be unrealistic to assume that lack of this knowledge among individuals from other cultural groups is a sign of low intelligence.*

AO2: Research methods

In Margaret Mead's research, identify one ethical issue that Mead should have considered. Suggest how she could have dealt with this ethical issue. (3 marks)

AO2: One for you to try

Mead (1935) observed three tribal communities in New Guinea and concluded that there were differences in gender roles between the three tribes which would suggest that gender was a product of environment/culture rather than biology. She found Arapesh men and women to be gentle, responsive and cooperative, and the Mundugumor men and women to be violent and aggressive, seeking power and position. By contrast, the Tchambuli exhibited gender role differences: the women were dominant, impersonal and managerial, whereas the men were more emotionally dependent.

Using your knowledge of cultural bias, identify one strength and one limitation of Mead's research. (4 marks)

How do I answer... description only (AO1) questions?

There is a fairly simple formula in answering description only questions. For 2 marks, say two things, for 3 marks say three things and so on.

Work through the sample questions below, using the advice that follows them. The AO1 material for these questions is on the opposite page.

Q1: Explain what is meant by 'cultural bias' in psychology. **(2 marks)**

Use the AO1 'Cultural bias' point to define cultural bias, then mention alpha and beta bias.

Q2: Using examples, explain how alpha bias and beta bias can affect the validity of conclusions from cross-cultural research. **(4 marks)**

Use four AO1 points, two for alpha bias and two for beta bias. You will need to explain how these affect validity, as the assumption of differences (or similarities) may be incorrect. You must use examples, as there will be marks specifically allocated for these.

Q3: Briefly describe the issue of ethnocentrism in psychological research. **(2 marks)**

Use both AO1 'Ethnocentrism' points, making sure you use them to explain how research is affected.

Q4: Describe how cultural bias can affect psychological research. **(6 marks)**

Use the first six or seven AO1 points, making sure you use them to explain how research is affected.

REVIEW

Cultural bias is a common issue in research, and possibly unavoidable, so this issue can be applied to research from many topics you have covered in your course. See how many you can think of, without looking them up, before going back through your notes/the Student Book. Remind yourself of research from each of the Year 1 topics, using the table on the right. Identify which type of bias there is, how it might affect the conclusions, and how it could have been dealt with by cultural relativism or researching a broader range of participants.

	Research	Type of bias	Effect on conclusions	How to deal with it
Social influence				
Memory				
Attachment				
Psychopathology				
Approaches				
Biopsychology				

Free will and determinism

RECAP

AO1 Description

Determinism

- **Determinism** is the view that our behaviour is governed by internal or external forces.
  - > **Biological determinism** suggests that behaviour is governed by our genes. For example, research by Hill *et al.* (1999) found a particular gene (IGF2r) in people with high intelligence, suggesting that intelligence may be biologically determined.
  - > **Environmental determinism** suggests that our behaviour is caused by previous experience, through classical and operant conditioning. For example, humans develop phobias through classical conditioning, where a conditioned response can be learned if a neutral stimulus (e.g. a bee) is paired with an unconditioned stimulus (e.g. being stung), suggesting that some phobias may be environmentally determined.
  - > **Psychic determinism** suggests that our behaviour is caused by innate drives and early experiences.
- These three types represent **hard determinism**. **Soft determinism** recognises that behaviour may be predictable but is not inevitable; individuals are free to choose their behaviour within cognitive and social constraints.

Free will

- **Free will** is the view that humans have complete control over their behaviour and have the ability to make a choice.
- Humanistic psychologists, such as Maslow and Rogers, claim that humans have free will and that self-determination is a necessary part of human behaviour and without self-determination, self-actualisation is not possible.

AO3 Evaluation/Discussion

No behaviour is completely biologically determined…

Studies that compare identical twins typically find 80 per cent concordance rates for intelligence and 40 per cent for depression.	However, identical twins share 100 per cent of their genes and even though there is an 80 per cent similarity in terms of IQ, the results suggest that 20 per cent is caused by environmental factors.	*This suggests that neither biological nor environmental determinism can fully explain any behaviour. There is usually an interaction.*

Determinism can provide an excuse for immoral behaviour…

Stephen Mobley, who killed a pizza shop manager in 1981, claimed that he was 'born to kill' due to a history of violence in his family.	However, this argument was rejected and he was sentenced to death.	*A truly determinist position may be undesirable because it would allow individuals to 'excuse' their behaviour, leading to issues of criminal responsibility.*

Free will is an illusion and a culturally relative concept…

Behavioural psychologist Skinner claimed that free will is an illusion, as our choices are actually determined by previous reinforcement experiences.	Furthermore, the idea of self-determination may only be relevant in individualistic societies, as collectivist cultures emphasise group needs.	*This suggests that our experience of free will is a product of socialisation and is not universal.*

Research challenge to free will from cognitive neuroscience…

Libet *et al.* (1983) recorded activity in motor regions of the brain, before a person had conscious awareness of the decision to move their finger.	In other words, the decision to move the finger was a predetermined action of the brain.	*However, the brain activity may simply represent a 'readiness to act', so this evidence has been challenged by other researchers.*

 APPLY

AO2: An example

SCENARIO Abbie gains a place at university and starts a degree course in Business Studies with Psychology. In spite of her best efforts, she fails her first year exams. Instead of retaking them, she drops Business Studies and starts again, this time just taking Psychology. This time she is much more successful.

Using what you know about free will and determinism, discuss reasons why Abbie behaved as she did. (**4 marks**)

ANSWER *Free will means that Abbie's initial course choice and subsequent change were entirely her choice, probably based on what she thought would give her the best chance of personal growth and self-actualisation. Soft determinism means that she would have some element of choice over her actions, within social or cognitive constraints. Maybe her school encouraged her to apply for Business Studies (social constraint) but she found that Psychology suited her abilities better (cognitive constraint) so she ended up choosing this course.*

AO2: One for you to try

Andrew has always got his own way at school, by bullying and fighting with other children. His older brother was excluded from school for hitting another student and last week Andrew was also excluded for hitting another student.

Using your knowledge of determinism, suggest two reasons why Andrew is aggressive. (4 marks)

AO2: Research methods

Explain how scientific research can draw conclusions about cause and effect. (3 marks)

How do I answer... evaluation only (AO3) questions?

Like the description only questions on the previous spread, evaluation questions come in all sorts of shapes and sizes. Terms like 'evaluate', 'discuss', 'explain', 'criticism', 'strength' and 'limitation' all indicate that AO3 is required. The AO3 material for these questions is on the opposite page. Let's look at some examples:

Q1: Give one criticism of determinism in psychology. **(2 marks)**

You could choose either of the first two AO3 points opposite as your material for this question. For 2 marks, you could use the lead-in phrase (e.g. 'No behaviour is completely biologically determined...'), followed by the material in the first two columns (i.e. the main critical claim and its expansion).

Q2: Explain one limitation of the concept of free will in psychology. **(3 marks)**

This requires a little more elaboration than **Q1**, but this time you are asked to evaluate free will as a concept. You could use either the third or fourth AO3 point, including material from all three columns to access 3 marks.

Q3: Discuss the free will and determinism debate in psychology. **(6 marks)**

You need to fully elaborate two points, and make sure you have one from each side of the debate. Choose either the first or second AO3 point and pair this with either the third or fourth AO3 point.

REVIEW

To become familiar with this debate, practise writing answers of different lengths. Make sure you know the definitions and can explain them clearly, for 2- or 4-mark AO1 questions. Then make an essay plan for 'Discuss free will and determinism in psychology' (16 marks), including all four AO3 points. Spaced retrieval is a well-evidenced effective method of learning; test yourself on your essay plan after some time doing something else (or getting a night's sleep), and check you can still recall all the definitions and discussion points.

The nature–nurture debate

RECAP

AO1 Description

Nature and nurture

- Nature refers to innate (genetic) influences.
- However, this does not just refer to characteristics present at birth, but to any characteristics determined by genes and passed on through **heredity**. Secondary sexual characteristics which appear at puberty and conditions like Huntingdon's disease are also genetically determined.
- For example, schizophrenia has a concordance rate of 40 per cent for MZ twins and 7 per cent for DZ twins. This suggests that nature is a contributing factor in schizophrenia.
- **Nurture** refers to environmental influences which are acquired through interactions with the environment, including both the physical and social world.
- Nurture can affect an infant before and after birth.
- Behaviourists suggest that certain behaviours can be explained in terms of experience alone. For example, attachment could be explained in terms of classical conditioning (the infant associating the mother with food) and operant conditioning (food reducing the discomfort of hunger).
- The **nature–nurture debate** examines the relative contribution of nature and nurture to a particular behaviour: the extent to which nature and nurture are responsible, and how they interact.

Taxi drivers' hippocampi change with driving experience.

AO3 Evaluation / Discussion

An interactionist approach gives the best explanation…

It is not possible to separate nature and nurture, as they both contribute to behaviour.	For example, the disorder phenylketonuria is a genetic (nature) disorder. If it is identified at birth, the infant can be given a restricted diet and brain damage can be avoided (nurture).	This highlights the importance of an interactionist approach in considering both nature and nurture.

The diathesis-stress model…

A person can be born with a biological vulnerability, for example a gene for schizophrenia; however the disorder will only develop if it is triggered by a stressor in the environment.	Research has found that not everyone with genes for schizophrenia goes on to develop symptoms and therefore a person's nature is only expressed under certain conditions of nurture.	This highlights the importance of taking an interactionist approach, such as the diathesis-stress model.

Reactive, passive or active influence of nature on nurture…

An innately aggressive child may provoke aggressive responses in others, which affects the child's experience – a *reactive* influence.	Alternatively, a mentally ill parent may pass on genes for a disorder as well as creating an unstable environment for the child – a *passive* influence.	Thirdly, children choose experiences that suit their genes, known as niche picking or active influence.

Neural plasticity demonstrates how nature and nurture interact…

Maguire *et al.* (2000) showed how taxi drivers' hippocampi responded to increased use.	In addition, Blakemore and Cooper (1970) found that kittens raised in a restricted visual environment had permanent changes to their visual cortex.	These examples show how experience (nurture) affects brain structure, which is originally coded for by genes (nature).

 **APPLY**

AO2: An example

SCENARIO Pharrel is in the first year of his GCSEs but he spends more time in the Head of Year's office than in his classes. He frequently gets into fights with the other children in his class and has recently been excluded after it was discovered he was bullying other children and stealing from them. When teachers look into his family background they discover that his father is currently in prison for aggravated burglary and his two brothers both have a history of violent assault charges.

Using your knowledge of the nature–nurture debate, outline possible explanations for Pharrel's violent behaviour at school. **(6 marks)**

ANSWER *'Nature' explanations refer to behaviour being caused by genes, and aggressive behaviour in three close male relatives suggests genetic factors may underlie Pharrel's aggression. Nurture is the contribution of experience or interaction with the environment. Behaviourists would explain the aggression as a learned/conditioned response; Pharrel received attention for his behaviour from the Head of Year, which he may have found reinforcing. Social learning theory (SLT) would look at aggressive role models in the family – maybe Pharrel saw his father and brothers receiving rewards for their behaviour, so he believes he will too (vicarious reinforcement).*

AO2: One for you to try

Look at the picture of the two cats. Rainbow (on the left) was cloned to produce a kitten called CC (on the right). They have identical genes but look quite different.

Using your knowledge of the nature–nurture debate, explain two reasons why CC is different to Rainbow, despite having exactly the same genes. (4 marks)

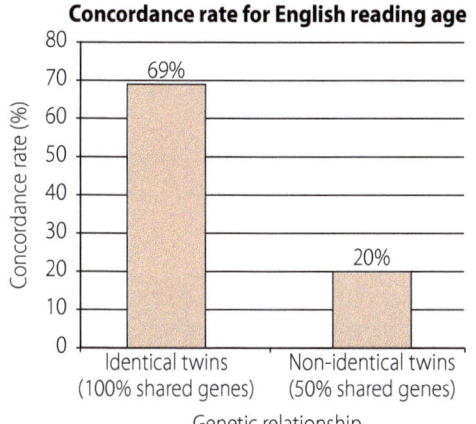

AO2: Research methods

Researchers used a test to examine the English reading age of pairs of identical and non-identical twins. If the twins had a similar reading age, then they were said to be concordant.

The results of the experiment can be found in the graph below.

Concordance rate for English reading age

[Bar chart: y-axis "Concordance rate (%)" from 0 to 80. Identical twins (100% shared genes) = 69%; Non-identical twins (50% shared genes) = 20%. x-axis "Genetic relationship".]

What can you conclude from the graph in relation to the nature–nurture debate? (4 marks)

 How do I answer... application questions (AO2)?

In the example about Pharrel in **AO2: An example**, you can see how to obtain all the marks in this type of question. For 6 marks, you need three pieces of psychology, each explicitly linked to the stem:

1 Find a bit of appropriate psychology. e.g. 'Nature explanations refer to behaviour being caused by genes.'

2 Use this to explain some aspect of the scenario, e.g. 'Aggressive behaviour in three close male relatives suggests genetic factors may underlie Pharrel's aggression.'

3 Find a second bit of psychology, e.g. 'Nurture is the contribution of experience or interaction with the environment. Behaviourists would explain the aggression as a learned/conditioned response.'

4 Use this to explain the scenario, e.g. 'Pharrel received attention for his behaviour from the Head of Year, which he may have found reinforcing.'

5 Find a third bit of psychology, e.g. 'SLT would look at aggressive role models in the family.'

6 Again link this to the scenario, e.g. 'Maybe Pharrel saw his father and brothers receiving rewards for their behaviour, so he believes he will too (vicarious reinforcement).'

 REVIEW

As with all the issues and debates, nature–nurture is very useful for high-level evaluation in many extended answers throughout the course. Whenever you see research about genes, twins or adaptive advantages of a characteristic, those are 'nature' explanations. These are related to biological determinism. 'Nurture' relates to experience or the environment, and links to environmental determinism. The interesting part of the discussion is about **how** nature and nurture interact. Think through each of the approaches and their position on the nature–nurture debate, then think of examples of different ways nature and nurture interact. You should prepare an essay plan (16 marks) for 'Discuss the relative importance of heredity and environment in determining behaviour'. Include some examples from different approaches. Which points would you select for an 8-mark question?

Holism and reductionism

RECAP

AO1 Description

- A **reductionist approach** involves breaking down complex phenomena and behaviours into their simplest components.

  > **Biological reductionism** reduces complex behaviours to the actions of neurons, neurotransmitters, hormones, etc. For example, biological psychologists suggest that schizophrenia is caused by excessive activity of the neurotransmitter dopamine.

  > **Environmental reductionism** reduces behaviours to simple stimulus-response links. For example, behavioural psychologists suggest that attachment is the result of an infant associating their mother with food, through classical conditioning.

- **Experimental reductionism** isolates and operationalises variables in order to determine causal relationships.

- **Levels of explanation:**

  > Highest level, which includes cultural and social explanations of how social groups affect behaviour.

  > Middle level, which includes psychological explanations of behaviour.

  > Lower level, including biological (hormone and genes) or environmental (stimulus-response units) explanations.

- A **holistic approach** suggests that we need to understand the whole experience, rather than the individual features, to fully understand complex phenomena and behaviours.

  > Humanistic psychologists believe that the individual reacts as an organised whole. What matters is a person's sense of a unified identity; and thus a lack of integration leads to mental disorder.

Dogs can be conditioned to imitate human behaviour, but the meaning of the behaviour may not be the same.

AO3 Evaluation / Discussion

The danger of lower levels of explanation…

In a reductionist approach, lower levels, in particular biological or behavioural levels, are taken in isolation and therefore the meaning of the behaviour might be overlooked.	For example, using the drug Ritalin as a treatment for ADHD may ignore the true cause of the child's hyperactive behaviour.	*This means we do not develop an accurate understanding of human behaviour and may only treat symptoms and ignore underlying causes.*

Biological reductionism has led to the development of drug therapies…

Drug therapies have led to treatments which have resulted in a considerable reduction in institutionalisation since the 1950s.	However, the success rates of drug treatments are highly variable and they treat the symptoms while ignoring the context and function of mental illness.	*On the other hand, psychological therapies have also produced many successful therapies.*

Environmental reductionism oversimplifies human behaviour…

A limitation of the behaviourist approach is that it was developed using experiments with non-human animals.	While it may be appropriate to explain non-human animals' behaviour in terms of simple components, reductionist explanations ignore other possible influences such as cognitive and emotional factors.	*This means that environmental reductionism ignores other possible influences on human behaviour, such as social context, intentions and emotions.*

Experimental reductionism limits the validity of conclusions…

Reducing behaviour to a form that can be studied has been productive but ultimately may not tell us much about everyday life.	For example, the findings from laboratory experiments investigating eyewitness testimony (Loftus and Palmer, 1974) are contradicted by studies of real-life eyewitnesses, whose memories were highly accurate (e.g. Yuille and Cutshall, 1986).	*The operationalisation of variables, such as eyewitness memory, may result in something that is measurable but bears no resemblance to the real thing.*

 **APPLY**

AO2: An example

SCENARIO Alex was addicted to smoking cigarettes and sought help. The nurse who helped her viewed smoking as a physical substance dependence. Some weeks afterwards, Alex had managed to stop smoking, but found that she had started eating too much chocolate instead.

Discuss Alex's difficulties, referring to reductionist and holistic explanations.
(6 marks)

ANSWER *The nurse took a biologically reductionist view, seeing smoking as an acquired dependence on nicotine which, once broken, results in complete cure. The apparent substitution of nicotine with chocolate could also be reduced to physically based substance dependence. However, the need to substitute one substance with another could be explained in a more holistic way; perhaps Alex needs some form of oral comfort to help her to control anxiety. A more effective treatment would take a holistic view, considering Alex's emotions and cognitions as well as social and cultural factors. The treatment could help her to deal with her thoughts and feelings in a healthier way, using psychological therapy to control her anxiety, and changing her circumstances if they were making her anxious.*

How do I answer... longer (16-mark) questions?

Q1: Discuss holism and reductionism in psychology.
(16 marks)

Q2: Discuss levels of explanation in psychology, referring to an area of psychology you have studied. **(16 marks)**

Any of the issues and debates are possible targets for an extended answer to a 'discuss' question, and they lend themselves well to a discursive type of writing. This may include evidence, counter-evidence, strengths and limitations, applications and implications.

Here are some tips:

1. Plan your answer carefully. Use the planning box – jot down key words for each of your paragraphs. Plan towards 6 marks of AO1 and four effective discussion points.

2. Think about a logical structure in your writing. For **Q1**, this might be defining the terms first, and referring to approaches or research that take a reductionist or holistic perspective, then evaluating each separately. **Q2** is a very similar essay, but you need to frame your answer within the concept of levels of explanation.

3. Develop your points thoroughly, using all three columns of the AO3 we have given you on the opposite page, to make your essay discursive. This may include link words such as 'however' or 'on the other hand'.

AO2: One for you to try

Fred and Mary are discussing their son's refusal to tidy his bedroom. Fred says, 'We should give him a reward each time he tidies his room, and punish him every day it is messy'. Mary objects to this view, saying, 'I think he needs more than just rewards and punishments. He needs to understand the benefits of a tidy room, and to see you tidying up the house, and to realise how lucky he is to even have a room, as so many children in the world don't.'

Use the concepts of reductionism and holism to explain Fred and Mary's different views. (4 marks)

AO2: Research methods

Christiansen and Hubinette (1993) questioned 58 victims and bystanders several months after they had witnessed bank robberies in Sweden. They found that the victims (assumed to be more anxious) had better recall than the bystanders.

a. **What type of experiment was this? (1 mark)**

b. **What can you conclude about the effect of anxiety on recall? (2 marks)**

c. **How was anxiety operationalised? (1 mark)**

d. **What ethical issues would the researchers need to consider in this research? (2 marks)**

e. **Suggest why findings of lab experiments into anxiety and eyewitness testimony have often contradicted the findings of this experiment. (3 marks)**

f. **State two advantages of conducting lab experiments such as these. (2 marks)**

g. **Explain how experimental reductionism can affect the findings of lab experiments. (3 marks)**

REVIEW

On a separate piece of paper, draw a line, where one end is labelled 'Reductionism' and the other is labelled 'Holism'.

'Reductionism' ◄─────────────► 'Holism'

Consider where the six key psychological approaches would fit on this continuum: behavioural, biological, humanistic, psychodynamic, cognitive and social learning theory. Write these labels in the appropriate place.

Once you have done this, you could add the key studies/theories you have encountered to your labels, e.g. Cognitive – Loftus and Palmer (1974).

Finally, you could state what type of reductionism (if any) the study demonstrates, e.g. Cognitive – Loftus and Palmer (1974) – Experimental reductionism. This would provide you with a great tool for evaluation in your Year 2 essays.

Idiographic and nomothetic approaches to psychological investigation

 **RECAP**

AO1 Description

- **The idiographic approach** to psychological research focuses on individuals and emphasises uniqueness.

- This approach is qualitative, because the focus is on developing an in-depth insight into human behaviour, and employs methods such as unstructured interviews, case studies and thematic analysis.

- For example, Freud (1909) used case studies in order to understand human behaviour. The case study of Little Hans consisted of approximately 150 pages of quotes recorded by Hans' father, plus Freud's own interpretations.

- Humanistic psychologists also favour the idiographic approach, as they are concerned with studying the person's subjective experience.

- **The nomothetic approach** is based on the study of large numbers of people and aims to make generalisations in order to formulate general theories of behaviour.

- This approach uses quantitative methods, analysing numerical data using statistical analysis.

- The biological approach takes a nomothetic approach and seeks to formulate general laws about how the brain works.

- Behaviourist psychologists produced general laws of behaviour, for example classical and operant conditioning, to explain learning in humans and animals.

- Cognitive psychology is also nomothetic, although case studies (such as HM) can be used to illustrate memory processes.

How do you know these are all dog faces? Focusing on similarities between many individuals and making general rules is a nomothetic approach.

AO3 Evaluation / Discussion

A strength of the idiographic approach is its focus on the individual…

Allport (1961), who was the first to use the term idiographic, argued that a drastic reorientation was needed as psychologists had lost sight of what it was to be human.

Allport argued that there was too much emphasis on measurement, and it is only by knowing the person as an individual that we can predict what that person will do in any situation.

This suggests that the focus on individuals can provide us with a more complete understanding.

How scientific is an idiographic approach…?

Case studies may not be replicable, but they still aim to be objective and evidence-based.

Qualitative approaches use reflexivity to identify biases: the researcher reflects on any factors that affect researchers' or participants' behaviour.

Idiographic approaches do embrace many of the aims of the scientific approach.

The idiographic approach is more time consuming…

Both approaches are based on large amounts of data, but idiographic research collects large amounts of data about one person whereas nomothetic research collects data from a large number of people.

Collecting large amounts of data from a group of people takes time but can be quicker because, once you have devised a questionnaire or psychological test, data can be generated and processed quickly.

This means that the idiographic approach is less efficient when it comes to data collection.

Combining idiographic and nomothetic methods…

Holt (1967) claimed that there is no such thing as a unique individual and that the idiographic approach is still used to generate principles of behaviour.

Millon and David (1996) argue that researchers should start with the nomothetic approach and can then focus on idiographic understanding.

Consequently, researchers suggest that both approaches should be used together.

APPLY

AO2: An example

SCENARIO The experience of elderly people who were losing their sight was researched by a psychologist. She interviewed five volunteers in their homes, and also interviewed their carers and other relatives, to find out how they felt their visual impairment had affected their life, and what their needs were.

This idiographic research yielded qualitative data. How could the researcher go on to collect further data using a nomothetic approach? **(6 marks)**

ANSWER *'Idiographic' refers to unique characteristics in each individual while 'nomothetic' refers to generalisations from a larger sample. The researcher should get a much larger sample of elderly people with visual impairments, maybe through an eye clinic. She could use questionnaires to obtain quantitative data about their lives and their needs, and also she could obtain secondary data about the visual impairments of the individuals. She could analyse the data using statistical methods and make generalisations, drawing conclusions about people in this situation, which would be useful for comparing other people's experiences to a norm, or for planning social care.*

AO2: One for you to try

Two educational psychologists decided to conduct some research in a local primary school. One researcher chose to conduct a case study on Jack, a pupil with extreme behavioural difficulties. The other researcher chose to examine the entire student population, to formulate a general theory in relation to mathematical ability and self-confidence.

Using your knowledge of idiographic and nomothetic, explain how the psychologists used these two different approaches. (4 marks)

AO2: Research methods

The psychologist conducting a case study on Jack (see **AO2: One for you to try**) used observations and interviews with Jack and his teachers.

a. **How could the researcher analyse this qualitative data? (4 marks)**

b. **Identify two ethical issues that the researcher would need to consider in this research. (4 marks)**

The psychologist researching mathematical ability had access to 400 children.

c. **What research methods could the researcher use to collect data about mathematical ability and self-confidence? (4 marks)**

d. **How could the researcher analyse this data and draw conclusions? (3 marks)**

e. **Discuss the strengths and limitations of the two psychologists' approaches. (6 marks)**

How do I answer... 'Distinguish between' questions (AO3)?

Distinguish between idiographic and nomothetic approaches to research. **(4 marks)**

If you are asked to 'compare' or 'distinguish between' two concepts, you must compare a specific aspect of them. Don't just describe one then describe the other. The process is:

1. Choose a feature which is relevant to both, e.g. their focus.

2. Explain the difference, using 'whereas' to connect the two ideas, e.g. 'Idiographic methods focus on the individual, whereas nomothetic methods study large numbers of people'.

3. Elaborate further to get more marks, e.g. 'This means that idiographic methods obtain deep, rich, descriptive qualitative data, whereas nomothetic methods collect quantitative data which can be analysed statistically'. Two clear comparisons will be enough for 4 marks.

REVIEW

When you are comparing two concepts, it is useful to make a table. This could be two theories, two explanations for a behaviour, two similar research studies, etc. In this case, we are comparing two approaches to research. Make a table and try to compare equivalent aspects of the approaches:

	Idiographic	Nomothetic
Focus		
Size of sample		
Possible research methods		
Type of data collected		
Purpose		
Examples from topics		

Ethical implications of research studies and theory

AO1 Description

- Researchers have a duty to balance the rights of individual research participants against the potential benefits for individuals and society.

- **Socially sensitive research** refers to studies in which there are potential social consequences or implications, either directly for the participants in research or the class of individuals represented by the research.

- **The research process** Sieber and Stanley (1988) identified four aspects of the research process at which ethical issues with social consequences may occur:

  > The research question. For example, the research question, 'Is homosexuality inherited?', could add credibility to a prevailing prejudice.

  > The treatment of the participants: ensuring confidentiality for participants.

  > The institutional context: ensuring that the data is not misused or misreported as research is often funded by private institutions.

  > Interpretation of findings. For example, an IQ test was used to demonstrate the inferiority of certain groups of people.

- They described 10 **ethical issues in socially sensitive research**.

- These include: privacy, confidentiality, methodology (invalid findings could shape social policy and harm those represented), deception, informed consent, equitable treatment (e.g. not withholding educational opportunities from one group), scientific freedom (scientists have a duty to conduct research, while not harming their participants), ownership of data, values, and risk/benefit ratio (it is difficult to identify risks).

SEVERE DANGER OF ETHICAL CONSEQUENCES

AO3 Evaluation / Discussion

The wider impact of research…

Even with socially sensitive research, there is the potential for an indirect impact on the participant's family and co-workers, which may not be taken into account.

Findings may also have implications for groups that the participant represents, e.g. addicts, women, the elderly.

Therefore, socially sensitive research should also take into account the likely impact of the research for the wider community.

Research may disadvantage marginalised groups…

Many groups are often excluded from, or misrepresented in, psychological research, e.g. disabled people.

This failure to represent and research such groups creates an additional ethical issue, as these people miss out on the benefits of research.

This means that our understanding of human behaviour has been limited by our failure to represent different groups.

Just avoid socially sensitive research…

Researchers could avoid researching sensitive areas like homosexuality, race, gender and addiction because the findings may have negative consequences for the participants.

However, this would probably leave psychologists with nothing to research but unimportant issues.

Sieber and Stanley (1988) argued that this is an avoidance of responsibility by psychologists, who have the duty to conduct socially sensitive research.

Engaging with the public and policymakers…

In order to reduce the likelihood of misuse of data, psychologists should take responsibility for their findings.

They should be aware of the possibility that their research might lend support to prejudices and lead to discrimination.

Sieber and Stanley (1988) recommend that researchers should promote evidence-based research in a socially sensitive way and not take a neutral position.

APPLY

AO2: An example

SCENARIO A psychologist believes that it is possible to identify patterns of electrical activity in the brain which identify children with exceptional mathematical ability. It is claimed that this is detectable before five years of age. The psychologist wants to see if this is correct and puts forward a research proposal for funding.

a. *Who might be adversely affected by this research and how?* **(3 marks)**

b. *Who might be positively affected by this research and how?* **(3 marks)**

ANSWER *a. 'Exceptional' children may be channelled into certain types of education too early and without choice, possibly at the expense of other attributes that may have been able to develop. Parents and educators may feel obliged to assess children and respond to exceptional ability in competitive ways. Assessment may not be available to all, so some children miss out. Educational systems may focus too heavily on mathematical ability at the expense of a balanced curriculum.*

b. Early recognition of exceptional ability fosters its development, possibly providing a fulfilling education for the child. Parents and educators may be better informed about how to deal with the child, e.g. in ensuring they have a well-rounded education. There may be wider benefits to society in the application of superior mathematical knowledge.

How do I answer... research methods questions?

Q1: How could the researchers obtain a random sample of participants for this study? **(3 marks)**

Q2: Why did the researchers obtain a random sample of participants for this study? **(3 marks)**

Remember that at least 25 per cent of your marks will be for research methods questions, which can appear in any section of any A Level paper, as well as the multi-part questions in Section C in Paper 2. They could include any aspect of research methods, data analysis or ethical issues. You must apply your knowledge to the specific study that is described, rather than just regurgitating definitions or strengths and limitations in a generic way. Here are some tips:

1. Take time to think, make sure you have understood the research scenario. Identify the IV and DV. Use a highlighter.

2. Read the question and be clear what it is asking you. In particular, is it asking 'how' researchers do something (**Q1** above), or 'why' (**Q2** above)? If the question is 'how', you need to give steps in a procedure. If it is 'why', you should focus on the benefits of the research design choice the researcher has made.

In **Q1**, for example, they could write all the names of potential participants on pieces of paper. Then put the pieces of paper in a bowl. Then take out 20 for each group.

In **Q2**, for example, the random sample is less biased than a volunteer or opportunity sample, and therefore will be more representative of the target population, so the results can be generalised.

AO2: One for you to try

In a study of intelligence and social background, researchers interviewed 100 children in two schools. They were classified in relation to their intelligence level. The researchers found that the majority of the 'low intelligence' children attended the state comprehensive school, while the majority of the other two groups attended the independent school.

Using your knowledge of social sensitivity, discuss how researchers could deal with the issues of social sensitivity in this study. (4 marks)

AO2: Research methods

a. **What level of measurement is being used in the AO2: One for you to try study? (1 mark)**

b. **Outline one issue with using this level of measurement. (2 marks)**

The children were then given IQ tests, and the results are shown in the table below.

IQ scores	State school	Independent school
Mean	97	111
Median	102	112
Mode	110	110

c. **Describe the distributions of intelligence in the two schools, and give a reason for your answer. (3 marks)**

d. **Which statistical test would be suitable to compare the mean IQ scores in the two schools? Explain your choice. (3 marks)**

REVIEW

You could be asked about ethical implications of any piece of research, and you need to be able to run through a mental checklist of ethical issues affecting individual participants, and more general issues relating to social sensitivity. Test yourself on these now, and come back to them at intervals (one day, one week, one month…) to ensure you can still remember them.

If you have completed the Issues and Debates topic, you should be prepared to write an 8-mark or 16-mark essay on any of the issues and debates, referring to examples from other topics. You should also be able to use issues and debates to evaluate theory or research in all the other topics from Year 1 or Year 2 of your course. Look out for the **Issues/Debates** tags in the Year 1 Revision Guide for some suggestions, and practise explaining **why** the issue or debate is relevant to that topic. In the Student Book for Year 2, we have made a list of suggestions of material from each topic that illustrate issues and debates. You may find this useful in your revision. (See Year 2 Student Book p.327–29.)

RECAP

AO1 Description

- **Sexual selection** explains the evolution of characteristics that confer a reproductive advantage as opposed to a survival advantage.

- **Intrasexual selection** Individuals of one sex must outcompete other members of their sex in order to mate and pass on their genes. Characteristics that lead to reproductive success (e.g. strength, intelligence) become more widespread in the gene pool because of the reproductive advantage to the winners.

- **Intersexual selection** Members of one sex evolve preferences for desirable qualities in potential mates. Members of the opposite sex who possess these characteristics (e.g. attractiveness, status, resources) gain a mating advantage over those who do not.

- **Sexual selection and long-term mate preferences** Low-quality mates (e.g. who are unattractive and unhealthy) are more likely to produce unattractive, unhealthy offspring. A high-quality mate leads to higher quality offspring and an individual's genes are more likely to be passed on.

  > For females, this means being attracted to males who are able to invest resources in her and her children, and shows promise as a good parent.

  > For males, this means being attracted to females who display signals of fertility, an indication of their reproductive value (Buss, 1989).

AO3 Evaluation/Discussion

Cultural traditions may be just as important as evolutionary forces…

Bernstein (2015) claims that gender differences in mate preference patterns might stem from cultural traditions rather than being the result of evolved characteristics.	Kassa and Sharma (1999) found that women valued potential mates' access to resources far more in cultures where women's status and educational opportunities were sharply limited.	This suggests that the role of social and economic factors are as important as evolutionary factors in establishing mate preference patterns.

Female preferences for high-status men may not be universal…

Buller (2005) claims that evolutionary psychologists are mistaken in their claims of a universal female preference for high-status men as mates.	Most studies on female mate preferences have been carried out on female undergraduate students. They would be expected to show a preference for men with similar interests, education and prospects to their own.	Buller concludes, therefore, that the evidence for a universal female mating preference for high-status men is weak or non-existent.

Mate choice in real life…

Studies such as Buss's survey of mate preferences may only give an indication of expressed preferences rather than a reflection of what happens in real life.	However, many real-life studies also support these mate-choice hypotheses. A study of actual marriages in 29 cultures (Buss, 1989) confirmed that men do choose younger women.	Despite this, questionnaires such as the ones used in Buss's study are more about partner preference than reflecting real relationships, particularly in cultures where arranged marriages are the norm.

Mate choice and the menstrual cycle…

Penton-Voak et al. (1999) suggests that, far from being constant, female mate choice varies across the menstrual cycle.	Typically, women choose a feminised version of a male face for long-term relationships. For short-term relationships, during the high conception risk phase of the menstrual cycle, more masculinised faces were preferred. This suggests genetic benefits in producing masculine offspring.	However, a meta-analysis (Wood et al., 2014) failed to support Penton-Voak's claim of a preference for masculine males when women were at their most fertile.

 **APPLY**

AO2: An example

SCENARIO Natasha is writing her online dating profile. She describes herself as young, kind and caring. She adds a photograph of herself at a recent wedding where she had her hair and make-up professionally done. Browsing through other people's profiles, she notices Billy, who describes himself as professional, ambitious and loving. She thinks he looks like a gentle person in his profile photo.

Discuss evolutionary explanations for partner preferences, making reference to Natasha and Billy in your answer. **(16 marks)**

ANSWER **An extract showing how you could address the AO2 requirements of this question:** *Natasha has promoted characteristics that males would be attracted to, e.g. men seek youth and physical attractiveness (hence her choice of photo) as an indication of fertility. She is drawn to Billy's profile by his 'gentle' appearance: a desirable trait in a long-term partner as it suggests good parenting. According to evolutionary explanations, females also seek a partner with resources as they will be able to provide for any offspring resulting from the union. Both males and females seek traits such as 'kind' and 'loving' in a mate as signs of future parenting skills. Buss's (1989) survey of over 10,000 people found the traits displayed by Natasha and Billy in their dating profiles to be universal, suggesting an innate preference for certain traits...*

AO2: One for you to try

Reuben and Tim are in Year 13 and very attracted to Ashiakia in their psychology class. While Ashiakia finds Reuben more attractive, once she discovers that Tim works for Waitrose and has a university place and that Reuben doesn't have a job and has no plans to go to university, she decides to start dating Tim.

Using your knowledge of evolutionary explanations for partner preferences, explain why Ashiakia decides to date Tim and not Reuben. (4 marks)

AO2: Research methods

It is often claimed that the best way to see these evolutionary forces in action is to browse the 'personal ads' in newspapers or online. This is where males and females looking for love 'advertise' their qualities whilst also stating the qualities they are looking for in a mate. Design a study that would research the male/female differences in this process.

a. **Based on what you know about evolutionary explanations for partner preferences, construct a directional hypothesis for your study. (2 marks)**

b. **What type of sampling method would you use? Briefly explain one limitation of this sampling method for this study. (3 marks)**

c. **Write the 'Procedure' section that would be appropriate if you were writing this up in a scientific report. (4 marks)**

 How do I answer... selection (multiple choice) questions?

> Which **one** of the following is a typical characteristic of sexual selection? **(1 mark)**
>
> A Males and females develop characteristics that increase their chances of survival.
>
> B Males learn from experience what makes a good mate and choose accordingly.
>
> C Females compete with other females for access to males.
>
> D Females choose males who are able to provide resources.

Usually these questions require you to pick out the **one** statement that is correct, matches or defines a concept or idea. They may also (on occasion) ask you to pick out the **one** statement that is *incorrect* or does *not* match or define a concept or idea.

Although these are generally worth only 1 mark, getting them correct is still important because that 1 mark can be the difference between one grade and another. So, some general advice on answering these:

- Read the question very carefully. Is it asking you to pick the statement that matches (as here) or the 'odd one out' that doesn't match?

- Make life easier by crossing out any that are obviously *not* going to be the correct answer given the specific demands of the question.

- Applying this to the question above we cross out **A** because that is describing *natural* selection rather than sexual selection. We can also cross out **B** because that is describing a learning process from than an evolutionary one. That leaves a choice of **C** and **D**, and, much as us males would love to think females fight over us, the opposite tends to be true, so **C** is out. That just leaves **D**, which is the right answer!

REVIEW

Knowing what is, and what is not, sexual selection (e.g. compared to natural selection), and the difference between intrasexual and intersexual selection is vital for all the questions you are likely to face on this topic. There are a few things that you can do to help you with this.

1 Can you come up with a couple of typical characteristics for each of these?

2 Can you highlight the *differences* between intrasexual and intersexual selection?

3 Try writing a few rough notes about how a researcher might test these ideas in a human population.

4 Try browsing the personal ads in your local newspaper. Do they support the idea that males offer resources and look for youth and personal attractiveness in a partner, and females offer youth and personal attractiveness and look for resources? Do you find evidence of males and females offering and looking for something other than these (e.g. intelligence, kindness, sense of humour, good parenting skills, etc.)?

Physical attractiveness

RECAP

AO1 Description

- Buss (1989) demonstrated that men in particular place great importance on physical attractiveness when choosing a mate. Physical appearance is an important cue to a woman's health and hence her fertility.

- Eastwick *et al.* (2011) suggests that physical attractiveness may also be important to women when choosing a partner for short-term relationships, but less important in choosing a long-term mate.

- **The matching hypothesis** claims that individuals seek out partners whose social desirability approximately equals their own (Walster and Walster, 1969).

  > According to this view, when choosing a partner, individuals first assess their own 'value' in the eyes of a potential partner and then select the best available candidates likely to be attracted to them.

  > This hypothesis has become associated with matching on physical attractiveness alone, suggesting that people pair up with those who are similar in terms of physical attractiveness.

  > Realistic choices must consider what the person desires, whether the other person wants them in return, and whether other desirable alternatives are available for either of them.

AO1 Key Study (Walster *et al.*, 1966)

- **PROCEDURE** Walster *et al.* randomly selected male and female students who purchased tickets for a 'computer dance'. Four accomplices rated each of them for physical attractiveness.

  > Participants completed a questionnaire to assess personality, intelligence, etc. and were told that this would be used to allocate their ideal partner for the evening (although pairing was done completely randomly).

  > During the intermission, participants were asked to complete a questionnaire about their dates, with a follow-up questionnaire distributed six months later.

- **FINDINGS** These did not support the matching hypothesis.

  > Regardless of their own physical attractiveness, participants responded more positively to physically attractive dates and were more likely to subsequently try to arrange dates with them.

  > Other factors, such as personality and intelligence, did not affect liking the dates or any subsequent attempts to date them.

AO3 Evaluation / Discussion

Speed dating and the challenge to traditional views of attraction…

Eastwick and Finkel (2008) claim that although men may value physical attractiveness more than women do, this does not predict real-life partner choice.

Prior to speed-dating sessions, participants showed traditional sex differences when stating the importance of physical attractiveness or earning prospects in an ideal partner. However, these preferences failed to predict their actual behaviour during and after the event.

They concluded that no significant sex differences emerged in the degree to which judgements of targets' physical attractiveness or earning prospects influenced participants' romantic interest in those targets.

Matching is more complex than mere physical attractiveness…

Sprecher and Hatfield (2009) explain why research often fails to find evidence of matching in terms of physical attractiveness. People offer many desirable characteristics of which physical attractiveness is just one.

A person may compensate for a lack of physical attractiveness with other desirable qualities such as a charming personality, kindness, status, etc. (i.e. 'complex matching').

This suggests that people are able to attract partners far more physically attractive than themselves by offering other assets.

Research support for sex differences in the importance of physical attractiveness…

If physical attractiveness in a partner is more important for males, then males with physically attractive partners should be more satisfied with their relationship.

Meltzer *et al.* (2014) provided support for this. Husbands' relationship satisfaction was positively related to objective ratings of their wives' physical attractiveness at the beginning and for at least the first four years of marriage.

In contrast, husbands' physical attractiveness was not related to wives' marital satisfaction, either initially or over time.

Implications of sex differences in the importance of physical attractiveness…

Research challenges the claim that women experience increased pressures to maintain their physical attractiveness in order to successfully maintain a long-term relationship.

However, men and women also desire partners who are supportive, trustworthy and warm. Those with partners who demonstrate these qualities tend to be more satisfied with their relationships (Pasch and Bradbury, 1998).

As a result, less physically attractive women who possess these other qualities tend to have partners who are just as satisfied as those with more physically attractive mates.

APPLY

AO2: An example

SCENARIO Gareth has arranged to meet his blind date at a local restaurant. He arrives early and decides to wait for his date by the bar. He sees a stunning woman walk through the door; while he hopes she is there to meet him, he tells himself she is 'out of my league'.

With reference to Gareth, outline the role of physical attractiveness in attraction. **(4 marks)**

ANSWER *Buss's cross-cultural research found men place particular importance on physical attractiveness when choosing a mate. This is seen as Gareth immediately notices the woman's appearance as she enters the restaurant. He hopes she is there to meet him – her 'stunning' appearance makes her a desirable potential partner as her attractiveness implies health and fertility. However, Gareth worries he may not be of a similar level of attractiveness. The matching hypothesis suggests we would expect people to pair up with someone who is similar in terms of physical attractiveness, and so while Gareth may wish for a relationship with the woman, she may not be so inclined.*

AO2: One for you to try

Craig and Lorraine divorced when they were in their late forties. One Friday evening when Craig went to Lorraine's house to pick up his children for the weekend, he was shocked when she opened the door. She was tanned, wearing clothes from a fashionable boutique and her hair was no longer grey but blonde. 'Wow', he said, 'You look sensational.' 'I've got a date tonight,' she explained, 'so I thought I'd try to impress him.' Craig told her she would have impressed him anyway as she was a very intelligent and accomplished woman. 'Ah well,' she replied, 'You know what men are like, they aren't interested in us oldies.'

Using insights from research into the role of physical attractiveness in attraction, explain why Lorraine felt the need to impress her date in the way she described above. (4 marks)

AO2: Research methods

A researcher used a questionnaire to assess the importance of four different qualities for partner selection, in males and females. The results are show in the graph below.

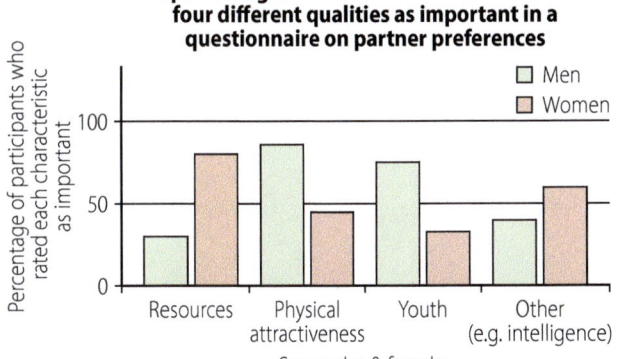

The percentages of males and females who rated four different qualities as important in a questionnaire on partner preferences

What does the bar chart show about partner preferences for men and women and how can psychology explain these findings? (4 marks)

How do I answer... description only (AO1) questions?

There is a fairly simple formula in answering description only questions. For 2 marks, say two things, for 3 marks say three things and so on.

So, working through the sample questions below, and using the AO1 material on the opposite page.

> **Q1:** Briefly explain what is meant by the matching hypothesis. **(2 marks)**

> **Q2:** Briefly explain the relationship between physical attractiveness and attraction in romantic relationships. **(3 marks)**

> **Q3:** Outline the matching hypothesis as it applies to attraction. **(4 marks)**

> **Q4:** Describe the relationship between physical attractiveness and attraction in romantic relationships. **(6 marks)**

Q1: Use the first two 'The matching hypothesis' points (The matching hypothesis claims…; According to this view…).

Q2: Use the first three 'Physical attractiveness' points.

Q3: Use all four 'The matching hypothesis' points

Q4: Use all six 'Physical attractiveness' points.

This approach adds an appropriate level of detail to each answer and gives the examiner a useful way of discriminating between your answer and one that would be worth fewer than the maximum marks for that question.

REVIEW

Being able to describe something concisely, while maintaining accuracy, is not as easy as it sounds. On the opposite page, we have stripped down the descriptive detail you will find in the main textbook to give you some guidance about how to do just that. Let's now play around with that content to make it a bit more familiar.

1 Try answering the four questions in **How do I answer...?** above using the advice given. How long did it take you and would you be able to reproduce this in exam conditions?

2 If the answer is 'no', then read over the material again and see how much you can reproduce just from memory.

3 Repeat step 2 frequently over the coming weeks until the whole process becomes second nature.

Self-disclosure

RECAP

A01 Description

- **Self-disclosure** refers to the extent to which a person reveals personal information about themselves (e.g. their intimate thoughts, feelings and experiences) to another person.
  - > Self-disclosure leads to greater feelings of intimacy, with people preferring those who disclose intimate details to those who self-disclose to a lesser extent.
- **Research on self-disclosure** Sprecher *et al.* (2013) found that level of self-disclosure *received* was a better predictor of liking and loving than level of self-disclosure *given*.
  - > Self-disclosure was found to be linked to relationship stability. The amount of disclosure in a relationship was predictive of whether couples stayed together for longer than four years.
- **Different types of self-disclosure** Researchers have found that it is not self-disclosure per se that predicts relationship satisfaction but the *type* of self-disclosure.
  - > Sprecher (1987) found that disclosure of personal disappointments and accomplishments have a greater influence on relationship satisfaction than more neutral self-disclosure.

- **Norms of self-disclosure** One norm is that people should engage in only a moderately personal level of self-disclosure in the early stages of a relationship.
  - > People possess a norm of reciprocity concerning self-disclosure. The more one person discloses to another, the more disclosure is expected in return.

A03 Evaluation/Discussion

Research support for self-disclosure…

A meta-analysis by Collins and Miller (1994) provided research support for the importance of self-disclosure.	People who engage in intimate disclosures are liked more than people who disclose at lower levels. The relationship between disclosure and liking was stronger if the recipient believed that the disclosure was shared only with them rather than shared indiscriminately with others.	*This supports the central role that self-disclosure plays in the development and maintenance of romantic relationships.*

Self-disclosure on the Internet: The 'boom and bust' phenomenon…

Cooper and Sportolari (1997) claim that relationships formed over the Internet involve higher levels of self-disclosure than in face-to-face relationships.	Because individuals on the Internet are often anonymous, relationships get intense very quickly (boom) but, because the underlying trust and knowledge of the other person are not there to support the relationship, it becomes difficult to sustain (bust).	*This would explain why many individuals who are certain they have found their 'soulmate' online may leave an established relationship to meet people who do not turn out to be what they first seemed.*

Self-disclosure may be greater in face-to-face than online relationships…

Knop *et al.* (2016) challenges the assumption that people self-disclose more in online relationships than in face-to-face relationships.	They found that people self-disclose more in face-to-face than online interactions and disclose more intimate information. This may be due to the lack of intimacy of the Internet as a context for personal self-disclosure.	*This suggests that individuals do not seize the opportunity to reveal personal information online as much as expected, contrary to the belief that people disclose too much personal information via the Internet.*

Cultural differences in patterns of self-disclosure…

Cultures differ in the extent to which various topics are considered appropriate for conversation.	In the West, people typically generally engage in more intimate self-disclosure than do non-Westerners (Chen, 1995). Nakanishi (1986) found that Japanese women show a lower preference for self-disclosure than do Japanese men. This is opposite to gendered self-disclosure patterns typically found in the West.	*This suggests that the importance of self-disclosure as an aspect of attraction is moderated by the influence of culture.*

 APPLY

AO2: An example

SCENARIO Ronnie is developing feelings for the newest employee in the office. They have been spending lunchtimes together and their conversations have moved from work-related topics to personal life such as hobbies, childhood experiences and, more recently, past relationships.

With reference to Ronnie, outline and evaluate the role of self-disclosure in attraction. **(16 marks)**

ANSWER **An extract showing how you could address the AO2 requirements of this question:** *Collins and Miller support the suggestion that self-disclosure is an important process in the development of romantic relationships. The conclusions of their meta-analysis would suggest Ronnie has growing feelings for her work colleague as those who disclose intimate information tend to be more liked by those who disclose at lower levels. Furthermore, as only the two of them spend lunchtime together, Ronnie may feel the disclosures are for her ears only and so her attraction would continue to grow...*

AO2: One for you to try

Bobby and Chelsea are on their first date. During the date, Bobby tells Chelsea about all of his previous relationships and dominates the conversation. Chelsea is a lot more reserved and only reveals a little information about herself and a recent holiday. The next day, Chelsea is discussing her date with Jocelyn. She explains that Bobby made her feel uncomfortable and that she probably won't see him again. Likewise, Bobby is talking to his friend Blessed and says that he doesn't think that Chelsea is into him.

Using your knowledge of self-disclosure, explain why Chelsea and Bobby are unlikely to see each other again. (4 marks)

AO2: Research methods

Two psychologists carried out a study looking at sex differences in the relationship between self-disclosure and liking. The psychologists were Kathryn Dindia and Mike Allen and in 1992 their article, `Sex differences in self-disclosure: a meta-analysis', was published on pages 106–124 of Issue 1, Volume 112 in the journal *Psychological Bulletin*.

Write an appropriate scientific reference for this study. (3 marks)

Another team of psychologists carried out a study called `Reflecting on connecting: Meta-analysis of differences between computer-mediated and face-to-face self-disclosure'. The psychologists were Erin Ruppel, Clare Gross, Arrington Stoll, Brittnie Peck, Mike Allen and Sang-Yeon Kim. They wrote an article that was published in Volume 22 of the *Journal of Computer-Mediated Communication* on 1 January 2017. It appeared on pages 18–34 of the first issue of this volume.

Write an appropriate scientific reference for this study. (3 marks)

 How do I answer... evaluation only (AO3) questions?

Like the description only questions on the previous spread, evaluation questions come in all sorts of shapes and sizes. Terms like 'evaluate', 'discuss', 'explain', 'criticism', 'strength' and 'limitation' all indicate that AO3 is required. The AO3 material for these questions is on the opposite page. Let's look at some examples:

Q1: Give **one** criticism of the role of self-disclosure in attraction. **(2 marks)**

'Criticisms' can be either negative or positive (and research support would count as a 'positive' criticism), so you could choose any one of the AO3 points opposite as your material. For 2 marks, you could use the lead-in phrase (e.g. 'There is research support for self-disclosure'), followed by the material in the first two columns (i.e. the main critical claim and its expansion).

Q2: Explain **one** limitation of the role of self-disclosure in attraction. **(3 marks)**

This requires a little more elaboration, but this time you are restricted to something that limits the value of self-disclosure as an explanation of attraction. The most obvious AO3 point to use would be the last one, ('Cultural differences in patterns of self-disclosure...') with material from all three columns being used to access all 3 of the marks on offer.

Q3: Evaluate the role of self-disclosure in attraction. **(6 marks)**

Take the same approach as for **Q2**, but this time use **two** of the AO3 points. Stick to two only, to avoid being superficial.

REVIEW

In order to feel comfortable with this topic you should practise using the material in all the different ways that might be assessed in your exam.

1 Try constructing 3-, 4- and 6-mark descriptions of the role of self-disclosure in relationships.

2 Write an essay plan showing how you would use the material on this spread to answer 8-, 10- and 16-mark extended writing questions.

3 If you are feeling really adventurous, try writing each of these six different questions on separate bits of paper. Put them in a suitable container and then, whenever you have a spare bit of time, pick one out and try to answer it, without notes, in the appropriate time. Keep doing this until you become confident in answering all of them.

 **RECAP**

AO1 Description

- **Kerckhoff and Davis (1962)** suggest we choose romantic partners by using a series of filters that narrow down the 'field of alternatives'.

  > In the early stages, demographic factors are important. As the relationship develops, similarity of attitudes and values become important. Finally, partners are assessed in terms of compatibility.

- **Social demography** Age, social background, geographical location, etc. reduce the number of people that are realistically available for us to meet.

  > These are the people we feel more at ease with; we find them more attractive because we have more in common with them.

- **Similarity in attitudes and values** These are of central importance at the start of a relationship and are the best predictor of the relationship becoming stable.

  > As a result of disclosures to each other, individuals weigh up whether to continue or end the relationship. Those who are very different to the individual are 'filtered out'.

- **Complementarity of needs** People are attracted to others whose needs are 'harmonious' with their own rather than conflicting with them.

  > Finding a partner who complements their needs (e.g. the need to be caring and the need to be cared for) ensures that their own needs are likely to be met.

AO3 Evaluation/Discussion

Lack of research support for filter theory…

Levinger *et al.* (1970) failed to replicate the results of the Kerckhoff and Davis study.

In a study of 330 couples who were 'steadily attached', Levinger *et al.* found no evidence that either similarity of attitudes and values or complementarity of needs influenced progress towards permanence in relationships.

They suggest that the questionnaires used in the Kerckhoff and Davis study would not have been appropriate given the changes in courtship patterns in the years between the two studies.

The real value of the filtering process…

Duck (1973) suggests that the filtering process is important because it stops people from investing in a relationship that 'won't work'.

Each person discloses some information about themselves. They then decide whether to continue with a relationship or decide that it will not work before they become too deeply involved with the other person.

This suggests that the real value of filtering is that it stops people making the wrong choice and then having to live with the consequences.

Complementarity of needs may not be that important…

Support for the importance of the complementarity of needs aspect of Kerckhoff and Davis's theory is scarce.

Dijkstra and Barelds (2008) studied 760 male and female singles who were looking for a long-term mate. Although initially participants indicated that they desired a complementary partner rather than a similar one, there were strong correlations between their own and their ideal partner's personality.

This finding lends support to the similarity attraction hypothesis rather than the complementarity of needs hypothesis.

A problem for filter theory…

The claim that relationships progress when partners discover shared attitudes and values with their partner and needs that complement their own may no longer be the case.

Thornton and Young-DeMarco (2001) found evidence of changed attitudes towards relationships in young American adults over a few decades, including more egalitarian attitudes towards gender roles in marriage.

They conclude that as attitudes and values are constantly changing over time, this weakens the relevance of filtering theory to mate selection.

⚙ APPLY

AO2: An example

 Katie is describing her new partner to her friends. She says, 'We work at the same hospital and agree that people should be better informed about how to look after their health through their lifestyle choices. Both of us have similar beliefs regarding marriage and children. He can sometimes be indecisive so he doesn't mind that I like to decide what we do at the weekend.'

Outline the filter theory of attraction. Refer to Katie's comments in your answer. **(6 marks)**

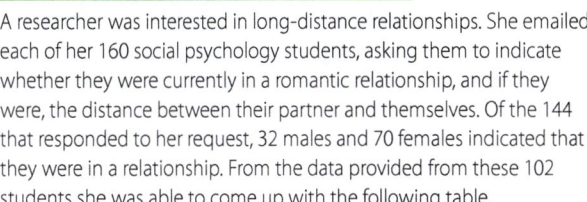 *The first filter the theory suggests people apply is social demography, i.e. variables such as age, background and geographical location. Katie and her partner work in the same hospital so they will feel similar and more at ease with each other; this will increase the attraction felt. The second filter involves similarity of attitudes and values. This is of central importance at the start of a relationship. Through encouraging self-disclosure, Katie has learnt her partner holds similar views to her regarding marriage and children. Finally, she has assessed the complementarity of needs as she mentions she likes to make decisions while her partner can be indecisive. Katie is attracted to her new partner as his needs are harmonious with her own.*

✎ AO2: Research methods

A researcher was interested in long-distance relationships. She emailed each of her 160 social psychology students, asking them to indicate whether they were currently in a romantic relationship, and if they were, the distance between their partner and themselves. Of the 144 that responded to her request, 32 males and 70 females indicated that they were in a relationship. From the data provided from these 102 students she was able to come up with the following table.

	Distance less than 50 miles	Distance more than 50 miles
Males	20	12
Females	22	48

a. What level of measurement is being used in this table? (1 mark)

b. Identify the most suitable statistical test to use in analysing this data. Give reasons for your choice. (3 marks)

c. What conclusions is the researcher likely to reach about long-distance relationships among her students? (4 marks)

✎ AO2: One for you to try

Tommy has just joined a new school and psychology class. There are many attractive female students in Tommy's new group but he is most drawn to a few of them who share his passion for Korean hip-hop. He likes to impress with his knowledge of the genre and talks enthusiastically about artists such as Jay Park, Gaeko and Dok2. He gets a bit frustrated that all but one of the girls think he's a bit too intense when it comes to music. However, one girl in particular respects his knowledge and listens intently when he talks about it all. He thinks maybe he should ask her out.

With reference to the three stages of filter theory, explain how Tommy has come to this decision about whom he would like to ask out. (6 marks)

🐾 How do I answer... application (AO2) questions?

Let's look again at the scenario of Tommy in the **AO2: One for you to try** above.

One way of answering questions such as this is to remember the 'say one thing for 1 mark' and 'say four things for 4 marks' strategy. So, for a 6-mark question we could say six things.

1 **Find a bit of appropriate psychology,** e.g. 'The first filter is social demography, as age, social background, geographical location, etc. reduce the number of people that are realistically available for us to meet.'

2 **Use this to explain some aspect of the scenario,** e.g. 'Tommy has transferred to a new school, and students in his psychology class are likely to be similar in age and social background to him.'

3 **Find a second bit of psychology,** e.g. 'Kerckhoff and Davis (1962) found that similarity in attitudes and values narrows down the field of alternatives.'

4 **Use this to explain the scenario,** e.g. 'Tommy discovers a few girls in his class that have similar attitudes about Korean hip-hop so is drawn to them.'

5 **Find a third bit of psychology,** e.g. 'The final filter is when people are attracted to others whose needs are "harmonious" with their own.'

6 **Use this to explain the scenario,** e.g. 'Tommy likes one girl more than the others because she respects his need to talk about his music and she appears to have a need to listen.'

🔄 REVIEW

You need to be able to answer questions with different mark allocations concisely while using enough detail to explain the concept clearly. Practise answering 3-mark, 4-mark and 6-mark descriptive questions on filter theory, spending about a minute and a quarter per mark, e.g. 5 minutes for a 4-mark question. Make sure you allow time to plan logical answers.

1 Practise recalling the material in the AO1 points opposite.

2 Practise actually writing the full answer, setting a timer to make sure you use the time available.

3 Check your answer is clear and logical, and has relevant key terms in each point.

Social exchange theory

A01 Description

- **Profit and loss** People exchange resources with the expectation that rewards received will exceed the costs incurred (Thibaut and Kelley, 1959).
  - > Rewards include companionship, being cared for and physical resources. Costs include effort, financial investment and missed opportunities with others.
  - > Rewards minus costs equal the outcome (profit or loss). Commitment to a relationship is dependent on the profitability of this outcome.
- **Comparison level (CL)** A standard against which all our relationships are judged, a product of experiences in other relationships and general views of what we might expect from this relationship.
  - > If the potential 'profit' in a new relationship exceeds our CL, the other person will be seen as being attractive as a partner.
  - > A romantic relationship is likely to be more successful if both partners' perceived profits are above their CL.
- **Comparison level for alternatives (CLA)** A person may weigh up a potential increase in rewards from a different partner minus costs associated with ending the current relationship.
  - > An individual will be committed to their current relationship when potential benefits in the new relationship are low and costs of ending the current relationship are high.
  - > If the benefits of being in a new relationship are high and the costs of leaving the current one relatively low then the person may be tempted to leave for the new relationship.

Profit and loss   CLA

A03 Evaluation/Discussion

Evidence for the influence of comparison level for alternatives...

Sprecher (2001) claimed that the exchange variable most highly associated with relationship commitment was partners' comparison level for alternatives.	She showed that when the CLA was high, commitment to, and satisfaction with, the current relationship tended to be low. This was the case for both males and females.	Sprecher suggests that those who lack alternatives are likely to remain committed and those who are committed to their relationship are more likely to devalue alternatives.

The problem of costs and benefits...

A problem for social exchange theory is the confusion of what constitutes a cost and a benefit in a relationship.	What is rewarding to one person (e.g. constant attention) can be perceived as irritating to another. What is a benefit at one stage of the relationship may later be seen as a cost as partners redefine what they previously perceived as rewarding (Littlejohn, 1989).	This suggests it is difficult to classify all events in a romantic relationship in such simple terms as 'costs' and 'benefits'.

The problem assessing value...

Nakonezny and Denton (2008) argue that social exchange may not be relevant to personal relationships.	'Value' is difficult to determine, as is the relative value of costs and benefits to individuals. This tends not to be the case in commercial and economic relationships, where social exchange theory is more typically applied.	The vagueness of terms such as costs and benefits and the difficulty in assessing their value suggests that this theory is less able to explain personal relationships.

Real-world application: Relationship therapy...

Individuals in unsuccessful marriages frequently report a lack of positive behaviour exchanges with their partner and an excess of negative exchanges.	Integrated Behavioural Couples Therapy (IBCT) attempts to increase the proportion of positive exchanges and decrease the proportion of negative exchanges, helping partners to break the negative patterns of behaviour that cause problems for the relationship.	This approach has been shown to be successful. Christensen et al. (2004) reported that about two thirds of couples reported significant improvements in the quality of their relationships as a result of using IBCT.

APPLY

AO2: An example

SCENARIO Jakub and Peter are talking about their marriages. Jakub describes his wife as his ideal companion. She is caring and always knows how to cheer him up, as well as being a wonderful mother to their children. Peter, on the other hand, fears his marriage is in difficulty. He and his wife always seem to argue and both appear more focused on spending time with friends rather than each other.

Discuss the social exchange theory of romantic relationships. Refer to Jakub and Peter's conversation in your answer. (16 marks)

ANSWER **An extract showing how you could address the AO2 requirements of this question:**

Jakub is describing the rewards he receives from his marriage. Social exchange theory would predict these rewards outweigh any costs incurred and so Jakub feels he is earning a 'profit'. The marriage is exceeding his comparison level and so he is committed to this relationship. Peter and his wife, however, both seem to be weighing up alternatives as they spend time with friends rather than each other. The more rewarding Peter finds this alternative, the less dependent he will be on his current relationship. The frequent arguments increase the negative exchanges in comparison to the positive exchanges. Gottman and Levenson (1992) found the ratio of positive and negative exchanges is 1:1 in unsuccessful marriages like Peter's, but successful relationships like Jakub's have a ratio of 5:1…

AO2: Research methods

A researcher has developed a measuring instrument to assess perceived 'outcomes' in romantic relationships, where respondents answer a series of questions and are then given a total score between 1 and 100. The more 'profitable' the relationship, the higher the score. He also asks his 24 respondents to complete a relationship satisfaction questionnaire, which also yields a numerical score. In his study, half of the respondents complete the 'outcomes' questionnaire first, and half complete the relationship satisfaction questionnaire first.

a. **Construct a non-directional hypothesis for this study. (2 marks)**

b. **Why did the researcher feel it important for half the respondents to complete the outcomes questionnaire first and the other half to complete the relationship satisfaction questionnaire first? (2 marks)**

After gathering the data, he decided to carry out a Spearman's *rho* correlation test to see if there was any relationship between outcomes and satisfaction. His calculation revealed a correlation of 0.47, which he then checked against the significance tables for this test.

n	0.01	0.05
23	0.353	0.416
24	0.344	0.407
25	0.337	0.398

c. **Using the significance table above, determine whether the researcher has achieved a significant result. Explain your answer. (2 marks)**

d. **What conclusion might the researcher draw about the relationship between 'outcomes' and 'relationship satisfaction' as a result of this study? (2 marks)**

AO2: One for you to try

Nick and Ekaterina have been married for just over a year. Nick was a widower when he and Ekaterina met at the law firm where they both worked, and she helped him deal with the distress of his wife's death. Although they get on fine, Ekaterina is ambitious and works a great deal on her legal cases when at home. Nick wishes he had the sort of relationship with Ekaterina that he had with his first wife, Ann, who always put him first. He has been phoning his sister-in-law quite a lot recently. It comforts him because she reminds him so much of Ann. He realises that he may have made a mistake with Ekaterina and wonders whether he and his sister-in-law would be better off together.

Explain Nick's situation in terms of the social exchange theory of relationships. (3 marks)

How do I answer... research methods questions?

Questions requiring research methods knowledge can appear in any section of any paper in the AS or A Level exams. They could include any aspect of research methods, data analysis or ethical issues. Doing well in research methods questions is as much a case of thinking clearly and using common sense as it is regurgitating knowledge. Let's look at the **AO2: Research methods** questions on the left:

a. You are asked to construct a 'directional' hypothesis but this is not an experiment, so don't say that one thing *causes* the other. Using words such as 'an association' between or a 'relationship between' would be fine.

b. This may not be immediately apparent, but think carefully what the problem might be in asking someone to consider how profitable their relationship is and *then* ask them about how satisfied they are. You also need to convince the examiner to give you both of the marks on offer so elaborate on your answer.

c. You should practise using these significance tables. You need to know what your 'n' (number of participants) is, what the appropriate level of significance is (0.05) and then *explain* whether you have achieved that level of significance and why.

d. Another 2-marker, so you need some elaboration beyond just saying that there *is* an association between the two measures. You might, for example, say something like 'There is a statistically significant association between…'

REVIEW

How much should I write? You should practise writing 3-, 4- and 6-mark descriptions of social exchange theory. For 3 marks, use three of the AO1 points on the opposite page ('Profit and Loss', CL and CLA), for 4 marks use four points and so on. For 6 marks you should be writing about 150–180 words. If you attempt to cover all aspects of the theory thoroughly, you will run out of time for AO3 in an extended answer, so be selective and concise. We have helped you by summarising the key content in the AO1 points. But you still need to include enough detail and specialist terminology if you want to get marks in the top band.

Equity theory

AO1 Description

- **Inequity and dissatisfaction** Equity theory assumes that people are most satisfied when they perceive that what they get out of a relationship is roughly equal to what they put in.

  > An equitable relationship should, according to the theory, be where one partner's benefits minus their costs equals their partner's benefits minus their costs. Such relationships are considered to be 'fair' for each partner.

  > If people feel over-benefited, they may experience pity, guilt and shame. If under-benefited they may experience anger, sadness and resentment. The greater the inequity, the greater the dissatisfaction.

- **A timetable of equity and inequity in marriages** Schafer and Keith (1980) found that, during the child-rearing years, wives reported being under-benefited and husbands over-benefited. In contrast, during the honeymoon period and when children left home, relationships were more equitable and couples reported greater satisfaction.

  > When couples are in the initial stages of a relationship, considerations of reward and equity are important. Once individuals become deeply committed to each other, they are less concerned about day-to-day reward and equity (Hatfield and Rapson, 2011).

  > Couples in equitable relationships are less likely to risk extramarital affairs than their peers, and their relationships are generally longer lasting than those of their peers (Byers and Wang, 2004).

AO1 Key Study (Stafford and Canary, 2006)

- **PROCEDURE** Stafford and Canary explored how equity and satisfaction predicted the use of maintenance strategies typically used in marriage.

  > Over 200 married couples completed measures of equity and relationship satisfaction. Each spouse was also asked questions about their use of relationship maintenance strategies such as assurances, sharing tasks and positivity.

- **FINDINGS** Satisfaction was highest for spouses who perceived their relationships to be equitable, followed by over-benefited partners and then under-benefited partners.

  > The relationship between equity and marital happiness was complementary. Spouses who were treated equitably were happier and so more likely to engage in behaviours that contributed to their spouse's sense of equity and happiness.

AO3 Evaluation / Discussion

Equity sensitivity…

Research challenges the assumption that everyone is equally sensitive to inequity.	Huseman *et al.* (1987) identified 'benevolents', who are 'givers' and so more tolerant of under-rewarded inequity; 'entitleds', who prefer to be over-rewarded, believing they are owed and so entitled to receive benefits; and 'equity sensitives', who experience tension when faced with inequity.	This concept of 'equity sensitivity' determines the extent to which an individual will tolerate inequity, and demonstrates individual differences in the impact of inequitable relationships.

Gender differences in the importance of inequity…

DeMaris *et al.* (2010) point out that men and women are not equally affected by inequity in romantic relationships.	Women's greater relationship focus may make them more sensitive to injustices and inequity. Women tend to perceive themselves as more under-benefited compared to men and are more disturbed by this.	A consequence of this is that women are more likely to be vigilant about inequity and more likely to react negatively to being exploited.

Cultural differences in the importance of inequity…

The concept of equity may not be as important in non-Western cultures given that most research has been carried out in the US and in Western Europe.	However, Aumer-Ryan *et al.* (2006) found that, in all the cultures studied, people considered it important that a relationship should be equitable. US participants claimed to be in the most equitable relationships, and participants from Jamaica claimed to be in the least equitable relationships.	This suggests that people in different cultures differ in how equitable they consider their relationships to be.

A problem of causality…

The nature of the causal relationship between inequity and dissatisfaction is not clear.	Clark (1984) claims dissatisfaction is the cause, not the consequence, of inequity. However, Van Yperen and Buunk (1990) found that people in inequitable marriages became less satisfied over the course of a year, with no evidence for the converse.	Hatfield and Rapson (2011) suggest that, when marriages are faltering, partners become preoccupied with the inequities of the relationship, and this can then lead to relationship dissolution.

 APPLY

AO2: An example

SCENARIO Greta declares the most successful relationships are ones where both partners feel equally rewarded. Tina disagrees, arguing relationships are more complex than a simple calculation of costs and rewards.

*Explain **one** criticism of using equity theory to explain romantic relationships. Refer to Greta and Tina's conversation in your answer.* **(3 marks)**

ANSWER *Tina may be right to disagree with Greta's statement, as people may differ in their perception of equality and inequality. For example, Huseman identified benevolents (tolerate inequality), equality sensitives (strive for equality) and entitleds (seek to be over-rewarded). This casts doubt on the claims made by equity theory which are echoed in Greta's comment. If Huseman is correct then some people seek to be over-rewarded rather than to provide an equal amount of rewards as their partner (entitleds) as predicted by equality theory.*

AO2: One for you to try

Emmanuela and Chris have been married for many years and their children Emily and Grace have just left home. While the children were growing up Emmanuela, who had a full-time job, did all of the chores while Chris relaxed in front of the TV every evening. Emmanuela put up with this while the children were growing up. However, now they have left home and she and Chris have retired. The situation has not changed and she is becoming increasingly dissatisfied with her marriage.

Using your knowledge of equity theory, explain why Emmanuela is becoming increasingly dissatisfied with her relationship with Chris. (4 marks)

AO2: Research methods

Researchers asked 10 married couples to complete two measures. The first of these was the Global Measure of Equity scale, which measures how fair and equitable people believe their relationships to be. The first was the 25-item Global Measure of Equity scale, where respondents indicate their judgements on a 7-point scale, with answers ranging from +3 (I am getting a much better deal than my partner), 0 (We get the same deal as each other) to -3 (My partner is getting a much better deal than I am). The second was the Kansas Marital Satisfaction Scale, a 3-item measure designed to assess marital satisfaction. Respondents answer each item on a 7-point scale ranging from 1 (extremely dissatisfied) to 7 (extremely satisfied). The results are shown in the tables below:

Table 1. Equity and satisfaction scores (males).

Participant number	1	2	3	4	5	6	7	8	9	10
Global Measure of Equity score	-54	+14	-23	-11	-8	+10	+12	-37	+8	+35
Kansas Marital Satisfaction score	7	15	10	12	11	18	14	8	17	9

Table 2. Equity and satisfaction scores (females).

Participant number	1	2	3	4	5	6	7	8	9	10
Global Measure of Equity score	-54	-17	-60	-16	-8	+4	-22	-37	+8	+17
Kansas Marital Satisfaction score	7	11	4	9	13	16	10	8	14	15

a. **Calculate the mean marital satisfaction scores for males and females. (2 marks)**

b. **What conclusion can you draw from these calculations? (2 marks)**

c. **From the data in Tables 1 and 2, what can you conclude about the relationship between equity and satisfaction for males and females? (4 marks)**

 How do I answer... 'Distinguish between' questions?

Distinguish between social exchange theory and equity theory. (3 marks)

There are some fairly simple rules for answering this sort of question. If you are asked to 'distinguish between…', 'compare…' or 'explain the difference between…', then these rules apply:

1. Don't just *describe* the two things you are being asked to distinguish between.

2. Pick a characteristic that applies to both but which is different for each and point that out (e.g. how does each explain satisfaction in relationships?). For example, social exchange theory claims satisfaction is about 'profitable' outcomes, i.e. when rewards received are greater than the costs expended. Equity theory explains satisfaction in terms of 'fairness' in outcomes, i.e. the rewards received should equal the costs expended.

3. Use words like 'whereas', 'however', 'on the other hand' to point out this difference. That gives us 'Social exchange theory claims satisfaction is about "profitable" outcomes, i.e. when rewards received are greater than the costs expended. However, equity theory explains satisfaction in terms of "fairness" in outcomes, i.e. the rewards received should equal the costs expended'.

4. Don't be over-ambitious; one point of difference is usually enough.

REVIEW

As you are probably aware, simply reading material is not the most effective way of learning it properly. So, using the material on the opposite page, try writing plans for 3-, 4- and 6-mark 'outline' questions on equity theory plus plans for 8- and 16-mark essay questions.

Test yourself on the key points of equity theory by covering up your plans and writing it out again. It's useful to have a supply of cheap paper for this, as the more times you practise retrieving the information, the better you will remember it.

Spaced practice is also very effective: come back to the same topic tomorrow and start your revision by seeing how many of the points you can remember before you look at your essay plan.

The investment model of relationships

AO1 Description

- **Satisfaction level** The balance of positive versus negative emotions experienced within a relationship, determined by the extent to which the other person fulfils the individual's most important needs.
- **Quality of alternatives** The extent to which the individual's most important needs (e.g. companionship, sexual needs) might be better fulfilled outside the current relationship.
  - > If better outcomes are likely in an alternative relationship, the individual may move towards that relationship. They may, however, stay in an unsatisfying relationship because of a lack of better options.
- **Investment size** A measure of all the resources attached to the relationship (e.g. time invested, shared possessions), which might be lost if the relationship were to end.
  - > Investments increase dependence on the relationship because they would be costly to break. This creates a psychological inducement to stay in a relationship.
- **Commitment level** Commitment is high in partners who have *high* levels of satisfaction and investment and *low* quality of alternatives.
  - > Commitment is low in partners who have *low* levels of satisfaction and investment and *high* quality of alternatives.

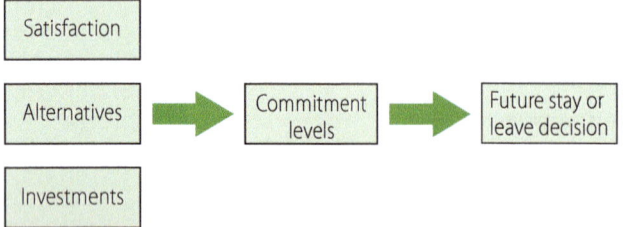

AO1 Key Study (Le and Agnew, 2003)

- **PROCEDURE** Carried out a meta-analysis of studies that had explored the different components of the investment model and the relationship between them.
  - > This produced a total sample of over 11,000 participants (54 per cent male and 46 per cent female) from five countries.
- **FINDINGS** Across all studies, satisfaction level, quality of alternatives and investment size were highly correlated with relationship commitment.
  - > Correlation between satisfaction level and commitment was stronger than any other correlation. Individuals with higher levels of commitment were also more likely to stay in a relationship and those with lower levels more likely to leave.

AO3 Evaluation/Discussion

Research support for the investment model...

The importance of commitment as an indicator of relationship stability is supported by a meta-analysis.	Le *et al.* (2010) analysed data from 137 studies. In line with predictions from Rusbult's investment model, commitment was a particularly strong predictor of whether a relationship would break up.	However, satisfaction, quality of alternatives and investment size were only modest predictors of the likelihood of staying in a relationship.

Problems in measuring the variables of the investment model...

A problem for this model is the difficulty of measuring commitment in a relationship and variables that lead to commitment.	Rusbult *et al.* (1998) developed the 'Investment Model Scale' to overcome this problem. This scale has been found to be high in both reliability and validity in the measurement of these variables.	A potential problem is that the scale relies on self-report measures, with respondents trying to present themselves in a good light. This raises the possibility of biased findings.

Real-world application: Explaining abusive relationships...

The investment model is able to explain why individuals may persist in a relationship with an abusive partner.	Victims of partner abuse experience low satisfaction, yet despite this, many stay in the relationship. They may lack alternatives or may have too much invested with that partner, making dissolution too costly.	In a real-world validation of this, Rusbult and Martz (1995) found that alternatives and investments predicted whether abused women remained committed to or returned to their partner.

Investment in the future is also important...

Goodfriend and Agnew (2008) suggest that 'investment' should also include any future plans that partners have made regarding the relationship.	In ending a relationship, an individual would lose any future plans they had made with that partner. Some relationships persist, therefore, not because of the current balance of investments made, but because of a motivation to see these plans come to fruition.	Their research showed that future plans were strongly predictive of commitment in romantic relationships, over and above past investments.

⚙ APPLY

AO2: An example

SCENARIO Tina is interviewing people in long-term relationships to determine whether there are common variables influencing the commitment each participant had to their partner.

With reference to the investment model, what variables is Tina likely to identify? **(4 marks)**

ANSWER *Tina will probably find that people in long-term relationships experience a high level of satisfaction, e.g. the participants may report that the needs that are most important to them are fulfilled by their partner. She may also find that the time and energy each participant has invested in their relationship as well as shared friends and possessions have built a strong foundation that enables the relationship to last. Finally, alternative potential partners may not offer anything better than their current relationship, so the individual chooses to stay with their current partner.*

AO2: One for you to try

Janice and Wendy are discussing their boyfriends. Both have been in their relationships for about a year but have had different experiences during that time. Wendy is irritated by her boyfriend's lack of interest in doing anything except going to the gym and spending time with his mates. Janice, on the other hand, has a boyfriend who never wants to be away from her, and is always texting her to check she's OK. Janice and her boyfriend have recently bought a flat together whereas Wendy and her boyfriend still live with their respective parents. Wendy admits that a doctor at the surgery where she works as a receptionist had asked her out. She feels very attracted to this new man, even though she would be letting her current boyfriend down.

Using your knowledge of the investment model of relationships, outline whether Wendy or Janice would be less committed to their current relationship and more likely to end it. Explain the reasons for your answer. (4 marks)

AO2: Research methods

Researchers were interested in exploring the relationship between investment size, quality of alternatives, satisfaction and how these contributed to commitment in romantic relationships. Six individuals, three male and three female, were interviewed by one of the researchers, who then carried out a thematic analysis based on their responses to her questions.

a. **Distinguish between quantitative and qualitative data. (3 marks)**

b. **Explain why qualitative data would be more revealing in this particular study. (2 marks)**

c. **Outline one question that the researcher might have asked concerning the relationship between investment size and commitment. (2 marks)**

d. **Outline what is meant by thematic analysis. (2 marks)**

e. **Explain how a thematic analysis might be carried out in this study. (3 marks)**

🐾 How do I answer... shorter (8-mark) essay questions?

Not all essays follow the 12- or 16-mark format. Some have a slightly lower tariff. Of these lower tariff essay questions, the 8-marker is the most common. It does help to know what you are dealing with, however, as they are not always straightforward. The AO1 and AO3 material for these questions is on the opposite page.

Q1: Outline and evaluate the investment model of relationships. **(8 marks)**

Although you could be forgiven for believing that this question would be worth 4 marks for AO1 and 4 marks for AO3, this is actually half of a 16-mark essay question, so there is a similar split of marks, i.e. 3 marks for AO1 and 5 marks for AO3 (instead of the 6- and 10-mark split for a 16-mark question).

Q2: Mark and Jemimah had been having problems for a few months, so it was time to take stock, particularly as they were about to leave on their dream trip travelling round Australia and New Zealand for a year. Mark was confiding in his parents, saying that he wasn't as sure about the relationship as he was when he and Jemimah had booked their trip a couple of months ago. Mark's parents reminded him that all relationships go through rocky patches and that he was ignoring all the positive times he and Jemimah had experienced together. They also claimed it wouldn't be easy to find someone as nice as Jemimah.

Discuss the investment model of relationships. Make reference to Mark in your answer. **(8 marks)**

This question includes a scenario that is referred back to in the question. This is an indication that there is an additional AO2 requirement in the question. AO2 marks tend to be 'stolen' from the AO3 allocation, so this question would be 3 marks of AO1, 3 marks of AO3, and 2 marks' worth of AO2. The scenario of Mark and Jemimah appears to involve concepts such as 'satisfaction', 'investment' and 'commitment', so the first point on the opposite page for each of 'Satisfaction level', 'Investment size' and 'Commitment level' would constitute the AO1 component. These concepts could then be used to interpret his dilemma (whether he should continue with the relationship or leave) and would constitute the AO2 component. Finally, you would include a full AO3 point from the opposite page, or two abridged AO3 points..

↻ REVIEW

To enhance your practical expertise in questions on this topic over and above selecting material to answer AO3 questions and completing the **AO2: Research methods** exercise above, there are a couple of other useful things you can do, including:

1 Write 2-, 3-, 4- and 6-mark outlines of the investment model of relationships.

2 Write a bullet-pointed answer plan (including both AO1 and AO3 material) for the following two questions.

Briefly discuss the investment model of relationships. **(8 marks)**

Discuss the investment model of relationships. **(16 marks)**

Relationship breakdown

A01 Description

Duck's (1982) model of relationship breakdown

- **Breakdown** This begins when one of the partners becomes dissatisfied (perhaps through realisation of inequity) with the way the relationship is conducted.

- **Intrapsychic phase** This is characterised by a brooding focus on the relationship and a consideration of whether they might be better off out of it.
  - > The individual may not say anything about their dissatisfaction to their partner, but may become withdrawn while they take stock of the relationship.

- **Dyadic phase** Individuals confront their partners and discuss their discontentment and the future of the relationship. They may discover that their partner also has concerns to air.
  - > The relationship might be saved if both partners are motivated to resolve the issues and so avoid a break-up.

- **Social phase** Dissatisfaction with the relationship spills over to friends and family, who may take sides or help in mending disputes between the two sides.
  - > 'Going public' makes it harder to deny there is a problem with the relationship and harder for them to subsequently bring about a reconciliation.

- **Grave-dressing phase** Partners construct a representation of the failed relationship that does not paint their contribution to it in unfavourable terms.
  - > Each partner attempts to justify their actions and present themselves as being trustworthy and loyal – important if they are to attract a new partner.

A03 Evaluation / Discussion

Fails to acknowledge the possibility of personal growth…

Duck's original model failed to reflect the possibility of personal growth following breakdown.	A new model with a final 'resurrection processes' phase (Rollie and Duck, 2006) stresses the opportunity to move beyond the distress associated with the ending of a relationship and instead engage in the process of personal growth.	There is support for this new phase. Undergraduates who had recently broken up with a partner typically reported that they had not only experienced emotional distress but also personal growth (Tashiro and Frazier, 2003).

The impact of the social phase varies by type of relationship…

Duck (2005) suggests that the nature and impact of the social phase depends on the type of relationship.	For teenagers and young adults, individuals may receive sympathy but no real attempt at reconciliation from their confidants as there are 'plenty more fish in the sea'. However, for older people in longer-term relationships, the consequences of a break-up are more significant (Dickson, 1995).	This suggests that, for this age group, the social phase may be characterised by more obvious attempts by others to rescue the current relationship.

Benefits of the grave-dressing phase…

Research supports the importance of the grave-dressing phase in dealing with the after-effects of relationship breakdown.	Tashiro and Frazier (2003) found that individuals are able to feel better about ending a relationship when they focus on how the situation, rather than their own flaws, was responsible for the break-up.	The benefit of grave-dressing, therefore, is that the individual is able to create stories that play down their role in the break-up and so do not threaten their psychological well-being.

Ethical issues in breakdown research…

Carrying out research in this area raises issues of vulnerability (distress from revisiting the issues that led to breakdown) and privacy (issues are of an intensely personal nature).	The impact of the research on participants must be considered. This is a particularly difficult issue when dealing with vulnerable individuals attempting to cope with the trauma and emotional distress associated with a relationship break-up.	Psychologists should consider whether they truly have the interests of the participants in mind when exploring their research question.

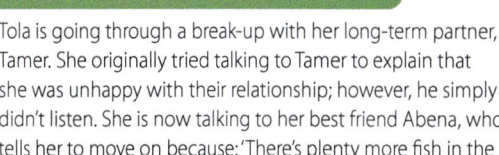
 **APPLY**

AO2: An example

SCENARIO Beverly is discussing with a work colleague a friend's recent break-up. Beverly says she had suspicions that her friend had been unhappy in the relationship for a while. She mentions her friend had hinted that the reason the relationship ended was because she thought he was having an affair. Beverly says she always knew he couldn't be trusted.

Outline and evaluate Duck's phase model of relationship breakdown. Include reference to Beverly's comments in your answer. **(16 marks)**

ANSWER **An extract showing how you could address the AO2 requirements of this question:**

Beverly mentions she felt her friend was unhappy for a while before publicly announcing the break-up. Duck's model would suggest the friend was in the intrapsychic phase (where she broods over her feelings towards her partner) or dyadic phase (where she shares her dissatisfaction with her partner). On telling Beverly about the break-up, her friend has entered the social phase and it seems Beverly is taking sides in saying she 'knew he couldn't be trusted'. Beverly's friend is grave-dressing by explaining the reason for ending the relationship. The mention of a possible affair justifies her actions and presents her as the loyal, trusting partner, which is a desirable trait to promote when seeking a new relationship...

AO2: One for you to try

Tola is going through a break-up with her long-term partner, Tamer. She originally tried talking to Tamer to explain that she was unhappy with their relationship; however, he simply didn't listen. She is now talking to her best friend Abena, who tells her to move on because: 'There's plenty more fish in the sea' and 'He was no good for you anyway.'

Which two of Duck's phases of relationship breakdown has Tola gone through? Justify your choice. (4 marks)

AO2: Research methods

A psychologist wanted to investigate Duck's phase model of relationship breakdown. The psychologists recruited 10 males and 10 females who had recently gone through a divorce, using a volunteer sampling method. The participants were all interviewed and asked a series of questions to explore whether or not their divorce followed the stages outlined by Duck.

Identify two ethical issues that the researcher would need to consider in this research. Suggest how the researcher could deal with each of these. (4 marks)

How do I answer... essay questions with an AO2 component?

The question in **AO2: An example** is an example of one of the trickiest types of question to answer, in that it has three distinct components, an AO1 descriptive component, an AO3 evaluative component and an AO2 application component. This type of question is reasonably common, so it pays to have an effective strategy for answering it. Essay questions with an AO2 (application) component are essentially the same as a straightforward essay (see p.51) but, for a 16-mark question, 4 of the marks available are diverted for your ability to explain the scenario outlined in the question in the context of the material you are discussing. These marks are always taken from the AO3 allocation, so there are still 6 marks for AO1, but now the AO3 component drops from 10 to 6 with the remaining 4 marks for AO2.

Let's look again at **AO2: An example**:

For 4 marks' worth of AO2, you should write approximately 100–120 words explaining the scenario (in this case Beverly's discussion of her friend's relationship break-up) using the prescribed psychological material. In this example, there are references to several phases in Duck's model, e.g. the intrapsychic phase ('her friend had been unhappy for a while') and the grave-dressing phase ('by explaining the reason for ending the relationship'). First and foremost this is an essay on Duck's model, but you should not ignore the AO2 content, which is not as difficult as you might think!

REVIEW

Craik and Lockhart (1972) proposed a theory of memory called the 'levels of processing model'. This model claimed that the more that information is elaborated, the more likely we will be able to access that information later on. There are many different ways of elaborating material, so let's try one.

Take a large sheet of paper (A3 works well here) and construct a mind-map so that all your material on relationship breakdown is linked together visually. This serves several purposes:

1. It elaborates the material, making it more memorable.

2. The act of constructing the mind-map counts as revision, again making it more likely you can recall the information in an exam.

3. You have a *visual* image of the material, which, for many people, is a much easier way of remembering complex material.

*Tip: There is a wealth of useful revision videos on the Internet – take a look for some on mind-map construction.

Virtual relationships in social media

AO1 Description

Self-disclosure in virtual relationships

- Individuals exercise different levels of self-disclosure online than with romantic partners. Self-disclosure in the public domain involves the individual presenting an 'edited' version of the self to others (Jourard, 1971).

- People feel more secure about disclosing intimate information in private than in public.

- People may compensate for the lack of control over the target audience by exercising increased control over what information they present.

- **Why do people self-disclose more on the Internet?** Individuals are more confident about self-disclosing online because of the relative anonymity offered by the Internet.

    > The anonymity of Internet interactions greatly reduces the risks of disclosure because people can share their inner thoughts and feelings with less fear of disapproval.

    > We are more likely to disclose personal information to strangers, because they do not have access to our social circle, so confidentiality is less of an issue (Rubin, 1975).

Absence of gating in virtual relationships

- **Gating in face-to-face relationships** In face-to-face relationships, we use available features such as attractiveness or age to categorise potential partners.

    > In online relationships there is an absence of 'gates' that would otherwise limit opportunities for the less attractive, shy or less socially skilled to form relationships in face-to-face encounters.

- **Absence of gating and its consequences** A consequence of removing gating features is that a person's true self is more likely to be active in Internet relationships than in face-to-face interactions.

    > The reduction of gating obstacles in the online environment allows people to 'stretch the truth a bit' in order to project a self that is more socially desirable than their real 'offline' identity.

    > Yurchisin et al. (2005) found that online daters tended to give accounts of both their real and better selves in dating profiles as a way of attracting potential partners.

AO3 Evaluation / Discussion

The absence of gating factors has been demonstrated in research…

McKenna et al. (2002) provided research support for the importance of gating factors in attraction.	University students engaged in two 20-minute meetings with a partner. When they interacted in an Internet chat room first and then met face-to-face, it was the initial quality of the interaction that determined subsequent liking. This was not the case when they interacted in person on both occasions.	*This finding is consistent with the notion that in face-to-face interactions, it is the more superficial gating features that dominate liking and overwhelm other factors.*

Virtual relationships can be as strong as offline relationships…

It is claimed that virtual relationships formed on the Internet are superficial and cannot compare with the richness of face-to-face relationships (Putnam, 2000).	For example, it is believed that relationships formed online are of lower quality and more temporary than relationships formed in more traditional ways.	*However, Rosenfeld and Thomas (2012) found no difference in the quality of online and offline relationships, nor did they find that online relationships were more fragile than relationships formed offline.*

A biological basis for self-disclosure on Facebook…

Tamir and Mitchell (2012) found evidence of a biological basis for the motivation to self-disclose on social media.	They found increased activity in two brain regions associated with reward, the nucleus accumbens and the ventral tegmental area. These were strongly activated when people were talking about themselves, less so when they were talking about someone else.	*These findings suggest that the tendency to share our personal experiences over social media may arise from the rewarding nature of self-disclosure.*

Facebook helps shy people have better quality friendships…

Baker and Oswald (2010) argue that shy individuals find particular value in virtual relationships.	They found that, for students who scored high for shyness, greater use of Facebook was associated with higher perceptions of friendship quality. In contrast, for those who scored low for shyness, Facebook usage was not associated with friendship quality.	*This suggests that, through social media sites, shy people are able to overcome the barriers they face when trying to form relationships in real life.*

APPLY

AO2: An example

SCENARIO Jimmy frequently posts on his Facebook wall. He has a large number of friends online and will happily accept new friend requests. He thinks nothing of posting his highs and lows with his online friends; from a great night out to sharing his worries. He often uses private messaging to have conversations with his online friends.

With reference to Jimmy, outline the nature of self-disclosure in virtual relationships.
(4 marks)

ANSWER *High levels of self-disclosure in virtual relationships can be explained by the anonymity the Internet provides. Jimmy is able to share personal information with less fear of disapproval or rejection than in a face-to-face relationship. As the online friends he chats to in private messages are likely to be acquaintances rather than members of his social circle, Jimmy is confident he will not see them and so confidentiality is less of a problem. Jimmy may be selective over the content he shares, e.g. posting only trivial worries in an attempt to compensate for the lack of control over those who view his profile.*

AO2: One for you to try

Dion has just started at a new sixth-form college and is rather shy. He finds it very difficult to talk to females and often says really silly things. However, he finds it much easier to talk to girls from college on social media and this makes him feel a lot more popular.

Using your knowledge of virtual relationships in social media, explain why Dion finds it easier to conduct his relationships online. (4 marks)

AO2: Research methods

Write a 100-word abstract for the McKenna *et al.* study used as an AO3 point on the opposite page. You should include details of the aim, procedure, results and any conclusions that might be drawn from this study.

How do I answer... description and evaluation (AO1 + AO3) questions?

1. Recognise what you need to do. Two different command words – e.g. 'outline' (an AO1 term) – and 'evaluate' (an AO3 term) –is a clue that this is a mixed AO1 + AO3 question.

2. Plan how much to write for the AO1 and AO3 parts. In mixed AO1 + AO3 questions up to 6 marks, the division is half and half (it is different with mark totals higher than this as we will see on p.51).

3. Decide what to write. The examples below show you how to put into practice the advice in the previous spreads. The AO1 and AO3 material for these questions is on the opposite page.

Q1: Briefly explain how the absence of gating is important in virtual relationships and give one criticism of research in this area. **(4 marks)**

Use the first two AO1 points under the 'Absence of gating in virtual relationships' heading together with an abridged version of the first AO3 point.

Q2: Outline and evaluate the role of self-disclosure in virtual relationships. **(6 marks)**

The AO1 requirement would be met by the first three AO1 points under the 'Self-disclosure in virtual relationships' heading. They would give a good 3-mark overview as required by the question. For the AO3 content you might use one complete AO3 point preferably the third point which is specifically about self-disclosure.

Q3: Outline and discuss findings from research into virtual relationships in social media. **(6 marks)**

Although 'discuss' is more commonly used as an AO1 + AO3 term in its own right, in **Q3** it is being used just as an AO3 term. You have a number of ways to answer this, but whichever route you take, there should be about 75–90 words of AO1 and 75–90 words of AO3. This time you should use the findings associated with research into virtual relationships (the third column of the AO3 points) plus abridged versions of either of these AO3 points 2 and 4.

REVIEW

Knowing what we mean by 'self-disclosure in virtual relationships' or 'absence of gating' and being able to describe what psychologists know about these processes is vital for your understanding of this topic. There are a few things that you can do to help you with this.

1. Try explaining each of these to someone else (or even the dog, cat or teddy bear who won't be critical or snigger while you are doing it!)

2. Go back and read your notes again and then explain each in even more detail until you think Rover, Fang or Teddy would (had they really been listening) have a good understanding of both processes.

3. Try writing (and answering) a few of your own exam questions on this topic to consolidate this understanding.

Parasocial relationships

A01 Description

An attachment theory explanation

- Parasocial relationships (PSRs) may function similarly to 'real-life' relationships as relationships with TV personalities show the properties of adult attachment.

  > **Proximity seeking** Fans exhibit many proximity-seeking behaviours between themselves and their attachment figure, e.g. attempting to contact them (Leets *et al.*, 1995).

  > **Secure base** With a PSR, where there is little or no chance of rejection from the attachment figure, the individual is able to create a secure base from which they can explore other relationships in a safe way.

  > **Protest at disruption** For example, the BBC's axing of Jeremy Clarkson from Top Gear was met by the sort of emotion typical of the loss of an attachment figure.

- Individuals with an anxious-ambivalent attachment style were most likely to enter into PSRs with their favourite TV personalities. These individuals turn to TV characters as a means of satisfying their often unmet relational needs (Cole and Leets, 1999).

  > Avoidant individuals were least likely to enter into PSRs, appearing to avoid not only relational intimacy but imagined intimacy as well. Securely attached individuals engaged in a moderate level of parasocial interaction.

The absorption addiction model

- PSRs might be appealing to some because there is no risk of criticism or rejection, as might be the case in a real relationship (Ashe and McCutcheon, 2001). Using the Celebrity Attitude Scale, Giles and Maltby (2006) identify three levels in this process:

  > **Entertainment-social** Fans are attracted to a favourite celebrity and will watch, keep up with and read about that celebrity for the purposes of entertainment and gossip.

  > **Intense-personal** This level involves a deeper level of involvement and reflects intensive and compulsive feelings about the celebrity.

  > **Borderline-pathological** Individuals at this level identify with the celebrity's successes and failures. However, they may also overidentify with the celebrity and display uncontrollable behaviours and fantasies about their lives.

- McCutcheon *et al.* (2002) suggest that initially interest in celebrities and the development of a PSR is via absorption, where fans are motivated to learn more about the object of their attention.

- This interest can turn into an addiction, driving the individual to more extreme behaviours in order to sustain satisfaction with the PSR they have developed with the celebrity.

A03 Evaluation/ Discussion

Research support for factors involved in PSRs…

Schiappa *et al.* (2007) provide research support for factors that are instrumental in the formation of PSRs. → They found that individuals with higher levels of PSRs also watched more television. The likelihood of forming a PSR with TV characters was also linked to those characters' perceived attractiveness and similarity to the viewer. → *A consequence is that the loss of a TV character may lead to feelings of 'bereavement', similar to the feelings experienced after the loss of a 'real' relationship.*

PSRs are linked to loneliness…

PSRs are believed to be a substitute for 'real' social relationships and therefore linked to feelings of loneliness. → Greenwood and Long (2009) found that individuals may develop PSRs as a way of dealing with feelings of loneliness or loss. However, Eyal and Cohen (2006) found evidence of loneliness following a parasocial 'break-up', e.g. the end of the show *Friends*. → *This suggests that PSRs may compensate for feelings of loneliness, but their loss can also create feelings of loneliness.*

The absorption addiction model: Links to mental health…

Maltby *et al.* (2003) found a relationship between PSR level and personality in a sample drawn from students and the community. → Whereas the entertainment-social level was associated with extraversion (i.e. sociable, lively, active), the intense-personal level was associated with neuroticism (i.e. tense, emotional, moody). → *As neuroticism is related to anxiety and depression, this provides a clear explanation of why higher levels of PSR are associated with poorer mental health.*

Loss of a PSR is linked to attachment style…

Cohen (2004) supported the claim that viewers would show the same negative response to loss of a PSR as to a real relationship. → Viewers expecting to lose their favourite characters anticipated negative reactions similar to those experienced after the loss of close personal relationships. → *This study supported the influence of attachment style, with anxious-ambivalent individuals anticipating the most negative responses.*

APPLY

A02: An example

SCENARIO Tammi loves the group PRETTYMUCH. She is a regular user of fan pages and has seen them in concert four times. She enjoys discussing the band members with her friend Verity. Verity is 'in love' with one of the members of the band, Brandon. She becomes angry if she reads Brandon is dating another celebrity and believes that, if she only had the chance to meet him, he would realise they were meant to be together. She spends a lot of time alone watching PRETTYMUCH's music videos over and over again.

With reference to Tammi and Verity, discuss explanations of parasocial relationships. **(4 marks)**

ANSWER *The absorption addiction model would place Tammi at the 'entertainment–social' level as her interest in the band provides entertainment and gossip with her friends. Verity, however, has a more intense PSR; she seems to be borderline–pathological as she holds unrealistic fantasies about what would happen if she met the band member she 'loves'. Verity seems isolated from others (she spends a lot of time alone), and so this loneliness may have led her to form a PSR. This is consistent with evidence from Greenwood and Long (2009), who found that individuals may develop PSRs as a way of dealing with feelings of loneliness...*

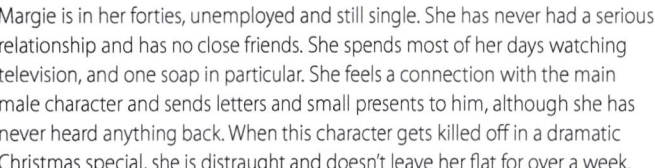

A02: One for you to try

Margie is in her forties, unemployed and still single. She has never had a serious relationship and has no close friends. She spends most of her days watching television, and one soap in particular. She feels a connection with the main male character and sends letters and small presents to him, although she has never heard anything back. When this character gets killed off in a dramatic Christmas special, she is distraught and doesn't leave her flat for over a week.

Explain Margie's behaviour in terms of the attachment theory explanation of parasocial relationships. (4 marks)

A02: Research methods

Researchers investigated the relationship between attachment and PSRs. In order to do this they had used a volunteer sample of 200 first-year students from their university. Students were asked to complete a questionnaire assessing their early attachment style, their friendships and relationships as young adults. In addition, they completed a questionnaire measuring their attitude toward celebrities.

a. **How might the researchers have obtained their volunteer sample? (2 marks)**

b. **Explain one limitation with the use of volunteer sampling in this study. (2 marks)**

c. **The researchers decided to debrief their participants at the end of the study. What is the purpose of debriefing and how might the researchers have done this? (4 marks)**

d. **Other than the need for debriefing, identify one other ethical issue that researchers would face in this study, and explain how they could deal with this. (3 marks)**

How do I answer... longer (16-mark) questions?

For a 16-mark question on PSRs, the demands are likely to be more general (e.g. 'explanations of parasocial relationships') rather than specific (e.g. 'the absorption addiction model'). The difference between the two questions below lies in how you approach the AO3 evaluation/ discussion. The AO1 and AO3 material for these questions is on the opposite page.

Q1: Outline and evaluate explanations of parasocial relationships. **(16 marks)**

The nominal mark division for AO1 (outline) and AO3 (evaluation) is 6 marks for the former and 10 marks for the latter. You could aim to include the first four AO1 points under 'An attachment theory explanation' heading and also the first four points under the heading, 'The absorption addiction model'. Note that this question does ask for 'explanations' in the plural, so just one explanation would not be sufficient. For the AO3 content, you should include all four of the AO3 points.

Q2: Discuss explanations of parasocial relationships. **(16 marks)**

The command word 'discuss' requires AO3 that is a bit more 'discursive', e.g. looking at applications, implications, counter-evidence, etc. We have tried to make some of our AO3 points 'discursive' to accommodate this. For example, the third AO3 point is 'discursive' because it goes beyond just stating strengths and/or limitations and looks at how the absorption addiction model might link to mental health.

REVIEW

In this final **Review** section of this chapter, it is time for some more 'revision accounting'. You should make a table like this for all 10 topics in this chapter. When you feel you have mastered the AO1 and AO3 components of these and can cope with any of the different types of question that we have covered in the **How do I answer... ?** sections, you will have earned a ✓ in the 'Got it!' column.

TOPIC	Got it!			Got it!	
	AO1	AO3		AO1	AO3
Evolutionary explanations for partner preferences	✓	✓	Equity theory		
Physical attractiveness			The investment model		
Self-disclosure			Relationship breakdown		
Filter theory			Virtual relationships in social media		
Social exchange theory			Parasocial relationships		

RECAP

AOI Description

- Sandra Bem first introduced gender schema theory, and Martin and Halverson (1981) developed sex-role stereotypes.
  - > Sex-role stereotypes, or gender stereotypes, are a set of social norms about how men and women should behave.
  - > Children learn sex-role stereotypes from explicit teaching by their parents and others in society, for example: 'boys don't cry'. Children also learn implicitly by imitating same-sex models.

Androgyny

- Bem introduced the concept of **androgyny** in the 1970s. She argued that it is psychologically healthy to avoid fixed sex-role stereotypes. People should be free to adopt a variety of typically masculine or feminine behaviours.
- Using the Bem Sex Role Inventory (BSRI), 100 US undergraduates rated personality traits as desirable for men or women. The BSRI includes 40 items. Individuals rate themselves on a 7-point Likert scale, and scores for masculinity and femininity are calculated.
- The BSRI includes items such as: 'independent', 'ambitious' (masculine items); 'compassionate', 'affectionate' (feminine items). They are rated on a scale from 'never or almost never true' to 'almost always true'.
- Individuals may be categorised as masculine (high masculine score, low feminine score), feminine (high feminine score, low masculine score), androgynous (high scores for both) or undifferentiated (low scores for both).

AO3 Evaluation / Discussion

Support for parental influence…

Smith and Lloyd (1978) showed that women played with babies differently, in line with sex-role stereotypes, depending on whether they were told they were boys or girls.	If they thought the baby was a boy, they encouraged more motor activity and offered stereotypically masculine toys (e.g. a squeaky hammer) rather than feminine toys (e.g. a doll).	This supports the influence of adults on children learning sex-role stereotypes.

Research support for androgyny being psychologically healthy…

Prakash *et al.* (2010) tested 100 married women in India.	Women with higher masculinity scores had lower scores for depression, anxiety, stress and physical health issues. Those with high femininity scores were less healthy.	This supports the psychoprotective effect of androgyny, as women with masculine and feminine traits were more physically and psychologically healthy.

Reliability and validity of the BSRI…

Test–retest reliability over a four-week period ranged from .76 to .94, which is a high correlation.	However, most adjectives in the BSRI are socially desirable, so people with high self-esteem score higher overall than those with low self-esteem (an intervening variable).	High reliability shows that individuals' scores for androgyny are stable over time. But the scale may measure self-esteem rather than androgyny.

Temporal validity of the BSRI…

Hoffman and Borders (2001) asked 400 undergraduates to rate the BSRI items.	Only two terms were still endorsed as masculine or feminine: the words 'masculine' and 'feminine'. All other items failed to reach 75 per cent agreement.	This suggests that people's attitudes have changed since the 1970s and the BSRI is no longer valid.

 **APPLY**

AO2: An example

SCENARIO Adam was given a toy toolkit for his sixth birthday. His younger sister, Evie, said she wanted one too because when she grows up she wants to be a builder. Adam laughed at Evie and said, 'You can't be a builder. You're a girl.'

Explain what is meant by a sex-role stereotype. Refer to Adam and Evie in your answer. **(4 marks)**

ANSWER *A sex-role stereotype is a set of shared expectations within a social group about what men and women should do and think. The society we live in teaches us expectations about how men and women should behave, such as expectations that men are doctors and women are nurses. Adam has a fixed sex-role stereotype about girls because he thinks they can't be builders. Evie does not hold the same stereotypes as her brother. She is more flexible in her thinking about what boys and girls can do. This may be because she has had different experiences from Adam, or it may be that her stereotypes are still forming as she is younger.*

AO2: One for you to try

Jim and Anne have decided to bring up their child, Robin, in a gender-neutral manner, ensuring Robin does not encounter sex-role stereotypes. Robin does not identify with either gender, but happily plays with children of both sexes, enjoys a wide variety of toys such as construction bricks, dolls, and painting. Robin also dresses in unusual combinations of clothes; dresses, trousers, T-shirts, and dressing-up costumes. Some of Jim and Anne's neighbours are very shocked and think that Robin's parents have been neglectful by not allowing their child to follow 'normal' boy or girl behaviour.

Referring to sex-role stereotypes, explain Robin's behaviour and the neighbours' reaction to it. (4 marks)

AO2: Research methods

The BSRI is a self-report scale to measure androgyny.

a. **What are the strengths and limitations of using a self-report scale to measure a personality trait such as androgyny? (6 marks)**

b. **How can the reliability of a self-report scale be assessed? (3 marks)**

c. **If the reliability is poor, how could it be improved? (3 marks)**

How do I answer... selection (multiple choice) questions?

The BSRI was developed by asking American undergraduates to rate adjectives. What were they asked? Tick **one** box only. **(1 mark)**

A Which traits were more masculine or feminine? ☐

B Which traits describe men or women? ☐

C Which words were used more in relation to males or females? ☐

D Which traits were more desirable for men or women? ☐

Multiple choice questions can seem simpler than they are. Here are some tips:

1 Take time to read the question carefully: are you asked to select one or two answers? Is it a positive choice, or an odd one out ('**not**') question? The question above asks for one answer.

2 Read all the answers and cross out any that are obviously not correct.

3 Think through which answer makes sense based on what you know.

4 Make your selection. Here, **D** is the correct answer, which fits with what we know about the BSRI's temporal validity – societal stereotypes about desirable traits for men and women have changed since the 1970s.

REVIEW

Look out for examples of sex-role stereotypes in the media. For example, in films or adverts, what roles are men and women shown in? Make a flow chart to show how these models can affect boys' or girls' behaviour, according to social learning theory.

Thinking psychologically like this at times when you are not actively studying will help you remember the key ideas better, such as sex-role stereotypes and androgyny.

The role of chromosomes and hormones in sex and gender

RECAP

A01 Description

The role of chromosomes

- Humans have 23 pairs of **chromosomes**. The sex chromosomes, XX (female) or XY (male), usually determine the sex of an individual.
- Intersex individuals may have a mismatch between sex chromosomes, hormones and phenotype, or may have ambiguous genitals.
- Atypical sex chromosome patterns: Klinefelter's syndrome, Turner's syndrome.
  - **Klinefelter's syndrome** (XXY) affects 1/1000 males. Physical characteristics include: reduced testosterone, infertility (not in all cases), less muscle, less facial hair and broader hips than typical males. Psychological characteristics often include: language difficulties and ADHD.
  - **Turner's syndrome** (XO, a missing X chromosome) affects 1/2000 females. Physical characteristics include: underdeveloped ovaries, meaning no menstruation. Psychological characteristics include: language fluency with social impairments and frequently difficulties with spatial and numerical tasks:

The role of hormones

- Most gender development is governed by **hormones**.
- More **testosterone** is produced in male foetuses from about 3 months in the testes, causing genitalia to develop. The surge of testosterone during puberty produces secondary sexual characteristics (deepening voice, body hair).
- Testosterone is produced by the adrenal glands in both sexes and relates to sex drive.
- Individuals with androgen insensitivity syndrome (AIS) may appear female.
- **Oestrogen** promotes secondary sexual characteristics (breasts, body hair) in females.
- Oestrogen is not required for development of female genitalia; these are the default option.
- **Oxytocin** promotes feelings of bonding and contentment. It causes milk to flow in a lactating mother, and has a role in orgasm in both sexes.

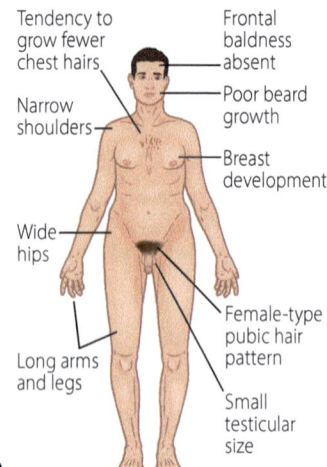

Tendency to grow fewer chest hairs

Narrow shoulders

Wide hips

Long arms and legs

Frontal baldness absent

Poor beard growth

Breast development

Female-type pubic hair pattern

Small testicular size

Typical features of Klinefelter's syndrome

A03 Evaluation / Discussion

Biological determinism…

Issues/Debates
Biological determinism

Reiner and Gearhart (2004) reported that, out of 14 genetic males raised as females, 8 had reassigned themselves by age 16.	The case of David Reimer is similar: his penis was damaged as a baby and he was raised as a girl, but he was unhappy and transitioned to a male as a teenager.	*This suggests that biological factors have a key role in gender development.*

A complex and unpredictable outcome of many factors…

For example, XX females with congenital adrenal hyperplasia (CAH) have unusually high levels of androgens and may be assigned male gender at birth.	Some people with CAH accept their assigned gender and some do not.	*Thus gender development is in part biologically determined (nature), but experience, personality and socialisation (nurture) also have a key role.*

Nature–nurture interaction: the Batista family from the Dominican Republic…

Issues/Debates
Nature-nurture

Imperato-McGinley et al. (1974) described four XY males born with female genitalia, due to androgen insensitivity, and raised as girls, who developed male genitalia during puberty.	The large amounts of testosterone produced during puberty caused their male genitalia to appear externally, and they were then treated as boys, adjusting easily to their new male role.	*This indicates the role of culture in gender, as well as the effect of testosterone.*

Treatment of intersex conditions

Intersex babies are not now treated surgically until they are older and can decide for themselves.	If identified at birth, girls with Turner syndrome can be given growth hormone so they reach normal height. Oestrogen replacement therapy helps them develop secondary sexual characteristics, and this also benefits their heart and bone health.	*It is useful to identify atypical chromosome patterns early, so the individual can be given hormone treatments.*

 **APPLY**

AO2: An example

SCENARIO Jolanta is 13, and her mother has taken her to see the GP as she is worried about her. She is very short compared to her friends and has not started to develop breasts. Her mother says that Jolanta talks fluently, and is doing fine at school. However, the doctor suspects that Jolanta may have Turner's syndrome.

Why does the doctor suspect Turner's syndrome, and how could she confirm this? What advice can she give to Jolanta and her mother?

(4 marks)

ANSWER *The doctor suspects this because Jolanta is short and has no sign of developing secondary sexual characteristics. The doctor could look for other physical signs such as short neck, low-set ears, etc. The doctor will have to do a chromosome test to find out. It may be too late to treat Jolanta with growth hormone, but she could be given oestrogen replacement therapy so she develops female characteristics, and this will protect her bones and heart too.*

AO2: Research methods

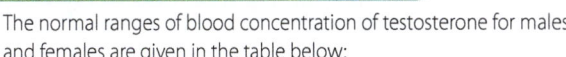

The normal ranges of blood concentration of testosterone for males and females are given in the table below:

	Blood testosterone concentration (nmol/L)
Males <50 years	8.6–29.0
Males >50 years	6.7–25.7
Females <50 years	0.29–1.67
Females >50 years	0.1–1.42

a. Calculate the median blood testosterone concentration (BTC) for males under 50 years? (2 marks)

b. The International Athletics Association Federation (IAAF) has set a maximum of 5nmol/L of testosterone for athletes competing as women (2018). Using the data in this table, explain why they have chosen this value. (2 marks)

c. South African Olympian Caster Semenya has been reported as having testosterone levels three times higher than most women. Suggest what her BTC could be, based on the data in this table. Would she be allowed to compete as a woman without using hormone suppression under these new rules? (2 marks)

AO2: One for you to try

Timmy is 15 and has always had difficulties at school. He has a diagnosis of ADHD and can be quite aggressive. He is referred to an adolescent mental health team. The specialist observes that Timmy is very tall (200cm) and overweight, and has some language difficulties. As a result of these observations, Timmy's chromosome type is analysed and his sex chromosomes are found to be atypical.

a. **Suggest what Timmy's chromosome pattern could be, and name the disorder. (2 marks)**

b. **What effect could this have on Timmy's future? (2 marks)**

 **How do I answer... description only questions (AO1)?**

Questions asking you to 'outline', 'describe' or 'explain' require AO1 answers. Take note of the marks available, and select that number of points from the AO1 material on the opposite page.

Q1: Outline the role of chromosomes in sex and gender. **(6 marks)**

Use the first point to describe typical chromosome patterns in males and females, then elaborate by describing atypical patterns (Klinefelter's and Turner's syndromes).

Q2: Outline the role of hormones in sex and gender. **(6 marks)**

Use the first six points under the heading, 'The role of hormones'.

Q3: Describe the physical and psychological characteristics of Klinefelter's syndrome. **(2 marks)**

Include one or two examples of each.

Q4: Explain the term 'intersex'. **(2 marks)**

This needs a definition, and you could also give examples, such as AIS or Klinefelter's syndrome.

REVIEW

Storytelling is a useful way to memorise information, and the stories of David Reimer and the Batista family may be fascinating to your family or friends, or your pet hamster. Prepare your story so that it is accurate, and use it to explain the role of chromosomes and hormones in determining sex and gender (which is not always straightforward!). You should then practise writing a two-sentence summary of each story, so that you can focus on the relevant points when including them as evidence in an exam answer. The temptation is to get carried away with too much detail; you need to write concisely and stay focused.

Cognitive explanations of gender development: Kohlberg's theory

RECAP

AO1 Description

Kohlberg's theory

- **Kohlberg** (1966) proposed that children gradually develop the ability to think about gender, progressing through stages, as they become capable of more complex and abstract thought.
- This is a cognitive developmental approach, like Piaget's theory of cognitive development, which proposes that brain maturation and experience interact to enable children's thinking to develop.
- Stage 1: **Gender labelling**
  > Age 2–3.
  > Children label themselves and others as boy/girl, man/woman, based on outward appearance (clothes, hairstyle).
  > Children change the labels as appearances change; 'he has long hair now, so he must be a girl'. This is **pre-operational** thinking.
- Stage 2: **Gender stability**
  > Age 4–7.
  > Children recognise that gender is stable over time (girls grow into women) but not over situations. They are still swayed by outward appearances.
  > McConaghy (1979) found that young children thought a doll in a dress was female even when male genitals were visible.

- Stage 3: **Gender constancy**
  > Age 6.
  > Children realise gender shows **conservation** across time and situations, and realise their gender will not change.

AO3 Evaluation/Discussion

Research evidence supports Kohlberg's three stages...

Slaby and Frey (1975) asked young children questions like 'were you a little girl or a little boy when you were a baby?'

They found that children didn't recognise gender stability until three or four years old. Also, children who scored highly on stability and constancy showed greater interest in same-sex models.

This supports Kohlberg's developmental stages and his prediction that children who have achieved constancy will pay more attention to same-sex models.

Methodological criticisms of studies with young children...

Martin and Halverson (1983) re-examined the responses, concluding that the children were in 'pretend' mode.

Bem (1989) argued that children use the cues that are most relevant in our society, such as clothes, and that many children who couldn't conserve didn't actually know what opposite-gender genitals look like.

This weakens the validity of the findings, and their support for the theory.

Gender differences...

Issues/Debates
Gender bias

Slaby and Frey found that boys tend to exhibit gender constancy before girls.

This may because boys are more likely to identify with same-gender role models as men are more powerful in society. In addition, boys are more likely to be punished for gender-inappropriate behaviour than girls.

Therefore, Kohlberg's theory is incomplete because principles of social learning theory are also involved.

Gender stereotypes without constancy...

Martin and Little (1990) showed that children under four display strong stereotypes about male and female behaviour.

For example, they had strong beliefs about what boys and girls were permitted to do. This was before they had developed gender stability, let alone gender constancy.

This supports gender schema theory rather than Kohlberg's theory (see next spread).

⚙ APPLY

AO2: An example

SCENARIO Jason's father is a soldier and hopes his son will want to be a soldier too. He is worried that Jason is not behaving like a proper boy. Jason likes wearing fairy dresses and prefers drawing pictures to fighting. However, Jason's mother thinks Jason will grow out of this phase. Jason is four years old.

Based on Kohlberg's theory of gender development, what advice could you give to Jason's parents? **(4 marks)**

ANSWER *Jason's parents could be advised that, as Jason is only four, he has not reached the stage of gender constancy, so may not realise that his behaviour is unusual for a male. He will probably change his tastes in clothes as he grows up and sees that men do not wear fairy dresses. If he is given opportunities to observe men fighting he may well imitate this behaviour as he learns to identify with men.*

AO2: Research methods

A researcher investigated children's stage of gender development, by asking them questions. For example, he asked: 'If you played football, would you be a boy or a girl?' He then categorised the children according to the stage they had reached. A tally of the results is shown in the table below. Each number represents the age of a child who has reached that stage.

Stage	Boys	Girls
Gender labelling	2 2 2 2 2 2 2 2 3 3	2 2 2 2 3 3
Gender stability	3 3 4 4 4 4 5	2 3 3 4 4 4 4 5 5 5 6 6 6
Gender constancy	4 4 5 5 5 5 5 5 6 6	5 5 5 5 6 6 6 6

a. **What percentage of boys had reached at least the gender stability stage? What percentage of girls had reached the same stage? Show your calculations. (2 + 2 marks)**

b. **Calculate the median ages for boys and for girls to reach gender constancy. Show your calculations. (2 marks)**

c. **The researcher tests the data for statistical significance. Which statistical test would be suitable for this data? Explain your answer. (3 marks)**

The researcher concludes that boys reach gender constancy earlier than girls.

d. **Briefly discuss the validity of this conclusion. (4 marks)**

✏ AO2: One for you to try

Phoenix, aged 3, is given a doll and asked, 'Is this doll a boy or a girl?' Phoenix answers, 'A boy.' Then a long-haired wig is placed on the doll, and Phoenix is asked again, 'Is this a boy or a girl?' Phoenix now answers, 'A girl.'

What kind of thinking is Phoenix demonstrating? Explain your answer using your knowledge of Kohlberg's theory of gender development. (6 marks)

Is this dog a boy or a girl?

🐾 How do I answer... evaluation only questions (AO3)?

Evaluation questions come in various shapes and sizes. Terms like 'evaluate', 'discuss', 'explain', 'criticism', 'strength' and 'limitation' all indicate that AO3 is required. Let's look at some examples. The AO3 material for these questions is on the opposite page.

Q1: Give one criticism of Kohlberg's theory of gender development. **(2 marks)**

A criticism can be positive or negative. The first AO3 evaluation point or the fourth are stand-alone points, so choose one of them, and use the lead-in statement and the first two columns for a 2-mark answer.

Q2: Explain one limitation of Kohlberg's theory of gender development. **(3 marks)**

You could select AO3 evaluation point 3 or 4, and fully elaborate it using all three columns.

Q3: Evaluate Kohlberg's theory of gender development. **(6 marks)**

This needs two effective AO3 points, and it would make sense to use the first one with the second or third so that you can make an effective discussion, linking them with 'however'. Or you could go for points 1 and 4. Use all three columns to elaborate the points fully.

🔄 REVIEW

You need to be able to answer questions with different mark allocations concisely while using enough detail to explain the concept clearly. Practise answering the questions above, spending about a minute and a quarter per mark: e.g. five minutes for a 4-mark question, 10 minutes for a 6-mark question. Make sure you allow time to plan logical answers.

1. Practise recalling the AO3 evaluation/discussion points opposite.

2. Practise writing the full answer, setting a time to make sure you use the time available.

3. Check your answer is clear and logical, and has relevant key terms in each point.

Cognitive explanations of gender development: Gender schema theory

 **RECAP**

AO1 Description

- Martin and Halverson (1981) developed this cognitive approach, in which a child seeks to acquire information about their own gender.

- A key difference between gender schema theory (GST) and Kohlberg's theory is that in GST gender labelling is sufficient for a child to pay attention to gender-appropriate behaviours. Kohlberg claimed this did not happen until after gender constancy was established.

- **Schemas** are mental representations of concepts. Children learn gender schemas at about age three, from interaction with other children and adults, and from the media. Gender schemas relate to cultural norms, and 'appropriate' behaviour for men and women.

- **Ingroup and outgroup schemas** Children identify with ingroup gender schemas and actively avoid outgroup behaviours. This leads to positive evaluation of the ingroup and negative evaluation of the outgroup: 'boys are better than girls'. This enhances self-esteem.

- **Resilience of gender beliefs** Children ignore information that is inconsistent with gender schemas, so it is very difficult to change stereotypes using counter-stereotypes.

- **Peer relationships** Children believe that same-sex peers are 'like me' and therefore more fun to play with. They also learn to avoid negative consequences of ignoring the schemas, such as being teased.

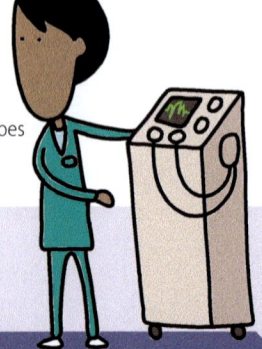

Gender counter-stereotypes

AO3 Evaluation / Discussion

Research supports gender schema theory…

Martin and Little (1990) found children under four had strong gender stereotypes about what boys and girls are allowed to do, despite a lack of gender stability or constancy.

Kohlberg's theory would require children to develop constancy before understanding gender roles, at about age six.

This shows that children have acquired information about gender roles earlier than Kohlberg suggested, supporting GST.

Gender schemas lead to cognitive distortions…

Martin and Halverson (1983) found children under six remembered more gender-consistent pictures (e.g. female teacher, male firefighter) than gender-inconsistent ones (e.g. female chemist, male nurse).

Schemas even caused distortion of memories, so that children shown a boy holding a doll (inconsistent, or counter-stereotypical) described it as a girl.

These cognitive distortions maintain ingroup schemas and this evidence supports GST.

Gender schemas organise new information…

Bradbard *et al.* (1986) told four- to nine-year-olds that gender-neutral items (burglar alarms, pizza cutters) were boy or girl items.

The children took a greater interest in items labelled as ingroup. They also remembered more of the 'ingroup' objects a week later.

This shows how gender schemas help children to organise new information in memory.

Changing stereotypes…

GST explains why children are frequently highly sexist, despite efforts of parents and teachers to provide counter-stereotypes.

However, Hoffman (1998) reported that children whose mothers work have less stereotyped views of what men do. This shows that children are receptive to non-stereotyped ideas of gender roles.

This suggests that practical approaches to changing stereotypes should involve direct experience of people who do not fit stereotypes.

APPLY

AO2: An example

SCENARIO Oli's parents both go out to work. Oli's mum enjoys doing DIY jobs at weekends, like assembling flat-pack furniture, and his dad never uses power tools but prefers to read a book. However, when Oli is shown a drill, and asked, 'Who would use this, Mummy or Daddy?', he replies, 'Daddy.' And when he is asked what Mummy and Daddy do all day, he says, 'Daddy goes to work and Mummy cleans the house.'

How does gender schema theory explain Oli's answers? **(4 marks)**

ANSWER *Oli has acquired his schema from films or stories or from other families in which the father goes out to work and the mother stays at home and carries out domestic tasks. He sees a power drill as a 'boy's toy' because of advertising or other factors, like the labelling of loud, powerful objects as masculine. He sees his mum and dad contradicting these gender schemas in their behaviour, but his schemas stay intact, and he answers according to the schemas rather than his observations.*

AO2: One for you to try

A primary school teacher wanted to challenge some of the stereotyping that featured in her class's play time.

How could the teacher break the stereotypes and encourage the children to explore a wider variety of roles in their play? (4 marks)

AO2: Research methods

Forty children were shown pictures of a firefighter, a teacher, a nurse and a chemist. There were equal numbers of men and women in each role. A week later, the same children were asked whether each job was being done by a man or a woman.

The results are shown in the bar chart.

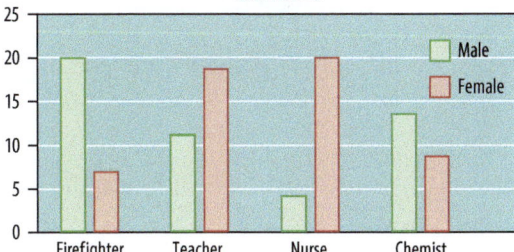

Number of models whose gender was correctly remembered

Firefighter | Teacher | Nurse | Chemist (Male / Female)

a. **What experimental design is used in this study? (1 mark)**

b. **State a possible hypothesis for this experiment. (3 marks)**

c. **How can gender schema theory explain these findings? (3 marks)**

d. **Explain how the results might have differed if the participants were adults? (2 marks)**

e. **Suggest an extraneous variable in this study, and explain how it could have affected the results. (3 marks)**

How do I answer... 'Distinguish between' questions?

> **Q1:** Distinguish between Kohlberg's theory and gender schema theory of gender development. **(4 marks)**

If you are asked to 'compare' or 'distinguish between' two concepts, you must compare a specific aspect of them. Don't just describe one and then describe the other. The process is:

1 Choose a feature which is relevant to both – e.g. the ages at which children pay attention to gender-appropriate behaviour.

2 Explain the difference, using 'whereas' to connect the two ideas. See second point ('A key difference between...') of AO1 material on the opposite page.

3 Choose a second point of difference – e.g. Children seek to acquire knowledge about gender from their experience (GST) whereas children's gender knowledge develops with maturity (Kohlberg).

Two clear comparisons will be enough for 4 marks.

REVIEW

Craik and Lockhart (1972) proposed a theory of memory called the 'levels of processing model'. This model claimed that the more that information is elaborated, the more likely we will be able to access that information later on. There are many different ways of elaborating material, so let's try one.

Take a large sheet of paper (A3 works well here) and construct a mind-map so that all your material on the cognitive explanations of gender development (Kohlberg's theory and GST) is linked together in a colourful, visual way. This serves several purposes: (1) It elaborates the material, making it more memorable; (2) The act of constructing the mind-map counts as revision, making recall in an exam more likely; and (3) It produces a visual image, which, for many people, is a much easier way of remembering complex material.

*Tip: There is a wealth of useful revision videos on the Internet – take a look for some on mind-map construction.

Psychodynamic explanation of gender development

AO1 Description

- **The Oedipus complex** Freud (1905) proposed that, during the phallic stage (ages three to six), boys:

  > Desire their mother and want her whole attention, see their father as a rival and wish he was dead. Develop anxiety about their wish for their father to die. This leads to castration fear, which is repressed.

  > Eventually resolve the conflict by **identification** with the father and **internalisation** of the father's gender identity. Identification means the boy wants to be like his father, and internalisation means the boy accepts his father's attitudes and behaviour and takes them on as his own.

- **The Electra complex** Jung (1913) proposed that girls:

  > Are initially attracted to their mother, but discover she doesn't have a penis. Blame their mother for their lack of a penis, believing they were castrated. This penis envy is later converted into a wish to have a baby, resolving anger against the mother. Transfer their sexual desires to their father.

  > Eventually **identify** with the mother and **internalise** her gender behaviours.

- **Unresolved phallic stage** Frustration and/or overindulgence may lead to fixation at the phallic stage, and an individual who is not capable of intimacy.

- Freud also claimed that fixation could be a root cause of amoral behaviour and homosexuality.

MUMMY!!!!

Freud suggested Little Hans was scared of horses because they represented his father

AO3 Evaluation / Discussion

Freud's theory is supported with case studies…

Issues/Debates
Psychic determinism

Freud (1909) described Little Hans, who developed a fear of horses due to repressing his desires for his mother.	Also Levin (1921) reported on 32 patients with bipolar disorder; 22 had unresolved Electra complex or penis envy.	However, these case studies are subjectively interpreted and selectively reported, to fit the researcher's expectations. This means that they are poor evidence, and the theories are unfalsifiable.

The theory lacks predictive validity…

It predicts that children in one-parent families or with same-sex parents would have difficulty acquiring a gender identity or normal gender-role behaviour, which is not supported by evidence.	Patterson (2004) found that children of lesbian parents develop gender identities in similar ways to children of heterosexual parents, and have normal social relationships.	This means that gender development does not depend on the Oedipus or Electra complex.

Alternative psychodynamic explanations…

Chodorow (1994) suggested that mothers and daughters are closer because they are the same sex, whereas boys become more independent.	This is supported by observations that mother-daughter pairs play more closely (Goldberg and Lewis, 1969). In addition, boys and girls attempt to identify with the father but only sons succeed.	The advantage of this alternative explanation is that it does not predict problems in families with same-sex parents.

Criticisms of Freud's idea of penis envy…

Feminists object to the idea that the resolution of the Oedipus complex is less satisfactory for girls, and Freud admitted he didn't really understand women.	However, Lacan (1966) suggested that penis envy can be considered as a symbolic envy of male power in a male-dominated society, rather than being taken literally.	So, although Freud can be accused of gender bias, his theories make more sense as metaphorical rather than literal descriptions.

Issues/Debates
Gender bias. Freud's theory is considered to be alpha biased as male sexual development is taken as the norm, and females are therefore seen as inferior.

APPLY

AO2: An example

SCENARIO Here are some key ideas from Freud's case study of Little Hans:

- At three years old, Hans was interested in his penis and liked playing with it, but his mother didn't like this behaviour and threatened to get a doctor to cut it off.
- He was very distressed by seeing a horse collapse and die in the street.
- Hans commented that horses had large 'widdlers' and assumed that his parents, being adults, must have the same. He was told that his mother didn't have one, and assumed she'd been castrated.
- At four, Hans developed a phobia of horses, which became generalised anxiety so that he didn't want to leave the house.
- At around the same time Hans's father started objecting to Hans climbing into his parents' bed in the morning to cuddle his mother.

Using this information, and your knowledge of Freud's psychoanalytic theory, how would Freud interpret the causes of Hans's phobia? **(4 marks)**

ANSWER *Hans was interested in his penis during the phallic stage (ages three to six) as his libido was focused on the genitals. His mother threatened to cut it off, leading to castration anxiety. The horse represented his father, whom he wished was dead, as he was a rival for his mother's love. This resulted in general anxiety from repressing his wish to kill his father, and a phobia of horses.*

Hans wanted to cuddle his mother in bed: this shows his sexual desire for his mother.

His father objected, reinforcing the rivalry.

AO2: One for you to try

To resolve little Hans's conflict and treat his phobia, what needs to happen, according to Freud's theory? Select one answer.

A His mother should apologise for threatening to castrate Hans, and he should forgive her.

B His father should reassure Hans that he will not be castrated, and Hans should identify with his father.

C Hans should be exposed to horses to desensitise him.

D His mother and father should explain to Hans that it is normal for a woman not to have a penis.

AO2: Research methods

Explain how these research issues can be used to evaluate psychodynamic explanations of gender development:

a. **Based on case studies. (3 marks)**

b. **Gender bias. (3 marks)**

c. **Unfalsifiable. (3 marks)**

d. **Lack of predictive validity. (3 marks)**

e. **Non-experimental methods. (3 marks)**

How do I answer... description and evaluation (AO1 + AO3) questions?

Step 1: In answering mixed AO1 + AO3 questions the first step is recognising that this is what you are being asked to do! Having two different command words, e.g. 'outline' (an AO1 term) and evaluate (an AO3 term) is usually a good clue.

Step 2: Plan how much you should write for each. In mixed AO1 + AO3 questions up to 6 marks, the division is half and half (it is different with mark totals higher than this as we will see on p.51).

Step 3: Decide what to write. Look at the examples below. The AO1 and AO3 material for these questions is on the opposite page.

Q1: Describe and evaluate the Oedipus complex as an explanation of gender development. **(4 marks)**

For **Q1**, this would mean using the AO1 points relating to the Oedipus complex, and the second AO3 point.

Q2: Outline and evaluate the psychodynamic explanation of gender development. **(6 marks)**

Use the AO1 points relating to the Oedipus complex and the final two points. The Electra complex is less relevant. Then use one fully elaborated AO3 point.

Q3: Discuss the findings of research into psychodynamic explanations of gender development. **(6 marks)**

Describe findings and evaluate the research, including about 75–90 words of AO1 and 75–90 words of AO3. Use only the findings of research, not the procedure. To make it a discussion, include some 'howevers' (AO3 evaluation point 1, and 2 or 3).

REVIEW

How much should I write? You should practise writing 3-, 4- and 6-mark descriptions of the psychodynamic explanation. For 3 marks, use three AO1 points, for 4 marks use four points and so on. For 6 marks you should be writing about 150–180 words. If you attempt to cover all aspects of the theory thoroughly, you will run out of time for AO3 in an extended answer, so be selective and concise. We have helped you by summarising the key content in the points on the opposite page. But you still need to include enough detail and specialist terminology if you want to get marks in the top band.

Social learning theory as applied to gender development

AO1 Description

- Bandura explained that we learn indirectly from other people (models) by observing and imitating their behaviour. This is **social learning theory** (SLT).

- **Indirect reinforcement** Children observe gender behaviour of others from home, school, and the media. They learn, from the consequences, whether the behaviour is worth repeating (vicarious reinforcement). Girls identify with other females and are more likely to imitate their behaviour. Boys may also observe their mothers' behaviour at home but are less likely to imitate it.

- **Direct reinforcement** Reinforcement (e.g. praise) of gender behaviour increases the likelihood that a child will repeat it. Punishment reduces it.

- **The role of mediational processes** Bandura called SLT a social cognitive theory. Children store information about reinforcements as mental representations which create an expectancy of future outcomes. They will then display the behaviour if the expectation of reward is greater than the expectation of punishment.

- **Direct tuition** When children acquire linguistic skills, they learn appropriate gender behaviour through explicit instructions such as 'be ladylike'.

- **Self-direction** Bandura believed that people internalise gender-appropriate behaviours and then actively direct their own behaviour. This is no longer dependent on external reinforcement.

AO3 Evaluation/Discussion

Research evidence supports modelling of gender...

Perry and Bussey (1979) showed children (aged 8–9) films of other children selecting apples or pears, then gave them fruit to choose.	The children preferentially selected the fruit they had observed a same-sex model choosing. However, the children only imitated same-sex behaviour if it was not counter to stereotypes (e.g. a man wearing a dress).	So it seems that the effects of modelling may be limited to existing stereotypes.

However, peers may not be important until later in childhood...

Gender identity is being formed in early childhood, when parents are the main influence. Later peer reinforcement may act as a reminder.	Lamb and Roopnarine (1979) observed that reinforcement of male-type behaviour in preschool girls was less long-lasting than reinforcement of male-type behaviour in boys.	This suggests that peer behaviour does not create gender-role stereotypes, but simply reinforces existing ones.

Direct tuition may be more effective than modelling...

Direct instruction is more important than modelling in preschool children, but both influence behaviour.	Martin et al. (1995) found that boys played with toys labelled 'boys' toys' even if they saw girls playing with them. However, they didn't play with 'girls' toys' even when they saw boys playing with them.	However, parents' and teachers' behaviour does not always match their direct tuition, and this contradiction weakens the effect of what is being taught (Hildebrandt, 1973).

Self-direction increases with age...

Bussey and Bandura (1992) showed children (aged 3–4) videos of other children playing with masculine or feminine toys.	The younger children disapproved of others but not themselves for gender-inconsistent behaviour, whereas older children disapproved of both. These evaluations were confirmed by the children's actual choices of toys in play.	This shows how self-regulation increases with age, as children learn to evaluate others' behaviour, and then their own.

Issues/Debates
Free will/determinism

APPLY

AO2: An example

SCENARIO Annabelle, aged 16, is often told by her parents that she is not being ladylike, and that she should wear a skirt when they go out as a family, not jeans. However, her friends rarely wear skirts and seem to have lots of fun.

Discuss the social learning theory explanation of gender development, and suggest how Annabelle is likely to behave. **(16 marks)**

ANSWER **An extract showing how you could address the AO2 requirements of this**

question: *Annabelle receives direct tuition from her parents, 'should wear a skirt', and also direct punishment – the criticism 'not being ladylike'. However, she also receives modelling from peers of wearing jeans, and vicarious reinforcement as they seem to be having fun. There is a conflict between these two influences; she is old enough to make her own choice and weigh up the likely punishment from her mother versus the expectation of reward she has gained from observing peers.*

Evidence from research by Martin et al. suggests that Annabelle may be more affected by direct tuition. Lamb and Roopnarine's research suggests that peers merely reinforce existing gender-role stereotypes, so Annabelle's peers may have less influence over her behaviour than she imagines.

AO2: Research methods

a. **A book was published by Taylor & Francis in 2001 called *Schooling the Boys: Masculinities and Primary Education. Educating Boys, Learning Gender*. The author was Christine Skelton and the place of publication was Florence, Kentucky (KY). A researcher found some interesting material on pages 47–51 of this book. Write a reference for this, suitable to include in the reference section of a scientific report. (2 marks)**

b. **The journal *Violence and Victims* published an article in 1992 called 'Dating Violence, Social Learning Theory, and Gender: A Multivariate Analysis'. This appeared on pages 3–14 of Volume 7, Issue No. 1 of the journal, which is published by Springer Publishing Company. The article's authors were Pamela Tontodonato from Kent State University and B. Keith Crew from the University of Northern Iowa. Write a reference for this article, suitable to be included in a reference section. (2 marks)**

AO2: One for you to try

Recent research found that male characters are twice as likely to take leading roles in children's picture books. In the 100 most popular children's picture books of 2017, researchers found that the stories were dominated by male characters, often in stereotypically masculine roles, while 20 books contained no female characters.

Use your knowledge of social learning theory to suggest how children may be affected by reading these books. (4 marks)

How do I answer... research methods questions?

Questions requiring research methods knowledge can appear in any section of any paper in the AS or A Level exams. They could include any aspect of research methods, data analysis or ethical issues. Don't be shocked if an unexpected question comes up, such as the referencing questions in **AO2: Research methods**. Just have a go, and try to use your general knowledge of research methods, which you have gained during your course. When a question like this came up in an A Level paper recently, very few students gained 2 marks, as many didn't even make an attempt. It's worth having a go, as getting 1 mark could make the difference between grades. You probably know that the author's surname comes first, then the date and title, and this would get you 1 mark.

It's also important to remember that you need to apply your knowledge to the study in research methods questions whenever possible, not just give generic points. Keep practising!

REVIEW

As you are probably aware, simply reading material is not the most effective way of learning it properly. So, using the material on the opposite page, try writing plans for 3-, 4- and 6-mark 'outline' questions on SLT and gender development, plus plans for 8- and 16-mark essay questions.

Test yourself on the key points of the topic by covering up your plans and writing them out again. It's useful to have a supply of cheap paper for this, as the more times you practise retrieving the information, the better you will remember it.

Spaced practice is also very effective: come back to the same topic tomorrow and start your revision by seeing how many of the points you can remember before you look at your essay plan.

Cultural and media influences on gender roles

RECAP

AO1 Description

- **Cultural influences** The gender rules of a culture underlie stereotypes and influence peer and parental reinforcement.
    - > Mead (1935) found cultural role differences between three social groups in Papua New Guinea; Arapesh men and women were gentle and cooperative, Mundugumor men and women were violent and competitive, whereas Tchambuli women were dominant.
- **Cultural differences** People across cultures believe that women are more conformist than men, but conformity actually varies (Berry *et al.*, 2002).
- Cultures can change with time, e.g. UK women perform more domestic duties than men but the gender gap is decreasing.
- **The influence of the media** Media role models perpetuate gender stereotypes.
- **Vicarious reinforcement** affects people's self-efficacy about their ability to master gender-consistent or inconsistent activities.
    - > Usually, men are portrayed as independent and directive, whereas women are shown as dependent, unambitious and emotional (Bussey and Bandura, 1999).
    - > Men are more likely than women to be shown controlling events (Hodges et al., 1981) and women in adverts are shown as more flawless and passive than men (Conley and Ramsey, 2011).
- On the other hand, the media can present **counter-stereotypes** which reduce children's adherence to stereotypes (Pingree, 1978).

GENDER ROLES EXAMINED

AO3 Evaluation / Discussion

Social role theory explains gender roles as a product of biological and social factors...

Issues/Debates
Nature-nurture

Because of biological differences between men and women, women have to bear and care for children, while men are generally physically stronger and more suited to traditional work requiring upper body strength.

According to social role theory (Eagly and Wood, 1999), in societies where childcare is available and work doesn't require strength, gender roles become more similar.

This explains gender differences in roles as a product of biological differences, not just cultural stereotypes.

Observer bias is a problem with cross-cultural research...

Freeman (1984) criticised Mead's research as invalid, as the indigenous people had told her what she wanted to hear, creating a false picture of their behaviour.

However, Freeman's account has also been criticised, and Mead subsequently changed her conclusions, noting that there were more similarities than differences between males and females.

This means that evidence from cross-cultural studies may be flawed, limiting the conclusions that can be drawn.

Evidence for the influence of TV...

The Notel study (Williams, 1985) was a longitudinal study which compared children's stereotypes before and after the introduction of TV to their remote Canadian valley.

After TV arrived, the children's views had become significantly more sex-stereotyped.

This shows that exposure to media can have significant effects on gender attitudes.

Counter-stereotyping and backlash...

Some research has shown that counter-stereotypes can change expectations. However, gender-inconsistent messages are often misremembered and have no effect. (Martin and Halverson, see p.58).

Additionally, Pingree (1978) found that preadolescent boys display stronger stereotypes after exposure to non-traditional models. This may be because boys this age want to take a view that contradicts adults' views.

This makes it difficult to use the media to change cultural stereotypes.

 **APPLY**

AO2: An example

SCENARIO A study of Harvard Law School classrooms found that, in a class with a male instructor, men spoke two-and-a-half times longer than their female classmates. However, when a female instructor led the classroom, they had 'an inspiring effect on female students', leading women to speak three times as much as they did with a male instructor.

Suggest why the difference occurred when a female instructor led the classroom. **(6 marks)**

ANSWER *The female instructor 'had an inspiring effect' on the female students, as she was a counter-stereotypical role model, a confident professional woman who took a lead and talked to the class a lot. As the instructor, she would probably be talking more than the students. This challenges stereotypes of female reticence or shyness, and enables female students to identify with her and imitate her behaviour. In contrast, male students may identify less with a female instructor and therefore be quieter. Also, there is the possibility that the female instructor was deliberately encouraging female students to talk, by targeting them with questions or by direct tuition, telling them that they need to practise talking to become successful lawyers.*

AO2: Research methods

Sasha was researching gender stereotypes in advertising.

a. Describe how he could carry out a content analysis to explore this topic. (4 marks)

He has gathered some data relating to advertisements for different products using male or female actors. He also analysed the roles of males and females in conversation in these advertisements. The data he collected is shown in the table below.

	Male actors	Female actors
Beauty product	2	15
Chocolate	4	8
Alcoholic drink	6	4
Starting a conversation	5	3
Giving information	11	3
Verbally expressing emotion	0	8

b. Draw a suitable chart to display the data. (4 marks)

c. What can you conclude about the roles displayed by males and females in conversation in these advertisements? (3 marks)

AO2: One for you to try

Referring to the study described in **AO2: An example**, answer the following questions.

a. If men spoke for a mean time of 1.5 minutes when there was a male instructor, how long was the mean time of women's comments? Show your working. **(2 marks)**

b. There were 60 men and 40 women in the classroom. When there was a male instructor, what percentage of the time taken up by students talking were females talking? **(3 marks)**

c. Assuming the total student talking time is the same, what percentage of student talking time was occupied by females when there was a female instructor? **(2 marks)**

 ## How do I answer... essay questions with an AO2 component?

In 16-mark essay questions with an AO2 (application) component, 4 of the marks are for explaining the question scenario in the context of the material you are discussing. These marks are always taken from the AO3 allocation, so there are still 6 marks for AO1, 4 marks for AO2 and 6 marks for AO3. The best idea is to link each AO2 point to a relevant point of AO1, as you do with a shorter application question (see p.51). Then you can evaluate or discuss as you would in a normal essay. If you are able to link any of the AO3 points to the scenario too, this shows that you are really thinking about the question, and looks impressive. Here is an example.

> The governors of a boarding school are considering whether to ban violent TV and computer games, hoping that this will reduce boys' aggressive behaviour in school. Discuss what advice you could give the governors, based on research into the influence of culture and media. **(16 marks)**

Explain how boys learn aggressive behaviour from models, which may be on TV, and cultural norms of masculinity. You must state what advice you would give – it doesn't matter whether you advise them to ban TV or to encourage the students to watch counter-stereotypical TV shows, as long as you back this up with evidence. You only need three evaluation points, so select points which you can link, particularly the Notel study.

REVIEW

To enhance your practical expertise in questions on this topic further, there are a couple of other useful things you can do, including:

1. Write 2-, 3-, 4- and 6-mark outlines of culture and media influences on gender. For a longer answer, you could include some key terms from SLT, as this is **how** gender roles are learnt from the media.

2. Write a bullet-pointed answer plan (including both AO1 and AO3 material) for the following two questions.

> Briefly discuss the role of culture and media in influencing gender roles. **(8 marks)**

> Discuss the role of culture and media in gender. **(16 marks)**

Atypical gender development

RECAP

AO1 Description

- **Gender dysphoria** is a psychiatric condition involving discomfort with one's assigned gender.

- **Biological explanations of gender dysphoria:**

  > The **brain-sex theory** suggests that transsexuals' brains do not match their genetic sex. For example, the BSTc area of the thalamus is larger in men than women, and its size correlates with preferred gender rather than biological sex (Zhou *et al.*, 1995).

  > A **'transsexual gene'**, a longer version of the androgen receptor gene, reduces sensitivity to testosterone and may under-masculinise the brain. Male to female (MtF) transsexuals are more likely to have this gene (Hare *et al.*, 2009).

  > Ramachandran suggested that gender dysphoria is due to innate **cross-wiring**, in which the sensory cortex is connected differently. So two thirds of FtM transsexuals report the sensation of a phantom penis.

  > Some **environmental pollutants**, such as pesticides, contain oestrogens, which could affect foetal development. Vreugdenhil *et al.* (2002) found that boys with mothers who had been exposed to dioxins displayed feminised play.

- **Social and psychological explanations of gender dysphoria:**

  > Overly close mother–son relationships could lead to greater female identification in boys.

  > Females with poor father–daughter relationships could identify as males, unconsciously hoping to gain acceptance from their father.

AO3 Evaluation / Discussion

Criticisms of the brain-sex theory…

Issues/Debates
Biological reductionism

Chung *et al.* (2002) noted that the BSTc is the same size in males and females until adulthood, whereas most transsexuals report their gender dysphoria as starting in early childhood.

Also, people in the BSTc studies had received hormone therapy, and this could have affected their BSTc size. Any differences could be an effect, rather than a cause, of gender dysphoria.

It is difficult to find consistent differences between the brains of males and females, let alone people with gender dysphoria, so there is inconsistent evidence for the brain-sex theory.

Research support for cross-wiring…

Ramachandran and McGeoch (2007) report that 60 per cent of non-gender dysphoria men and only 30 per cent of gender dysphoria men experience a phantom penis after penis amputation (e.g. for cancer).

In addition, only 10 per cent of FtM patients experience phantom breasts after surgery to remove breasts.

This suggests that some transsexual adults have differently wired brains.

Mixed evidence for social explanations…

For example, Zucker *et al.* (1996) found that 64 per cent of boys with gender dysphoria were also diagnosed with separation anxiety disorder, compared to 38 per cent of boys who had some gender concerns but were not diagnosed with gender dysphoria.

However, Cole *et al.* (1997) studied 435 people with gender dysphoria and found no greater incidence of psychiatric conditions than in a normal population.

This suggests that the development of gender dysphoria is generally unrelated to trauma or pathological family relations.

Socially sensitive research…

There are potential social consequences for individuals with gender dysphoria, if causes are found.

If a biological cause is identified, it might help society to be more accepting. On the other hand, a biological cause might harm individuals if it is assumed that transsexualism is inevitable.

Either way, the outcomes of research have likely consequences for individuals concerned. A simple cause-and-effect relationship is unlikely, however.

Issues/Debates
Ethical implications of research

 APPLY

AO2: An example

SCENARIO Nina is 12 years old. Ever since she can remember, she has much preferred socialising with boys rather than girls. Most of her hobbies are typically masculine, and she is often mistaken for a boy because of the way that she dresses. She has recently told her parents that she is considering renaming herself Nathan, and wants to be referred to as 'they'.

Discuss both biological and social explanations of gender dysphoria. Refer to the case of Nina as part of your answer. **(16 marks)**

ANSWER **An extract showing how you could address the AO2 requirements of this question:** *There may be biological factors causing Nina to identify as a boy: differences in brain areas, or 'cross-wiring', giving the sensation of a phantom penis (Ramachandran).*

According to a social psychological explanation, they may have a poor father–daughter relationship and feel rejected by their father as a girl, hoping to be more affirmed as 'Nathan'. Or there may be a social/cultural explanation: they feel they do not fit cultural stereotypes of femaleness because of their typically masculine hobbies and clothing, Nina gets on better with boys, and identifies more with boys and wants to be one...

AO2: One for you to try

Carol wrote a message on an Internet forum, 'I desperately wanted to be a boy until aged about 10 yrs, dressed as one, prayed I would wake up as one. Only did "boys stuff", was better than my brothers at football, tree climbing, etc. Aged about 13 I suddenly thought being a girl wasn't sooo bad. However, still am not "girly"'.

Adam replied, 'I paint, love music, etc. and was bullied for being intuitive and creative. It's the stereotyping we should fight!'

Becks added, 'Being tall, late developing, analytical and bossy meant I never felt properly feminine, and was surprised to discover I could produce babies!'

Using these examples, explain how sex-role stereotypes could lead to feelings of gender dysphoria. (8 marks)

AO2: Research methods

Sam was born a girl but has experienced gender dysphoria since early childhood, and is attending a gender clinic. Sam has been taking hormone treatment for two years and identifies as a man, and is now planning surgery. A researcher wants to publish Sam's case as a case study.

a. **How could the researcher collect information for the case study? (4 marks)**

b. **Evaluate the use of a case study in studying gender dysphoria. (6 marks)**

The researcher sends the case study to a journal for publication.

c. **Explain the process of peer review that the case study will go through. (3 marks)**

d. **What is the purpose of peer review of this case study? (2 marks)**

How do I answer... longer (16-mark) questions?

The difference between the two questions below lies in how you approach the AO3 evaluation/discussion. The AO1 and AO3 material for these questions is on the opposite page.

Q1: Outline and evaluate explanations of atypical gender development. (16 marks)

For a 16-mark question on atypical gender development, you can also include the intersex conditions you met in the Chromosomes and hormones topic (see p.94 of the Year 2 Student Book). The nominal mark division for AO1 (outline) and AO3 (evaluation) is 6 marks for the former and 10 marks for the latter. You could aim to include the four 'Biological explanations of gender dysphoria' points and also the **two** 'Social and psychological explanations of gender dysphoria' points. Note that this question does ask for 'explanations' in the plural, so just one explanation would not be sufficient. For the AO3 content, you should include all four of the AO3 points opposite.

Q2: Discuss what research has told us about gender dysphoria. (16 marks)

In this question, the focus is gender dysphoria, so intersex conditions would not be so relevant (except where they can lead to gender dysphoria, such as in the case of Klinefelter's syndrome). The command word 'discuss' requires AO3 that is a bit more 'discursive', e.g. looking at applications, implications, counter-evidence, etc. We have tried to make some of our AO3 points 'discursive' to accommodate this. The brain-sex evidence and counter-evidence are useful here. The fourth AO3 point is also 'discursive' because it goes beyond just stating strengths and/or limitations and looks at ethical implications of research. You could also contrast with a social psychological explanation about stereotypes.

REVIEW

Now you have reached the end of the Gender topic, it would be useful to review how your revision is going. Make a table like the one below, and tick the boxes when you are confident with each of the sections.

TOPIC	Got it!			Got it!	
	A01	A03		A01	A03
Sex-role stereotypes and androgyny			The role of chromosomes and hormones in sex and gender		
Kohlberg's theory			Gender schema theory		
Psychodynamic explanations			SLT as applied to gender		
Culture and media influences			Atypical gender development		

Piaget's theory of cognitive development

 RECAP

A01 Description

Mechanisms of cognitive development

- **Schemas** are mental structures that represent a group of related concepts. They can be behavioural (such as grasping objects) or cognitive (such as classifying objects).

- Some schemas are innate, but new experiences lead to new schemas being developed. Schemas become more complex by assimilation and accommodation.

  > **Assimilation** The process of incorporating new information into an existing schema. For example, when a baby is given a new toy car to play with, they may grasp it in the same way they grasped a rattle.

  > **Accommodation** This occurs when a child adapts an existing schema to understand new information that doesn't seem to fit into existing knowledge. This new information cannot be assimilated into the existing schema, so the child's schema must alter to 'accommodate' new information, and so a new schema is formed.

- **Equilibration** The intellect strives to maintain a sense of balance (i.e. equilibrium). If an experience cannot be assimilated into existing schemas then imbalance occurs. Individuals seek to restore balance through equilibration.

- **Cognitive development**, in Piaget's theory, is a result of maturation and interaction with the environment, so children's understanding becomes more complex.

Young children assimilate new information into schemas, such as 'cat'.

ACCOMMODATION

A03 Evaluation / Discussion

Issues/Debates
Nature–nurture

There is evidence to support innate schemas…

For example, Fantz (1961) found that four-day-old infants show a preference for a human face with all its features (e.g. nose) correctly positioned, rather than a 'jumbled up' human face.	This preference indicates that it is the unique configuration of a face, rather than merely a complex pattern, that is important.	An innate preference for faces makes sense as it is adaptive, allowing an infant to elicit attachment and caring.

Piaget's theory has important applications in education…

For example, if knowledge is gained through equilibration, then true understanding only occurs if children make their own accommodations.	Although children taught by formal methods do better in reading, maths and English, this could be because discovery learning requires more experience on the teacher's part.	Therefore it is not discovery learning that is problematical, but its application by teachers.

Some aspects of Piaget's theory are difficult to demonstrate…

There is actually little research to support Piaget's ideas about the effects of disequilibrium.	Inhelder *et al.* (1974) did show that children learnt better when there was a conflict between their expectations and what happened, but Bryant (1995) argues that this wasn't the major dissonance that Piaget proposed.	Some aspects of the theory are not really testable because concepts (such as assimilation) are difficult to operationalise.

A comprehensive theory…

Piaget produced the first comprehensive theory of children's cognitive development.	Piaget's theory combines both nature (biological maturation) with nurture (experience from the physical environment) to explain how thinking changes with age.	It has also changed ideas about children, had an influence on educational practice, and generated much research interest.

APPLY

AO2: An example

SCENARIO

Alisha takes her two nephews, aged three and six, to the zoo. Her youngest nephew shouts out 'cat' whenever he sees animals with four legs, fur and a long tail. Her older nephew, who has been to the zoo before, is able to distinguish between lions, tigers and leopards.

How might Piaget's theory of cognitive development explain the difference between Alisha's two nephews? **(3 marks)**

ANSWER

Alisha's younger nephew has a schema for 'cat' which he is using to understand the new animals he meets at the zoo. As these animals also have four legs, fur and a long tail, he can assimilate them into his existing schema. Alisha's older nephew's previous visit to the zoo led to his existing 'cat' schema changing to accommodate new information, e.g. mane = lion, stripes = tiger and spots = leopard. When he began to notice the difference between the creatures a state of imbalance would have been experienced.

AO2: Research methods

Fantz (1963) tested infants to see at what age they preferentially look at faces rather than other patterns. Some of his findings are shown in the table below.

Age group	N	Mean percentage of fixation time — Faces	Mean percentage of fixation time — Concentric circles	p
Under 48 hours	8	29.5	23.5	<0.01
Two to five days	10	29.5	24.3	<0.01
Two to six months	25	34.3	18.4	<0.01

a. **What does N mean? (1 mark)**

b. **Name a suitable statistical test that could be used to compare the times spent looking at faces or circles at each age. Give reasons for your choice. (3 marks)**

c. **What do the values of p tell you about the findings? (2 marks)**

d. **What do the findings show about infants' preferential looking at faces or circles? (3 marks)**

e. **Referring to Piaget's theory of cognitive development, write a conclusion for this study. (2 marks)**

AO2: One for you to try

Mark took his two-year-old child to the park. He saw his friend Girish approaching. Girish was bald on the top of his head and had long frizzy ginger hair on the sides. As Girish approached, Mark's son shouted 'Clown, clown!' much to Mark's embarrassment.

a. **Using your knowledge of Piaget's theory of cognitive development, explain the toddler's behaviour. (3 marks)**

b. **Using Piaget's theory explain how Mark could make sure that his toddler wouldn't call Girish a clown again. (4 marks)**

How do I answer... selection (multiple choice) questions?

Which **one** of the following best describes equilibration? Tick one box. **(1 mark)**

A It is a state of cognitive imbalance. ☐

B It is experienced as an unpleasant state. ☐

C It involves fitting new experiences into existing schemas without making any change. ☐

D It is a way of restoring cognitive balance. ☐

Multiple choice questions can seem simpler than they are, as you don't have to write anything. However, it's worth thinking carefully and making sure you don't make errors by misreading the question. Here are some tips:

- Take time to read the question carefully: are you asked to select one or two answers? Is it a positive choice, or an odd one out ('not') question? The question above asks for one answer.
- Read all the answers and cross out any that are obviously not correct. **C** is clearly wrong as schemas will have to change in response to new experiences.
- See what else makes sense. **A** and **D** are saying the opposite of each other, whereas **A** and **B** are both about the unpleasant state of cognitive imbalance.
- Make your selection. Here, **D** is the correct answer, as equilibration means achieving a new equilibrium – restoring the balance.

REVIEW

Graphic organisers include mind-maps, flow charts, tables and charts, and there is good evidence that using these helps you to learn. Making concepts visual can give them a structure which works well with the cognitive links and schemas used in memory. This topic lends itself to becoming a flow chart, so make one like this, and add descriptions of each stage of the process:

Schema ⟶ assimilation

⟶ equilibration

⟶ equilibrium

⟶ accommodation

Piaget's stages of intellectual development

 **RECAP**

A01 Description

- **Sensorimotor stage (0–2 years):**
  - > The infant learns to coordinate sensory input with motor actions by repeating movements.
  - > Infants assume objects no longer exist if they cannot be seen. At around 8 months old, they realise objects still exist even if they can't be seen – **object permanence**.

- **Pre-operational stage (2–7 years):**
  - > Children don't understand that volume or number stays the same – **conservation** – even if their appearance changes.
  - > Piaget's conservation task: A child is shown two identical glasses of water. One is then poured into a taller, narrower glass. Pre-operational children think the quantity of water has changed.
  - > **Egocentrism** Children see the world from their perspective and are unaware of other perspectives.
  - > Piaget's three mountains task (1956): A child is asked to select a picture which shows the view that a doll would have. Young children select the picture matching their own view, as they find taking another's perspective difficult.
  - > **Class inclusion** Young children can classify objects into categories, but not subgroups. Children shown three black cows and one white cow will say there are more black cows than cows.

- **Concrete operational stage (7–11 years):**
  - > Children acquire the rudiments of logical reasoning such as conservation.

- **Formal operational stage (11+ years):** Children can now develop and test hypotheses and solve abstract problems. Children also display idealistic thinking, imagining how things could be.

Piaget's three mountains task

Are there more white puppies or more puppies? Is this a confusing question?

A03 Evaluation / Discussion

Piaget's methodology was flawed…

Piaget invented an impressive range of tasks to test the abilities of young children. However, a number of researchers have criticised these methods.	When Hughes (1975) tried Piaget's three mountain tasks using familiar ideas for children, such as a naughty boy hiding from a policeman, they did not show egocentricity.	It has been argued that Piaget's tasks confuse young children, and may suffer from demand characteristics.

The idea of biologically driven stages is broadly correct…

Replications of Piaget's research still support the biologically driven sequence of development.	However, Dasen (1994) claims only a third of adults ever reach the formal operational stage, and even then, not during adolescence.	The evidence still supports the view that there are qualitative changes in cognitive development as a child matures, although these are not rigid.

Cultural bias…

For example, Piaget's middle-class European background valued thinking about abstract ideas.	Other cultures may place greater value on concrete operational abilities, such as making things.	This suggests that Piaget's theory may not be universally applicable, and is culturally biased.

Issues/Debates
Cultural bias

Important applications…

Piaget's stage theory had a strong influence on the shape of primary education in the UK.	For example, abstract mathematical calculations are difficult to teach pre-operational children. Piaget thought this was because the children are not 'biologically ready'.	However, there have been some challenges to this. For example, Bryant and Trabasso (1971) found that training did improve performance.

 ## APPLY

AO2: An example

SCENARIO Last year Mr Sampa taught the Year 6 class at Merrydale Primary School. This year he has taken over the school's Reception class. By his own admission he sometimes finds he overestimates the Reception children's abilities and has had to replan a number of his lessons.

With reference to Mr Sampa's experience, discuss Piaget's stages of intellectual development. **(16 marks)**

ANSWER An extract showing how you could address the AO2 requirements of this question: *The children in Mr Sampa's Year 6 class would be at the concrete operational stage of intellectual development (7–11 years) and so would be able to understand the basics of logical reasoning. For example, if Mr Sampa showed the class two glasses each containing the same amount of water, then poured one of the glasses into a tall, thin glass, the children would know the new glass still holds the same amount of water. The children in Reception class would not be able to understand this conservation task as they are in the pre-operational stage (2–7 years) meaning their reasoning is based on what they see rather than what is reality. Mr Sampa has to replan his lessons as, according to Piaget, children are not biologically ready to be taught certain concepts until they have reached a certain age...*

AO2: Research methods

A researcher was interested in testing the claim that pre-operational children can solve class inclusion tasks if the task is presented in a different way to usual. A large sample of six-year-old children were shown four toy cows, three of which were black and one white. The cows were laid on their side and the children were told they were 'sleeping'. Half of the children were asked, 'Are there more black cows or more cows?' The other half were asked, 'Are there more black cows or more *sleeping* cows?' The results are shown in the table below.

	Are there more black cows or more cows?	Are there more black cows or more sleeping cows?
Number of children answering correctly	25	48
Number of children answering incorrectly	75	52

a. What level of measurement was used in this study? (1 mark)
b. Identify a suitable statistical test that could be used to analyse the data in the table. Give two reasons why this test would be appropriate. (3 marks)
c. The test showed that the null hypothesis could be rejected at $p<0.05$. What conclusions would you draw from this study's findings? (4 marks)

AO2: One for you to try

Rona took her two grandchildren to her local pizza restaurant. The waiter brought Rona's pizza over first and asked her if she wanted it cut into six or eight pieces. Rona said: 'Oh, you'd better make it six, I could never eat eight pieces.' Rona's 10-year-old grandchild laughed so much he spluttered his fizzy drink all over the table. However, her 6-year-old grandchild did not react to what Rona had said.

Using your knowledge of Piaget's stages of intellectual development, explain why Rona's two grandchildren reacted differently to what she said. (4 marks)

How do I answer... description only questions (AO1)?

Questions asking you to 'outline', 'describe' or 'explain' require AO1 answers. Take note of the marks available, and select that number of bullet points from our summary. The AO1 material for these questions is on the opposite page.

Q1: Using an example, explain Piaget's concept of 'class inclusion'. **(2 marks)**

The definition counts for 1 mark, and an example (such as the cows) gets you the second mark.

Q2: Outline one study where Piaget investigated conservation. Include details of what he did and what he found. **(4 marks)**

You need to give a brief description of the procedure and findings. The 'Piaget's conservation task' point includes the outline of this study, and you can use the first point about conservation (Children don't understand that…) to explain what the findings show.

Q3: Outline Piaget's stages of intellectual development. **(6 marks)**

The maximum amount of AO1 you need to answer any question is 6 marks' worth, and so **Q3** requires six points of ages and stages. Select your points to make sure you have sufficient detail but without writing too much or losing focus. You have four stages to cover, and you should include key terms for each, without going into details about Piaget's research, as this question is focused on theory. For example, you could include both points under 'Sensorimotor stage…', the first point and one other point (such as 'Egocentrism') under 'Pre-operational stage…' and the brief outline points of the 'Concrete operational…' and 'Formal operational…' stages.

REVIEW

You can use your sensorimotor or kinaesthetic learning to help you memorise these stages. To do this, replicate Piaget's cognitive tests with a friend or relative, preferably a small child! Gather suitable materials or pictures. Test the stages in order: object permanence, then egocentric thinking and class inclusion, followed by conservation, and finally an abstract or imaginative problem such as thinking about an ideal world. Can you recall which tasks relate to each stage of Piaget's stages of development?

Vygotsky's theory of cognitive development

A01 Description

Savage-Rumbaugh taught bonobos to communicate with symbols.

- **Elementary mental functions** are innate and biological, and are a form of natural development. Cultural influences transform them into **higher mental functions**, which are exclusively human.

- **The role of experts** Children learn through problem-solving with a more competent individual (an 'expert'), who guides problem-solving but gradually the child takes over.

- **The role of language** Experts transmit culture to children using language. Language begins as shared dialogues between an expert and child, but as the skill of mental representation develops, an internal dialogue occurs.

- **The social and individual level** Every function in cognitive development appears on the social level, and later on the individual level. Social experiences depend on language, enabling higher mental functions to develop.

- **The zone of proximal development (ZPD)** Cognitive development takes place in the region between what children can achieve alone and what they could potentially achieve with an expert's help. Cognitive development must occur just beyond current development, as new challenges aren't useful if they are too far from current knowledge.

- **Scaffolding** is the process of assisting a child through the ZPD. The expert creates a scaffold which is gradually withdrawn. The expert responds to success or failure by providing either less, or more, explicit instructions.

A03 Evaluation / Discussion

Evidence for the role of culture…

Gredler (1992) discovered that the counting system used in Papua New Guinea is very different from our own. ➤ This system involves counting from one thumb, up the arm and down to the fingers, ending at 29, making it difficult to add and subtract large numbers. ➤ *This shows how culture can limit cognitive development.*

Research with non-human animals supports Vygotsky's claims…

Some psychologists believe that elementary mental functions can be transformed into higher mental functions by immersing animals in human culture. ➤ Savage-Rumbaugh (1991) exposed Bonobo apes to a language-rich culture and found they can communicate using a symbol system. ➤ *This suggests that higher mental functions (a symbol system) can be transmitted through culture.*

Evidence for the role of language…

Carmichael et al. (1932) gave participants one of two labels for certain drawings. For example, a kidney shape was called either a kidney bean or a canoe. ➤ When participants were subsequently asked to draw the shape, it differed according to which label they had been given. ➤ *This shows that words can affect the way we think about and remember things.*

Evidence for the role of the ZPD…

For example, McNaughton and Leyland (1990) observed young children working with their mothers on jigsaw puzzles of increasing difficulty. ➤ The mothers offered help in line with Vygotsky's predictions. If the puzzle was easy (below the ZPD): little help. If it was difficult (beyond the ZPD): more help. ➤ *This supports Vygotsky's theory, and shows that experts do adjust their input according to where a learner is in relation to the ZPD.*

⚙ APPLY

AO2: An example

SCENARIO Terry is helping his daughter learn to ride a bike. She can ride easily with stabilisers but now Terry has removed them she is really struggling. Terry decides to hold the back of the bike seat with one hand and the handle bars with the other to help his daughter understand the need to balance. When she is able to pedal in a straight line he tries just holding the back of the seat.

Using your knowledge of Vygotsky's theory, explain how Terry is supporting his daughter's cognitive development. **(3 marks)**

ANSWER *Terry would be seen as an expert as he understands how to ride a bike. His daughter can ride a bike with stabilisers (her current area of development) but cannot yet ride without assistance (this is beyond what she can do independently). Terry is scaffolding her learning as he is assisting her through her zone of proximal development. Terry knows balance is important when riding so he uses strategies that will help his daughter develop her balance. She is learning about the importance of maintaining her balance before she develops this skill for herself.*

AO2: Research methods

A researcher carried out a study in which mothers were observed helping children solve a puzzle. The researcher was interested in how much direct help was given to the children by the mothers. 'Direct help' was operationally defined as phrases such as, 'Try that piece here'. Two observers recorded the amount of direct helping they saw in 10 children over a one-hour-period. The results are shown in the table below.

Child	First observer	Second observer
1	5	6
2	7	6
3	7	8
4	8	7
5	12	14
6	17	15
7	14	15
8	6	5
9	2	1
10	19	18

a. **Display the findings in the table above in the form of a suitably labelled scattergram. (4 marks)**

b. **The researcher used the scattergram to initially assess how reliable the observers were. What is the name of this method of reliability assessment? (1 mark)**

c. **Name a parametric test that could be used to determine whether the observations are reliable or not. (1 mark)**

✎ AO2: One for you to try

Beth was learning how to make cakes. At first, her mum gave her lots of help. For example, her mum gave her clear instructions on what she should do, and helped her to use the scales to weigh out the ingredients correctly. Beth enjoyed making cakes, but the more cakes she made, the less help her mum gave her. After six months, Beth's mum would get on with other things while Beth made cakes.

Use your knowledge of scaffolding to explain why Beth's mum's behaviour changed over time. (6 marks)

🐾 How do I answer... 'Distinguish between' questions?

Q1: Distinguish between Piaget's and Vygotsky's theories of cognitive development. **(4 marks)**

Q2: Discuss similarities and differences between Piaget's and Vygotsky's theories of cognitive development. **(8 marks)**

If you are asked to 'compare' or 'distinguish between' two concepts, you must compare a specific aspect of them. Don't just describe one then describe the other. For **Q1** the process is:

1 Choose a feature which is relevant to both – e.g. children's active learning about the world.

2 Explain the difference, using 'whereas' to connect the two ideas – e.g. Piaget thought children learnt by experimentation, whereas Vygotsky thought children learn more from experts… (elaborate using the second and sixth points from the AO1 material on the opposite page: 'The role of experts'; 'Scaffolding').

3 Choose a second point of difference – e.g. Piaget considered that children's thinking develops in stages with maturation, whereas Vygotsky focused on the way children learn via language.

Two clear comparisons will be enough for 4 marks.

Q2 asks for a similarity as well as a difference, so you can describe how Piaget and Vygotsky both emphasise the complex interactions between nature (innate programmes of development) and nurture (learning experiences), with the child as an active agent in their own learning. Alternatively you could explain how Piaget and Vygotsky both saw abstract, scientific thought as the final stage of cognitive development.

🔄 REVIEW

Craik and Lockhart (1972) proposed a theory of memory called the 'levels of processing model'. This model claimed that the more that information is elaborated, the more likely we will be able to access that information later on. There are many different ways of elaborating material, so let's try one.

Take a large sheet of paper (A3 works well) and construct a mind-map linking together all of the material on the theories of cognitive development (Piaget and Vygotsky). This serves several purposes: (1) It elaborates the material, making it more memorable; (2) The act of constructing the mind-map counts as revision, making recall in an exam more likely; and (3) It produces a visual image, which can be a much easier way of remembering complex material.

*Tip: There is a wealth of useful revision videos on the Internet – take a look for some on mind-map construction.

Baillargeon's explanation of early infant abilities

RECAP

A01 Description

Baillargeon's research

- Baillargeon argues that the reason infants don't search for hidden objects is not because they lack object permanence.
- She developed techniques to measure infants' reactions to impossible events, known as **violation of expectation research (VOE)**.

Infants' knowledge of the physical world

- Piaget did not believe an innate mechanism existed in children.
- Baillargeon showed infants have an innate **physical reasoning system (PRS)** helping them understand the physical world and learn to reason about novel physical phenomena. This is a **nativist approach**.
- Infants form an 'all-or-none' concept about physical phenomena, and then incorporate variables that affect it.
- Children aged 9.5 months show surprise when a cover with a bulge is removed to reveal nothing. By 12.5 months children express surprise if the object is smaller than the bulge suggested.

Infants' knowledge of the psychological world

- Baillargeon has also used the VOE to research infants' understanding of **false beliefs** in others and their sense of fairness.
- Infants as young as 14.5 months show surprise when someone chooses the 'wrong' box in a toy choosing task.

Violation of expectation (VOE) (Baillargeon and DeVos, 1991)

Babies are surprised when their expectations are violated.

- **PROCEDURE** This tests for object permanence, and assumes that infants will express surprise at an impossible event.
- **FINDINGS** Following habituation events (to get used to the activity), infants expressed no surprise when a short object failed to appear in a high window. However, when a tall object failed to appear (the impossible event), they did.
- **CONCLUSION** Three-month-olds show object permanence and understand the principle of occlusion, when an object is hidden behind another.

A03 Evaluation / Discussion

Carefully controlled research…

For example, Baillargeon has studied children from various social classes, and not just the middle class. → Her research also controls for the influence of parental behaviour while infants perform the tasks, and uses observers unaware of a study's purpose. → This means that her research has both population and experimental validity.

Alternative explanations of an infant's knowledge of the physical world…

Issues/Debates
Nature–nurture

Baillargeon has been challenged by Spelke *et al.* (1992) who propose that infants are born with a core knowledge, including a basic understanding of the physical world. → However, research findings indicate that infants do not show expectations about all events related to one core principle (e.g. covering objects). → This supports Baillargeon's view that infants are born with the ability to acquire certain kinds of knowledge very quickly rather than with a core knowledge itself.

Do children understand object permanence?…

Bremner (2013) argues that demonstrating object permanence does not imply that an infant has a real understanding of it. → For Piaget, cognitive development involves understanding a principle, not just acting in accordance with it, as Baillargeon's research shows. → This suggests that Baillargeon may only have shown that Piaget underestimated children's abilities, rather than disproving his views about maturation.

Baillargeon's research lacks cultural validity…

Baillargeon has not specifically studied the capabilities of very young children raised in cultures other than America. → If there were differences in abilities related to culture, this would challenge Baillargeon's views about innate mechanisms. → This suggests that further research is needed before we can accept Baillargeon's claims that infants' abilities are innately driven.

Issues/Debates
Cultural bias

APPLY

AO2: An example

SCENARIO Sami is planning a violation of expectation study to investigate whether infants have an understanding of object permanence.

What advice would you offer Sami to improve the validity of his research?
(4 marks)

ANSWER *First Sami needs to avoid a biased sample. For example, Piaget is criticised for using infants from middle-class families. Sami could approach families who place birth announcements in newspapers to obtain a more diverse sample. Second, Sami needs to reduce the possibility of parents unconsciously communicating cues to the child during the VOE procedure. He should instruct parents to close their eyes and not to talk to their child. Finally, he should use a double-blind study. The observers should only see the infant's face when judging whether surprise is shown, and they should not be able to see the event the child can see so that they do not know whether it is possible or impossible, as this knowledge may bias their observations.*

AO2: One for you to try

Charlotte had taken her five-month-old daughter to the childminder. When she picked her up, the childminder said: 'I put a on DVD called "Larry the Lucky Lemming" to amuse her. It showed cartoon lemmings walking off a cliff and falling to earth. She got bored very quickly, so I paused the DVD. When I put the DVD back on she saw Larry the Lucky Lemming walk off the cliff but remain suspended in the air. I couldn't believe your daughter's reaction! It really grabbed her attention, but I have no idea why.'

Use your knowledge of Baillargeon's research to explain to the childminder why Charlotte's daughter behaved the way she did. (6 marks)

AO2: Research methods

In Baillargeon's VOE research, babies are tested sitting on their mother's lap. The mothers are asked not to interact with their babies, and are additionally asked to keep their eyes shut during the task.

Explain why this apparently unusual request is made of the mothers. (2 marks)

How do I answer... evaluation only questions (AO3)?

Evaluation questions come in various shapes and sizes. Terms like 'evaluate', 'discuss', 'explain', 'criticism', 'strength' and 'limitation' all indicate that AO3 is required. The AO3 material for these questions is on the opposite page. Let's look at some examples:

Q1: Give **one** criticism of Baillargeon's explanation of early infant abilities. **(2 marks)**

Remember that a criticism can be positive or negative. You could use any of the AO3 points and use the lead-in statement and the first two columns for a 2-mark answer.

Q2: Explain **one** limitation of Baillargeon's research into the abilities of newborn infants. **(3 marks)**

You could select AO3 point 2, 3 or 4, and fully elaborate it using all three columns.

Q3: Evaluate Baillargeon's research into the abilities of newborn infants, and refer to Piaget's research in your answer. **(6 marks)**

You need two effective AO3 points, and you will need to use point 2 as one of them, as it refers to Piaget. Use all three columns to elaborate the points fully.

REVIEW

You need to be able to answer questions with different mark allocations concisely while using enough detail to explain the concept clearly. Practise answering the questions above, spending about a minute and a quarter per mark: e.g. 5 minutes for a 4-mark question, 10 minutes for a 6-mark question. Make sure you allow time to plan logical answers.

1 Practise recalling the material in the points opposite.

2 Practise writing the full answer, setting a timer to make sure you use the time available.

3 Check your answer is clear and logical, and has relevant key terms in each point.

The development of social cognition: Selman's theory

A01 Description

Selman's levels of perspective-taking

- Selman's theory of social development focused on perspective-taking. He used dilemmas to explore children's reasoning when faced with conflicting perspectives.
- He analysed responses and constructed a five-stage model:
- **Stage 0: Undifferentiated perspective-taking (3–6 years)**
  > Children can distinguish between self and others.
  > They are governed by their own perspective.
- **Stage 1: Social-informational perspective-taking (6–8 years)**
  > Children are aware of perspectives that are different to their own.
  > However, they assume that this is because others have different information.
- **Stage 2: Self-reflective perspective-taking (8–10 years)**
  > Children view their own thoughts and feelings from someone else's perspective.
  > They also recognise that others can do the same.
- **Stage 3: Mutual perspective-taking (10–12 years)**
  > Children can imagine how they and others are viewed by a third, impartial party.
  > They can also consider two viewpoints simultaneously.

- **Stage 4: Societal perspective-taking (12–15+ years)**
  > Personal decisions are now made with reference to social conventions.
  > For example, treating animals humanely is seen as an important social convention.
- **Relation to deception** Children are able to deceive others and plant a false belief in someone else's mind at around age three.

'It wasn't me!'

A03 Evaluation / Discussion

Research support for the stage theory…

For example, Cooney and Selman (1978) found that 40/48 boys made gains in their level of perspective-taking over two years.	Later analysis of the same boys by Gurucharri and Selman (1982) confirmed this progressive developmental sequence over the next three years.	This supports Selman's belief that perspective-taking is a progressive age-related developmental sequence.

Research support for the role of experience…

For example, Fitzgerald and White (2003) found that growth in perspective-taking skills was related to parenting style.	Children showed more growth when their parents encouraged them to take a victim's perspective when the child had hurt someone.	This shows that social experience can lead to changes in perspective-taking skills.

One weakness of research in this area is that much of it is correlational…

Just because perspective-taking skills and social competence are correlated, does not necessarily mean that the former causes the latter.	For example, more popular children interact with more people, and this could help them develop perspective-taking skills.	This means that we cannot be sure of the direction of causation.

Real-world applications…

For example, some criminals lack empathy so are more willing to harm others.	Social skills training programmes encourage prisoners to learn perspective-taking skills.	This aims to increase their empathetic concern and stop them reoffending.

APPLY

AO2: An example

SCENARIO Freddie was recently involved in a playground fight and would not apologise to the other boy. His parents were called and Freddie was asked to explain his actions. Freddie knew his parents would be disappointed in him but felt when they knew that the other boy was bullying his friend they would understand why he was fighting.

With reference to Freddie's behaviour, discuss Selman's levels of perspective-taking. **(16 marks)**

ANSWER An extract showing how you could address the AO2 requirements of this question:

Freddie seems aware that others may hold a different view to him (he expects his parents to be disappointed when he feels it was acceptable to fight) but that this may be because they do not realise the other boy was a bully. This suggests Freddie is at stage 1, social informational perspective-taking, and we could presume he is aged between six and eight. Research suggests a progressive age-related developmental sequence with children moving from egocentrism to deeper levels of insight into the feelings of others. While this may be biologically driven, social experiences also play a role (FitzGerald and White, 2003), e.g. if Freddie's parents had previously encouraged Freddie to take the perspective of the victim when he harmed another, he might show some remorse towards the boy he was fighting with...

AO2: Research methods

A psychologist was interested in studying whether experience plays a role in the development of perspective-taking. She interviewed parents about their reactions to their children hurting other children. Ten children of parents who encouraged them to see things from their victim's perspective were assessed for their perspective-taking by means of a questionnaire (Group A). Their scores on the questionnaire were compared with those of 10 children whose parents did not encourage them to see things from their victim's perspective (Group B). The questionnaire scores are shown in the table below. The higher the score, the better the perspective-taking.

| Group A | 5 | 5 | 7 | 5 | 8 | 6 | 7 | 9 | 2 | 9 |
| Group B | 4 | 4 | 5 | 1 | 2 | 7 | 3 | 3 | 3 | 1 |

a. **Calculate the mean perspective-taking score for each group. (2 marks)**

b. **Calculate the median perspective-taking score for each group. (2 marks)**

c. **Calculate the modal perspective-taking score for each group. (2 marks)**

d. **The standard deviation for Group A was 2.2 and for Group B it was 1.8. What do these standard deviations suggest about the variability of performance in the two groups? (2 marks)**

The researcher decided to see if there was a significant difference between the two sets of scores.

e. **Suggest an appropriate statistical test that could be used. (1 mark)**

f. **Give two reasons why this test would be appropriate. (2 marks)**

AO2: One for you to try

Frank, who is 9 years old, and his 13-year-old sister, Lisa, were watching a children's TV programme. One of the children in the programme had seen a boy steal another boy's bag and run away down a busy street. The child knew he could run fast enough to catch the thief, but in an earlier scene his father had told him never to run down busy streets because of the danger from cars. The child hesitated. 'Why doesn't he chase him?' said Frank. 'His dad would only get angry if he thought his son was running down the street for fun.' His sister replied, 'It's a little more complex than that, Frank. His dad won't be angry because he knows that stealing is wrong.'

Explain Frank and Lisa's different views in terms of Selman's perspective-taking stages. (6 marks)

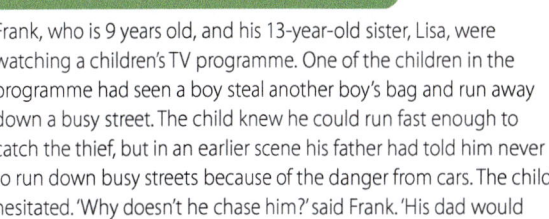

How do I answer... description and evaluation (AO1 + AO3) questions?

1 Recognise what you need to do. Two different command words – e.g. 'outline' (an AO1 term) – and 'evaluate' (an AO3 term) – is a clue that this is a mixed AO1 + AO3 question.

2 Plan how much to write for the AO1 and AO3 parts. In mixed AO1 + AO3 questions up to 6 marks, the division is half and half (it is different with mark totals higher than this as we will see on p.87).

3 Decide what to write. Look at the examples below. The AO1 and AO3 material for these questions is on the opposite page.

Q1: Describe and evaluate one study that has investigated levels of perspective-taking. **(4 marks)**

Use the first two AO1 points, which describe Selman's research (procedure and findings), and the first AO3 point.

Q2: Outline and evaluate Selman's research into levels of perspective-taking. **(6 marks)**

You could select 3 marks' worth of AO1 (three or four points) and one fully elaborated evaluation point or two briefer ones, whichever relates to your AO1.

Q3: Briefly discuss Selman's research into levels of perspective-taking. **(8 marks)**

Describe findings and evaluate the research, including about 75–90 words of AO1 and 75–90 words of AO3. Use only the findings of research, not the procedure. To make it a discussion, include some 'howevers' (evaluation point 1, and 2 or 3).

REVIEW

How much should I write? You should practise writing 3-, 4- and 6-mark descriptions of the psychodynamic explanation. For 3 marks, use three AO1 points, for 4 marks use four points and so on. For 6 marks you should be writing about 150–180 words. If you attempt to cover all aspects of the theory thoroughly, you will run out of time for AO3 in an extended answer, so be selective and concise. We have helped you by summarising the key content in the points on the opposite page. But you still need to include enough detail and specialist terminology if you want to get marks in the top band.

The development of social cognition: Theory of mind

AO1 Description

- **Theory of mind (ToM)** is our understanding that others have separate mental states to us. Social relationships require a ToM, which appears at around three to four years old.

- ToM is tested using false belief tasks. These measure the understanding that others may hold, and act on, mistaken (false) beliefs. Children can do these tasks successfully by four to six years old.

- In the Sally–Anne test, Sally puts her ball in a basket before leaving the room. Anne then moves the ball to a box. When Sally returns, children are asked where she will look for the ball.

- Baron-Cohen *et al.* (1985) found 20 per cent of children who don't have autism, including those with Down's syndrome, and 80 per cent of autistic children fail the test.

- Children with ASD may find social interaction difficult as they lack a ToM.

- High-functioning adults with ASD pass the Sally–Anne test, but show poorer performance than control adults on the Eyes Task, which tests the ability to identify emotions from pictures of eyes.

- As ToM develops at a particular age and is absent in many autistic children, Baron-Cohen (1995) suggests that a ToM module exists. This is a specific mechanism that enables people to understand others' mental states.

Sally puts her ball in her basket and leaves the room.

Anne moves the ball to her box.

Sally returns. Where will she look for the ball?

The Sally–Anne test procedure (Baron-Cohen *et al.*, 1985)

AO3 Evaluation / Discussion

Evidence for the role of experience and biology…

Issues/Debates
Nature–nurture

Perner *et al.* (1994) found that ToM appears earlier in children from large families, with older siblings.	In these circumstances, a child is challenged to think about the feelings of others when resolving conflicts.	This means that the development of ToM is probably a combination of biology and social environment.

Criticisms of Baron-Cohen's research…

Baron-Cohen *et al.* (1997) claim that the Eyes Test measures 'mindreading', which is essentially the same thing as ToM.	However, Wellman and Woolley (1990) argue that knowing someone else's internal state (mindreading) is not the same as knowing how they experience the world (ToM).	This suggests that the Eyes Task lacks internal validity as a measure of true ToM.

Issues with ToM as an explanation for autism…

Not all autistic children fail the Sally–Anne test, which is hard to explain if lack of ToM is central to the condition.	Also, autistic children may lack social skills and language and may therefore lack experiences which would help them develop ASD.	The research is based on quasi-experiments so causal explanations are not justified, and ToM is not a complete explanation for autism.

Cultural bias in research…

For example, Baron-Cohen's research was from a very Western perspective and used only British participants.	The higher rates of autism diagnosed in the West may be because its symptoms are not considered abnormal in other cultures.	The view that a lack of social interaction is a problem may be a Western rather than universal perspective.

Issues/Debates
Cultural bias

APPLY

AO2: An example

SCENARIO Tanya and her friend Tilly were using plastic counters to work on maths problems. As it was nearly break time the teacher said the quickest group to tidy up could be first out to play. Tilly hid the counters under the maths books so they could go out to play. When the teacher realised this she called Tilly back into the classroom to put the counters in the box where they should have been stored.

Where would an autistic child suggest Tanya should look for the counters after playtime? Explain your answer with reference to theory of mind research. **(4 marks)**

ANSWER *An autistic child would expect Tanya to look in the box the counters had been moved to as they would not realise that Tanya would hold a false belief – the counters were still under the maths books. This scenario is similar to the Sally–Anne task which showed the majority of children without autism and including those with Down's syndrome children understood the concept of false beliefs but only 20 per cent of autistic children did. Research such as this suggests autistic children do not have theory of mind: they do not understand that others may see the world from a different point of view than their own and so would not realise that Tanya would still believe the counters to be under the maths books as she did not know Tilly had moved them.*

AO2: Research methods

A research team used the Sally–Anne test with 20 autistic children spectrum disorders (ASD) whose mean age was 11 years and 11 months. The test was also used with a control group of 27 children who did not have ASD, whose mean age was four years and five months. The team found that 23 of the children in the control group completed the test successfully, and 16 of the autistic children failed it.

a. **Fill in the contingency table below using the information presented in the passage above. (4 marks)**

	Control group	Autistic children
Successful at the test		
Unsuccessful at the test		

b. **Display the findings in the contingency table above in the form of a suitably labelled bar chart. (4 marks)**

c. **Name a statistical test that could be used to analyse the data in the contingency table. (1 mark)**

d. **Give two reasons for your choice of statistical test. (2 marks)**

e. **Explain what is meant by a Type I error. (2 marks)**

f. **The research team used the *p*<0.05 significance level in their study, and found a statistically significant difference between the children with ASD and control group's performance on the task. What is the likelihood of a Type I error being made in this study? (2 marks)**

AO2: One for you to try

Kirsty likes to play tricks on her sisters. One day she placed some buttons into an empty sweets tube and asked her three- and six-year-old sisters, 'What do you think is in here?' Both of her sisters were surprised when Kirsty showed them the buttons. 'I know,' said Kirsty. 'Let's put the buttons back and ask Dad what he thinks is in the tube. What do you two think he'll say?'

What do you think Kirsty's two sisters would have said? Explain your answer with reference to theory of mind research. (6 marks)

How do I answer... research methods questions?

Questions requiring research methods knowledge can appear in any section of any paper in the AS or A Level exams. They could include any aspect of research methods, data analysis or ethical issues. You should be prepared to have to select or use a statistical test somewhere in Paper 3, as in the **AO2: Research methods** question on this page. Tips for answering research methods questions:

1. Read the description of the research carefully, and think about the IV and DV, levels of measurement of data, and experimental design. These are important for many questions about data analysis as well as other things you could be asked to do, such as writing a hypothesis.

2. Work your way steadily through the question parts, and keep looking back at the description of the research to make sure you've understood what it's about and not gone off course.

3. If you are really stuck on a particular question part, have an educated guess, trusting in your experience over the whole of the course, then don't fret but move on to the next part.

4. It's also important to remember that you need to apply your knowledge to the study in research methods questions whenever possible, not just give generic points.

Keep practising!

REVIEW

As you are probably aware, simply reading material is not the most effective way of learning it properly. So, using the material on the opposite page, try writing plans for 3-, 4- and 6-mark 'outline' questions on ToM, plus plans for 8- and 16-mark essay questions.

Test yourself on the key points of the topic by covering up your plans and writing it out again. It's useful to have a supply of cheap paper for this, as the more times you practise retrieving the information, the better you will remember it.

Spaced practice is also very effective: come back to the same topic tomorrow and start your revision by seeing how many of the points you can remember before you look at your essay plan.

The development of social cognition: The mirror neuron system

RECAP

A01 Description

- **Mirror neurons (MNs)** react when a person performs an action and when we see another person perform the same action.
  - > Rizzolatti *et al.* (1996) first observed these neurons in the F5 area of the premotor cortex in macaque monkeys.
- **Imitation** is important in acquiring skilled behaviours and is the beginning of the development of social cognition. MNs explain how imitation occurs.
  - > MN activity is usually 'offline', so imitation usually doesn't occur because the observation-response link is 'off'. However, if the observation-response link is 'online', a behaviour is repeated immediately.
  - > Damage to the frontal cortex (responsible for inhibitory control) leads to compulsive imitation, presumably because the link is 'on'.
- **Understanding intention** MNs in the inferior frontal cortex are concerned with intention. These neurons are active when we see someone intending to perform a behaviour.
- **Perspective-taking and ToM** Gallese and Goldman (1988) claim that MNs enable us to feel empathy. MNs might therefore be the mechanism for understanding another's perspective.

- **Language acquisition** MNs may play a role in language development since language acquisition involves imitation. There are MNs in Broca's area, which is involved in speech production.
- **The basis of human uniqueness** Ramachandran (2000) believes that MNs have enabled us to excel in social relationships, explaining the success of our species.

Bonobos may also be able to recognise themselves in a mirror and understand others' intentions.

A03 Evaluation/Discussion

Research evidence from individual neurons…

For example, Mukamel *et al.* (2010) found single neurons in people with epilepsy that were active when they performed an action and when they observed the task being performed. ▶ Other neurons responded when participants performed an action but were inhibited when they observed it being performed ('anti-mirror'). ▶ *Anti-mirror neurons are important as they enable us to think about another person's actions without simultaneously performing those actions.*

Research evidence from individuals with brain damage…

For example, Tranel *et al.* (2003) studied people with damage to the left premotor area. ▶ They could not retrieve words for motor actions. However, they could identify pictures of those motor actions. ▶ *This indicates that disruption to MN areas does cause action deficits.*

Issues/Debates
Biological determinism

Gender differences…

Research suggests that women are generally better than men at understanding people's feelings. ▶ Cheung *et al.* (2009) have found physiological evidence of stronger MN activity in women than men. ▶ *This suggests that gender differences in social sensitivity have a biological rather than a social basis.*

Exaggeration of the importance of MNs…

Heyes (2009) suggests that MNs are just the outcome of associative learning (classical conditioning) rather than the result of evolutionary adaptation. ▶ Heyes argues that neurons become paired because they are both 'excited' at the same time or because one regularly precedes the other. ▶ *This suggests that MNs could actually be the result of experience rather than being innate.*

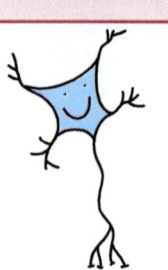
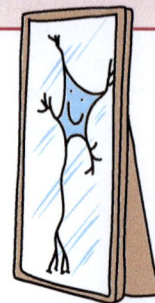

APPLY

AO2: An example

SCENARIO Researchers studying neural activity in humans found the same patterns of activity in certain brain areas when participants watched an origami demonstration and when they later made the origami figures themselves.

With reference to this example, discuss the role of mirror neurons in social cognition. **(16 marks)**

ANSWER **An extract showing how you could address the AO2 requirements of this question:** *The patterns of brain activity are likely to have been located in the premotor cortex, a brain area identified by researchers as containing mirror neurons. For example, Rizzolatti et al. (1996) recorded neural activity in the F5 area of the premotor cortex in macaque monkeys when they observed another monkey tear up paper. The same neural activity was seen when the monkeys then performed the action. Similarly, the people watching origami demonstrations showed activity in the same region as when they made the origami figures themselves. MNs have a role in social cognition as the ability to imitate is important in skill development, e.g. Meltzoff and Moore found newborns were able to imitate the facial movements of adults....*

How do I answer... essay questions with an AO2 component?

In 16-mark essay questions with an AO2 (application) component, 4 of the marks are for explaining the question scenario in the context of the material you are discussing. These marks are always taken from the AO3 allocation, so there are still 6 marks for AO1, 4 marks for AO2 and 6 marks for AO3. The best idea is to link each AO2 point to a relevant point of AO1, as you do with a shorter application question (see p.83). Then you can evaluate or discuss as you would in a normal essay. If you are able to link any of the AO3 points to the scenario too, this shows that you are really thinking about the question, and looks impressive. Here is an example.

> Annie's grandfather had a stroke which affected his frontal cortex. Annie noticed that he now imitates behaviour, so if she waves her right hand, he imitates this, and if she shakes her head he also copies her. The doctor has described this symptom as echopraxia.
>
> Outline and evaluate research into the mirror neuron system, referring to Annie's grandfather's condition in your answer. **(16 marks)**

Explain what we have learnt from research into the mirror neuron system generally, including the points about imitation and damage to the frontal cortex. Six marks' worth of AO1 equates to about six of our points from the AO1 material opposite. You only need three evaluation points, so select points which you can link to Annie's grandfather's imitation behaviour if you can, although general discussion of mirror neuron research is also fine.

AO2: One for you to try

Paresh was watching the big football match on TV, with his takeaway pizza on his lap. A player was just about to shoot when an opposition player kicked him hard on the knee. Paresh winced, his leg straightened, and his pizza went flying through the air. 'What are you doing?' asked his girlfriend. 'Anybody would think it was you who'd been kicked, not some bloke on the TV.'

Using your knowledge of the mirror neuron system, how could Paresh's reaction be explained? (6 marks)

AO2: Research methods

A researcher recorded the activity of 184 individual neurons in the F5 motor area of a macaque monkey. All of the neurons responded when the monkey performed some kind of action. Of these, 87 also responded to some type of visual stimuli. Forty-eight of the neurons that responded to visual stimuli responded only to seeing objects, and 39 responded to seeing actions. Of these 39 neurons, 12 responded when the monkey grasped an object and when it observed the researcher performing the same action.

a. **What percentage of the total number of neurons responded when the monkey grasped an object and observed the researcher performing the same action? Show your calculations. (2 marks)**

b. **What percentage of the number of neurons that responded to some type of visual stimuli responded only to seeing actions? Show your calculations. (2 marks)**

c. **What percentage of the neurons that responded to seeing actions responded when the monkey grasped an object and when it observed the researcher performing the same action? Show your calculations. (2 marks)**

REVIEW

Now you have reached the end of the Cognitive Development topic, it would be useful to review how your revision is going. Make a table like the one below, and tick the boxes when you are confident with each of the sections.

TOPIC	Got it!			Got it!	
	AO1	AO3		AO1	AO3
Piaget's theory					
Piaget's stages					
Vygotsky's theory			Baillargeon's explanation		
Selman's theory – social cog			Theory of mind		
Mirror neuron system					

Classification of schizophrenia

RECAP

AO1 Description

Diagnosis of schizophrenia

- **Criterion A – Two (or more) of the following symptoms:**
  - > Delusions; hallucinations; disorganised speech; grossly disorganised or catatonic behaviour; negative symptoms, i.e. affective flattening, alogia or avolition.
  - > Only one of the characteristic symptoms is required 'if delusions are bizarre'.
- **Criterion B – Social/occupational dysfunction:**
  - > For a significant portion of the time since onset, one or more major areas of functioning, e.g. interpersonal relations or self-care are markedly below the level achieved prior to the onset.
- **Criterion C – Duration:**
  - > Continuous signs of the disturbance persist for at least six months, including at least one month of symptoms that meet Criterion A.

Positive symptoms

- Schizophrenia is a type of psychosis, a severe mental disorder in which thoughts and emotions are so impaired that contact is lost with external reality.
- **Positive symptoms** are those that appear to reflect an excess or distortion of normal functions. They include the following:
  - > **Hallucinations** are bizarre, unreal perceptions of the environment that are usually auditory (e.g. hearing voices) but may also be visual (e.g. seeing lights), olfactory (smelling things) or tactile (e.g. feeling something touching the skin).
  - > **Delusions** are bizarre beliefs that seem real to the person with schizophrenia, but they are not real. Sometimes these delusions can be paranoid (i.e. persecutory) in nature. Delusions may also involve inflated beliefs about the person's power and importance (delusions of grandeur).
  - > **Disorganised speech** is the result of abnormal thought processes, where the individual has problems organising his or her thoughts and this shows up in their speech.
  - > **Grossly disorganised or catatonic behaviour**, including the inability or lack of motivation to initiate a task, or to complete it once it is started, leads to difficulties in daily living and can result in decreased interest in personal hygiene.

Negative symptoms

- **Negative symptoms** appear to reflect a reduction or loss of normal functions. Negative symptoms weaken the person's ability to cope with everyday activities, and their ability to manage without significant outside help. They include the following:
  - > **Speech poverty** (alogia) Characterised by the lessening of speech fluency and productivity, this is thought to reflect slowing or blocked thoughts.
  - > **Avolition** is a reduction of interests and desires as well as an inability to initiate and persist in goal-directed behaviour (e.g. sitting in the house for hours every day, doing nothing).
  - > **Affective flattening** is a reduction in the range and intensity of emotional expression, including facial expression, voice tone, eye contact and body language.
  - > **Anhedonia** is a loss of interest or pleasure in all or almost all activities, or a lack of reactivity to normally pleasurable stimuli. It may be pervasive (i.e. all-embracing) or confined to a certain aspect of experience.

APPLY

AO2: An example

SCENARIO Joel is studying chemistry at university. For the last month or so, his family and friends have noticed him behaving increasingly bizarrely and talking to himself in whispers even though there was nobody there. Lately, he has refused to answer or make calls on his mobile phone, claiming that, if he does, it will activate a chip in his brain that was implanted by the security forces. Then he stopped leaving his flat for days on end.

Using your knowledge of the classification of schizophrenia, explain why Joel would be likely to be given a diagnosis of schizophrenia. **(4 marks)**

ANSWER *Joel's behaviour shows some positive symptoms of schizophrenia: talking to himself could mean he is hearing voices (auditory hallucinations); he has delusions about a chip in his brain; and his behaviour appears bizarre. This is Criterion A. He has had these symptoms for a month, which is Criterion C. He also has negative symptoms: stopping leaving his flat could be a sign of avolition or anhedonia, and shows that he is not functioning, as he is meant to be studying. This is Criterion B.*

AO2: One for you to try

The following is an extract from an interview between Charlotte and her psychiatrist.

Psychiatrist: *How are you feeling today?*

Charlotte: *[long pause] Well, I'm okay but the prices in the shops... and my flat is green and white. I have clothes and I keep an eye open for dogs and cats.*

Psychiatrist: *Did you have a good weekend?*

Charlotte: *[long pause] No... didn't want to do anything. I sit... a lot of the time.*

Using your knowledge of the symptoms of schizophrenia, identify and briefly explain two symptoms that are evident in Charlotte's response. (4 marks)

AO2: Research methods

Shah and Nakamura (2010) reported on a case study of a 19-year-old male patient who believed that a device had been planted into his wrist by the Central Intelligence Agency (CIA) and that this was being used to control his actions. The patient also believed that his friends, neighbours and professors were working with the CIA by watching and abusing him. Furthermore, he claimed that he often received commands that instructed him to harm his friends or family and that these orders came either from the implant or the people who were abusing him.

a. **Explain why the findings of this case study suggest a diagnosis of schizophrenia. (2 marks)**

b. **Is this case study an example of an idiographic or a nomothetic approach? Explain your answer. (3 marks)**

c. **Outline one strength and one limitation of case studies to investigate the nature of schizophrenia. (2 marks + 2 marks)**

How do I answer... 'Distinguish between' questions?

> **Distinguish between positive and negative symptoms in the context of schizophrenia. (3 marks)**

There are some fairly simple rules for answering this sort of question. If you are asked to 'distinguish between...', 'compare...' or 'explain the difference between...', then these rules apply:

1. Don't just *describe* the two things you are being asked to distinguish between.

2. Pick something that applies to both (e.g. both affect normal functions in some way) yet which is different for one compared to the other (e.g. one leads to an excess of normal functions, the other a reduction). For example, 'Positive symptoms are those that appear to reflect an excess or distortion of normal functions such as experiencing hallucinations.' 'Negative symptoms appear to reflect a reduction or loss of normal functions, such as the lessening of speech fluency and productivity (alogia).'

3. Use words like 'whereas', 'however' and 'on the other hand' to point out this difference. That gives us 'Positive symptoms are those that appear to reflect an excess or distortion of normal functions such as experiencing hallucinations, whereas negative symptoms appear to reflect a reduction or loss of normal functions, such as the lessening of speech fluency and productivity (alogia).'

4. Note that we have included an example of each just to drive home the point. This 'belt and braces' approach will ensure (if you have time) that you have enough for the full 3 marks available for this question.

5. Don't be too ambitious; one point of difference is usually enough.

REVIEW

You should know what schizophrenia is and how it is diagnosed. You should also know about positive symptoms (particularly hallucinations and delusions) and negative symptoms (particularly alogia and avolition) and the difference between positive and negative symptoms. There are a few things that you can do to help you with this.

1. Try looking up some case studies of schizophrenia on the Internet. Can you detect any of the diagnostic criteria of schizophrenia in the behaviour being described?

2. Can you highlight the *differences* between positive and negative symptoms (see the above **How do I answer... ?** if not)?

3. Practice writing 2- and 3-mark descriptions of (each of) hallucinations, delusions, alogia and avolition. To turn your 2-mark description into a 3-mark description, you could add an example. So... make sure you have a suitably detailed example for each!

Reliability and validity in diagnosis and classification

 **RECAP**

AO1 Description

Reliability

- **Diagnostic reliability** means that clinicians must be able to reach the same conclusions at two different points in time (test–retest reliability), or different clinicians must reach the same conclusions (inter-rater reliability).

  > In DSM-V field trials, the diagnosis of schizophrenia had only moderate inter-rater reliability (Regier *et al.*, 2013).

- **Cultural differences in diagnosis** Research suggests there is a significant variation between countries when it comes to diagnosing schizophrenia, i.e. culture has an influence on the diagnostic process.

  > Copeland (1971) gave US and British psychiatrists a description of a patient. Sixty-nine per cent of the US psychiatrists diagnosed schizophrenia, but only 2 per cent of the British ones gave the same diagnosis.

  > Luhrmann *et al.* (2015) interviewed 60 adults diagnosed with schizophrenia in Ghana, India and the US. Many of the African and Indian subjects reported positive experiences with the voices they heard, whereas US patients were more likely to report these voices as being violent and hateful.

Validity

- **Gender bias** This occurs when the accuracy of a diagnosis is dependent on the gender of an individual. The accuracy of diagnostic judgements can vary for a number of reasons:

  > Some diagnostic categories may be biased towards pathologising one gender rather than the other.

  > Mentally healthy 'adult' behaviour associated with mentally healthy 'male' behaviour in the US, with a tendency for women to be perceived as less mentally healthy (Broverman *et al.*, 1970).

- **Symptom overlap** Many of the symptoms of schizophrenia are also found in many other disorders, such as depression and bipolar disorder.

  > Most people who are diagnosed with schizophrenia have sufficient symptoms of other disorders that they could also receive at least one other diagnosis (Read, 2004).

- **Co-morbidity** This refers to the extent that two (or more) conditions co-occur. Psychiatric co-morbidities (e.g. substance abuse, depression) are common among patients with schizophrenia.

  > A meta-analysis by Swets *et al.* (2014) found that 12 per cent of patients with schizophrenia also fulfilled the diagnostic criteria for OCD and 25 per cent displayed significant obsessive-compulsive symptoms.

AO3 Evaluation / Discussion

Reliability

Lack of inter-rater reliability…

Despite claims for increased reliability, there is still little evidence that DSM is routinely used with high reliability by mental health clinicians.

Whaley (2001) found inter-rater reliability correlations in the diagnosis of schizophrenia as low as 0.11. Rosenhan's study also illustrated the lack of inter-rater reliability in the diagnosis of schizophrenia.

Because psychiatric diagnosis lacks the more objective measures enjoyed by other branches of medicine, this means that it inevitably faces additional challenges with inter-rater reliability.

Unreliable symptoms…

For a diagnosis of 'schizophrenia', only one of the characteristic symptoms is required 'if delusions are bizarre'. However, this creates problems for reliability of diagnosis.

When 50 psychiatrists were asked to differentiate between 'bizarre' and 'non-bizarre' delusions, they produced inter-rater reliability correlations of only around 0.40 (Mojtabi and Nicholson, 1995).

This suggests that if this central diagnostic requirement lacks sufficient reliability, it cannot be an accurate method of distinguishing between schizophrenic and non-schizophrenic patients.

Validity

Research support for gender bias in diagnosis…

Loring and Powell (1988) found evidence of gender bias among psychiatrists in the diagnosis of schizophrenia.

Male and female psychiatrists read two case vignettes of patients' behaviour. If patients described as 'males' or no information was given about gender, 56 per cent of the psychiatrists gave a diagnosis of schizophrenia. However, when the patients were described as 'female', only 20 per cent were given this diagnosis.

This gender bias was not as evident among the female psychiatrists, suggesting diagnosis is also influenced by the gender of the clinician.

The consequences of co-morbidity…

Many studies of co-morbidities with schizophrenia have involved relatively small sample sizes.

However, Weber *et al.* (2009) looked at nearly 6 million hospital discharge records, finding evidence of many co-morbid non-psychiatric diagnoses, including asthma and hypertension.

The authors concluded that patients with schizophrenia tend to receive a lower standard of medical care, which in turn adversely affects their prognosis.

 **APPLY**

AO2: An example

SCENARIO Harrison *et al.* (1997) reported that the incidence rate for schizophrenia was eight times higher for Afro-Caribbean groups (46.7 per 100,000) than white groups (5.7 per 100,000) in the UK.

How could issues with the validity of diagnosis of schizophrenia contribute to this difference? **(4 marks)**

ANSWER *Research (e.g. Chien et al., 2008) has shown that rates of schizophrenia are roughly the same across different cultures, yet schizophrenia is repeatedly diagnosed at a higher rate in the Afro-Caribbean population in the UK. It is possible that psychiatrists (mostly white, middle class) may misdiagnose people because of their cultural differences in behaviour or the way they talk. For example, hearing voices may be a more normal experience in some cultures but could be thought of as 'bizarre' by a psychiatrist. Certain cultural beliefs may seem like bizarre delusions to someone from a different culture, therefore it may lead to invalid diagnosis of schizophrenia.*

AO2: Research methods

A researcher asked a class of her students to present themselves to psychiatric hospitals claiming to be hearing voices saying 'empty', 'hollow' and 'thud'. All of the students were psychologically healthy. In the first part of the study, 14 out of 20 were admitted and diagnosed as schizophrenic. In the second part of the study, the hospitals were told to be aware that other students would be trying to gain admission, and they should be on the lookout for these 'imposters'. However, the researcher did not send any more students. Of 35 people who were genuinely disturbed and sought admission, 12 were not diagnosed as schizophrenic.

a. **Use the data above to complete the following contingency table. (2 marks)**

	Genuinely schizophrenic	Not schizophrenic
Schizophrenia diagnosed		
Schizophrenia not diagnosed		

b. **What percentage of the total number of people studied were genuinely schizophrenic? (1 mark)**

c. **What percentage of those who were genuinely schizophrenic were not diagnosed as schizophrenic? (1 mark)**

d. **What percentage of those who were not schizophrenic were correctly diagnosed? Show your calculations. (2 marks)**

AO2: One for you to try

One criticism of the diagnosis of schizophrenia is that whilst diagnosis is reliable, in that a patient might be given the same diagnosis of schizophrenia by different psychiatrists, this does not necessarily suggest that the diagnosis is valid.

Explain why reliability of diagnosis does not necessarily indicate that such diagnoses are valid. (4 marks)

How do I answer... shorter (8-mark) essay questions?

Not all essays follow the 12- or 16-mark format. Some have a slightly lower tariff. Of these lower tariff essay questions, the 8-marker is the most common. It does help to know what you are dealing with, however, as they are not always straightforward. The AO1 and AO3 material for these questions is on the opposite page.

> **Outline and evaluate the issue of reliability in the diagnosis and classification of schizophrenia. (8 marks)**

Although you might believe that this question would be worth 4 marks for AO1 and 4 for AO3, this is actually half of a 16-mark essay question, so there is a similar split of marks i.e. 3 marks for AO1 and 5 marks for AO3 (instead of the 6- and 10-mark split for a 16-mark question). The AO1 and AO3 material for these questions is on the opposite page.

> Carlos has been feeling 'depressed' for over a year and it has had quite an effect on his personal life and his work life. His sister Maria, who studied psychology at university, sees him on a regular basis and believes that he has enough symptoms to be classified as having depression. She tells him that he should go to the doctor to be put on a course of antidepressants. However, when he goes to see the doctor, he is diagnosed as having schizophrenia, particularly when he tells the doctor about hearing voices (something he hadn't told Maria about). Carlos is puzzled because Maria is usually right about things like this, so he questions the doctor, who tries to explain about something called 'co-morbidity'.
>
> **Outline and evaluate the issue of validity in the diagnosis and classification of schizophrenia. Make reference to Carlos in your answer. (8 marks)**

This question includes a scenario that is referred back to in the question. This is an indication that there is an additional AO2 requirement in the question. AO2 marks tend to be 'stolen' from the AO3 allocation, so this question would be 3 marks of AO1 (first three bullet points), 3 marks of AO3 (one complete AO3 point) and 2 marks' worth of AO2. The Carlos scenario could be explained in terms of co-morbidity – e.g. Buckley *et al.* (2009) estimate that co-morbid depression occurs in 50 per cent of patients with schizophrenia.

REVIEW

One way of making sure you understand all the appropriate aspects of reliability and validity in the diagnosis and classification of schizophrenia is to do a bit of 'revision accounting'. When you feel you have mastered these different aspects, you have earned a tick in the 'Got it!' column. This list might include:

TOPIC	Got it!		Got it!
Reliability (AO1)		Symptom overlap (AO1)	
Reliability (AO3)		Comorbidity (AO3)	
Gender bias in diagnosis (AO1)		Validity (AO3)	

Biological explanations for schizophrenia

 **RECAP**

AO1 Description

The dopamine hypothesis

- An excess of the neurotransmitter dopamine in certain regions of the brain is associated with the positive symptoms of schizophrenia. The key role played by dopamine was highlighted in two sources of evidence:
  - > 'Normal' individuals exposed to large doses of dopamine releasing drugs such as amphetamines develop the characteristic symptoms of a schizophrenic episode.
  - > Antipsychotic drugs block the activity of dopamine in the brain, eliminating symptoms such as hallucinations and delusions.
- **The revised dopamine hypothesis** Davis and Kahn (1991) proposed that positive symptoms are caused by an excess of dopamine in subcortical areas of the brain. Negative and cognitive symptoms arise from a deficit of dopamine in the prefrontal cortex.

Genetic factors

- The risk of developing schizophrenia among individuals who have genetically related family members with the disorder is higher than it is for those who do not.
- **Family studies** show that schizophrenia is more common among biological relatives of a person with schizophrenia, and that the closer the degree of genetic relatedness, the greater the risk.
- **Twin studies** Joseph (2004) calculated that the pooled data for all schizophrenia twin studies carried out prior to 2001 showed a concordance rate for MZ twins of 40.4 per cent and 7.4 per cent for DZ twins.
- **Adoption studies** Tienari et al. (2000) found that of 164 adoptees whose biological mothers had been diagnosed with schizophrenia, 11 (6.7 per cent) also received a diagnosis of schizophrenia, compared to just 4 (2 per cent) of the 197 control adoptees (those born to non-schizophrenic mothers).

Neural correlates

- **The pre-frontal cortex** (PFC) is the area of the brain involved in executive control. This is impaired in schizophrenia patients (Weinberger and Gallhofer, 1997).
- **The hippocampus** Deficits in the nerve connections between the hippocampus and the PFC correlate with the degree of working memory impairments, a cognitive impairment in schizophrenia (Mukai et al., 2015).
- **Grey matter** Individuals with schizophrenia have a reduced volume of grey matter in their brain. Many people displaying negative symptoms have enlarged ventricles, a consequence of the loss of grey matter in nearby parts of the brain.
- **White matter** Du et al. (2013) found reduced myelination of white matter pathways in schizophrenic patients. This was particularly the case in the neural pathways between the PFC and the hippocampus.

AO3 Evaluation / Discussion

Genetic factors
MZ twins encounter more similar environments

A crucial assumption underlying all twin studies is that the environments of MZ twins and DZ twins are equivalent, therefore differences between MZ and DZ twins can be attributed to genetic factors.

However, MZ twins encounter more similar environments and experience more 'identity confusion' (i.e. being treated as 'the twins' rather than as two distinct individuals) than DZ twins (Joseph, 2004).

This suggests that differences in concordance rates between MZ and DZ twins reflect nothing more than environmental differences that distinguish the two types of twin.

Adoptees may be selectively placed…

Parents who adopt children with a schizophrenic biological parent may be different to those who adopt children with more normal backgrounds.

Given the belief in the 1960s that schizophrenic mothers would give birth to children prone to 'insanity and degeneracy', it is unlikely that such children would have been placed into the same type of adoptive families as children without such a background (Joseph, 2004).

This suggests we cannot accept conclusions from adoption studies regarding the role of genetics in schizophrenia.

The dopamine hypothesis
Evidence from treatment…

Evidence supporting the dopamine hypothesis comes from the success of drugs that change levels of dopamine activity in the brain.

Leucht et al. (2013) concluded that all the antipsychotic drugs tested in their meta-analysis were significantly more effective than placebo in the treatment of positive and negative symptoms.

These findings also challenge the classification of antipsychotics into typical and atypical groupings because differences in their effectiveness were small.

Challenges to the dopamine hypothesis…

Noll (2009) claims there is strong evidence against the original dopamine hypothesis and the revised dopamine hypothesis.

Antipsychotic drugs do not alleviate hallucinations and delusions in one third of people, and in some people, hallucinations and delusions are present despite levels of dopamine being normal.

This suggests that, rather than dopamine being the sole cause of positive symptoms, other neurotransmitter systems may also produce the positive symptoms associated with schizophrenia.

Neural correlates

Support for the influence of grey matter deficits…

Support for the significance of grey matter deficits in schizophrenia comes from a meta-analysis by Vita et al. (2012).

→

Patients with schizophrenia, compared with healthy controls, showed a higher reduction in cortical grey matter volume over time. This was specific to discrete cortical areas in the frontal, temporal and parietal lobes.

→

This loss of grey matter was especially active in the first stages of the disease, consistent with the relatively early onset of schizophrenia (late teens/early 20s).

Implications for treatment…

The importance of neural correlates for schizophrenia is that early intervention might prevent development of the later stages of this disorder.

→

This concept of 'treatment as prevention' is seen in the North American Prodrome Longitudinal Study, which uses neuroimaging to predict who will develop psychoses such as schizophrenia.

→

With a better understanding of how schizophrenia develops, researchers can detect loss of brain tissue early and treat at-risk patients before psychosis develops.

 **APPLY**

AO2: An example

SCENARIO When schizophrenia patients were given drugs that lowered their dopamine levels, they showed improvement in some symptoms (e.g. hallucinations) but a worsening in others (e.g. cognitive impairment). When the same patients took psychostimulants, which raised dopamine levels, the opposite pattern emerged, with increased hallucinations but reduced cognitive impairment.

Explain how this evidence supports the dopamine hypothesis of schizophrenia. **(4 marks)**

ANSWER *Positive symptoms of schizophrenia (such as hallucinations) are caused by an excess of dopamine in mesolimbic pathways in the brain. Drugs that lowered dopamine levels in this study would have blocked dopamine transmission in these areas and so reduced these positive symptoms. Negative symptoms, such as cognitive impairment, are caused by a depletion of dopamine in the mesocortical pathways. Drugs that lowered dopamine levels would have mimicked this depletion and caused cognitive impairments. Reversing this by the use of psychostimulants would have increased positive symptoms and cognitive impairments, which is what was found in this study.*

AO2: One for you to try

Ruby and Pearl are identical twins, whereas Amber and Jade are non-identical twins. Ruby and Amber have both been diagnosed with schizophrenia.

Assuming that both sets of twins are raised in broadly similar environments, would Pearl or Jade be more likely to develop schizophrenia? Explain your choice. (3 marks)

AO2: Research methods

When rats are given substances which deplete dopamine in the prefrontal cortex, they show cognitive impairment (e.g. memory deficits). These impairments can be reversed using olanzapine, an atypical antipsychotic drug thought to have beneficial effects on the negative symptoms of schizophrenia in humans.

What is the major limitation of using non-human animals to study the causes of schizophrenia? (2 marks)

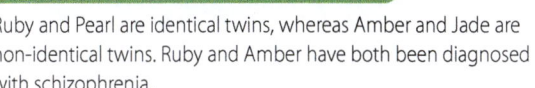 How do I answer… description only (AO1) questions?

There is a fairly simple formula in answering description only questions. For 2 marks, say two things, for 3 marks say three things and so on. This approach adds an appropriate level of detail to each answer and gives the examiner a useful way of discriminating between your answer and one that would be worth fewer than the maximum marks for that question.

Work through the sample questions below, using the advice that follows them. The AO1 and AO3 material for these questions is on the opposite page.

Q1: Briefly explain what is meant by the dopamine hypothesis of schizophrenia. **(2 marks)**

Q1: Use the first sentence of the first point under the AO1 heading for the 'dopamine hypothesis', plus one example, e.g. 'Antipsychotic drugs block the activity of dopamine in the brain, eliminating positive symptoms.'

Q2: Explain the role of neural correlates in schizophrenia. **(3 marks)**

Q2: Use the first **two** points under the AO1 heading for 'neural correlates' plus *either* the third or fourth point.

Q3: Outline the dopamine hypothesis of schizophrenia. **(4 marks)**

Q3: Use all **four** points under the AO1 heading for the 'dopamine hypothesis'.

Q4: Describe the role of genetic factors in schizophrenia. **(6 marks)**

Q4: For a 6-mark question, you should aim for about 150–180 words. Use all **four** points under the AO1 heading for 'genetic factors' but *add* the first sentence from the first AO3 point ('A crucial assumption underlying all twin studies is that the environments of monozygotic twins and dizygotic twins are equivalent therefore differences between MZ and DZ twins can be attributed to genetic factors') at the beginning of your 'Twin studies' bullet.

REVIEW

In order to feel comfortable with this topic you should practise using the material in all the different ways that might be assessed in your exam.

1. Try constructing 3-, 4- and 6-mark descriptions of the dopamine hypothesis, neural correlates and genetic factors in schizophrenia using the advice given in the **How do I… ?** section above.

2. Write an essay plan showing how you would use the material on this spread to answer 10- and 16-mark extended writing questions that combine any two of the three types of explanation covered on this spread.

Psychological explanations for schizophrenia

 **RECAP**

AO1 Description

Family dysfunction

- **Double bind theory** Bateson *et al.* (1956) suggest that children who frequently receive contradictory messages from their parents are more likely to develop schizophrenia.

    > A child may receive conflicting messages about their relationship from a parent, one which suggests affection and acceptance, another which suggests animosity and rejection.

    > The child's ability to respond appropriately is incapacitated by these contradictions because one message invalidates the other.

    > These interactions prevent the development of an internally coherent construction of reality, and in the long run this manifests itself as schizophrenic symptoms (e.g. flattened affect and withdrawal).

- **Expressed emotion (EE)** Family members talk to the patient in a critical manner or in a way that indicates emotional over-involvement or over-concern with the patient or their behaviour.

    > Research by Kuipers *et al.* (1983) found that high EE relatives talk more and listen less. High levels of EE are most likely to influence relapse rates (i.e. an increase in symptoms).

    > A patient returning to a family with high EE is about four times more likely to relapse than a patient whose family is low in EE (Linszen *et al.*, 1997).

    > The negative emotional climate in these families arouses the patient and leads to stress beyond their already impaired coping mechanisms, thus triggering a schizophrenic episode.

Cognitive explanations

- **Cognitive explanations** emphasise the role of **dysfunctional thought processing**, particularly in the positive symptoms of schizophrenia such as delusions and hallucinations.

- **Cognitive explanations of delusions** The patient's interpretations of their experiences are controlled by inadequate information processing. They relate irrelevant events to themselves and arrive at false conclusions.

    > Patients are unable to consider that they may be wrong or to substitute more realistic explanations for events (Beck and Rector, 2005).

- **Cognitive explanations of hallucinations** Individuals focus excessive attention on auditory stimuli and have a higher expectancy for the occurrence of a voice than normal individuals. They find it difficult to distinguish between imagery and sensory-based perception.

    > Patients with schizophrenia are more likely to misattribute the source of a self-generated auditory experience to an external source (Baker and Morrison, 1998).

AO3 Evaluation / Discussion

Family dysfunction
Family relationships are important…

The importance of family relationships in schizophrenia was demonstrated by Tienari *et al.* (1994).	Adopted children with schizophrenic biological parents were more likely to become ill themselves than were children with non-schizophrenic parents, but only where the adoptive family was disturbed.	*This suggests that the illness only manifests itself under appropriate environmental conditions, therefore genetic vulnerability alone is not sufficient.*

Individual differences in vulnerability to EE…

Not all patients who live in high EE families relapse, and not all those who live in low EE homes avoid relapse.	Lebell *et al.* (1993) claims it is how patients appraise the behaviour of their relatives that is important. In cases where high EE behaviours are not perceived as being negative or stressful, patients are less affected by them.	*This shows that not all patients are equally vulnerable to high levels of expressed emotion within the family environment.*

Cognitive explanations
Supporting evidence for the cognitive model of schizophrenia…

Sarin and Wallin (2014) supported the claim that the positive symptoms of schizophrenia have their origins in faulty cognition.	Delusional patients showed faulty information processing, e.g. lack of reality testing. Patients with hallucinations had impaired self-monitoring and tended to experience their own thoughts as voices.	*A consequence of this is that a therapist can use this information when choosing techniques for the treatment of patients.*

Support from the success of cognitive therapies…

The claim that the symptoms of schizophrenia have their origin in faulty cognition is reinforced by the success of cognitive-based therapies for schizophrenia.	The effectiveness of cognitive behavioural therapy was demonstrated in a review of treatments (NICE, 2014). This found that CBTp was more effective than antipsychotic medication in reducing symptom severity.	*This supports the view that faulty cognitions have an important causal influence in the development of schizophrenia.*

APPLY

AO2: An example

SCENARIO Emmanuel has been diagnosed with schizophrenia. His family are very stressed by his odd behaviour and are trying to find someone to blame. Emmanuel's father blames his mother, as he thinks she was too soft on him as a little boy. Meanwhile she claims it was inherited from his father's family, as there were several relatives in his father's family who had schizophrenia. Emmanuel's sister keeps telling him his delusions and hallucinations are not real, but it doesn't seem to help.

Discuss psychological explanations of schizophrenia, referring to Emmanuel's family's ideas. **(16 marks)**

ANSWER **An extract showing how you could address the**

AO2 requirements of this question: *The family may display high levels of expressed emotion (EE), as they have become stressed by Emmanuel's odd behaviour. Also, Emmanuel's father thinks his mother was too soft on him, so Emmanuel may have received inconsistent messages from his parents, simultaneously communicating affection and animosity, which fits the double bind theory. Emmanuel's sister is attempting to take a cognitive approach, identifying the faulty cognitions that led to him experiencing delusions and hallucinations. An integrated approach may be a better explanation, as there is evidence of genetic links and Emmanuel's father's family had several incidences of schizophrenia. This model proposes an interaction between Emmanuel's genetic vulnerability and the family dysfunction experienced as high levels of expressed emotion...*

AO2: One for you to try

Jack was diagnosed with schizophrenia while in the final year of his university course. He had to return home to live with his mother. Although she seemed glad to be able to look after him, he doesn't find their relationship to be an easy one. During one argument over the state of his room his mother says, 'Jack, you are driving me mad with all your mess, I just can't have you living here any more.' Jack suggests he might be better off moving to a hostel. Her response is, 'I can't see why you think you would be better off in a hostel. You don't look after yourself now and I'm here to help you. Did you brush your teeth this morning? Have you taken your medication?'

Identify and explain the psychological explanation for schizophrenia demonstrated in the above scenario. (3 marks)

AO2: Research methods

In some families, members are frequently hostile towards each other, critical of each other, and over-involved and over-concerned with each other's lives. These families are said to be high in expressed emotion (high EE). Other families do not show these characteristics and are said to be low in expressed emotion (low EE).

The table below shows the results from four studies conducted in different countries.

	Study location	Number of participants	Follow-up period (months)	Percentage relapse rate in high EE participants	Percentage relapse rate in low EE participants
Vaughn and Leff (1976)	UK	37	9	50	12
Vaughn et al. (1984)	USA	54	9	56	28
Cazzullo et al. (1989)	Italy	45	9	58	21
Barrelet et al. (1990)	Switzerland	41	9	32	0

a. **Calculate the average percentage relapse rate found in high EE participants across the studies. (2 marks)**

b. **What do the differences in relapse rates between the high and low EE participants suggest? (2 marks)**

c. **Calculate the range for relapse rates in high EE participants and in low EE participants. (2 marks)**

d. **What do the differences between the ranges for the high and low EE participants suggest? (2 marks)**

How do I answer... selection (multiple choice) questions?

Which one of the following is true of the family dysfunction explanation of schizophrenia? (1 mark)

A Parents are under-involved in the lives of a family member with schizophrenia.

B A patient in a family with high levels of expressed emotion is less likely to relapse than a patient in a family with low levels of expressed emotion.

C The individual receives conflicting messages about their relationship from their parents.

D The individual engages in dysfunctional thought processing, which gives rise to the positive symptoms of schizophrenia.

- Read the question very carefully. Is it asking you to pick the statement that matches (as here) or the 'odd one out' that doesn't match?
- Make life easier by crossing out any that are obviously *not* going to be the correct answer given the specific demands of the question.

Applying this to the question above, we cross out **D** because that is describing a cognitive explanation rather than one based on family dysfunction. We can also cross out **A** because family dysfunction explanations emphasise the over-involvement of family members. That leaves choices **B** and **C**. You should know that high levels of EE make relapse more likely, so **B** cannot be true either. That just leaves **C**, which is the right answer!

REVIEW

Practise answering 3-, 4- and 6-mark AO1 questions on family dysfunction explanations and the same for cognitive explanations of schizophrenia. You should spend about a minute and a quarter per mark, so for a 3-mark question you have just under 4 minutes, for a 4-mark question you have 5 minutes and for a 6-mark question you have 10 minutes.

Drug therapy

 **RECAP**

A01 Description

- Antipsychotic drugs work by reducing the action of the neurotransmitter dopamine in areas of the brain associated with the symptoms of schizophrenia thus increasing people's feelings of subjective well-being.

- **Typical antipsychotics** (such as chlorpromazine) are dopamine antagonists in that they bind to, but do not stimulate, dopamine receptors, thus blocking their action.

  > By reducing stimulation of the dopamine system in the mesolimbic pathway, antipsychotic drugs such as chlorpromazine eliminate the hallucinations and delusions experienced by people with schizophrenia.

  > There are several dopamine pathways in the brain. Blocking dopamine receptors in only the mesolimbic pathway is useful, whereas blocking dopamine receptors in the remaining pathways may be harmful for the person.

- **Atypical antipsychotics** (such as clozapine) carry a lower risk of extrapyramidal side effects, have a beneficial effect on negative symptoms and cognitive impairment, and are suitable for treatment-resistant patients.

  > These drugs only temporarily occupy dopamine receptors and then rapidly dissociate to allow normal dopamine transmission.

  > It is this 'rapid dissociation' associated with atypical antipsychotics that is responsible for the lower levels of extrapyramidal side effects found with these drugs compared to conventional antipsychotics.

A03 Evaluation / Discussion

Antipsychotics versus placebo...

Support for the effectiveness of antipsychotics comes from studies comparing relapse rates for antipsychotics and placebos.	A meta-analysis (Leucht *et al.*, 2012) used patients taken off their antipsychotic medication and given a placebo instead, and patients who remained on their regular antipsychotic. Within 12 months, 64 per cent of the placebo group had relapsed, compared to 27 per cent of those who stayed on the antipsychotic drug.	*This study demonstrates the superiority of antipsychotic drugs compared to placebo in preventing relapse.*

Ethical problems with typical antipsychotics...

The problems associated with antipsychotic medication raise significant ethical issues relating to their use.	In the US, a large out-of-court settlement was awarded to a tardive dyskinesia sufferer on the basis of the Human Rights Act, which states that 'no one shall be subjected to inhuman or degrading treatment or punishment' (Chari *et al.*, 2002).	*This suggests that if side effects and other consequences were taken into account, a cost–benefit analysis of typical antipsychotics would probably be negative.*

Advantages of atypical over typical antipsychotics...

A key advantage of atypical antipsychotics is that patients experience fewer side effects.	Atypical antipsychotics, particularly newly developed drugs, such as olanzapine and quetiapine, are less likely to produce the extrapyramidal effects commonly found with typical antipsychotics.	*As a result, patients are more likely to continue with their medication, which in turn means they are more likely to see a reduction in their symptoms.*

Are atypical antipsychotics actually better?...

It is claimed that atypical antipsychotics are superior to the older 'typical' antipsychotics.	A meta-analysis (Crossley *et al.*, 2010) found no significant differences between atypical and typical drugs in terms of their effect on symptoms. However, patients on atypical antipsychotics gained more weight and those on typical antipsychotics experienced more extrapyramidal side effects.	*They concluded that, although there was no difference in efficacy, there was a clear difference in the side-effect profile of the two types of antipsychotic.*

APPLY

AO2: An example

SCENARIO Your cousin Jasmine has schizophrenia and has been prescribed antipsychotic medication. She has noticed her 'voices' have gone away, but she says she feels lonely without them, and is also experiencing hand tremors which embarrass her. She says she's going to stop her medication as she feels unhappy and has no energy, and is blaming this on the drugs. She doesn't want to go back to the doctor as she thinks they don't understand her.

Discuss drug therapies in the treatment of schizophrenia. What advice could you give Jasmine, based on your knowledge of such drug therapies?
(16 marks)

ANSWER An extract showing how you could address the AO2 requirements of this question:

The drugs were helping with Jasmine's positive symptoms (auditory hallucinations) but not her negative symptoms (avolition, anhedonia). She may also have co-morbid depressive symptoms. The tremors could be Parkinsonism, a sign of extrapyramidal side effects. If she is currently taking typical antipsychotics, you could tell her that there are other drugs, atypical antipsychotics, which might give her fewer side effects and could also benefit her negative symptoms (although evidence for this is inconclusive). You could offer to go to the doctor with her, as she may be feeling socially isolated and the social/cognitive factors are also important in her treatment. There is a high risk of relapse if she stops taking the drugs without medical support – 64 per cent of patients going onto a placebo relapsed within a year compared to 27 per cent who stayed on antipsychotics, and if she stops she won't even have the placebo effect...

AO2: Research methods

In a study designed to compare the relative effectiveness of different antipsychotic drugs, a researcher randomly assigned 100 schizophrenics, who had not been previously treated, to one of four groups. Each group were given one of four typical antipsychotics. The researcher asked a colleague who was familiar with antipsychotic medication to rate the participants in terms of how much they had improved on a 7-point scale (1 = no improvement, 7 = large improvement). The table below shows the mean ratings of improvement in each of the four groups.

	Drug A	Drug B	Drug C	Drug D
Mean improvement rate	4.6	3.8	5.9	6.2

a. **Identify the independent and dependent variables in this study. (2 marks)**

b. **The researcher's colleague was 'familiar with antipsychotic medication'. Explain one weakness of using this colleague to make the ratings. (2 marks)**

c. **The researcher concluded that all of the drugs were effective in treating schizophrenia. Explain why this conclusion may not be justified. (3 marks)**

d. **The researcher wanted to know if Drug A and Drug B had significantly different effects. Name a statistical test that she could have used, and give three reasons for choosing this test. (4 marks)**

AO2: One for you to try

Tomasz has been taking anti-psychotics for the last five years, ever since he was diagnosed with schizophrenia in his late teens. He takes quetiapine, a typical antipsychotic, but has had problems with mood swings and weight gain which he believes have something to do with the drug. His doctor suggests that changing his medication to an atypical antipsychotic might help.

Outline and evaluate the use of typical and atypical antipsychotics in the treatment of schizophrenia. Explain why the doctor believes that changing medication might benefit Tomasz. (16 marks)

How do I answer... essay questions with an AO2 component?

This type of question is one of the trickiest types to answer, in that it has three distinct components, an AO1 descriptive component, an AO3 evaluative component and an AO2 application component. Such questions are essentially the same as a straightforward essay (see p.105) *but*, for a 16-mark question, 4 of the marks available are diverted for your ability to explain the scenario outlined in the question using the material you are discussing. These marks are always taken from the AO3 allocation, so there are still 6 marks for AO1, but now the AO3 component drops from 10 to 6 with the remaining 4 marks for AO2.

Let's look again at the **AO2: One for you to try** question above:

> **Outline and evaluate the use of typical and atypical antipsychotics in the treatment of schizophrenia. Explain why the doctor believes that changing medication might benefit Tomasz. (16 marks)**

For 4 marks' worth of AO2, you should write approximately 100–120 words explaining the scenario (in this case Tomasz's change of medication) using the material on the opposite page. In this example, there are references to the side effects associated with typical antipsychotics such as quetiapine, and the doctor's belief that an atypical antipsychotic might not have the same side effects. You could explain the basis for this belief and consider evidence that might support it. First and foremost this is an essay on drug therapy as a treatment for schizophrenia, but you should not ignore the AO2 content, which is not as difficult as you might think!

REVIEW

Knowing what we mean by 'typical' and 'atypical' antipsychotics and being able to describe how these drugs work is vital for your understanding of this topic. There are a few things that you can do to help you with this.

1 Try explaining each of these to someone else (or even the dog, cat or teddy bear who won't be critical or snigger while you are doing it!).

2 Go back and read your notes again and then explain each in even more detail until you think Rover, Fang or Teddy would (had they *really* been listening) have a good understanding of both processes.

3 Try writing (and answering) a few of your own exam questions on this topic to consolidate this understanding.

Cognitive behavioural therapy

A01 Description

Cognitive Behavioural Therapy for Psychosis (CBTp)

- **Basic assumption** People often have distorted beliefs, which influence their feelings and behaviour in maladaptive ways.

- Delusions result from faulty interpretations of events. CBTp is used to help the patient identify and correct these faulty interpretations

- CBTp aims to help people establish links between their thoughts, feelings or actions and their symptoms and general level of functioning.

- By monitoring their thoughts, feelings or behaviours with respect to their symptoms, patients are better able to consider alternative ways of explaining why they feel and behave as they do.

- Patients are encouraged to trace back the origins of their symptoms to get a better idea of how they might have developed. They might be set behavioural assignments to improve their general level of functioning.

- The therapist lets the patient develop their own alternatives to these maladaptive beliefs, looking for alternative explanations and coping strategies that are already present in the patient's mind.

How does it work?

- CBTp usually proceeds through the following phases:

  > **Assessment** The patient expresses their thoughts about their experiences. Realistic goals for therapy are discussed.

  > **Engagement** The therapist empathises with the patient's perspective and their feelings of distress, and stresses that explanations for their distress can be developed together.

  > **The ABC model** The patient gives their explanation of the activating events that cause their distress. These beliefs can then be rationalised, disputed and changed.

  > **Normalisation** By placing psychotic experiences on a continuum with normal experiences, the patient feels less alienated and the possibility of recovery seems more likely.

  > **Critical collaborative analysis** The therapist uses gentle questioning to help the patient understand illogical deductions and conclusions.

  > **Developing alternative explanations** The patient develops their own alternative explanations for their previously unhealthy assumptions in cooperation with the therapist.

A03 Evaluation / Discussion

Advantages of CBTp over standard care…

The NICE (2014) review of treatments for schizophrenia found that, compared to antipsychotic medication, CBTp was more effective in reducing rehospitalisation.

CBTp was also effective in reducing symptom severity and, when compared with patients receiving standard care, there was evidence for improvements in social functioning.

However, most studies have been conducted with patients treated at the same time with antipsychotic medication. It is difficult, therefore, to assess the effectiveness of CBTp independent of this medication.

Effectiveness of CBTp is dependent on the stage of the disorder…

CBTp appears to be more effective when it is made available at specific stages of the disorder.

In the initial phase of schizophrenia, self-reflection is not particularly effective. Following stabilisation of the psychotic symptoms with antipsychotic medication, however, individuals are more likely to benefit from CBTp (Addington and Addington, 2005).

Research has shown, therefore, that it is individuals with more experience of their schizophrenia and a greater realisation of their problems that benefit more from CBTp.

Problems with meta-analyses of CBTp as a treatment for schizophrenia…

Meta-analyses in this area may reach unreliable conclusions because they fail to take into account study quality.

Some studies fail to randomly allocate participants to either a CBTp or control condition. Others fail to mask the treatment condition for interviewers assessing symptoms and general functioning. Despite such differences, all such studies are grouped together for a meta-analysis.

This suggests that the problems associated with methodologically weak studies translate into biased findings about the effectiveness of CBTp.

The benefits of CBTp may have been overstated…

More methodologically sound meta-analyses of the effectiveness of CBTp as a sole treatment suggest that its effectiveness may actually be lower than originally thought.

One recent large-scale meta-analysis (Jauhar et al., 2014) revealed only a 'small' therapeutic effect on the key symptoms of schizophrenia, such as hallucinations and delusions.

This uncertainty over whether CBTp really does offer superior outcomes to antipsychotic medication has led to conflicting recommendations within the UK about its use as a treatment for schizophrenia.

 # APPLY

AO2: An example

SCENARIO *Jon has been offered cognitive behavioural therapy as part of his treatment for schizophrenia. Outline what Jon should expect to experience during his treatment, and how it could help him.* **(6 marks)**

ANSWER *He will be working with a therapist, probably one-to-one, although a group may be more helpful if he feels isolated and will help to normalise his experience when he meets other people with similar symptoms. He will probably have 16 sessions, and will be encouraged to find alternative explanations for events, using the ABC model to challenge his faulty beliefs about activating circumstances, so that his emotional and behavioural consequences are improved. This should help to reduce his distress as he will have some sense of control over his cognitive symptoms. It can be effective and reduce symptom severity and rehospitalisation. CBTp is only part of his treatment, so he is probably taking antipsychotic drugs too. He should wait until hallucinations and delusions settle down before he starts the CBTp, as it is more effective in the non-acute stage, once he is less delusional.*

AO2: Research methods

Meta-analysis is a method for systematically combining data from different studies. The aim is to produce a single conclusion that is stronger than the conclusion drawn by any of the individual studies. It is a useful technique when lots of studies have been done on a topic but have produced conflicting results. However, there are several weaknesses associated with meta-analysis. An important question to ask of any meta-analysis is whether the studies that have been combined are all similar in type.

Explain why meta-analytic studies of CBTp's effectiveness as a treatment for schizophrenia should be treated with caution. (3 marks)

AO2: One for you to try

Jack was reading a case study of an individual with schizophrenia who claimed that he knew what people were going to say before they said it. 'Wow!' said Jasper, 'that's some ability.' 'Don't be daft,' said Jack. 'He couldn't really. He just believed that he could. They used CBTp to show him that he didn't really have that ability.' 'Really?' said Jasper. 'How did they do that?'

Using your knowledge of the aims of CBTp, suggest a way in which the false beliefs of the individual with schizophrenia could have been challenged. (4 marks)

How do I answer... evaluation only (AO3) questions?

Evaluation questions come in all sorts of shapes and sizes. Terms like 'evaluate', 'discuss', 'explain', 'criticism', 'strength' and 'limitation' all indicate that AO3 is required. The AO3 material for these questions is on the opposite page. Let's look at some examples:

Q1: Give **one** criticism of cognitive behavioural therapy as a treatment for schizophrenia. **(2 marks)**

Remembering that 'criticisms' can be either negative or positive (so research support would count as a 'positive' criticism), you could choose any one of the AO3 points as your material for **Q1**. For 2 marks, you could use the lead-in phrase (e.g. 'There are advantages of CBTp over standard care… '), followed by the material in the first two columns (i.e. the main critical claim and its expansion).

Q2: Explain **one** limitation of cognitive behavioural therapy as a treatment for schizophrenia. **(3 marks)**

Q2 requires a little more elaboration than **Q1**, but this time you are restricted to something that limits the value of self-disclosure as an explanation of attraction. For example, you might choose to use the final AO3 point ('The benefits of CBTp may have been overstated… ') with material from all three columns being used to access all 3 of the marks on offer.

Q3: Evaluate cognitive behavioural therapy as a treatment for schizophrenia. **(6 marks)**

For **Q3**, you would take the same approach as with **Q2**, but this time using **two** of the AO3 points. Trying to use more than two would make your treatment of them too superficial.

REVIEW

As you are probably aware, simply reading material is not the most effective way of learning it properly. So, using the material on the opposite page, try writing plans for 3-, 4- and 6-mark 'outline' questions on cognitive behavioural therapy as a treatment for schizophrenia plus plans for 8- and 16-mark essay questions.

Test yourself on the key points of cognitive behavioural therapy by covering up your plans and writing them out again. It's useful to have a supply of cheap paper for this, as the more times you practise retrieving the information, the better you will remember it.

Spaced practice is also very effective: come back to the same topic tomorrow and start your revision by seeing how many of the points you can remember before you look at your essay plan.

Family therapy

AO1 Description

- Schizophrenics in families characterised by high levels of criticism, hostility or over-involvement have more frequent relapses than those who live in families that are less expressive in their emotions.

- Family therapy aims to: reduce expressions of anger and guilt by family members and maintain reasonable expectations among family members for patient performance.

- During family therapy, the individual with schizophrenia is encouraged to talk to their family and explain what sort of support they find helpful – and what makes things worse.

- Family-based interventions aim to reduce the family's level of expressed emotion (expressed emotion shown to increase likelihood of relapse).

- Family therapy involves providing family members with: information about schizophrenia, finding ways of supporting an individual with schizophrenia and resolving practical problems.

- Family therapy improves relationships because the therapist encourages family members (including the person with schizophrenia) to listen to each other and work towards solutions.

How does it work?

- Family therapy makes use of a number of strategies, including:

  > **Psychoeducation** Helping the person and their carers to understand and be better able to deal with the illness.

  > **Forming an alliance with relatives** who care for the person with schizophrenia.

  > **Reducing the emotional climate** within the family and the burden of care for family members.

  > **Enhancing relatives' ability** to anticipate and solve problems.

  > **Reducing expressions of anger and guilt** by family members.

  > **Maintaining reasonable expectations** among family members for patient performance.

- Family therapy is commonly used in conjunction with routine drug treatment and outpatient clinical care.

- The individual with schizophrenia is encouraged to talk to their family and explain what sort of support they find helpful, and what makes things worse for them.

Pharoah *et al.* (2010)

- **PROCEDURE** Review of 53 studies to investigate the effectiveness of family therapy.

  > Studies compared outcomes from family therapy to 'standard' care (antipsychotic medication) alone.

  > The researchers concentrated on studies that were randomised controlled trials.

- **FINDINGS** The main results were:

  > *Mental state* – Some studies reported an improvement in the overall mental state of patients compared to those receiving standard care, whereas others did not.

  > *Compliance with medication* – The use of family intervention increased patients' compliance with medication.

  > *Social functioning* – family therapy did not appear to have much of an effect on concrete outcomes such as living independently or employment.

  > *Reduction in relapse and readmission* – There was a reduction in the risk of relapse and a reduction in hospital admission in the 24 months after.

AO3 Evaluation / Discussion

Why is family therapy effective?...

The improvements found in the Pharoah *et al.* study may not be a direct result of family therapy.	The authors suggest that the main reason for its effectiveness may have more to do with the fact that it increases medication compliance.	*This suggests the main benefit of this therapy is that it makes people more likely to comply with their medication regime, leading to improvements in their mental state and social functioning.*

A methodological limitation: Lack of blinding…

In the Pharoah *et al.* meta-analysis, quality was compromised in studies where raters were not 'blinded' to type of therapy used.	In half of the studies reported, raters were either aware whether patients had received family therapy or standard care, or failed to mention whether blinding had been used.	*This is problematic in studies with longer follow-ups where participants tend to unintentionally reveal the type of therapy received.*

Economic benefits of family therapy…

An additional advantage of family therapy is that it has considerable economic benefits associated with the treatment of schizophrenia.	The extra cost of family therapy is offset by a reduction in costs of hospitalisation because of lower relapse rates associated with this form of intervention.	*This means that the cost savings associated with family therapy are even higher.*

Impact on family members…

An additional advantage of family therapy is that it can have a positive impact on family members as well.	Lobban *et al.* (2013) analysed the results of 50 studies that included an intervention to support relatives. Sixty per cent reported a significant positive impact for relatives.	*However, the methodological quality of the studies was generally poor, making it difficult to distinguish effective from ineffective interventions.*

 **APPLY**

AO2: An example

SCENARIO Kyle is 18 and was diagnosed with schizophrenia about six months ago. His family find it very stressful and worry that they are doing the wrong thing and that nothing they do helps Kyle. As a result, Kyle's psychiatrist has recommended that family therapy might be provided to help Kyle and his family deal effectively with Kyle's illness. His parents are very apprehensive about this and don't really understand what it is or why they need it, so they ask you to explain because you study psychology.

Using your knowledge of family therapy, explain what you could tell Kyle's parents about why family therapy will help them all deal with Kyle's schizophrenia. **(6 marks)**

ANSWER *Kyle's parents' anxiety is a reason why family therapy may help. It aims to reduce anxiety and stress around the illness within a family. Getting information about schizophrenia can help them to understand what's going on with Kyle, and how they can help him. Family therapy has been shown to improve outcomes for patients by increasing compliance with medication; it will help Kyle's family to remind Kyle to take his medication if they understand how much he needs it, and how it can help him. Also, Kyle will have a chance to talk to his family about what support he wants, so they know they are doing the best for him. Family therapy will help them to feel able to support him effectively, which will reduce their anxiety, guilt and stress levels, in turn improving the caring environment for Kyle. They may be worried that they are going to be told they are doing things wrong, but family therapy actually aims to help everyone improve their relationships and solve problems more effectively, so it can be a positive experience for the family as well as for Kyle himself.*

AO2: Research methods

A researcher wanted to know if family therapy could reduce the relapse rate for schizophrenic family members. One hundred high-stress families were identified. Half of the schizophrenic family members received standard aftercare therapy, whilst the other half received supportive family therapy. This therapy encourages the family to convene a family meeting whenever an issue arises, in order to discuss and specify the exact nature of the problem, to consider alternative solutions, and to select and implement the consensual best solution. A year after the study began, the researcher identified which schizophrenic family members had been readmitted to hospital and which had not. The findings are shown in the table below.

	Number readmitted to hospital	Number not readmitted to hospital
Standard aftercare therapy	53	47
Supportive family therapy	9	91

a. Draw a suitably labelled bar chart of the data in the above table. **(4 marks)**

b. The researcher decided to analyse the results using a statistical test. Identify a suitable test that could have been used. Give two reasons for your choice of test. **(3 marks)**

c. The researcher set the significance level at $p<0.05$. What is the likelihood of a Type I error being made? **(1 mark)**

d. The statistical test showed that the null hypothesis could be rejected. What conclusion would be drawn about the effectiveness of supportive family therapy as compared with standard aftercare therapy? **(3 marks)**

AO2: One for you to try

Joe was diagnosed with schizophrenia two years ago. However, he admits that he finds home life very stressful. 'Mum is always fussing around me. I know she constantly worries what I might be doing and keeps lecturing me about taking my medication. Dad really doesn't seem to understand what I'm going through. I swear he thinks I'm just making it all up. He is always having a go at me and telling me to get my act together.'

Explain why family therapy would be a suitable treatment for Joe. (6 marks)

 How do I answer... application questions?

Let's look again at the scenario of Joe above. One way of answering this is to remember the 'say one thing for 1 mark' and 'say four things for 4 marks' strategy. So, here, we could say six things.

1 **Find a bit of appropriate psychology,** e.g. 'Schizophrenics in families characterised by high levels of criticism, hostility or over-involvement have more frequent relapses than those who live in families that are less expressive in their emotions.'

2 **Use this to explain some aspect of the scenario,** e.g. 'Joe complains that he finds home life very stressful, with his mother's constant fussing and the high levels of criticism from his father.'

3 **Find a second bit of psychology,** e.g. 'Family-based interventions reduce the level of expressed emotion within the family, as expressed emotion has been shown to increase the likelihood of relapse.'

4 **Use this to explain the scenario,** e.g. 'The high levels of stress Joe is experiencing could be reduced by working with the family to reduce levels of expressed emotion, and decreasing odds of a relapse.'

5 **Find a third bit of psychology,** e.g. 'Family therapy improves relationships within the household because the therapist encourages family members to listen to each other and openly discuss problems and negotiate potential solutions together.'

6 **Use this to explain the scenario,** e.g. 'Family therapy would be appropriate for Joe because his mother would learn that she could be supportive without being over-involved and his dad would become more aware of the nature of Joe's disorder and become more sympathetic toward him.'

REVIEW

To enhance your practical expertise on this topic, there are a couple of useful things you could do:

1 Write 3-, 4- and 6-mark outlines of family therapy as a treatment of schizophrenia.

2 Write a bullet-pointed answer plan for the following two questions.

Briefly discuss family therapy as a treatment of schizophrenia. (8 marks)

Discuss family therapy as a treatment of schizophrenia. (16 marks)

Token economy and the management of schizophrenia

RECAP

A01 Description

- A token economy is a form of behavioural therapy where clinicians set target behaviours that will improve the patient's engagement in daily activities. Tokens are awarded whenever the patient engages in one of the target behaviours.

- Ayllon and Azrin (1968) gave schizophrenic patients plastic tokens for behaviours such as carrying out domestic chores. These tokens were then exchanged for privileges such as being able to watch a movie. This procedure was effective in maintaining patients' adaptive behaviours as long as the token economy remained in effect.

- To give the neutral token some 'value', it is repeatedly presented alongside or immediately before the reinforcing stimulus. By pairing the neutral tokens with the reinforcing stimulus, the neutral token eventually acquires the same reinforcing properties.

- When a token can be exchanged for a variety of different privileges and rewards (i.e. a generalised reinforcer), the more powerful it becomes.

- During the early stages of the token economy, frequent exchange periods mean that patients can be quickly reinforced and target behaviours can then increase in frequency.

- The effectiveness of the token economy may decrease if more time passes between presentation of the token and exchange for the backup reinforcers (Kazdin, 1977).

How does it work?

- The behavioural principles employed in token systems are based mainly on the theory of operant conditioning. The principles of operant conditioning describe the relationship between a behaviour and environmental events. Key within this relationship is the idea of positive reinforcement, i.e. an increase in the frequency of a particular behaviour when it is followed by a desirable event.

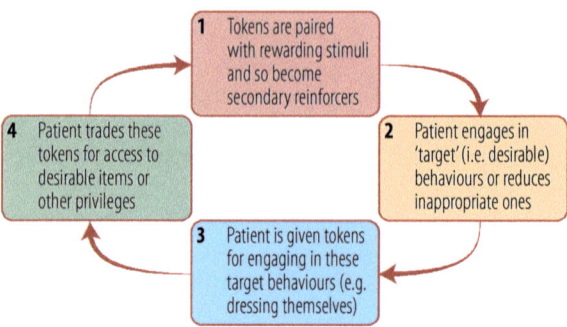

A03 Evaluation / Discussion

Research support…

| Dickerson *et al.* (2005) provided research support for the effectiveness of token economies in a psychiatric setting. | They reviewed 13 studies of the use of token economy systems in the treatment of schizophrenia, eleven of which reported beneficial effects that were directly attributable to the use of token economies. | *However, the authors cautioned that many of the studies reviewed had significant methodological shortcomings that limited their impact in the overall assessment of token economies.* |

Difficulties assessing the success of a token economy…

| A problem in assessing the effectiveness of token economies is that studies of their use tend to be uncontrolled. | Typically, all patients on a ward are on the programme rather than having an experimental group and a control group. As a result, patients' improvements can only be compared with their past behaviours rather than with those of a control group. | *This comparison may be misleading, as other factors (e.g. an increase in staff attention) could be causing patients' improvement rather than the token economy.* |

Less useful for patients living in the community…

| Although the token economy has shown to be effective, it has only really been shown to work in a hospital setting. | There are problems administrating a token economy with outpatients. Within a psychiatric ward, staff are able to monitor and reward patients appropriately. This is not possible with outpatients living in the community. | *Therefore, even if the token economy does produce positive results within the ward setting, these results may not be maintained beyond that environment.* |

Ethical concerns…

| There are ethical concerns about the use of token economy programmes in psychiatric settings. | Clinicians may withhold important primary reinforcers such as food, privacy or access to activities that alleviate boredom. Patients gain access to these rewards by exchanging tokens awarded for demonstrating target behaviours. | *However, human beings have certain basic rights (to food, privacy, etc.) that cannot be violated regardless of the positive consequences that might be achieved by manipulating them within a token economy programme.* |

APPLY

AO2: An example

SCENARIO Annie is a clinical psychologist who is asked to talk to staff at a local psychiatric unit about setting up a token economy in one of the wards. It is a ward of eight female patients between the ages of 30 and 45. These women have been on antipsychotic medication for an average of 12 years and display a variety of negative symptoms including speech poverty and avolition.

Outline what advice Annie might give to staff in the unit about setting up a token economy to address these two particular symptoms. **(6 marks)**

ANSWER *First, suitable rewards should be identified as primary reinforcers. A variety of rewards should be chosen which the women will be able to choose from, such as watching movies or food treats, as this is more effective than simple food rewards. Then the staff should start presenting tokens every time these rewards are given. This will create an association between the reward and the token. Then the staff should give the women tokens every time they carry out a positive behaviour, such as talking or making an effort to do something (the opposite of speech poverty and avolition). These tokens must be exchanged quite quickly for rewards in the early stages, so that the connection is made. Staff will need to be consistent in rewarding positive behaviour very promptly so that the tokens reinforce the desired behaviour, not an intervening one.*

AO2: Research methods

Psychologists wanted to investigate the effectiveness of the token economy in the management of schizophrenia. They obtained permission from a regional NHS trust to study two wards of long-term patients prior to them being transferred into the community. One group were subjected to a token economy programme alongside their antipsychotic medication for a period of one month, the second group received only their antipsychotic medication over the same period. The groups were then followed up for three months after their transfer back into the community.

a. **Identify one ethical issue that the researchers would need to consider in this research. Suggest how the researchers could deal with this issue. (3 marks)**

b. **Explain how the researchers might have assessed whether the token economy had produced better outcomes than antipsychotic medication alone. (2 marks)**

AO2: One for you to try

A token economy ward was set up in a psychiatric ward of a hospital. The staff took time to associate tokens with desired outcomes (e.g. sweets from the hospital shop), so that the tokens became secondary reinforcers. Tokens were awarded whenever a patient helped out around the ward or showed courteous behaviour to another patient. In the evenings, the token economy system was suspended and the ward was under the supervision of nursing auxiliaries. Three weeks into the new system, two new patients joined the ward and immediately were given tokens for any display of the desired behaviours. The results from the token economy system were disappointing, with patients reverting to their old ways at the start of every day. The outcome for the new patients was even worse, with no improvements at all that could be attributed to the token economy.

Identify and explain reasons for the disappointing results of the token economy used in this scenario. (4 marks)

How do I answer... description and evaluation (AO1 + AO3) questions?

1 Make sure you can spot a mixed AO1 + AO3 question. Having two different command words, e.g. 'outline' (an AO1 term) and 'evaluate' (an AO3 term) is a good clue.

2 Plan how much you should write for each. In mixed AO1 + AO3 questions up to 6 marks, the division is half and half.

3 Decide what to write. (The AO1 and AO3 material for these questions is on the opposite page.)

Q1: Briefly explain how the token economy technique has been used in the management of schizophrenia and give one criticism of this approach. **(4 marks)**

Use the first two AO1 points, together with an abridged version of the first AO3 point.

Q2: Outline and evaluate the token economy technique as used in the management of schizophrenia. **(6 marks)**

The AO1 requirement would be met by the first three AO1 points. They would give a good 3-mark overview as required by the question. For the AO3 content you might use one complete AO3 point or two abridged AO3 points.

Q3: Outline and evaluate findings from research into the use of the token economy technique in the management of schizophrenia. **(6 marks)**

This question is included as an example to show how sometimes you need to be creative in the material you use in your response. Bearing in mind that research findings can be used as AO1 or as an explanation of research support, we can do a bit of detective work to find 3 marks' worth that we can use as AO1. The Ayllon and Azrin (1968) and Kazdin (1977) studies are relevant, as is the description of the Dickerson *et al.* (2005) findings. The fact that these appear in our AO3 section is irrelevant because we are only using the second column, which is a statement of the research finding. The most obvious AO3 point to use for this question would be 'Difficulties assessing the success of a token economy'.

REVIEW

Take a large sheet of paper (A3 works well here) and construct a mind-map so that all your material on the token economy is linked together visually. This serves several purposes: (1) It *elaborates* the material, making it more memorable; (2) The act of constructing the mind-map counts as *revision*, again making it more likely you can recall in an exam; (3) You have a *visual* image of the material, which, for many people, is a much easier way of remembering complex material.

An interactionist approach

 **RECAP**

AO1 Description

The diathesis-stress model

- The diathesis-stress model sees schizophrenia as the result of an interaction between genetic (the diathesis) and environmental (stress) influences.

- **Diathesis** Schizophrenia has a genetic component in terms of vulnerability, e.g. the identical twin of a person with schizophrenia is at greater risk of developing schizophrenia than a sibling or fraternal twin.

  > Because half of identical twins in which one twin is diagnosed with schizophrenia never become schizophrenic themselves, this indicates that environmental factors must also play a role in determining whether they develop the disorder.

- **Stress** Stressful life events that can trigger schizophrenia include stresses associated with living in a highly urbanised environment.

  > Children who experienced severe trauma before the age of 16 were three times as likely to develop schizophrenia in later life compared to the general population (Varese *et al.*, 2012).

  > Relatively minor stressors may lead to the onset of the disorder for an individual who is highly vulnerable, or a major stressful event might cause a similar reaction in a person low in vulnerability.

Tienari *et al.* (2004)

- **PROCEDURE** Records for 20,000 women admitted to Finnish psychiatric hospitals were checked to identify those diagnosed with schizophrenia. Those who had one or more of their offspring adopted away were selected from this list. A sample of 145 adopted-away offspring (high-risk) was matched with a sample of 158 adoptees without this genetic risk (low-risk).

  > Both groups of adoptees were assessed after 12 years, with a follow-up after 21 years. The interviewing psychiatrists were kept blind as to the status of the biological mother (i.e. schizophrenia or no schizophrenia).

- **FINDINGS** Of the 303 adoptees, 14 had developed schizophrenia. Of these, 11 were from the high-risk group and three from the low-risk group. Being reared in a 'healthy' adoptive family appeared to have a protective effect even for those at high genetic risk for schizophrenia.

  > High-genetic-risk adoptees reared in 'healthy' and supportive families were significantly less likely to have developed schizophrenia than high-genetic-risk adoptees reared in families that were less healthy and supportive.

AO3 Evaluation/Discussion

Diatheses may not be exclusively genetic...

Diathesis-stress models emphasise 'vulnerability' due to genetic influences alone, which are assumed to result in an increased risk for schizophrenia.	However, this increased risk can also result from brain damage caused by obstetric complications at birth. Verdoux *et al.* (1998) estimated the risk of developing schizophrenia later in life after obstetric complications is four times greater than for those who experience no such complications.	However, researchers claim that birth complications are caused by an already compromised foetus (Weinberger, 1995).

Urban environments are not necessarily more stressful...

Not all research has agreed with the finding that living in densely populated urban environments was a significant stress factor for schizophrenia.	For example, Paykel *et al.* (2000), although finding evidence of urban–rural differences, showed that these differences disappeared after adjusting for the socio-economic differences for the two groups.	This suggests that, although social adversity may well be a significant trigger for schizophrenia, the claim that social adversity and urbanisation are synonymous is likely to be an oversimplification.

Difficulties in determining causal stress...

It is possible that stressors earlier in life can also influence how people respond to later stressful events and increase their future susceptibility to the disorder.	Maladaptive methods of coping with stress in childhood means that the individual fails to develop effective coping skills, which in turn compromises their resilience and increases vulnerability to schizophrenia (Hammen, 1992).	Ineffective coping skills may, therefore, make life generally more stressful for the individual and so trigger mental illness.

Implications for treatment...

If the onset of schizophrenia is a result of the additive effect of genetic vulnerability and environmental stress, this has implications for its treatment.	Børglum *et al.* (2014) found that women infected with cytomegalovirus during pregnancy were more likely to have a child who developed schizophrenia, but only if both mother and child carried a particular gene defect.	This suggests that antiviral medicine during pregnancy may prevent the onset of schizophrenia in the offspring of women known to have this gene defect.

⚙ APPLY

AO2: An example

SCENARIO Carla has a history of schizophrenia. It began when she smoked cannabis as a teenager, to deal with the stress of her alcoholic father who was subsequently imprisoned for violence against her mother and her younger sister. Carla's mental health has been more stable for the last few years, and she has stopped taking her medication because she wants to have a baby. She manages her symptoms with the help of skills she learnt in CBTp. She is worried that her baby might inherit her vulnerability to schizophrenia.

Discuss the diathesis–stress model of schizophrenia. Suggest reasons why Carla had developed schizophrenia and explain how she could reduce her baby's chances of developing the disorder.
(16 marks)

ANSWER **An extract showing how you could address the AO2 requirements of this question:** *Carla's schizophrenia was probably caused by an interaction between biological factors (genetic susceptibility) and environmental stress (the stress of having an alcoholic father, the violence in the family, and the court case against her father). The cannabis may also have made her more vulnerable to the disorder. The biological factors (the diathesis) interacted with the stress to cause the onset of her schizophrenia. Her baby could have the same faulty gene, but if she cares for the baby well there is no reason the schizophrenia will necessarily develop. It is important for Carla to avoid the double bind situation or the critical or hostile style, or the over-involvement associated with high expressed emotion (EE) families, so that her baby's genetic vulnerability is not accompanied by family stress...*

AO2: One for you to try

The diagram below is a hypothetical illustration of the diathesis-stress model. 'Biological vulnerability' has been measured in terms of a person's family history of schizophrenia, whilst 'stress' has been measured in terms of life events that a person can experience.

On the 'biological vulnerability' axis, 'low' indicates that a person has no family history of schizophrenia, 'medium' indicates that one of their parents is schizophrenic, and 'high' indicates that both of their parents are schizophrenic. On the stress scale, being overdrawn at the bank has a stress value of 50, going away to university has a stress value of 75, and being made unemployed has a stress value of 100.

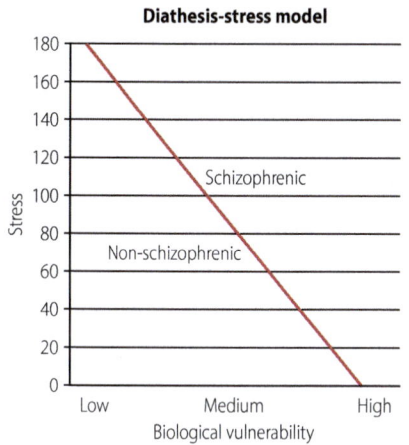

Adrian has one schizophrenic parent and is overdrawn at the bank. Both of Barry's parents are schizophrenic, and he has recently been made redundant. Chris has no family history of schizophrenia, but he is overdrawn at the bank and has just gone away to university. Dave has one schizophrenic parent and has just gone away to university. Six months into his course, Dave's bank manager tells him that he has reached his overdraft limit. To make matters worse, Dave has lost his job at the local burger bar.

Using the diagram and information above, identify whether each person is likely to be schizophrenic or likely to develop it. Explain your decisions. (8 marks)

AO2: Research methods

Write a 100-word abstract for the Tienari *et al.* key study on the opposite page. You should include details of the aim, procedure, results and any conclusions that might be drawn from this study. **(4 marks)**

🐾 How do I answer... longer (16-mark) questions?

A 16-mark question on schizophrenia might ask you to 'discuss…' an explanation (or two) of schizophrenia or a therapy (or two) used in the treatment of schizophrenia. Whilst all of these instructions indicate that both AO1 *and* AO3 are required in your answer, the 'discuss…' command word requires you to go a little further than just writing about strengths and/or limitations. Let's look at these different types of question as they might appear in the context of the interactionist approach. The AO1 and AO3 material for these questions is on the opposite page.

Q1: Outline and evaluate the interactionist approach to schizophrenia. (16 marks)

The nominal mark division for AO1 (outline) and AO3 (evaluation) is 6 marks for the former and 10 marks for the latter. You could aim to include the six AO1 points to cover the 'outline' component of this question. For the AO3 content, you should include all four of the AO3 points.

Q2: Discuss the interactionist approach to schizophrenia. (16 marks)

The command word 'discuss' requires AO3 that is a bit more 'discursive', e.g. looking at applications, implications, counter-evidence, etc. We have tried to make some of our AO3 points 'discursive' to accommodate this. For example, the second AO3 point is 'discursive' because it challenges the belief that urban environments are more stressful. Likewise, the fourth point is 'discursive' because it discusses the implications of an interactionist perspective for treatment.

🔄 REVIEW

In this final Review section of this chapter, it is time for some more 'revision accounting'. You should make a table. Include all nine topics from this chapter on schizophrenia as rows of one column (headed 'Topic'). Add another two columns (headed 'Got it!') for the AO1 and AO3 on each topic. When you feel you have mastered the AO1 and AO3 components of each topic and can cope with any of the different types of question that we have covered in the **How do I answer… ?** sections, you will have earned a tick in the 'Got it!' columns.

The evolutionary explanation for food preferences

RECAP

A01 Description

- **Evolutionary explanations for food preferences** focus on the adaptive benefits that certain foods would have offered our ancestors in the environment of evolutionary adaptation (EEA).

- **Early diets** Preferences for fatty food was adaptive for early humans, because energy resources were vital to stay alive and to find the next meal.

  > The diet of early humans was derived primarily from animal-based foods. A meat diet, full of nutrients, provided the catalyst for the growth of the brain.

  > The taste of sweetness is associated with a high concentration of sugar and calories. More calories meant children were more likely to grow and to survive.

- **Taste aversion** is a learned response to eating toxic or poisonous food. The animal avoids eating the food that made it ill or that they associate with the illness.

  > Rats made ill through radiation shortly after eating saccharin developed an aversion to the saccharin (Garcia *et al.*, 1955).

  > The development of taste aversions helped our ancestors to survive because, if they survived eating poisoned food, they would not make the same mistake again.

- **Food neophobia**, a reluctance to consume new or unusual foods, protects animals from the risk of being poisoned by something that is potentially harmful.

  > Species restricted to just a few specific food sources tend not to exhibit food neophobia, whereas species that have varied diets do display food neophobia.

  > Neophobia explains reluctance to consume new or unusual foods. This is stronger for animal products than non-animal products because of the illness threat posed by rotting meat.

A03 Evaluation / Discussion

Are all food preferences a product of evolution?...

Not all food preferences can be traced back to the adaptive pressures of the EEA.	A preference that is beneficial today (e.g. for low cholesterol foods) would not have evolved because of any beneficial effects for our ancestors. Many things that were important to our ancestors (e.g. animal fats) are nowadays harmful to our health, so we are more likely to avoid them.	*Krebs (2009) suggests that modern-day health epidemics are a consequence of a 'mismatch' between evolved preferences (e.g. for fatty foods) and modern environments.*

Support for evolved preferences for sweet foods...

Early exposure to a sweet taste is not necessary for children to develop a preference for sweet-tasting foods.	When a culture with no experience of sweet foods and drinks has come into contact with cultures that regularly consume these, in no case has the culture without sugar rejected the sugar-containing foods and drinks of the other culture (Bell *et al.*, 1973).	*This provides support for the claimed evolutionary preference for sweet foodstuffs in our distant ancestors in the EEA.*

Real-world application: Taste aversion and chemotherapy...

Research on taste aversion can explain the food avoidance that can occur during cancer treatment.	Chemotherapy can cause gastrointestinal illness. When this illness is paired with food consumption, taste aversions can result. The 'scapegoat technique' involves giving cancer patients a novel food along with some familiar food just prior to their chemotherapy. The patient forms an aversion to the novel food and not the familiar food.	*These findings are consistent with a neophobia explanation of the adaptive avoidance of unfamiliar foods.*

Support for the heritability of neophobia...

If food neophobia has adaptive advantages, then there should be a strong genetic component for this characteristic.	Knaapila *et al.* (2007) measured food neophobia in 211 MZ and 257 DZ adult twin pairs. The heritability estimate for food neophobia in this sample was 67 per cent, suggesting that two thirds of the variation in food neophobia is genetically determined.	*This lends support to the view that neophobia evolved among humans because it protected them from potentially harmful foods.*

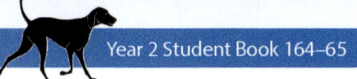

APPLY

AO2: An example

SCENARIO Sonia will happily eat mashed potato, carrots and peas. But when her mum tries to introduce her to Brussels sprouts she refuses to take even a tiny bite. She tells her mum she is not eating them as they look and smell funny.

With reference to Sonia's behaviour, briefly outline neophobia as an explanation for food preferences. **(3 marks)**

ANSWER *Sonia is reluctant to consume the Brussels sprouts as they are a new and unusual food that looks and smells different to the foods she considers to be 'acceptable'. This neophobic response is a naturally occurring reaction that has evolved to protect a species from the risk of consuming potentially harmful substances. Humans as a species have a varied diet and so are more likely to display neophobia than animals with a more restricted diet, such as koalas who mostly eat eucalyptus leaves. This suggests Sonia's mum will have difficulty introducing a range of new foods to Sonia.*

AO2: Research methods

Anthropologists studying the Pirahã people, an indigenous Amazonian hunter-gatherer tribe, are able to gather together information gathered from people who have traded with Pirahã and early explorers who have encountered this tribe in the past. Because the Pirahã have minimal contact with the outside world, this information potentially offers a valuable insight into the diet of our hunter-gatherer ancestors.

a. **The anthropologists decide to use a content analysis on the written and verbal (tape-recorded) material gathered on the lives and diet of the Pirahã. What is meant by a content analysis? (2 marks)**

b. **Explain how the anthropologists might carry out a content analysis on this material. (3 marks)**

c. **Outline one strength and one limitation of content analysis as a method of investigation. (4 marks)**

AO2: One for you to try

Alex had never tried sushi before, but agreed to give it a go on a night out with friends. That night he was violently sick and had to take the next day off work. When he spoke to his friends the next day he told them it must have been the sushi. However, his friends told him that one of them, Jack, had been recovering from norovirus, the vomiting bug, and had most probably passed on the bug to Alex. Despite knowing that it wasn't the sushi that had made him ill, Alex still felt ill at the sight and smell of sushi for quite a while afterwards.

Using your knowledge of the evolutionary explanation for food preferences, explain why Alex feels sick at the sight and smell of sushi. (4 marks)

How do I answer... selection (multiple choice) questions?

Which **one** of the following is indicative of taste aversion in food preference? **(1 mark)**

A   Animals show a preference for sweet-tasting foods, and avoid those that lack this taste.

B   Animals made ill though radiation shortly after eating a food later show a preference for that food.

C   Animals who survive eating poisoned food learn to avoid that food in the future.

D   Many animals show a tendency to avoid unusual foods.

Usually these questions require you to pick out the **one** statement that is correct, matches or defines a concept or idea. They may also (on occasion) ask you to pick out the one statement that is *incorrect* or does *not* match or define a concept or idea.

Although these are generally worth only 1 mark, getting them correct is still important because that 1 mark can be the difference between one grade and another. So, some general advice on answering these:

*   Read the question very carefully. Is it asking you to pick the statement that matches (as here) or the 'odd one out' that doesn't match?
*   Make life easier by crossing out any that are obviously *not* going to be the correct answer given the specific demands of the question.
*   Applying this to the question above we cross out **D** because that is describing food neophobia rather than taste aversion. Alternative **A** is actually just describing a preference for sweet foods, which is nothing to do with taste aversion. Alternative **B** suggests that animals later show a *preference* for any food that has made them sick. Hard to see the adaptive benefits of that! That just leaves **C**, which is the right answer!

REVIEW

You should be able to use the material on this spread to answer any question on the topic of evolutionary explanations for food preference. This means being able to write descriptive answers worth 2, 3 and 4 marks on early food diets, taste aversion and food neophobia: 2 marks (50 words approx.); 3 marks (75 words); and 4 marks (100 words). You should be able to write one AO3 point (75 words approx.) for each of these three topics and four AO3 points overall.

Throughout this chapter we show you how to use this sort of material flexibly to answer all the different types of questions you might be asked. The more you practise using different parts of the same material in response to different questions, the more effective you will be in the exam.

RECAP

AO1 Description

Social influences

- **Parental influences** Children acquire their **food preferences** by observing their parents' behaviour. Brown and Ogden (2004) reported correlations between parents and their children in terms of their eating behaviour and attitudes to food.

  > Parents may manipulate the availability of certain foods, as a reward (e.g. special treats) or because of a perceived health gain (e.g. foods with reduced fat).

- **Peers** The behaviour of same-age peers has an influence on the food preferences of children. Greenhalgh *et al.* (2009) found that children exposed to positive modelling (i.e. peers eating novel foods) were more likely to try these foods themselves.

  > Exposure to another child can change food preferences. Birch (1980) showed that children changed their vegetable preference after sitting next to another child who chose a different vegetable at lunchtimes to the one they preferred.

Cultural influences

- **Media effects** The role of **social learning** is also evident in the impact of television and other media on food preferences. The media have a major impact both on what people eat and their attitudes to certain foods (MacIntyre *et al.*, 1998).

  > People learn from the media about healthy eating, but must place this information within the broader context of their lives (i.e. what they can afford and what is freely available).

- **The context of meals** In the UK, 'grazing' and the desire for convenience foods are increasingly common. Maguire *et al.* (2015) found that the number of takeaway restaurants had risen by 45 per cent in the previous 18 years; areas of the highest deprivation saw the highest increase.

  > Gillman *et al.* (2000) suggest that eating more 'informally' leads to a learned preference for quickly prepared snack foods rather than more elaborate meals.

AO3 Evaluation / Discussion

Social influences

Limitations of the parental influence view…

Research into the role of parental influences on food preferences is quite limited.	Typically, studies have been small-scale and carried out on a highly selective sample of white Americans. For example, research by Robinson *et al.* (2001) revealed a complex association between the behaviour of parents and the food preferences of their children, with girls being more influenced than boys.	*It is unclear, however, whether the findings of these studies generalise to other populations.*

Not all parental influences are effective…

Not all the methods used by parents are effective in influencing food preferences in their children.	Russell *et al.* (2015) found that some methods used by parents (e.g. parental modelling) were effective in promoting healthy eating in their children, whilst others (e.g. restricting food access) were ineffective.	*This supports the claim that children do learn food preferences from their parents, but also that some attempts at influence are more effective than others.*

Cultural influences

Research support for media influences on food preferences…

Boyland and Halford (2013) provided supporting evidence that exposure to food advertising on television influences food preferences in children.	They found that children who had the greatest preference for high-carbohydrate and high-fat foods were also the ones that watched the most television.	*However, as research has mostly focused on the negative consequences of media influences on children's diets, the potential for television and social media to encourage the development of healthier dietary choices is under-investigated.*

Real-world application: Implications of media influences on food preferences…

Research has shown that television is the dominant medium for children's exposure to food marketing, particularly unhealthy foods (Cairns *et al.*, 2013).	This has led to a number of countries developing regulations that limit the quantity of TV advertising of unhealthy food to children or reduce the effect of such advertising on children.	*This suggests that a ban on TV advertising for this type of food could significantly reduce the number of overweight children.*

⚙ APPLY

AO2: An example

SCENARIO Andre is not a healthy eater. His parents give him money to spend in the school canteen but he often skips lunch and visits the local chip shop with his friends on the way home. He always pesters his parents for chocolate bars and will only drink fizzy pop. His parents have tried to improve his eating habits by restricting the amount of treats in the house and refusing to let him leave the table until he has eaten some of the vegetables on his plate.

Outline and evaluate the role of learning in food preference, making reference to Andre in your answer. **(16 marks)**

ANSWER An extract showing how you could address the AO2 requirements of this question: *Andre may have learned his unhealthy habits from his peers who would be influential role models. Greenhalgh et al. (2009) found negative modelling (the model refusing to eat novel food) had an effect on eating behaviour (the observer also refused). In this case Andre is avoiding a healthy school lunch to eat chips (high fat and salt) with his friends. His parents' attempts to improve his diet may be unsuccessful – Russell et al. (2015) found that forcing consumption and restricting access are not effective. Andre's parents would be better advised to model consumption of vegetables themselves...*

AO2: Research methods

In the Brown and Ogden study mentioned opposite, a sample of children aged between 9 and 13 were recruited from two schools in southern England. A total of 260 children were approached and asked to give a consent form to their parents. From these, 112 parents and 112 children returned completed questionnaires about their eating habits. The researchers found significant correlations between parents' and their children's consumption of healthy snacks ($\rho = 0.392$ $p = 0.01$) and a correlation between parents' and their children's consumption of unhealthy snacks ($\rho = 0.317$ $p = 0.001$).

a. **Construct a directional hypothesis that might have been used in this study. (2 marks)**

b. **Identify the type of sampling method used in this study and give one limitation of this sampling method. (3 marks)**

c. **Explain why a consent form was necessary in this study. (3 marks)**

d. **Explain what the correlation of 0.317 tells the researchers about the relationship between parents' consumption of unhealthy snacks and their children's consumption of unhealthy snacks. (2 marks).**

e. **Explain the difference between the significance levels of $p = 0.01$ and $p = 0.001$ found for healthy and unhealthy snacks. (2 marks)**

AO2: One for you to try

A celebrity chef, popular on television, is determined to change the eating habits of children in the UK.

Using your knowledge of social and cultural influences, outline two ways in which this chef could influence the eating behaviour of children. (4 marks)

🐾 How do I answer... 'Distinguish between' questions?

> Explain the difference between social and cultural influences in food preference. **(3 marks)**

There are some fairly simple rules for answering this sort of question. If you are asked to 'distinguish between...', 'compare...' or 'explain the difference between...', then these rules apply:

1 Don't just *describe* the two things you are being asked to distinguish between.

2 Pick something that applies to both (e.g. that they both influence food preferences) yet *how* they do this is different for one compared to the other. For example, 'Social influences, such as parents, may exert their influence by directly manipulating the availability of "healthy" foods and "unhealthy" foods." Cultural influences, such as the media, may present role models eating healthy or unhealthy food, so the child acquires their preference through observational learning.'

3 Use words like 'whereas', 'however' and 'on the other hand' to point out this difference. That gives us, 'Social influences, such as parents, may exert their influence by directly manipulating the availability of "healthy" foods and "unhealthy" foods. However, cultural influences, such as the media, may present role models eating healthy or unhealthy food, so the child acquires their preference through observational learning.'

4 Don't be too ambitious; one point of difference is usually enough.

🔄 REVIEW

One way of making sure you understand all the different aspects of the role of learning in food preferences is to do a bit of 'revision accounting'. When you feel you have mastered these different aspects, you have earned a tick in the 'Got it!' column. This list might include:

TOPIC	Got it!		Got it!
Parental influences (AO1)		Parental influences (AO3)	
Peer influences (AO1)		Peer influences (AO3)	
Media influences (AO1)		Media influences (AO3)	
The context of meals (AO1)		The context of meals (AO3)	

Neural and hormonal mechanisms

AOI Description

Neural mechanisms in the control of eating

- **Homeostasis** is the mechanism by which an organism maintains a steady internal environment, detecting whether the body has enough nutrients and correcting the situation if this is not the case.
    > A decline in glucose levels in the blood activates the lateral hypothalamus (LH), resulting in feelings of hunger. A rise in glucose levels activates the ventromedial hypothalamus (VMH), leading to feelings of satiation.
- **The lateral hypothalamus** Damage to the LH in rats causes aphagia ('absence of eating'). Stimulation of the LH elicits feeding behaviour.
    > Neuropeptide Y (NPY), when injected into the LH of rats, causes them to begin feeding, even when satiated (Reynolds and Wickens, 2000).
- **The ventromedial hypothalamus** Damage to the VMH causes rats to overeat, leading to hyperphagia ('overeating'). Stimulation of this area inhibited feeding.
    > It is now believed that damage to a specific area of the VMH (the paraventricular nucleus) causes hyperphagia.

Hormonal mechanisms in the control of eating

- The two main hormones involved in the control of eating are ghrelin and leptin. Ghrelin increases appetite when we are hungry, and leptin decreases appetite when the body has enough stored energy.
- **Ghrelin** is released in the stomach and stimulates the hypothalamus to increase appetite. If a person's bodily resources are low, then ghrelin levels increase.
    > Ghrelin is important in the development of obesity because, on stimulating the appetite, it leads to an increase in body weight.
- **Leptin** is produced by fat tissue and secreted into the bloodstream, where it travels to the brain and decreases appetite. Short-term fluctuations in leptin levels provide information regarding changes in calorific intake.
    > By binding to receptors in the hypothalamus, leptin counteracts the effects of the feeding stimulant neuropeptide Y. Leptin also increases sympathetic nervous system activity, stimulating fatty tissue to burn energy.

AO3 Evaluation/Discussion

Limitations of a homeostatic explanation...

For a hunger mechanism to be adaptive, it must be able to anticipate energy deficits, not just react to them.	A truly adaptive mechanism must promote levels of consumption that maintain bodily resources well above the optimal level to act as a buffer against future lack of food availability.	This suggests that explanations of food intake based solely on homeostatic mechanisms offer only a limited perspective on eating behaviour.

Problems with the role of the lateral hypothalamus...

The view that the LH served as an 'on switch' for eating turned out to have a few problems.	Damage to the LH caused deficits in other aspects of behaviour (e.g. thirst) rather than just hunger. Research has also shown that eating behaviour is controlled by neural circuits that run throughout the brain, not just the hypothalamus.	This shows that although the LH plays an important role in controlling eating behaviour, it is not the brain's 'eating centre'.

Research support for the role of ghrelin in appetite control...

Wren *et al.* (2001) provided research support for the role of ghrelin in appetite control.	Nine volunteers either received intravenous ghrelin or a saline infusion and one week later the same participants received the other condition. The results showed a significant increase in food consumption in the ghrelin condition compared to the saline infusion condition.	This study demonstrates that ghrelin is an important signal that stimulates food intake in human beings.

Leptin resistance...

Some people develop resistance to leptin and so it fails to control appetite and weight gain.	One reason is that leptin receptors stop functioning properly and so cells fail to respond to the hormone. Leptin resistance is often found in overweight and obese people, making it even harder for them to lose weight.	As leptin resistance appears to be a heritable trait, this offers a credible explanation of why obesity has been found to run in families (Silventoinen et al., 2017).

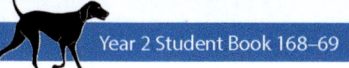

 APPLY

AO2: An example

SCENARIO Researchers interested in the neural control of eating caused damage to the LH in a group of rats. In a separate study, the VMH in a second group of rats was damaged. Finally, either the LH or the VMH was stimulated in a third group of rats.

What changes to eating behaviour would you expect researchers to observe as a result of their interventions? **(4 marks)**

ANSWER *The rats with damage to their LH are likely to show an absence of eating (aphagia) while those whose LH was stimulated will show increased feeding. This is because the LH is thought to be the 'on' switch for eating, causing feelings of hunger to encourage food consumption. VMH damage would lead to hyperphagia (increased eating), but rats whose VMH was stimulated would stop eating. This is because the VMH creates satiety to discourage further eating.*

AO2: One for you to try

After years of trying to lose weight, Max has volunteered to take part in a trial of a new leptin drug treatment for obesity. Max is worried about taking the drug and, as you are studying this area of psychology, he asks you to explain what effects it is likely to have on his eating behaviour.

Outline what you would tell Max about the effects that leptin treatment is likely to have on his eating behaviour. (3 marks)

AO2: Research methods

The study that Max is taking part in is successful and so the researchers decide to publish their findings. Before publication, their article is sent for peer review.

a. **Outline the purpose of peer review in psychological research. (3 marks)**

b. **Explain how research into leptin treatment for obesity could have implications for the economy. (3 marks)**

 How do I answer... description only (AO1) questions?

There is a fairly simple formula in answering description only questions. For 2 marks, say two things, for 3 marks say three things, and so on. This approach adds an appropriate level of detail to each answer and gives the examiner a useful way of discriminating between your answer and one that would be worth fewer than the maximum marks for that question.

Work through the sample questions below, using the advice that follows them. The AO1 and AO3 material for these questions is on the opposite page.

Q1: Briefly explain the role of **one** hormone in the control of eating. **(2 marks)**

Q1: Choose *either* ghrelin *or* leptin and use the **two** AO1 points associated with that hormone.

Q2: Outline the role of neural mechanisms in the control of eating. **(3 marks)**

Q2: Use **three** points under the AO1 heading for 'neural mechanisms'. These could be the three main points (homeostasis, lateral hypothalamus, ventromedial hypothalamus).

Q3: Explain the role of neural mechanisms in the control of eating. **(4 marks)**

Q3: Use **four** points under the AO1 heading for 'neural mechanisms'. This could be as for **Q2**, but adding in the second 'hypothalamus' point as well.

Q4: Describe the role of neural and hormonal mechanisms in the control of eating. **(6 marks)**

Q4: For a 6-mark question, you should aim for about 150–180 words. Use the same material as for **Q3** *plus* **three** points under the AO1 heading for 'hormonal mechanisms'. These could be the first, second and fourth points.

REVIEW

In order to feel comfortable with this topic you should practise using the material in all the different ways that might be assessed in your exam.

1. Try constructing 3-, 4- and 6-mark descriptions of neural mechanisms of the control of eating, and the same for hormonal mechanisms of the control of eating, using the advice given in the **How do I... ?** section above.

2. Write an essay plan showing how you would use the material on this spread to answer 8-mark extended writing questions for neural mechanisms and for hormonal mechanisms.

3. Write an essay plan showing how you would use the material on this spread to answer a 16-mark extended writing question for neural *and* hormonal mechanisms.

Biological explanations for anorexia nervosa

 **RECAP**

AO1 Description

Genetic explanations

- **Family studies** First-degree relatives of individuals with **anorexia nervosa** (AN) have a 10-times greater lifetime risk of having AN than relatives of unaffected individuals (Strober *et al.*, 2000).
    > People may inherit a more general vulnerability to eating disorders rather than AN specifically (Tozzi *et al.*, 2005).
- **Twin studies** Comparing the similarity of MZ twins to DZ twins provides a measure of the relative contributions of genetic and environmental factors in the development of AN.
    > Twin studies generally suggest moderate to high heritability of AN, with heritability estimates varying between 28 per cent and 74 per cent (Thornton *et al.*, 2010).
- **Adoption studies** avoid the problem of MZ twins sharing similar environments because they study biological relatives reared apart.
    > Klump *et al.* (2009) studied adopted sibling pairs (adopted females and 'sisters' from their adoptive family) and biological sibling pairs (adopted females and their biological sisters reared in a different family). Heritability estimates ranged from 59 per cent to 82 per cent for disordered eating, with non-shared environmental factors accounting for the remaining variance.

Neural explanations

- **Serotonin** Disturbances in levels of serotonin appear to be a characteristic of individuals with eating disorders.
    > Bailer *et al.* (2007) compared serotonin activity in women recovering from binge-eating/purging AN with healthy controls. They found significantly higher serotonin activity in the AN group compared to the control group.
- **Dopamine** Studies suggest a role for dopamine in AN. Kaye *et al.* (2005) used a PET scan to compare dopamine activity in the brains of women recovering from AN and healthy women.
    > In the AN group, they found overactivity in dopamine receptors in the basal ganglia, where dopamine plays a part in the interpretation of pleasure. This explains why AN individuals find it difficult to associate pleasure with food.
- **Limbic system dysfunction** Research suggests the neural roots of AN are related to a dysfunction in the limbic system, particularly the subcallosal cingulate and the insular cortex.
    > Lipsman *et al.* (2015) claim that dysfunction in these areas, whose normal functioning is to regulate emotion, can lead to the pathological thoughts and behaviours that are typical of AN.

AO3 Evaluation / Discussion

Problems with genetic explanations...

Despite evidence for a genetic component in AN, the actual heritability of this disorder is still unknown.	Fairburn *et al.* (1999) point out that studies are inconsistent in their estimates of the heritability of AN, giving widely contrasting heritability ranges. Studies also violate the 'equal environments assumption', as MZ twins tend to be treated more similarly than DZ twins.	This invalidates the claim that the greater concordance for AN in MZ compared to DZ twins must be due to greater genetic similarity.

Genetic explanations ignore the role of the media in AN...

Genetic explanations assume environmental factors such as the media do not play a significant role in the development of AN.	Representations of ultra-thin females in the media is a risk factor for eating disorders. However, Bulik (2004) suggests that genetically vulnerable individuals seek out images of thin role models to reinforce their body image.	This is supported by Vaughn and Fouts (2003). Girls whose symptoms' severity increased over a 16-month period also reported significantly greater fashion magazine reading.

Problems with the serotonin explanation...

A problem for serotonin explanations is that SSRIs, which alter levels of available brain serotonin, are ineffective with AN patients.	Ferguson *et al.* (1999) found no difference in outcomes between AN patients taking an SSRI and patients not taking an SSRI. However, Kaye *et al.* (2001) found that SSRIs were effective in preventing relapse in recovering AN patients.	This suggests that malnutrition-related changes in serotonin function negates the action of SSRIs, which only become effective when weight returns to a normal level.

Research support for the dopamine–AN relationship...

Research has provided support for the role of dopamine in AN symptoms.	Food aversion, weight loss and distorted body image cognitions are related to increased activity in dopamine pathways. Increased eye-blink (indicative of higher levels of dopamine activity in the brain) has been found in AN individuals compared to controls (Barbato *et al.*, 2006).	Barbato et al. also found a correlation between blink rate and duration of AN, suggesting the relationship between dopamine activity and AN symptoms develops over time.

 **APPLY**

AO2: An example

SCENARIO Tanya and her friends are discussing what they believe to be the cause of anorexia nervosa. Some of her friends suggest the media's promotion of ultra-thin models as the ideal female form is to blame. Tanya disagrees, suggesting anorexia nervosa has an internal rather than an external cause. She mentions she has read the disorder seems to run in families and thinks the brain functions differently in individuals with the disorder.

With reference to Tanya's claims, discuss biological explanations for anorexia nervosa. **(16 marks)**

ANSWER *An extract showing how you could address the AO2 requirements of this*

question: *By claiming AN runs in families Tanya is referring to research into genetic explanations which have suggested heritability rates between 28 per cent and 74 per cent. Adoption studies further support the involvement of genes in the disorder, as Klump et al. (2009) reported heritability estimates ranging from 59 per cent to 82 per cent for various aspects of disordered eating. However, Tanya should not discount the effect of environmental influences as the actual heritability of the disorder is still unknown. MZ twins are often treated more similarly than DZ twins, which might explain the greater concordance seen in MZ twins compared to DZ twins...*

AO2: One for you to try

Eileen is receiving counselling to overcome her anorexia nervosa. She explains that she gets very anxious about her weight, her studies, and her relationships but when she starves herself she feels less anxious. If she starts eating again she starts to feel anxious again so has to starve herself to feel better.

Using Eileen's story, explain the role of serotonin in anorexia nervosa. (3 marks)

AO2: Research methods

Researchers developed a new measuring instrument for anorexia nervosa, the 'Disordered Eating Inventory'. In order to demonstrate that this inventory has both reliability and validity, the researchers need to assess:

a. Test–retest reliability.

b. Inter-observer reliability.

c. Face validity.

d. Concurrent validity.

Briefly explain how the researchers could assess each of these four types of reliability/validity. (2 marks each)

 How do I answer... shorter (8-mark) essay questions?

Not all essays follow the 12- or 16-mark format. Some have a slightly lower tariff. Of these lower tariff essay questions, the 8-marker is the most common. It does help to know what you are dealing with, however, as they are not always straightforward. The AO1 and AO3 material for these questions is on the opposite page.

Q1: **Outline and evaluate the role of genetic explanations for anorexia nervosa. (8 marks)**

Although you might believe that this question would be worth 4 marks for AO1 and 4 for AO3, this is actually half of a 16-mark essay question, so there is a similar split of marks, i.e. 3 marks for AO1 and 5 marks for AO3 (instead of the 6- and 10-mark split for a 16-mark question). So, you would be aiming for 75–90 words of AO1 and about 125–150 words of AO3. This would mean the first four AO1 points for genetic explanations and the **two** AO3 points for genetic explanations.

Q2: **Charlotte's mother is worried about her. Charlotte's older sister has suffered from an eating disorder for years, and so her mother is always on the lookout for any signs of her other two daughters having the same problem. She has noticed a change in Charlotte since she started at university. She has lost a lot of weight, which her mother puts down to a student diet, but when she comes home, she has very little interest in food, even those foods that she had previously found so enjoyable.**

Outline and evaluate the role of neural explanations for anorexia nervosa. Make reference to Charlotte in your answer. (8 marks)

This question includes a scenario that is referred back to in the question. This is an indication that there is an additional AO2 requirement in the question. AO2 marks tend to be 'stolen' from the AO3 allocation, so this question would be 3 marks of AO1 (first three points), 3 marks of AO3 (one complete AO3 point) *and* 2 marks' worth of AO2. The Charlotte scenario could be explained in terms of overactivity in dopamine receptors in the basal ganglia. Dopamine plays a part in the interpretation of pleasure, which might explain why Charlotte finds it difficult to associate pleasure with food.

REVIEW

You need to be able to answer questions with different mark allocations concisely while using enough detail to describe these two biological explanations clearly. Practise answering 3-, 4- and 6-mark AO1 questions on genetic explanations and the same for neural explanations of anorexia nervosa. You should spend about a minute and a quarter per mark, so for a 3-mark question you have just under 4 minutes, for a 4-mark question you have 5 minutes and for a 6-mark question you have 10 minutes. Make sure you allow time to plan logical answers. You could use a timer to make sure you keep to time.

Family systems theory and anorexia nervosa

AO1 Description

Family systems theory and the 'psychosomatic family'

- **Family systems theory** claims that individuals cannot be understood in isolation from each other but rather as part of a family.

- The psychosomatic family model states that the prerequisite for the development of AN is a dysfunctional family occurring alongside a physiological vulnerability in the child (Minuchin *et al.*, 1978).

- **Enmeshment** Enmeshed family members are over-involved with each other and so the individual 'gets lost in the system'. Enmeshment stifles the development of children's skills to deal with social stressors and makes the development of AN more likely.

- **Autonomy** Enmeshed families place constraints on their members because, unlike non-enmeshed families, they are not allowed to become independent and develop age-appropriate autonomy.

- **Control** Overprotectiveness can retard individuals' beliefs regarding the extent to which they are able to control their lives. An adolescent may rebel against this control by refusing to eat.

- **Rigidity** A characteristic of pathological families who, in the face of stress, increase the rigidity of their patterns of behaviour and resist any exploration of alternatives.

- **Lack of conflict resolution** Minuchin believed AN families were in a state of constant but unresolved conflict, with conflicts being abandoned at their most intense level without resolution of the issues that caused them.

An enmeshed family

AO3 Evaluation/Discussion

Support for the concept of enmeshment…

Manzi *et al.* (2006) demonstrated a distinction between family factors that promote positive emotional development and those that stifle it.	Family cohesion was indicative of supportive family interactions, whereas enmeshment was rooted in manipulation and control. Cohesion among family members was linked to psychological well-being among adolescents; enmeshment had the opposite effect.	These findings, in line with Minuchin et al.'s predictions, applied across different cultural groups and demonstrate the universality of this explanation.

Problems with the psychosomatic family model…

Research testing the predictions of the psychosomatic family model has produced generally disappointing and inconsistent findings.	For example, Kog and Vandereycken (1989) failed to find the characteristics predicted by the psychosomatic family model in families of individuals with AN.	It remains unclear if such characteristics, if they do exist, are present prior to the onset of AN, or whether they are part of the family's response to having a family member with the disorder.

Inconclusive support from family-based therapy…

Although family dysfunction is only one potential cause of AN, the success of family therapies has shown that families are a key part of the recovery process.	For example, Carr (2009) concluded that there is compelling evidence for the effectiveness of family interventions for adolescent AN.	However, while there is some evidence that family therapy produces changes in family functioning, these are not necessarily the changes predicted by the psychosomatic family model (le Grange and Eisler, 2009).

Gender bias in family systems theory…

Gremillion (2003) claims there is a gender bias in family systems theory because it focuses almost exclusively on the mother–daughter relationship.	Enmeshment is nearly always seen as maternal in origin. As a result, therapy to reduce enmeshment in families focuses on reforming 'dysfunctional' mothers rather than acknowledging the role played by fathers.	However, fathers also contribute to the enmeshment process. Their tendency to demand action and change from the individual is often overlooked in the development of AN symptoms.

APPLY

AO2: An example

SCENARIO When analysing transcripts of AN patients discussing their home life, Morgan noticed that a number of individuals mentioned intense family interactions, a lack of freedom and overprotective parents.

How might family systems theory interpret these findings? **(6 marks)**

ANSWER *The AN patients' comments could be seen as evidence of the psychosomatic family. One characteristic of this family type is enmeshment. As mentioned in the transcripts that Morgan is analysing, enmeshed families show an extreme form of proximity and intense family interactions. This over-involvement stifles children's development in terms of their ability to deal with common stressors. The AN patients also report a lack of freedom within their families, which further suggests they are living in a psychosomatic family as the family is resisting making the necessary changes to allow the adolescent a sense of autonomy. Finally, the overprotectiveness of the parents would reduce the individual's sense of control over their own life, which may in turn lead them to rebel by refusing to eat.*

AO2: One for you to try

Demelza has anorexia. Her family are extremely close and her mother insists on knowing everything about her children and has even been known to read their diaries. Whenever Demelza has a problem at school, her mum will often turn up at the school to complain, without consulting Demelza first. Furthermore, her father is very protective towards her and her sisters. He insists on dropping them off and picking them up whenever they go out with their friends and will often call multiple times to check that they're okay.

Using your knowledge of family systems theory, explain two factors that might have contributed to Demelza's AN. (4 marks)

AO2: Research methods

A psychologist investigated the relationship between enmeshment, autonomy and control with AN. They decided to conduct interviews with patients experiencing AN and their immediate family members in their own homes.

Identify two ethical issues the researcher would need to consider in this research, and suggest how the researcher could deal with each of these ethical issues. (4 marks)

How do I answer... essay questions with an AO2 component?

This type of question has three distinct components, an AO1 descriptive component, an AO3 evaluative component and an AO2 application component. Such questions are essentially the same as a straightforward essay (see p.125) *but*, for a 16-mark question with an AO2 component, 4 of the marks available are used to assess your ability to explain the scenario outlined in the question using the material you are discussing. These marks are always taken from the AO3 allocation, so there are still 6 marks for AO1, but now the AO3 component drops from 10 marks to 6 marks with the remaining 4 marks for AO2.

Let's look at an example of this type of question.

> Narin is a vulnerable adolescent whose family life is characterised by a great deal of stress and tension. Her parents seem to interfere in every part of her life. They monitor her use of social media and tell her who is and who is not suitable to be a contact. They drive her to college every day and pick her up after classes so she never gets the chance to build social relationships with her friends. Even her brothers and sisters have an opinion on every part of her life. She just wishes they would all leave her to make her own decisions and find her own way in life.
>
> Outline and evaluate the family systems theory explanation of anorexia nervosa and explain why Narin is at risk of developing anorexia. **(16 marks)**

For 4 marks' worth of AO2, you should write approximately 100–120 words explaining the scenario (in this case Narin's risk of developing AN) using the psychological material on this spread. In the scenario above, there are references to *enmeshment* (her parents and siblings being over-involved in her life), *autonomy* (she is unable to develop age-appropriate autonomy because her parents drive her everywhere) and *control* (her parents control who she communicates with via social media). First and foremost this is an essay on the family systems theory explanation of AN, but you should not ignore the AO2 content, which is not as difficult as you might think!

REVIEW

Knowing what we mean by 'enmeshment', 'autonomy' and 'control' and being able to describe how these impact on the development of anorexia nervosa is vital for your understanding of this topic. There are a few things that you can do to help you with this.

1. Try explaining each of these to someone else (or even the dog, cat or teddy bear who won't be critical or snigger while you are doing it!).

2. Go back and read your notes again and then explain each in even more detail until you think Rover, Fang or Teddy would (had they *really* been listening) have a good understanding of both processes.

3. Try writing (and answering) a few of your own exam questions on this topic to consolidate this understanding.

Social learning theory and anorexia nervosa

RECAP

AOI Description

- **Social learning theory** claims that people learn by observing the attitudes and behaviours of role models, and observing the outcomes of those behaviours (Bandura, 1977).

- **Modelling** Models may be parents or peers, or someone in the media. They provide examples of attitudes to food that can be imitated.

- **Reinforcement** Positive reinforcement from others makes the individual feel good and makes them want to continue losing weight. They may also witness others being reinforced for their thinness (vicarious reinforcement).

- **Maternal role models** Research has highlighted the mother–daughter relationship, e.g. studies show similarities between mothers' and daughters' restraint and dieting behaviours (Hill *et al.*, 1990).

- **Peer influences** Adolescents are particularly susceptible to peer influence. Dieting among friends was related to unhealthy weight control behaviours (Eisenberg *et al.*, 2005).

  > A specific mechanism of peer influence is teasing. Jones and Crawford (2006) found that overweight girls and underweight boys were most likely to be teased by their peers.

- **Media influences** The portrayal of thin models in the media is a significant contributory factor in body image concerns and the drive for thinness among Western adolescent girls.

  > The media do not influence everyone in the same way, e.g. individuals with low self-esteem are more likely to compare themselves to idealised images portrayed in the media (Jones and Buckingham, 2005).

AO3 Evaluation / Discussion

Maternal influence is more complex than social learning...

Research on the role of mothers as models for eating disorders for their daughters has not produced consistent results.	Pike and Rodin (1991) found no evidence for daughters imitating the weight concern of their parents. Ogden and Steward (2000) found no association between mothers and daughters in terms of their restrained eating or body dissatisfaction.	Ogden and Steward suggest that it may be the nature of the mother–daughter relationship that is important, particularly the degree to which they are enmeshed.

Research support for peer influences...

The claim that adolescent girls are influenced by the perceived weight of their peers is supported by research.	Costa-Font and Jofre-Bonet (2013) found that individuals who had peers with a larger BMI had a lower likelihood of subsequently developing an eating disorder such as AN.	This suggests that having peers with average or higher than average BMI 'protects' individuals from AN, whereas having peers with a lower than average BMI makes the development of AN more likely.

Research support for media influences...

Evidence for the role of the media in shaping perceptions of body image comes from studies of societies where television has been introduced.	Eating attitudes and behaviours were studied among Fijian girls following the introduction of television to Fiji (Becker *et al.*, 2002). After exposure to TV the girls stated a desire to lose weight to become more like Western television characters.	This suggests that the media can be a powerful influence in the development of eating disorders.

Not all forms of media have the same effects...

Some studies have found that reading magazines is a more consistent predictor of the development of eating disorders than television viewing.	Harrison and Cantor (1997) found no association between television exposure and eating disorders, but did find a significant association between reading fitness magazines and attitudes to food and dieting.	This demonstrates social learning because of the relationship between drive for thinness and magazines that provide fitness advice. Television's influence is undermined by advertisements promoting foods high in fat and sugar.

APPLY

AO2: An example

SCENARIO Anouchka's mother is very careful about the media her daughter is exposed to. Even though Anouchka is 14 years old, her mother does not let her read fashion magazines and discourages her from watching TV shows with very slim actresses. Although her mother follows a strict diet, she tries not to discuss her eating habits or share her body dissatisfaction with Anouchka.

Outline and evaluate the social learning theory explanation of anorexia nervosa. Make reference to Anouchka's mother in your answer. **(16 marks)**

ANSWER **An extract showing how you could address the AO2 requirements of this question:** *Anouchka's mother believes the celebrities and fashion models presented in the media may act as a role model to encourage Anouchka to try to lose weight to receive the same praise and status associated with thinness. Research by Harrison and Cantor found no association between TV exposure and eating disorders but did find reading of fashion magazines was linked to a preference for lower weight. This suggests Anouchka's mother should continue to limit her daughter's exposure to such magazines. Her mother also realises she can be a role model for her daughter and so tries to avoid expressing her own weight concerns and eating patterns. However, she may not need to worry as much as she does as Ogden and Stewart found it was the degree of enmeshment that was influential rather than the presence of the mother as a role model in the development of eating disorders such as AN...*

AO2: Research methods

A psychologist examined the influence of the media before the introduction of the television on a remote island (1995) and three years after (1998). The results can be found in the table below.

Table 1: The mean BMI score for males and females, before the introduction of the TV (1995) and after (1998).

	1995		1998	
	Females	**Males**	**Females**	**Males**
Mean BMI	22.5	23.8	19.8	22.2
Standard Deviation	2.2	1.4	4.8	5.6

a. **What do the results suggest about the influence of the media? (3 marks)**
b. **Why is standard deviation a useful measure for psychologists when carrying out research in areas such as this? (2 marks)**

AO2: One for you to try

Denise is obsessed with fitness magazines and often reads magazines for diet tips and fitness strategies. She has recently started going to the gym seven days a week and often skips meals to ensure that she is controlling her calories. Her boyfriend Fayaz keeps telling her how great she looks and giving her lots of attention. However, her family are concerned that she is developing an eating disorder.

Using your knowledge of social learning, explain why Denise is showing signs of an eating disorder. (4 marks)

How do I answer... evaluation only (AO3) questions?

Evaluation questions come in all sorts of shapes and sizes. Terms like 'evaluate', 'discuss', 'explain', 'criticism', 'strength' and 'limitation' all indicate that AO3 is required. Let's look at some examples. The AO3 material for these questions is on the opposite page.

Q1: Give **one** criticism of the social learning theory explanation of anorexia nervosa. **(2 marks)**

Remembering that 'criticisms' can be either negative or positive (so research support would count as a 'positive' criticism), you could choose any one of the AO3 points as your material for **Q1**. For 2 marks, you could use the lead-in phrase (e.g. 'Not all forms of media have the same effects...'), followed by the material in the first two columns (i.e. the main critical claim and its expansion).

Q2: Explain **one** limitation of the social learning theory explanation of anorexia nervosa. **(3 marks)**

Q2 requires a little more elaboration than **Q1**, but this time you are restricted to something that limits the value of self-disclosure as an explanation of attraction. For example, you might choose to use the second AO3 point ('Research support for peer influences...') with material from all three columns being used to access the 3 marks on offer.

Q3: Evaluate the social learning theory explanation of anorexia nervosa. **(6 marks)**

Take the same approach as for **Q2**, but this time use **two** of the AO3 points. Don't try to use more than two; it would make your treatment of them too superficial.

REVIEW

Simply reading material is not the most effective way of learning it properly. So, using the material on the opposite page, try writing plans for 3-, 4- and 6-mark 'outline' questions on the social learning theory explanation of anorexia nervosa plus plans for 8- and 16-mark essay questions.

Test yourself on the key points of this explanation by covering up your plans and writing them out again. It's useful to have a supply of cheap paper for this, as the more times you practise retrieving the information, the better you will remember it.

Spaced practice is also very effective: come back to the same topic tomorrow and start your revision by seeing how many of the points you can remember before you look at your essay plan.

Cognitive theory and anorexia nervosa

 **RECAP**

AO1 Description

- **Cognitive distortions** Errors in thinking that cause the individual to develop a negative body image, e.g. comparisons with thin models in the media, lead to feelings of self-disgust and an attempt to lose weight.

- **Irrational beliefs** Individuals develop self-defeating habits because of faulty beliefs about themselves and the world around them, e.g. they must be thin for others to like them.

I have to stay thin to be accepted

- **Cognitive behavioural model of AN (Garner and Bemis, 1982)** Anorexia patients have a number of characteristics in common, e.g. they are typically high-achieving perfectionists and full of self-doubt.

  > These characteristics, coupled with exposure to cultural ideals of thinness, lead them to form ideas about the importance of body weight, causing them to develop the irrational belief that losing weight will reduce their distress.

  > Distorted thinking and interpretation of events convinces them that weight and thinness is the sole referent for judging self-worth and that complete control over these is desirable.

- **The transdiagnostic model (Fairburn et al., 2003)** The underlying cause of all eating disorders is the same set of cognitive distortions, i.e. the overestimation of body weight, appearance and an emphasis on self-control.

  > The experience of being able to control eating, compared to the relative failure they may have in controlling other areas of their lives, makes the control of eating particularly important.

  > An enhanced sense of self-control leads to increased self-esteem. Any weight gain leads to increased efforts to restrict food even more to regain self-control and self-esteem.

AO3 Evaluation/Discussion

Research support for the role of cognitive factors in AN...

Lang et al. (2015) provided research support for the role of cognitive factors in anorexia nervosa.	They compared performance of children and adolescents diagnosed with AN with healthy control participants on neuropsychological measures. Compared to the controls, AN individuals displayed a more inflexible and inefficient cognitive processing style.	*As inefficient cognitive processing in the AN group was independent of any clinical or demographic factors, this suggests it represents an underlying characteristic of AN.*

CBT-E (cognitive behavioural therapy for eating disorders): Support from the success of therapy...

Support for cognitive factors in AN comes from the success of cognitive behavioural therapies used in its treatment.	Fairburn et al. (2015) compared CBT-E with interpersonal psychotherapy (IPT), a treatment with no cognitive element. At the end of 20 weeks of treatment, two thirds of CBT-E participants met the criteria for remission compared with one third of IPT participants.	*The findings indicate that CBT-E is an effective treatment and that cognitive issues are a root cause of AN.*

Methodological limitations of cognitive theories of AN...

Viken et al. (2002) claim that a limitation of cognitive theories of AN is the over-reliance on self-reports of cognitive processing.	Self-reported cognitions tend to be assessed retrospectively. However, it is unlikely that individuals can accurately represent cognitions they have experienced at a previous point in time.	*This suggests that our understanding of the cognitive distortions thought to occur in AN are limited because of the problems associated with the methods used to access them.*

Limitations of the cognitive approach...

Cooper (1997) claims that cognitive models of AN are largely the result of clinical observation rather than being based on empirical research.	She points out that there has been comparatively little research carried out that tests the hypotheses derived from cognitive models of anorexia.	*As a result, claims Cooper, the development of a cognitive approach to anorexia nervosa has lagged behind the development of cognitive theory in other disorders, such as depression and anxiety disorders.*

APPLY

AO2: An example

SCENARIO Fran has been diagnosed as suffering from anorexia nervosa. Even when looking at recent photos of her thin frame, Fran continues to see herself as overweight and constantly compares herself to catwalk models. Despite friends trying to keep in contact, she claims they organise social activities without her because they find her huge body embarrassing to be around.

Distinguish between the distortions and irrational beliefs Fran is experiencing. **(4 marks)**

ANSWER *Fran holds irrational beliefs about herself and the world around her in that she feels her peers are leaving her out because of the way she looks. These beliefs are not based on fact and are unrealistic, given that her friends are trying to keep in contact with her. Fran is also showing distorted thinking, leading her to develop a negative body image. By comparing herself to fashion models she is experiencing self-disgust which drives her desire to lose weight.*

AO2: Research methods

A psychologist used the 'Food Stroop' test to examine cognitive distortions. The results are shown in Table 1.

Table 1: The time taken to state food and non-food words on a 'Food Stroop' test for 10 patients with AN.

	Time taken for food-related words	Time taken for non-food words
1	3	1
2	3.2	1.2
3	4.1	1.8
4	2.9	1.9
5	2.8	1.5
6	3.6	2.5
7	3.8	1.6
8	2.7	1.7
9	2.5	1.3
10	4	2
Mean		

1. **Calculate the mean score for both conditions. (4 marks)**
2. **What can the psychologist conclude from the results? (3 marks)**

AO2: One for you to try

Asha is doing her work experience at *Fashion Diva* magazine. She is in awe of all the models that come in to be photographed. They are all so tall and so slim, and everybody makes such a fuss of them. Asha feels quite depressed at the end of each day and is now convinced that the reason she doesn't have that many friends is that she is too fat. Her mum always calls her 'cuddly' but now she feels she really means 'fat'. She decides to go on a crash diet because if she can get slim like the models then she will be popular like them.

Using your knowledge of the cognitive theory explanation of anorexia nervosa, explain why Asha thinks the way she does, and why this makes her more vulnerable to developing an eating disorder such as anorexia. (4 marks)

How do I answer... application (AO2) questions?

Let's look again at the scenario of Asha in **AO2: One for you to try** above.

One way of answering questions such as this is to remember the 'say one thing for 1 mark' and 'say four things for 4 marks' strategy.

1. **Find a bit of appropriate psychology,** e.g. 'Cognitive distortions cause an individual to develop a negative body image, e.g. comparisons with thin models in the media lead to feelings of self-disgust and an attempt to lose weight.'

2. **Use this to explain some aspect of the scenario,** e.g. 'Asha has started comparing herself to the slim models she sees at the magazine and becomes depressed that she is not slim like them.'

3. **Find a second bit of psychology,** e.g. 'Individuals develop self-defeating habits because of faulty beliefs about themselves and the world around them, e.g. they must be thin for others to like them.'

4. **Use this to explain the scenario,** e.g. 'Asha believes that if she loses weight as a result of her crash diet and is no longer "fat" then she will be popular like the slim models at the magazine.'

REVIEW

Craik and Lockhart (1972) proposed a theory of memory called the 'levels of processing model'. This model claimed that the more that information is elaborated, the more likely we will be able to access that information later on. There are many different ways of elaborating material, so let's try one.

Take a large sheet of paper (A3 works well here) and construct a mind-map so that all your material on the cognitive theory explanation of anorexia nervosa is linked together in a wonderfully visual way. This serves several purposes: (1) It *elaborates* the material, making it more memorable; (2) The act of constructing the mind-map counts as *revision*, again making it more likely you can recall it in an exam; (3) You have a *visual* image of the material, which, for many people, is a much easier way of remembering complex material.

*Tip: There is a wealth of useful revision videos on the Internet – take a look for some on mind-map construction.

Biological explanations for obesity

AO1 Description

- **Genetics** A meta-analysis of twin studies involving 75,000 individuals (Maes *et al.*, 1997) found heritability estimates for BMI of 74 per cent in MZ twins and 32 per cent in DZ twins.
  > Even when MZ twins are reared apart (and experience dissimilar environmental influences), they are more alike in terms of their BMI than are DZ twins reared together (Stunkard *et al.*, 1990).

- **Adoption studies** Researchers have studied individuals who have been adopted as infants and raised by biologically unrelated families. Adoption studies allow researchers to look separately at the influence of biological parents (genetics) and adoptive parents (environment).
  > Stunkard *et al.* (1986) found a strong relationship between the weight category of adopted individuals and that of their biological parents but no significant relationship with their adoptive parents' weight category.

- **Neural explanations** The hypothalamus plays a key role in regulating metabolism and energy expenditure. One particular part of the hypothalamus, the arcuate nucleus, plays a key role in appetite and obesity.
  > The arcuate nucleus monitors circulating sugar levels in the blood, and acts when energy levels are low, producing the desire to eat. Any malfunction with this area can lead to overeating and obesity.
  > Leptin, a hormone secreted by fat cells, inhibits food intake by acting on receptors in the appetite control centres in the brain. Disruption of leptin signalling in the hypothalamus results in obesity (Bates and Myers, 2003).

AO3 Evaluation / Discussion

The expression of genetic influences varies with age...

Research suggests that the genetic contribution to BMI is not stable across a person's lifetime.	A meta-analysis of 88 studies by Elks *et al.* (2012) found that heritability estimates varied according to the age group of individuals studied. It was highest during childhood and decreased during adulthood.	This is most probably due to the greater gene expression during childhood, compared to adulthood, by which time individuals have adopted individual dietary and exercise habits.

The problem of time and geography...

Statistics show a sharp increase in obesity rates in the UK over the last 20 years, although the nature of the gene pool has remained constant over the same period.	In China, obesity rates are below 5 per cent in the countryside, but higher than 20 per cent in cities. Such differences are likely to be due to the availability of fast food in urban areas rather than genetic factors.	The rapid increase in obesity rates in urban areas poses problems for genetic explanations, as the gene pool changes at a much slower rate.

Research support for the leptin–obesity relationship...

Some humans do not produce leptin, or produce it in very low levels, which predisposes them to obesity.	Gibson *et al.* (2004) reported on a child from Pakistan who suffered from severe obesity. After four years of treatment with leptin injections, the child experienced dramatically beneficial effects on appetite, metabolism and weight.	This study supports the role of leptin in regulating appetite and its deficiency as a risk factor in obesity.

Advantages of biological explanations...

Biological explanations offer explanations of obesity that are perceived as being out of the individual's control and are therefore less stigmatising.	This is in sharp contrast to many psychological explanations of obesity that highlight the personal failing of the individual (e.g. overeating or lack of exercise).	A consequence of recognising biological influences in obesity is that it offers individuals some hope of dealing with their disorder, e.g. through treatments based on remedial leptin injections.

⚙ APPLY

AO2: An example

SCENARIO Collette and her friends are talking about a recent news story where a family of obese people had been interviewed about the impact their weight had on their physical and mental health. Collette's friends said the parents were responsible as they had developed poor eating habits over a period of time and passed these onto their children. Collette disagreed, suggesting the weight gain was beyond the control of the family members.

Discuss biological explanations for obesity. **(16 marks)**

ANSWER **An extract showing how you could address the AO2 requirements of this question:** *By saying the weight gain was 'beyond the family's control', Collette may have been referring to genetic and neural causes of obesity. As a number of family members were obese, their situation may be a result of genetic inheritance predisposing the family to a higher BMI. For example, twin studies have reported heritability rates ranging from 40 per cent to 74 per cent. However, research also suggests genetic influence varies with age. Elks et al. (2012) found heritability figures were highest during childhood, with the decrease in adulthood being linked to diet and exercise. This means Collette's friends may have identified a contributing factor in the development of obesity when they mention the adults of the family may have poor eating habits...*

AO2: Research methods ✏

Researchers investigating leptin treatment for obesity decided to carry out a replication of an earlier study. They recruited a sample of 200 men and women, classified as clinically obese, through a newspaper advert. These were split into an experimental group, who received the drug under test, and a control group, who received a placebo. Participants were not aware whether they were receiving the drug or the placebo. After six months, they were assessed to see how much weight they had lost.

a. **Why is replication of research an important feature of science? (2 marks)**

b. **What is the purpose of a control group in studies such as this? (2 marks)**

c. **Identify one possible problem with the design of this study and explain how this problem could be overcome. (3 marks)**

d. **Identify one potential ethical issue in this study and explain how this issue might be dealt with. (3 marks)**

AO2: One for you to try ✏

Daniel has always had a problem with his weight. His mum, dad and sister are also overweight and he has given up trying to lose weight because he believes that his weight problem is 'not his fault'.

Using research, outline two biological explanations that could support Daniel's claim that his weight problem is not his fault. (4 marks)

🐾 How do I answer... description and evaluation (AO1 + AO3) questions?

1 Step 1 To answer mixed AO1 + AO3 questions, you need to recognise that this is what you are being asked to do! Having two different command words, e.g. 'outline' (an AO1 term) 'and evaluate' (an AO3 term) is usually a good clue.

2 Step 2 is planning how much you should write for each. In mixed AO1 + AO3 questions up to 6 marks, the division is half and half (it is different with mark totals higher than this as we will see on p.125).

3 Step 3 Decide *what* to write. If you have followed the advice in the previous spreads, this should be easy to work out. Let's look at some examples. The AO1 and AO3 material for these questions is on the opposite page.

Q1: Briefly explain genetic explanations of obesity. **(4 marks)**

Use the first and third AO1 points, together with an abridged version of the first AO3 point.

Q2: Outline and evaluate neural explanations of obesity. **(6 marks)**

The AO1 requirement would be met by the three AO1 points for 'neural explanations'. They would give a good 3-mark overview as required by the question. For the AO3 content you might use *either* the third AO3 point or abridged versions of the third and fourth AO3 points.

Q3: Outline and evaluate findings from research into genetic explanations of obesity. **(6 marks)**

We have included this type of question to show how sometimes you need to be creative in the material you use in response to a question. Bearing in mind that research findings can be used as AO1 or as an explanation of research support, we can do a bit of detective work to find 3 marks' worth that we can use as AO1. The Elks *et al.* (2012) findings in the first AO3 point would be suitable for this purpose. The fact that these appear in our AO3 section is irrelevant because we are only using the second column, which is a statement of the research finding.

🔄 REVIEW

As well as AO1 + AO3 questions, you could be asked straightforward AO1 questions, straightforward AO3 questions and all the other types of question covered in this chapter.

- Try writing a plan for 4- and 6-mark 'outline' questions on biological explanations for obesity.

- Plan an 8- and a 16-mark essay on biological explanations for obesity.

Test yourself on the key points by covering up your plan and writing it out again. It's useful to have a supply of cheap paper for this as the more times you practise retrieving the information, the better you will remember it.

Spaced practice is also very effective: come back to the same topic tomorrow and start your revision by seeing how many of the points you can remember before you look at your essay plan.

Psychological explanations for obesity

 **RECAP**

A01 Description

- **Restraint theory** suggests that attempting not to eat increases the probability of overeating. Rather than restraint leading to weight loss, it leads to weight gain and increases the risk of becoming obese (Herman and Mack, 1975).
  - > **Rigid restraint** The all-or-nothing approach to dieting is positively associated with amount of body fat and BMI. Flexible restraint (fattening foods eaten in limited quantities without guilt) is negatively associated with these measures of obesity (Provencher *et al.*, 2003).
- **The boundary model** Food intake is regulated along a continuum. When energy levels are low, we experience hunger, giving rise to eating. At the other extreme, we experience feelings of fullness, and stop eating. In between these points (the 'zone of biological indifference'), food intake is determined by social factors (Herman and Polivy, 1984).
  - > Restrained eaters (dieters) have a larger zone of biological indifference, with a lower threshold for hunger and a higher threshold for satiation. They are less sensitive to feelings of hunger and feelings of fullness, and so are more likely to overeat.

- **Disinhibition** can occur when the normal inhibitions that prevent us from eating too much are removed, and so is strongly associated with adult weight gain and BMI.
  - > **Habitual disinhibition** The tendency to overeat in response to daily life circumstances has been shown to be the most important correlate of weight gain and obesity because of the high number of daily overeating opportunities people face in the typical Western food environment (Hays and Roberts, 2008).

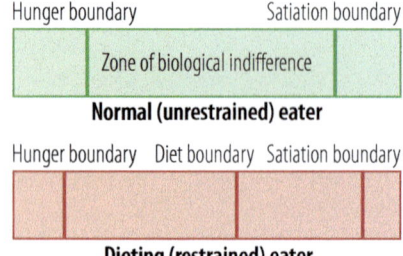

The boundary model

A03 Evaluation/Discussion

Support for restraint theory…

Support for the claim that dietary restraint can lead to overeating comes from Wardle and Beales (1988).

They randomly assigned 27 obese women to either a diet group (focusing on restrained eating patterns), an exercise group or a non-treatment group. After six weeks, food intake was assessed under stressful conditions.

As predicted by restraint theory, at both assessment sessions women in the diet condition ate more than women in the exercise and non-treatment groups.

A challenge to restraint theory…

Tomiyama *et al.* (2009) argued that most research relating to restraint theory has been restricted to the laboratory.

Such research typically shows that restrained eaters overeat after they violate their diet. Tomiyama *et al.* challenged this view of restraint, showing in their study that, outside of this artificial setting, restrained eaters were able to control their eating.

These findings appear to dispel the belief that diet violations lead to overeating in everyday life.

The 'what the hell' effect: Motivational collapse or rebellious reaction?…

Herman and Polivy describe the 'what the hell' effect, when a person gives in to overpowering urges to eat if they go past their self-imposed diet boundary.

However, Ogden and Wardle (1991) argue that rather than passively giving in to a desire to eat, the individual may actively decide to overeat as a form of rebellion against their self-imposed food restrictions.

This view is supported by Loro and Orleans (1981), who found that obese binge eaters frequently reported bingeing as a way of 'unleashing resentment' against their diet.

Disinhibition may not be important in all groups…

Most research on disinhibition is restricted to white women, which means that conclusions about men or other racial groups cannot be made.

Atlas *et al.* (2002) found restraint and disinhibition scores to be significantly lower in African American students compared to white students. Bellisle *et al.* (2004) found that restraint and disinhibition scores were lower in men compared to women.

This suggests that disinhibition might be a more important influence in adult weight gain in some groups compared to others.

APPLY

AO2: An example

SCENARIO Chad and his GP are discussing a weight loss plan to help Chad reduce his waist circumference and BMI as his current measurements suggest he is obese. Chad explains he finds it difficult to follow a strict diet plan as in times of stress or when he is feeling down he turns to food for comfort. He says as soon as he eats one 'banned food' he just thinks 'what the hell' and eats more, telling himself he will restart the diet tomorrow.

Briefly outline two psychological explanations for obesity. Make reference to Chad's experience in your answer. **(6 marks)**

ANSWER *Chad is finding the diet plan hard to maintain, which can be explained by restraint theory. This suggests that denial of food can actually lead to overeating. A number of studies (e.g. Herman and Mack, 1975) have found that following an all-or-nothing (strict diet plan) regime is positively associated with increased waist circumference and BMI. Placing a cognitive boundary (for example, Chad talks about 'banned foods') can lead to the 'what the hell effect' as once Chad has broken his self-imposed boundary he overeats to the point of satiation. This overeating is often higher than in unrestrained eaters as dieters have a higher threshold for fullness. Chad also seems to be engaging in emotional disinhibition as he mentions he tends to eat in times of stress or when he is feeling down. In these circumstances, Chad is less responsive to feelings of satiation and so is more likely to overeat.*

AO2: Research methods

Researchers investigated whether individuals on a restrained eating diet lost more weight than individuals on a physical exercise regime. Participants were matched in terms of gender, age and BMI and randomly allocated to either the restrained eating group or the exercise group. After three months, participants returned to the lab and again had their BMI measured. Researchers calculated the amount by which BMI had decreased and used a statistical test to analyse whether there was a difference between the two groups.

a. What type of experimental design did the researchers use in this study? (1 mark)

b. Briefly explain one strength and one limitation of this type of design. (4 marks)

c. Identify an appropriate statistical test that the researchers could use and explain your reasons for picking this test. (3 marks)

AO2: One for you to try

Helen went to the cinema to watch *Fantastic Beasts: The Crimes of Grindelwald*. Although she is trying to be healthy and resist the urge to eat, she still spent over £5 on pick-and-mix sweets, which weighed over 400g! She tells herself that she will save some for when she gets home. However, while watching the film she consumes the entire bag.

Using your knowledge of the boundary model, explain why Helen ate the entire bag of sweets. (4 marks)

How do I answer... research methods questions?

Questions requiring research methods knowledge can appear in any section of any paper in the AS or A Level exams. They could include any aspect of research methods, data analysis or ethical issues. Doing well in research methods questions is as much a case of thinking clearly and using common sense as it is regurgitating knowledge. Let's look at the **AO2: Research methods** questions on this page.

a. You are asked to identify the experimental design used in the study. This is a straightforward identification so no detail other than the name is necessary. The word 'matched' should give you a clue!

b. These questions will sometime be set within the context provided by the scenario, but in this case, it is a straightforward 'strength and limitation' question. So, identify a strength and say why that is a strength and do the same for a limitation.

c. There is a very useful test choice chart on p.24 of the Year 2 Student Book. Practise using this chart until it becomes second nature. As this is 'matched pairs' design and the researchers are looking for a 'difference' between the two groups, either a 'related *t*-test' or a 'Wilcoxon test' would be appropriate.

REVIEW

How much should you write? You should practise writing 2-, 3- and 4-mark descriptions of restraint theory, the boundary model and disinhibition in the development of obesity. Here is what you should aim for:

- 2 marks: 50 words.
- 3 marks: 75 words.
- 4 marks: 100 words.

There is some work to be done here to get 100 words of description for each of these explanations. Remember that you can extract outlines of research studies from the AO3 points to use to extend your description. For example, to push your description of restraint theory up to 4 marks' worth you could add a brief description of the Wardle and Beales (1988) study.

Explanations for the success and failure of dieting

A01 Description

- **A theory of hedonic eating** Stroebe (2008) suggests that restrained (i.e. dieting) eaters' problems in maintaining their diets might begin with the fact that they are more sensitive to the hedonic (i.e. pleasurable) properties of food. As a result, restrained eaters' cognitive processes will be geared towards pursuing this goal, and any conflicting goals (i.e. maintaining their diet) will be inhibited.

  > **Attention allocation** (Mischel and Ayduk, 2004) Exposure to attractive food triggers pleasurable thoughts, which result in selective attention to these items and the inhibition of thoughts of dieting.

- **The role of denial** Research in cognitive psychology has shown that attempting to suppress or deny a thought frequently has the opposite effect, making it even more prominent.

- **The theory of ironic processes of mental control** Attempts to suppress thoughts of foods such as pizza and chocolate only serve to increase the dieter's preoccupation with the very foods they are trying to deny themselves. As soon as a food is denied, therefore, it becomes more attractive. (Wegner, 1994).

- **Detail – the key to a successful diet** Research by Redden (2008) suggests that the secret of successful dieting lies in the attention we pay to what is being eaten. People usually like experiences (such as sticking to a strict diet) less as they repeat them. To overcome this, dieters should focus on the specific details of a meal (e.g. tomato, apple, etc.) to avoid getting bored and be able to maintain their diet.

  > **The jelly beans experiment** To test this idea, Redden gave 135 people 22 jelly beans each, one at a time. As each bean was dispensed, information about it was flashed onto a computer screen. One group saw general information (e.g. 'bean number 7'), whereas the other group saw specific flavour details (e.g. 'cherry flavour number 7'). Participants got bored with eating beans faster if they only saw the general information, and enjoyed the task more if they saw the specific flavour details. This shows that details of the food consumed cuts down on any repetitive feeling, which in turn would make sticking to a diet more likely.

A03 Evaluation / Discussion

Research support for ironic processes of mental control…

Soetens *et al.* (2006) provided experimental support for this theory.

A restrained group of dieters (i.e. who tried to eat less but who would often overeat) used more thought suppression related to food than unrestrained dieters, and also showed a rebound effect (i.e. thought more about food) afterwards.

However, Wegner (1994) admits that, generally, the 'ironic effects' observed in research are not particularly huge. As experimental effects go, they are detectable but far from overwhelming.

Support for the hedonic theory…

Support for the claim that restrained eaters are more likely to focus on the pleasurable aspects of food comes from studies of physiological reactions to food.

Brunstrom *et al.* (2004) tested salivary reactivity when participants were in close proximity to hot pizza. Participants who were dieting (i.e. restrained eaters) showed a greater salivary response to the pizza than participants who were not dieting (i.e. unrestrained eaters).

This difference between restrained and unrestrained eaters in their perception of food supports the hedonic theory of dieting.

Real-world application: Anti-dieting programmes…

Concerns about the ineffectiveness of many diets has led to the development of programmes aimed at replacing dieting with conventional healthy eating.

These emphasise regulation by hunger and satiety signals and the prevention of inappropriate attitudes to food. A meta-analysis of anti-dieting programmes (Higgins and Gray, 1999) found that participation in these programmes led to improvements in eating behaviour and psychological well-being.

This suggests that eating only when hungry and stopping when satiated is more likely to be successful than trying to restrict food intake.

Limitations of anecdotal evidence…

Many studies of dieting success or failure rely on the personal accounts of individuals, which are used to justify claims concerning particular dieting strategies.

However, memory is not 100 per cent accurate, nor is assessment of the success or failure of dieting entirely objective, which creates problems for the reliability of the evidence provided by these personal accounts.

An additional problem is that causal connections between a particular approach to dieting and weight loss are made without the control over extraneous variables that is possible with randomised controlled trials.

APPLY

AO2: An example

SCENARIO Demi always seems to be on a diet but never seems to lose much weight. At the start of each diet she makes a list of 'forbidden foods' and tries her best to avoid temptation. However, it's not long before she gets bored and finds herself longing for sweet, sticky cakes and the rich, cheesy taste of hot pizza.

Outline and evaluate one or more explanations for the success and/or failure of dieting. **(16 marks)**

ANSWER **An extract showing how you could address the AO2 requirements of this question:** *Demi may be more sensitive to the pleasurable properties of food like pizza and cake which trigger her desire to eat these foods. The theory of hedonic eating suggests that eating enjoyment is incompatible with eating control, meaning Demi's increasing thoughts of the pleasure of eating will reduce the likelihood of maintaining her diet. Brunstrom et al. (2004) support this explanation of diet failure as they found that, when presented with a hot pizza, female restrained eaters showed a greater salivary response than unrestrained eaters. Creating a list of 'forbidden foods' may result in Demi thinking more about these foods, which may increase the likelihood of consuming them. Soetens et al. (2006) found that dieters who often overate (disinhibition restrained eaters) used more thought suppression than restrained eaters with low levels of disinhibition, and also more thought suppression than unrestrained eaters...*

AO2: One for you to try

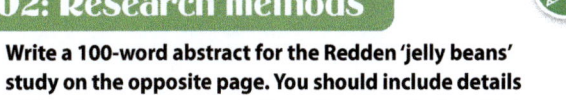

Jasmine is becoming increasingly frustrated with her weight. She has tried several diets that she has found in women's magazines and each has failed within two weeks.

Using your knowledge of the success and failure of dieting, explain why Jasmine's diets fail and provide a strategy that Jasmine could use to be more successful. (4 marks)

AO2: Research methods

a. **Write a 100-word abstract for the Redden 'jelly beans' study on the opposite page. You should include details of the aim, procedure, results and any conclusions that might be drawn from this study. (4 marks)**

b. **Write an appropriate reference for this study. The author of the study was Joseph P. Redden, and the title was 'Reducing Satiation: The Role of Categorization Level.' It was published in 2008 on pages 624–634 in Issue 5 of Volume 34 of the *Journal of Consumer Research*. (2 marks)**

How do I answer... longer (16-mark) questions?

For a 16-mark question on the success and failure of dieting, the command words might require you to 'outline (or describe) and evaluate'. Alternatively, a question might ask you to 'discuss' explanations for the success and failure of dieting. Whilst all of these instructions indicate that you should include both AO1 *and* AO3 in your answer, the 'discuss' command word requires you to go a little further than just writing about strengths and/or limitations. Let's look at these different types of question as they might appear in the context of the interactionist approach. The AO1 and AO3 material for these questions is on the opposite page.

> **Q1:** Outline and evaluate explanations for the success and failure of dieting. **(16 marks)**

The nominal mark division for AO1 (outline) and AO3 (evaluation) is 6 marks for the former and 10 marks for the latter. You could aim to include the six AO1 points to cover the 'outline' component of this question. For the AO3 content, you should include all four of the AO3 points.

> **Q2:** Discuss explanations for the success and failure of dieting. **(16 marks)**

The command word 'discuss' requires AO3 that is a bit more 'discursive', e.g. looking at applications, implications, counter-evidence, etc. We have tried to make some of our AO3 points 'discursive' to accommodate this. For example, the third AO3 point is 'discursive' because it discusses real applications of research evaluating approaches to dieting. Likewise, the fourth point is 'discursive' because it challenges the validity of evidence used to evaluate the success (or failure) of various approaches to dieting.

REVIEW

In this final Review section of this chapter, it is time for some more 'revision accounting'. You should make a table like this with all 10 topics from this chapter on eating behaviour. When you feel you have mastered the AO1 and AO3 components of these and can cope with any of the different types of question that we have covered in the **How do I answer... ?** sections, you will have earned a tick in the 'Got it!' column.

TOPIC	Got it!			Got it!	
	AO1	AO3		AO1	AO3
Evolutionary explanation for food preferences	✓		Social learning theory and anorexia nervosa		
The role of learning in food preference			Cognitive theory and anorexia nervosa		
Neural and hormonal mechanisms			Biological explanations for obesity		
Biological explanations for anorexia nervosa			Psychological explanations for obesity		
Family systems theory and anorexia nervosa			Explanations for the success and failure of dieting		

RECAP

A01 Description

Short- and long-term stress responses

- **Response to short-term (immediate) stress:** the **sympathomedullary pathway (SAM)**
  > The hypothalamus activates the sympathetic branch (S) of the autonomic nervous system (ANS). **Adrenaline** (A) and **noradrenaline** are released by the adrenal medulla (M).
  > Adrenaline and noradrenaline cause physiological responses including increased heart rate and muscle tension. These prepare us to deal with the stressor. (The fight-or-flight response.)
  > When the threat has passed, the parasympathetic branch of the ANS dampens down the stress response and returns the body to its normal resting state.

Response to long-term (ongoing) stress: the hypothalamic pituitary-adrenal system (HPA)

- The hypothalamus (H) activates the pituitary gland (P), stimulating the adrenal cortex (A) to release **cortisol**.
- The hypothalamus uses corticotrophin releasing hormone (CRH) to activate the pituitary gland. The pituitary gland activates the adrenal cortex using adrenocorticotrophic hormone (ACTH).

General adaptation syndrome (GAS)

- The GAS response enables the body to cope with extreme stress, but can lead to stress-related illnesses.
- Selye's (1936) three stages to the GAS response:
  > Alarm reaction – SAM and HPA.
  > Resistance – the body appears to be coping with the stressor's demands. However, as sugars, hormones, and neurotransmitters are depleted, the immune system becomes less effective.
  > Exhaustion – the immune system is suppressed. The adrenal glands may be damaged. Stress-related illnesses and mental impairments may occur.

Issues/Debates
Gender bias

A03 Evaluation / Discussion

Gender differences in the stress response…

Conclusions drawn from earlier research into the stress response may reflect a male bias due to reliance on data from male animals (added complication: fluctuating female hormones).

Stressed female rats release oxytocin. This increases relaxation and inhibits the fight-or-flight response. Taylor *et al.* (2000) argue that 'tend and befriend' evolved as a more adaptive response for women caring for infants.

Such differences mean that the standard description of the SAM and HPA systems is a gender-biased account.

The transactional model of stress…

Richard Lazarus (1999) argued that a physiological account alone is not sufficient to explain how we respond to stressors.

Lazarus found that participants expecting a film to be 'exciting' for the actors showed less physiological activity than those expecting the film to be 'painful'.

Lazarus and Folkman's (1984) transactional model proposes that cognitive appraisal moderates our body's response.

Research support for GAS…

A strength of Selye's model is that it was based on his observations working with human patients and non-human animals.

For example, research shows that both non-human and human bodies produce the same physiological responses to any stressor.

These findings support Selye's 'doctrine of specificity', which says that there is a non-specific response of the body to any demand made on it.

Stress-related illness may not be due to depletion of resources…

Research indicates that 'resources' such as sugars, neurotransmitters, hormones and proteins are not depleted even under conditions of extreme stress.

Sheridan and Radmacher (1992) found that it is more likely to be increases in the activity of hormones, such as cortisol, which lead to stress-related illness.

This shows that Selye's explanation of stress-related illnesses in terms of a depletion of the body's 'resources' appears to be wrong.

APPLY

AO2: An example

SCENARIO Sophie has a new job as a PA for the boss of a chain of restaurants, who expects her to work long hours and take on much more responsibility than she had anticipated. She appeared to be coping for the first few weeks, but after four weeks she is exhausted and feels unable to cope.

Using your knowledge of the general adaptation syndrome, explain why Sophie feels the way she does. **(4 marks)**

ANSWER *Sophie's stress response is activated to enable her to work hard and meet her boss's expectations – this is the alarm reaction stage. Next her body adapts to the needs of ongoing stress of long hours and responsibility, and uses up resources in maintaining the stress response, like sugars, proteins, neurotransmitters, etc. – the resistance stage. Finally, she becomes exhausted as she has depleted resources, and this will lead to health problems.*

AO2: Research methods

On the day of their A Level examinations, a psychologist asked 24 students to complete a questionnaire measuring how much stress they perceived themselves to be experiencing. A measure was also taken of how much adrenaline their bodies were producing compared with a baseline measurement taken before they started their revision. A scattergram of the findings is shown below:

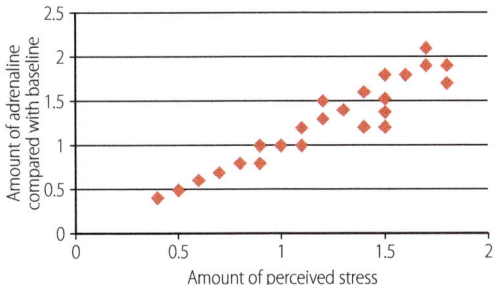

Amount of adrenaline compared with baseline (y-axis), Amount of perceived stress (x-axis)

a. **Explain why the data in this study is primary data rather than secondary data. (2 marks)**

b. **Explain one strength of primary data compared with secondary data. (3 marks)**

c. **What kind of relationship is shown in the scattergram? (2 marks)**

d. **Identify one statistical test that could be used to determine the strength of the relationship between the two variables. Give two reasons for your choice. (3 marks)**

e. **The researcher concluded that high levels of perceived stress were causing higher levels of adrenaline to be produced. Explain why this conclusion cannot be justified. (2 marks)**

AO2: One for you to try

Susie, aged nine, saw a clip of a horror movie on a friend's phone, in which a zombie was attacking a child. She felt sick and started shaking, and took a few minutes to calm down. She felt like this again every time she remembered the video for the next week.

Explain how Susie's body responded to seeing the zombie in terms of what you know about the role of the autonomic nervous system in response to stress. (4 marks)

How do I answer... research methods questions?

Questions requiring research methods knowledge can appear in any section of any paper in the AS or A Level exams. They could include any aspect of research methods, data analysis or ethical issues. Let's look at the **AO2: Research methods** example questions on the left:

a. There isn't a mark for saying 'primary data' as you were told this, but there are 2 for the explanation, so make it clear that you are saying two things: 'because it was collected by the psychologist directly from the students, and it was collected specifically for the purpose of this study'.

b. You should state a strength, for example 'Primary data is more relevant to the research aims of the current study' and make the comparison explicit: 'whereas secondary data may have been collected to answer a different research question, so may not be tailored perfectly to the current research'. Finally make sure you have explained why this is a strength 'so primary data will give more valid findings'.

c. Scattergrams always show correlational relationships. You should describe it as strong/moderate/weak/zero correlation and positive/negative. See the Year 1 Book if you need to revise this.

d. You should know how to select a statistical test confidently. State the name of the test and explain how the criteria for choosing that test fit the data from this particular study. For example: 'It is correlational data as it looks at the relationship between two covariables, the stress scores and adrenaline levels.'

e. Remember that correlation does not show causation! Explain why.

REVIEW

Organising your information into graphical form will help you learn it more effectively, and it is then straightforward to convert your mental diagram into words and sentences. For this topic, there are three flow charts you can make: SAM pathway, HPA system and GAS. Draw them out using the material on this spread, then practise drawing them from memory. Keep practising until you know each step securely. Make sure you know which steps in the two pathways involve hormones and which are part of the nervous system's response.

The role of stress in illness

RECAP

AO1 Description

- **Immediate stress: Adrenaline and cardiovascular disorders**
  - > High adrenaline levels increase heart rate, constrict blood vessels, and dislodge plaque on blood vessel walls.
  - > This causes the heart to work harder, increases blood pressure, and blocks arteries.
  - > This can lead to coronary heart disease, hypertension and strokes.
- **Ongoing stress: Cortisol and immunosuppression**
  - > One effect of cortisol is to reduce the body's immune response.
  - > This **immunosuppression** increases the chances that someone will become ill because invading bacteria and viruses are not attacked by the immune system.

- Williams *et al.* (2000) found that of 13,000 initially healthy people, the highest scorers on an anger scale were 2.5 times more likely to have had a heart attack six years later compared with those with the lowest scores.
  - > Even people with 'moderate' anger scores were more likely than the lowest scorers to experience a coronary event, suggesting that adrenaline level increases are closely associated with cardiovascular disorders.
- Kiecolt-Glaser *et al.* (1984) found that natural killer cells were less active in medical students while they were revising than before they started. This is evidence that ongoing stressors reduce immune system functioning.

AO3 Evaluation/Discussion

Self-report data should be treated with caution…

Stress and cardiovascular outcomes are often measured using self-report questionnaires.	People who remember more unpleasant than pleasant events are likely to score more highly on stress measures and cardiovascular outcomes.	This means that self-report measures might produce an unjustified correlation between higher perceived stress and cardiovascular symptoms.

Research support linking stress with cardiovascular disease…

A large body of research has linked stress with cardiovascular disease (CVD).	For example, Sheps *et al.* (2002) found that people with CVD had erratic heartbeats when public speaking. They were more likely to die from heart disease than those with stable heartbeats.	This shows that psychological stress dramatically increases the risk of death in at least some people with poor coronary artery circulation.

Individual differences in cardiovascular effects…

Individuals respond differently to stress because of gender, age and reactiveness of their sympathetic nervous system.	For example, women show more adverse immunological and hormonal changes when stress is caused by marital conflict.	There are also age differences; as people age, stress has a greater effect on immune system functioning, making it harder for the body to regulate itself (Segerstrom and Miller, 2004).

Stress may sometimes enhance immune system activity…

Evans *et al.* (1994) found lower levels of an antibody protecting against infection with a chronic stressor, but higher levels of that antibody when the stress was acute.	Segerstrom and Miller's (2004) meta-analysis also showed that acute stressors promote the body's ability to fight infection.	This means that stress may sometimes be beneficial to the body's immune system.

 **APPLY**

AO2: An example

SCENARIO A group of students studied the role of stress in illness over two months. Every week they asked their friends to rate how stressed they felt and whether they had been ill in the previous week. They calculated a stress score and an illness score for each participant. The students found a positive correlation between stress and illness scores.

Discuss the use of self report scales to measure stress. Refer to the scenario above in your answer. **(8 marks)**

ANSWER **An extract showing how you could address the AO2 requirements of this question:** *The students tested their friends, who may not be a representative sample... The correlation does not imply causation; it is possible that being ill made their friends more stressed as they had work to catch up... The self-report measures may be biased by negative perceptions, so some people would consistently score high on both measures, artificially strengthening the correlation. However, the findings do concord with other research such as Kiecolt-Glaser...*

AO2: Research methods

A researcher decided to investigate whether stress affected how quickly wounds heal. Groups of participants agreed to undergo a small skin biopsy on their arms. A non-stressed control group were compared with a group who were caring for an elderly relative with dementia. It was hypothesised that the wounds would take longer to heal in the group caring for an elderly relative. The mean time for the biopsy wounds to heal are shown below.

	Participants not caring for a relative	Participants caring for a relative
Mean time for wound to heal (days)	54	63

The researcher used a Mann-Whitney U test to analyse the data. The difference in wound healing time was significant at $p<0.05$.

a. **Was the hypothesis directional or non-directional? Give one reason for your answer. (2 marks)**

b. **Give two reasons why the researcher chose the Mann-Whitney U test to analyse the data. (2 marks)**

c. **The Mann-Whitney U test is a non-parametric statistical test. Identify a parametric alternative to the Mann-Whitney U test. (1 mark)**

d. **The researcher set the significance level at $p<0.05$. What is a Type I error, and what is the probability of a Type I error being made in this study? (2 marks)**

e. **The researcher concluded that caring for relatives with dementia is stressful, and stress suppressed the immune system which caused the difference in wound-healing times. Give one criticism of the conclusion the researcher drew. (2 marks)**

AO2: One for you to try

In a study of supporters of Premiership football teams, researchers analysed the results of hundreds of games played by Sunderland. They looked at the results of each match and at how many deaths from heart attacks and strokes occurred in the health authority area on the days that Sunderland played. They found that male death rates increased by 66 per cent when Sunderland lost on their home ground. Although there was an increase when the team lost and were playing away from home, it was much less than when they lost at home. There was no increase in female deaths, irrespective of how well the team did.

Use your knowledge of the relationship between stress and illness to explain these findings, and suggest a reason why defeats at their home ground led to a greater increase in supporters' death rates than defeats on other grounds. (4 marks)

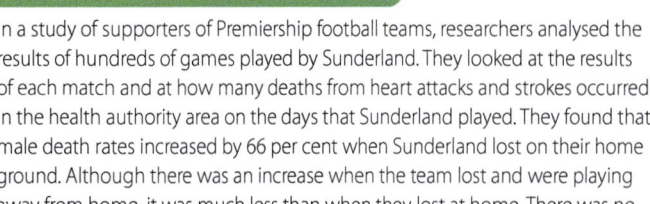 **How do I answer... description only questions (AO1)?**

There is a fairly simple formula in answering description only questions. For 2 marks, say two things, for 3 marks, say three things, and so on.

Work through the sample questions below, using the advice that follows them. The AO1 material for these questions is on the opposite page. This approach adds an appropriate level of detail to each answer while keeping it within the time restriction of 1 ¼ minutes per mark.

Q1: Briefly describe the role of stress in immunosuppression. (2 marks)

Use the first **two** points under the AO1 'ongoing stress' section.

Q2: Briefly outline how immunosuppression and cardiovascular disorders relate to stress. (4 marks)

Use **four** points, such as two from 'immediate stress' and two from 'ongoing stress'. You must touch on both types of illness in your answer because of the word 'and' in the question.

Q3: Outline research into the role of stress in illness, referring in your answer to immunosuppression and cardiovascular disorders. (6 marks)

Use **six** AO1 points. Choose points that are clearly findings of research, although any knowledge of the role of stress in illness on this page does come from research. Keep checking back, looking at the question to make sure you have not lost focus, and have answered all the requirements. You could tick them off on the question paper in an exam, to make sure you cover them all.

REVIEW

The Stress option contains many topics, and you will need a strategy to ensure you have covered them all. Condensing notes onto revision cards or mind-maps means that you process the content and pick out key terms, which will help you to memorise them. It also enables you to elaborate points in your mind as you review them, rather than just skimming over your class notes or Revision Guide. Practise now, by writing out the key terms or section headers from this page:

- Immediate stress: adrenaline and cardiovascular disorders.
- Ongoing stress: cortisol and immunosuppression.

Then mentally elaborate each point before you check back to see how well you did. You also need to know details of research evidence for each.

Sketching little pictures will also help you remember the key points, even if you aren't good at drawing (Fernandes *et al.*, 2018).

Sources of stress: Life changes

 **RECAP**

AO1 Description

- **Life changes** are events that require major adjustment in some aspect of our life, and are believed to be significant sources of stress. Life changes may be positive or negative, such as marriage or bereavement.

- The stress of life changes can be measured using the **Social Readjustment Rating Scale (SRRS)**. Each event has a **Life Change Unit (LCU)** score associated with it. 'Death of a spouse' is listed 'most stressful' and scores the maximum of 100 LCUs.

- A person identifies which of the 43 life events has occurred within some time period (e.g. a year). The scores for each event are added up to give a total LCU score.

Rahe *et al.* (1970)

- **PROCEDURE** Rahe *et al.* (1970) used a modified SRRS, called the Schedule of Recent Experiences (SRE), to study the relationship between stress and illness in naval personnel.

- **FINDINGS** SRE scores were positively correlated with scores on a measure of ill-health.
  > Since the SRE included both positive and negative events, it seems it is change, rather than the negativity of change, that requires effort to adapt, creates stress and may affect our health.
  > Other studies have also shown that higher LCU scores are associated with increased likelihood of illness.

AO3 Evaluation / Discussion

The life changes approach has provided insights…

| Large amounts of research has explored life changes and stress. | For example, Heikkinen & Lonnqvist (1995) found family and financial troubles, loss and unemployment prior to suicides in Finland. | This suggests these life changes may have been a causal factor in suicide. |

Recall of life events may be unreliable…

| For example, Rahe (1974) found that the recall reliability depends on the time interval between test and re-test. | However, Hardt *et al.* (2006) found moderate to good reliability of recall for most childhood experiences. | Since most findings are similar to Hardt et al.'s, this suggests that reliability levels for retrospective reports of life events are good. |

It ignores the different significance of events for different people…

| The SRRS assigns the same score to an event regardless of how it is perceived by a person. | For example, the death of a spouse may be more stressful if it is untimely than if it occurs after a long and painful illness. | The score ignores the fact that the same life changes may be more stressful for some than others |

Correlation, not causation…

|]The correlation between life changes and illness may be spurious. Instead, both may be caused by another variable. | People with high anxiety levels may be more prone to illness and more likely to report negative life events, so the causal variable is high anxiety. | In addition, people who are ill may be looking for a cause, and report more stressful events. |

⚙ APPLY

AO2: An example

SCENARIO In the past, mothers of children with Down's syndrome reported far more traumatic events in their pregnancy than did mothers of non-Down's children – at that time they didn't know that Down's was a chromosomal abnormality.

Discuss how the SRRS could be used to analyse a relationship between stressful life events and a birth disorder. Refer to issues of reliability and validity in your answer. **(16 marks)**

ANSWER **An extract showing how you could address the AO2 requirements of this question:** *Mothers of babies with a birth disorder could complete the SRRS and compare with a control group of mothers without a birth disorder. An association could show a causal link. However, the reliability of SRRS depends on the time interval, so it should be completed as soon as possible after the pregnancy. Also, mothers of babies with a birth disorder may look for a cause and recall more stressful events, so this could be a confounding factor, reducing the validity of the findings. Birth disorders could be caused by chromosome abnormalities, or by the mother's behaviour during pregnancy, e.g. using drugs or alcohol – these behaviours may be affected by anxiety so a link between LCU scores and birth disorders could be due to anxiety and alcohol use rather than the events themselves...*

AO2: Research methods

An A Level student decided to investigate for herself the relationship between stress and ill-health. She placed an advertisement in her local shop asking for people to take part in her study. Each of the 12 people who took part in the study completed the SRRS and estimated the number of days they had taken off through sickness in the previous year. A scattergram of the data she collected is shown on the right:

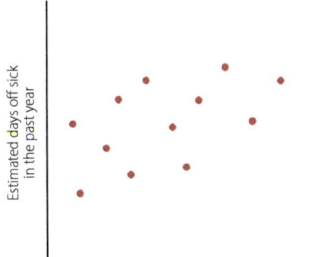

Estimated days off sick in the past year

Score on the SRRS

a. **Write an operationalised directional hypothesis for this study. (2 marks)**

b. **It has been claimed that the SRRS has internal validity. What is meant by the term 'internal validity'? (1 mark)**

c. **Name the sampling method used by the student. (1 mark)**

d. **Outline one limitation of this sampling method. (2 marks)**

e. **The student used Spearman's *rho* test to analyse her data. Give two reasons why this test was used. (2 marks)**

f. **Name a parametric alternative to Spearman's *rho* test. (1 mark)**

g. **The student found a correlation of +.27 with the alternative test and had set her significance level as $p < 0.05$. Use the relevant table in your textbook to decide if there is a significant correlation between the two variables. Explain how you reached your decision. (3 marks)**

✏ AO2: One for you to try

Munya and Nadia were discussing the SRRS. 'I think it makes a lot of sense as life events like moving house or breaking up a relationship or doing exams are clearly stressful,' said Nadia. 'I think it's way too simplistic,' said Munya. 'It doesn't apply to students like us, and it relies on you having a really good memory, which I don't!' he continued.

Using Nadia's and Munya's comments in your answer, evaluate the SRRS as a measure of stressful life changes. (6 marks)

🐾 How do I answer... (8-mark) essay questions?

Not all essays follow the 12- or 16-mark format. Some have a slightly lower tariff. Of these lower tariff essay questions, the 8-marker is the most common. It does help to know what you are dealing with, however, as they are not always straightforward. The AO1 and AO3 material for these questions is on the opposite page.

Q1: Outline and evaluate life changes as a source of stress. **(8 marks)**

Although you might believe that this question would be worth 4 marks for AO1 and 4 for AO3, this is actually half of a 16-mark essay question, so there is a similar split of marks, i.e. 3 marks for AO1 and 5 marks for AO3 (instead of the 6- and 10-mark split for a 16-mark question).

Q2: Jess has recently left her husband after a 30-year marriage, and moved to a different city. She is also experiencing pressure in her work as an author, with deadlines that are challenging to meet. She is now suffering from a cold and feeling tired, even though she is very happy with her new life.

Discuss how Jess may have been affected by her recent life changes. **(8 marks)**

- The scenario indicates an AO2 requirement, so the answer needs 3 marks of AO1 (first three points), 3 marks of AO3 *and* 2 marks' worth of AO2.
- The scenario is about having a cold, so you could link Jess' life events to the evidence about LCU scores and illness. For example, 'Jess has experienced several major life changes recently, and this may have affected her immune system and made her more susceptible to a cold.'
- You can take this to a higher level by referring to the methodological issues with this research too: 'However, the research is correlational which means that we can't conclude cause and effect: it could be that Jess would have got a cold anyway, or that the cold is making Jess feel more stressed as it is affecting her sleep and making her tired'.
- You could also link AO3 point 3 to Jess's story, as 'it ignores the significance of events for different people' and Jess is 'feeling happy about her new life'.

🔄 REVIEW

Can you complete the sentences below?

- Life changes can be defined as...
- An example of a life change is...
- The researchers who devised the SRRS are...
- The number of life changes on the SRRS is...
- A life change unit is...
- The life change which has the highest life change unit score is...
- An alternative to the SRRS is...
- Researchers who used this scale in their study are...

Sources of stress: Daily hassles

AO1 Description

- Kanner *et al.* (1981) define daily hassles as 'the irritating, frustrating, and distressing demands that to some degree characterise everyday transactions with the environment'. These include everyday work concerns and issues arising from family life.

- **Daily hassles** and **daily uplifts** were measured using the Hassles and Uplifts Scale (HSUP).

- Lazarus's (1999) explanation for the effects of daily hassles is that an accumulation of them creates persistent irritations, frustrations, and overloads, which cause more serious stress reactions such as anxiety and depression.

- An alternative explanation is that chronic stress due to major life changes make us more vulnerable to daily hassles, and amplify the stress they cause us.

- Major life changes might also deplete a person's resources making them less able to cope with daily hassles than usual.

Kanner *et al.* (1981)

- **PROCEDURE** Kanner *et al.* studied 100 participants aged 45–67.

- **FINDINGS** He found a negative correlation between the frequency of reported daily hassles and psychological well-being. Importantly, daily hassles were also a better predictor of well-being than life changes were.

AO3 Evaluation / Discussion

Research shows daily hassles are more stressful than life changes…

For example, Ruffin (1993) found that daily hassles were linked to greater physical and psychological dysfunction than were major life changes.	Additionally, Flett *et al.* (1995) reported that people seek more social and emotional support from significant others during life changes.	This means that daily hassles could be more stressful because other people provide less social and emotional support for them than for life changes.

Reliability of recall can be a problem…

For example, people's recall of events that happened a month ago may not always be accurate.	Charles *et al.* (2013) found that keeping a daily diary of hassles led to a more accurate record of events than retrospective recall.	This suggests that there are methodologies available which may avoid the problems of retrospective recall, and provide more valid data.

Validity of self-report data can also be an issue…

Social desirability bias is always possible when data are collected using self-report methods.	People may be embarrassed to admit that certain things (e.g. looking after their children) are hassles for them, and so do not report them.	Also, we cannot conclude that daily hassles are causing problems such as depression: negative thinking may cause people to report more hassles.

Gender differences in what constitutes a 'hassle'…

For example, Miller *et al.* (1992) found that, for men, pets are associated with hassles such as the money needed to care for them.	However, for women, pets are associated with uplifting feelings such as a lack of psychological pressure.	This shows that it is difficult to define something as a 'hassle' objectively because of individual differences in how things are perceived.

 **APPLY**

AO2: An example

SCENARIO People who reported a difficult day at work subsequently tended to report higher levels of stress on their commute home, and admitted shouting at other road users.

Using your knowledge of daily hassles and stress, explain the relationship between stress during the day and increased road rage on the commute home. **(4 marks)**

ANSWER *A difficult day at work constitutes an experience of daily hassles, and according to Lazarus these frustrations accumulate so that the person can then respond badly to further stressors, such as heavy traffic or diversions on the way home. In addition, if the person is going through major life changes this can amplify the effect of minor hassles – so if they have a new job or even a promotion with more responsibility, this extra stress makes them more vulnerable to road rage on the way home.*

AO2: Research methods

A research team asked 20 students (10 males, 10 females) to wear headcams for the whole of their first day at college. Two of the researchers used content analysis to identify the number of hassles each student experienced during the day. They predicted that male and female students would differ in the number of hassles they experienced.

a. What is 'content analysis'? (2 marks)

b. Explain how the researchers could have carried out content analysis on the data collected to find the information they wanted. (4 marks)

c. Explain how the researchers could have assessed the reliability of their content analysis. (3 marks)

d. Was the researchers' prediction directional or non-directional? Explain your answer. (2 marks)

e. Identify a non-parametric test that could have been used to analyse the results. Give two reasons why you chose this test. (3 marks)

f. The researchers found a significant difference between the number of hassles experienced by the males and females. The difference was significant at $p<0.01$. Explain why the researchers did not think that they had made a Type I error in relation to the difference they found. (2 marks)

In a follow-up study, the researchers asked each student to rate how stressful they had found the day. They used a Spearman's *rho* test to discover if daily hassles and stress were significantly correlated. For males, the correlation was .66, whereas for females it was .63.

g. Use the table below to decide if the two correlation coefficients are significant at $p<0.02$. Explain your answer. (4 marks).

Table of critical values for Spearman's *rho*

Level of significance for a one-tailed test	0.05	0.01
Level of significance for a two-tailed test	0.10	0.02
$N = 4$	1.00	
10	.564	.648
20	.380	.447
25	.337	.398

Observed value of *rho* must be EQUAL TO or GREATER THAN the critical value in this table for significance to be shown.

AO2: One for you to try

Liza has had a cold that she can't seem to shake off, and frequently has to see the college nurse because of headaches and problems with sleeping. Liza has a Twitter account, and updates her followers daily about the good and bad things that have happened to her. Sasha is a devoted follower of Liza and sent the following tweet: '@Liza Have you noticed that when you moan about how rubbish the day's been you don't go to college next day?' Liza replied: '@Sasha But if I have a good day, I'm OK for college. What's that all about?'

Using your knowledge of psychology, briefly explain Liza's problem. (3 marks)

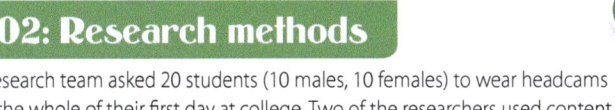 **How do I answer... questions about statistical testing?**

The more you practise questions about choosing and using inferential statistical tests, the better and quicker you will get at this. Remember there are three **Decisions** you need to make, and you can remember them with the 3 'D's:

- Are we testing a **Difference** or a correlation?
- Is the **Design** independent groups or repeated measures?
- What level of measurement is the **Data**?

These help you to choose the right test, and also give you the basis for your explanation of the reasons why you chose this test.

It would be very useful to learn an effective answer to **AO2: Research methods f.**, and also to a similar question, 'Why did the researchers choose a significance level of $p<0.05$?' Check the Probability page of the Research methods section of this Revision Guide, p.16 for suggested phrasing.

REVIEW

Being able to describe something concisely, while maintaining accuracy, is not as easy as it sounds. On the opposite page, we have stripped down the descriptive detail you will find in the main textbook to give you some guidance about how to do just that. Let's now play around with that content to make it a bit more familiar.

1 Write two different 6-mark 'describe' or 'outline' questions on the AO1 content.

2 Next think of four different short answer (2- to 3-mark) questions.

3 Finally, and possibly the hardest, write a multiple choice question.

After you've written the questions, you should write the mark schemes. This will make you think hard about which points you would include in different length answers.

You could pair up with a study buddy and each write questions like these for different topics, then swap.

Sources of stress: Workplace stress

RECAP

AO1 Description

Workload and control

- **Workplace stress** has enormous economic implications, with 10.4 million days lost due to staff absenteeism related to stress, costing an estimated £6.5 billion to the economy in 2012.
- **Workload** is defined as the amount of activity involved in a job, while **job control** is the extent to which people feel they can manage aspects of their work, such as meeting deadlines.
- The job-strain model proposes that high workload and low job control cause workplace stress.

Marmot *et al.* (1997)

- **PROCEDURE** Marmot *et al.* studied over 10,000 civil servants. Senior grade staff have a high workload and high control, while junior grade staff have a low workload and low control. Stress is therefore experienced by both grades, but for different reasons.
- **FINDINGS** Coronary heart disease (CHD) was associated with low job control, but not with high workload.

Johansson *et al.* (1978)

- **PROCEDURE** Johansson *et al.* studied 28 manual labourers at a Swedish sawmill.
- **FINDINGS** They found that workers with a high workload and low control (high-risk group) had higher adrenaline levels and illness rates than those with a low workload and high control (low-risk group).

Working dogs can also experience stress

AO3 Evaluation/Discussion

Individual differences in the way people cope with stress…

Schaubroek *et al.* (2001) found that some workers are actually less stressed by having no control or responsibility, and have better immune system functioning.	Lazarus' (1995) 'transactional model' proposes that whether a workplace stressor is perceived as stressful depends largely on a person's coping abilities.	*This indicates that the job-strain model is an oversimplification.*

Work underload can also be stressful…

Shultz *et al.* (2010) found that employees who reported work underload also reported low job satisfaction and significant absenteeism due to stress-related illness.	This suggests that work underload (dull or low skilled work) can cause similar problems to those associated with work overload.	*The stressful nature of work underload supports the idea that the job-strain model may be an oversimplification.*

Self-report data suffers from social desirability bias…

Most of the studies of workplace stress covered here have made use of questionnaires.	Keenan and Newton (1989) found that interviews could identify additional stressors such as interpersonal conflicts.	*This suggests that interviews may be a more valid way of assessing the impact of workplace stressors.*

Workplace stress and mental health…

Stress at work, combined with difficulties at home or daily hassles, can make depression more likely.	Warr (1987) suggested that positive aspects of work are like vitamins. When these are lacking, poor mental health may result.	*This suggests that workplace stress is just one of a number of daily hassles, which jointly lead to mental health problems.*

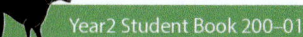

 **APPLY**

AO2: An example

SCENARIO Tom is at college and works in a call centre in the evenings, which he finds very boring and frustrating. He has to meet targets for numbers of contacts, but people usually put the phone down before he has explained why he is calling. He tries to do his homework at the weekend but is often too tired to concentrate.

Using your knowledge of workplace stress, explain why Tom is struggling to do his homework at the weekend. **(4 marks)**

ANSWER *Tom is under pressure at work, to meet targets, which gives him a high workload. It is difficult to make the contacts, which gives him low job control. High workload and low job control combine to make high job strain and this causes stress, according to the Swedish sawmill study by Johansson. This makes Tom tired. Tom is at risk of becoming physically ill and is too tired to do his homework because his experience of work is negative. If he had work satisfaction he might feel happier and have more energy, but he finds his work very boring and frustrating.*

AO2: Research methods

1. Twenty employees in a small company were divided into those that had a low degree of control in the workplace and those that had a high degree of control. Each employee was asked to rate how stressed they felt at work using a 10-point rating scale, where 1 = not at all stressed and 10 = extremely stressed. The raw data are shown below.

a. **Calculate the means for the two groups of participants. (2 marks each)**

b. **Identify one weakness of using the mean to describe the stress reported by the low degree of control employees. (2 marks)**

c. **Name two alternative measures of central tendency that could have been used instead of the mean. (2 marks)**

d. **Identify one measure of dispersion that could have been used to describe the variability in the ratings of stress given by the participants. (1 mark)**

e. **Identify a parametric test of difference that the researcher might have considered using to analyse the data. (1 mark)**

f. **Identify a suitable non-parametric alternative to the test you identified in (e) above. (1 mark)**

g. **At what level of measurement are the ratings provided by the participants? (1 mark)**

Low degree of control employees	8	7	8	6	1	6	6	8	6	9
High degree of control employees	4	5	3	3	2	2	3	5	5	2

2. Workplace stressors such as overload and control have been linked with potentially harmful behaviour in those affected by them. Chen and Spector (1992) gave 400 employees questionnaires about job stressors, frustration, satisfaction, and potentially harmful behaviours including sabotage, theft, and substance abuse. The researchers wanted to see if job stressors were correlated with any of the potentially harmful behaviours.

Identify one ethical issue the researchers needed to address, and suggest a way they could have dealt with it. (3 marks)

AO2: One for you to try

Homer and Moe were discussing their jobs. 'I think being a Nuclear Safety Inspector is too hard for me. I'm worried something will go wrong and I won't be able to deal with it', said Homer. 'I wish I had a job like yours,' said Moe. 'At least it would stimulate me. Serving beer all day is just so boring, but at least I'm my own boss, unlike you!' Lenny and Karl walked in. 'Sorry we're late,' said Karl, 'but I've just had way too much to do and not enough time to do it in.' 'I'm late because I fell asleep,' said Lenny. 'I've been sitting at my desk with nothing to do at all.'

Using your knowledge of workplace stress, identify the kind of workplace stressors for each of the four employees are experiencing (e.g. work overload). (4 marks)

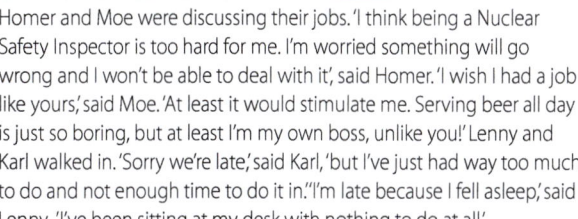 **How do I answer... application (AO2) questions**

Q1: Georgia is on a graduate training scheme in an international business, which involves six-month placements in different departments. Her first placement was in London. She found it very challenging as she had a long journey to work and she had to work extra hours to keep on top of things. However, she enjoyed having control of an area of work and had some exciting opportunities to travel abroad and work with colleagues from other departments. She had looked forward to her second placement, thinking it would be more relaxing and less stressful, as it was outside London. However, she was surprised to find that she was very stressed about not having enough to do.

Explain Georgia's experiences of workplace stress, referring to the effects of workload and control. (6 marks)

Remember the 'say one thing for 1 mark' and 'say four things for 4 marks' strategy. Here, we could say six things.

1. Find a bit of appropriate psychology, e.g. 'Workload is the amount of activity involved in a job'.

2. Use this to explain some aspect of the scenario, e.g. 'Georgia had high workload in her first placement, as she had to work long hours to keep on top of things'.

3. Find a second bit of psychology, e.g. 'Job control is the extent to which people feel they can manage their work'.

4. Use this to explain the scenario, e.g. 'Georgia enjoyed feeling in control in her first placement and this balanced out her heavy workload, so overall she had low job strain in this placement.'

5. Find a third bit of psychology, e.g. 'Work underload can also be stressful…'.

6. Use this to explain the scenario, e.g. 'Georgia seemed to experience work underload in her second placement, as she didn't have enough to do'.

REVIEW

Practise using the material on this topic in all the different ways that might be assessed in your exam.

1. Try constructing 3-, 4- and 6-mark descriptions of workplace stress.

2. Write an essay plan showing how you would use the material on this spread to answer a 16-mark extended writing question, then highlight which points you would include in an 8-mark version of the question.

Measuring stress: Self-report scales and physiological measures

RECAP

A01 Description

Self-report scales

- **Social Readjustment Rating Scale** (SRRS: Holmes and Rahe, 1967) consists of 43 life events, each associated with a Life Change Unit. Adding up the LCUs for each event experienced in some time period gives a total score.
- **Hassles and Uplifts Scale** (HSUP: Kanner *et al.*, 1980) consists of 117 'hassles' and 135 'uplifts', relating to work, health, family, friends, the environment and practical considerations.

Physiological measures

- **Skin conductance response** Adrenaline and noradrenaline cause sweating. The palms of the hands contain glands which are partly responsive to emotional stimuli, and produce a strong sweat response. This makes the skin conduct more electricity. The index and middle fingers have 0.5V applied across them, and the current that flows gives a skin conductance measure.
- **Other physiological measures** Blood pressure and heart rate are also measures of the adrenaline response. Cortisol can be measured in saliva or urine.

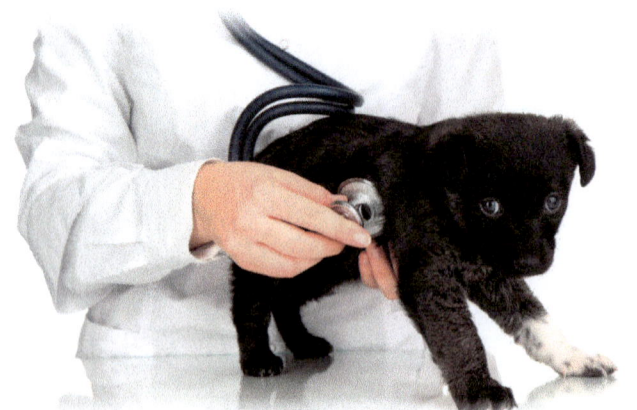

A03 Evaluation / Discussion

Self-report scales

Criticism of the SRRS…

A criticism is that the same event may have a different meaning for different people.	For example, 'divorce' may be stressful if a marriage was happy, but less stressful if it was unhappy.	This means that the SRRS's use of a fixed LCU for each event doesn't take individual differences in the perception of an event into account.

The HSUP scale is time-consuming for participants to complete…

The scale consists of 252 items (117 hassles and 135 uplifts) and participants may not maintain thoughtful, focused attention when completing it.	This is supported by low test–retest correlations (.48 on the hassles scale and .60 on the uplifts scale). Poor reliability means validity is also questionable.	However, DeLongis et al. (1988) have produced a shorter version with only 53 items.

Issues/Debates
Biological reductionism. Physiological measures reduce the stress response to effects on the body, ignoring the meaning to the individual.

Physiological measures avoid the problems of self-report measures…

Direct physiological measures avoid social desirability bias or positive response bias.	It is also the only way to measure stress with certain groups of participants, such as young children or non-human animals.	On the other hand, as Lazarus has pointed out, stress is not just a physiological response – the way it is perceived may be very much part of the experience.

The physiological response measures emotional arousal, not just stress…

Many emotions can cause arousal of the sympathetic nervous system. Also temperature, humidity and certain medications can increase skin conductance.	Oshumi and Ohira (2010) found that fear, anger, surprise and sexual arousal all increase sympathetic activity and produce an increased skin conductance response.	The influence of these other factors means that skin conductance might not be a valid measure of stress.

 **APPLY**

A02: An example

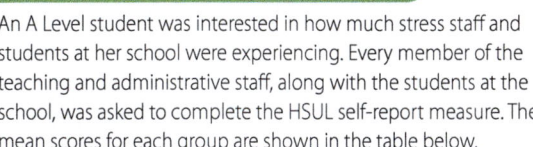 Janette is interested in conducting a study into stress levels of students taking exams.

Outline and evaluate methods of measuring stress. Refer to Janette's study in your answer. **(16 marks)**

ANSWER An extract showing how you could address the AO2 requirements of this question: *Janette could use multiple methods, to gain a variety of measures of stress. She could measure the students' skin conductance before, during and after the exam, although the equipment might be intrusive, so it would be difficult to measure during the exam. She could attach heart rate or blood pressure monitors to students to provide continuous data during the exam. She could measure cortisol in their saliva before and after exams. These physiological measures depend on other factors, however, so...*

In order to test the students' own perception of their stress levels, it would be better to use self-report measures. The SRRS and HSUP scales could be used to test the students' general levels of stress, to see whether life events or hassles and uplifts affect their response to exam stress. However, these scales...

A02: Research methods

An A Level student was interested in how much stress staff and students at her school were experiencing. Every member of the teaching and administrative staff, along with the students at the school, was asked to complete the HSUL self-report measure. The mean scores for each group are shown in the table below.

Group	Hassles score	Uplifts score
Teaching staff	210	45
Administrative staff	150	60
Students	105	270

a. **Which group has the highest hassles and lowest uplifts scores? (2 mark)**

b. **Hassles and uplifts are each rated on a 3-point scale. There are 117 hassles and 135 uplifts in the HSUP. What are the maximum possible hassles and uplifts scores? (2 marks)**

c. **Calculate the teaching staff's mean hassles score as a percentage of the maximum possible hassles score. (2 marks)**

d. **Which group has a hassles score two-and-a-half times its uplifts score? (1 mark)**

e. **Draw a suitably labelled bar chart of the data in the above table. (4 marks)**

f. **What conclusions can be drawn from the findings of this study? (3 marks)**

A02: One for you to try

Sadie is researching young children's stress responses in the Strange Situation procedure.

Suggest how she might measure the young children's stress levels. (4 marks)

How do I answer... 'Distinguish between' questions?

Q1: Distinguish between the Social Readjustment Ratings Scale and the Hassles and Uplifts scale in measuring stress. **(4 marks)**

If you are asked to explain the difference between the SSRS and HSUP, as in **Q1**, you need to give direct comparisons between aspects of each; for example, number of items in the scale, examples of items, the timescale reported on, the way the score is calculated.

1 First identify the point of comparison.

2 Secondly, explain the position of each scale in relation to that point.

3 Link it with 'whereas'.

For example, for **Q1**, 'The SRRS consists of scores for 43 major life events which may have taken place in the last six months or year, whereas the HSUP asks about 252 smaller events which may have occurred over the previous week.'

Q2: Compare the strengths and limitations of self-report scales and physiological measures such as skin conductance in measuring stress. **(8 marks)**

Q2 is looking for evaluation points, so you will need the AO3 material that is on the opposite page.

But again, as for **Q1**, you need to present them as a comparison between the two types of measure. For example, you could use the third AO3 point to compare self-report and physiological measures. You could point out limitations of physiological measures using the fourth AO3 point, and make the comparison with self-report measures which enable participants to report the meaning of their emotional state (stress or excitement for example).

REVIEW

Graphic organisers, including tables, flow charts and mind-maps, are highly effective for learning, and also enable you to easily find comparison points for a 'distinguish between ...' question. Complete the following table, which summarises information about the SRRS and HSUP self-report scales. You should also prepare to think of comparison points between self-report and physiological measures.

Scale	Who produced it?	Number of items	How score is calculated	Strengths	Limitations
SRRS					
HSUP					

Individual differences in stress: Personality

A01 Description

Personality types A, B and C

- The **Type A** personality is made up of three characteristics:
  - › competitiveness and achievement striving
  - › impatience and time urgency
  - › hostility and aggressiveness.
- Friedman and Rosenman believed these characteristics lead to increased blood pressure and stress hormone levels, both of which are linked to coronary heart disease (CHD).
- **Type B**s are patient, relaxed, and easy-going. These characteristics are believed to decrease a person's risk of stress-related illness.
- **The Type C** personality strongly suppresses negative emotions and is an unassertive and likeable person who rarely gets into arguments and is generally helpful to others. Type Cs cope with stress in a way that ignores their own needs in order to please others. This behaviour has been linked to cancer, possibly because of its effects on the immune system.
  - › Morris *et al.* (1981) found that women with cancerous breast lumps were more likely than women with non-cancerous lumps to have Type C personalities. The sample consisted of 75 women who were interviewed about their Type C behaviour by an interviewer 'blind' to initial cancer diagnoses.

Friedman and Rosenman (1959, 1974)

This study is known as the Western Collaborative Group (WCG) study.

- **PROCEDURE** Friedman and Rosenman (1959, 1974) used interviews to classify men as either Type A or B. The sample consisted of over 3,000 initially healthy Californian men aged 39–59.
- **FINDINGS** After an interval of nearly nine years, 12 per cent of Type As had experienced a heart attack compared with only 6 per cent of Type Bs.
  - › Type As had higher blood pressure and cholesterol levels, and twice as many Type As actually died from heart attacks.

A03 Evaluation / Discussion

Subsequent research challenged the conclusions of the WCG study…

Ragland and Brand (1988) conducted a 22-year follow-up of the participants originally studied by Friedman and Rosenman.	The results showed there was little evidence of a relationship between Type A and mortality. Age, smoking and high blood pressure were much more important factors.	*Although the Type A participants may have modified their behaviour, the lack of a relationship challenges the claim that Type A is a significant risk factor in CHD.*

Hostility is the key factor in the negative effects of Type A…

Myrtek's (2001) meta-analysis identified 'hostility' as the key characteristic of Type A and the development of CHD.	There was no association between 'time pressure' and 'competitiveness' and the development of CHD.	*This suggests that it is 'hostility' alone that is contributing to CHD rather than the Type A personality.*

Gender bias in research…

The original WCG research only studied men, but women can also have Type A personalities.	Friedman *et al.* (1986) found that both men and women with CHD reduced their risk of further problems when given Type A counselling alongside cardiac counselling.	*This suggests that both men and women experience Type A behaviours and benefit from strategies to reduce them.*

Challenges to the concept of Type C…

Giraldi *et al.* (1997) found no association between emotional suppression and cancer progression.	However, they did find more stressful life events in the months before a cancer diagnosis.	*This suggests that environmental variables (life events) may be more important than the Type C personality in causing some of the negative effects of stress.*

 **APPLY**

AO2: An example

SCENARIO Liam has a degree in psychology, and has started work in the human resources department of a city trading company employing 80 per cent male traders. Liam wants to improve their health and well-being. He has noticed that many seem to be very competitive and stressed, and believes that their Type A personality is putting them at risk of heart disease.

Outline how Type A personality might affect the trader's health. Explain how Liam could help the traders improve their health and well-being? **(4 marks)**

ANSWER *If the traders are male and competitive, they could fit the Type A personality profile, so they would be at risk of heart attacks, according to the findings of the WCG study. If they are stressed, it could cause high blood pressure, leading to cardiovascular disease. Liam could provide relaxation classes or counselling to help them to be less stressed, or address workplace issues like lack of job control to help reduce stress. In particular, the traders may need to be less hostile, as hostility is the biggest risk factor for coronary heart disease. He should strongly advise them not to smoke, as this is an even bigger factor according to Ragland and Brand's follow-up study of the WCG men.*

AO2: One for you to try

Ben, Sanya and Oliver were discussing their forthcoming exams. Ben had devised a detailed revision timetable, which identified what subject he should be revising, on what day, at what time, and for how long. He set the alarm on his phone to remind him when he should stop revising one subject and switch to another. Sanya liked to please his fellow psychology students, and so he helped Ben construct his timetable, even though he hadn't made his own yet. Oliver wasn't worried about revision. After all, the exams were a month away. That would be plenty of time to revise for his exams.

a. **Which student is most likely to be Type A? (1 mark)**

b. **Which student is most likely to be Type B? (1 mark)**

c. **Which student is most likely to be Type C? (1 mark)**

After the exams, the three students met up for a game of pool in their local leisure centre.

d. **Which student probably wouldn't care if he won or lost? (1 mark)**

e. **Which student would probably be unhappy if he lost, but would hide his disappointment from the other two? (1 mark)**

f. **Which student would probably try hardest to win? (1 mark)**

AO2: Research methods

The table below shows the data obtained by the Western Collaborative Group study into the relationship between personality and coronary heart disease (CHD).

Nature of CHD	Percentage Type A	Percentage Type B
Heart attacks	12.8	6.0
Recurring heart attacks	2.6	0.8
Fatal heart attacks	2.7	1.1

What do these findings show about the Type A and B personalities and CHD? (4 marks)

 ## How do I answer... description and evaluation (AO1 + AO3) questions?

1 Recognise what you need to do. Two different command words – e.g. 'outline' (an AO1 term) – and 'evaluate' (an AO3 term) – is a clue that this is a mixed AO1 + AO3 question.

2 Plan how much to write for the AO1 and AO3 parts. In mixed AO1 + AO3 questions up to 6 marks, the division is half and half (it is different with mark totals higher than this as we will see on p.141).

3 Decide what to write. Look at the examples below. The AO1 and AO3 material for these questions is on the opposite page.

Q1: Briefly explain what is meant by 'Type A behaviour' and give **one** criticism of Type A personality as a cause of stress. **(4 marks)**

Use the first two AO1 points and one AO3 point.

Q2: Outline and evaluate **one** study that has investigated Type A and Type B personality. **(6 marks)**

The AO1 needs to relate to a study, and the WCG study by Friedman and Rosenman is the obvious one. The three points describing the procedure and findings of this study would be perfect for this. To evaluate, use one AO3 point fully elaborated or two briefer ones. Any of points 1, 2 or 3 will be relevant.

Q3: Briefly discuss personality types in relation to stress. **(6 marks)**

'Discuss' means you need to outline and evaluate. You have a number of ways to answer this, but whichever route you take, there should be about 75–90 words of AO1 and 75–90 words of AO3. 'Personality types' could also include hardiness, so you could use material from the next spread if you happen to remember it better in the exam. If you are going down the Type A/ Type B route, you need to explain the behaviours, so use all the AO1 points relating to these. You can then use one or two AO3 evaluation points (as for **Q2**), or use the WCG findings as supporting evidence.

Q4: Outline and evaluate research into Type C behaviour. **(6 marks)**

In this case you need to focus just on Type C, so use the final two AO1 points and further evaluation from AO3 point 4.

 ## REVIEW

Practise application questions for this topic, so that you are used to linking the characteristics of Type A, Type B and Type C to descriptions of people. You can do this in everyday life too; when you see a character on tv or in a film, decide which personality type they would fall into, and mentally rehearse the risks associated with their behaviour. Then think to yourself what the evidence shows about the link between each response to stress and CHD.

RECAP

AO1 Description

- The three characteristics of the hardy personality are the 'three Cs':
  - > **Challenge** (seeing change as a challenge rather than a threat).
  - > **Commitment** (seeing a role as being meaningful rather than meaningless).
  - > **Control** (being in control of events rather than being controlled by the circumstances).
- These characteristics enable people to resist, and cope with, the negative effects of stress.
- Kobasa's findings have been replicated by Maddi (1987), who studied employees at an American telephone company that was making redundancies. Two thirds of employees suffered stress-related health problems, but the remaining third thrived, and were found to have more 'hardiness' attributes.
- Lifton *et al.* (2006) studied American university students who either completed their courses or 'dropped out' without graduating. Those with high hardiness scores were more likely to complete their degree.

Kobasa (1979)

- **PROCEDURE** Kobasa measured stress using the SRRS, and illness using self-report measures. Eighty-six participants were identified as high stress/low illness and 75 as high stress/high illness.
- **FINDINGS** He found that 'highly stressed' American male executives who were not often ill scored high on measures of the three Cs, whereas those who reported frequent illness were low scorers on those measures.

AO3 Evaluation/Discussion

Problems with measuring hardiness…

| Early research used lengthy and awkwardly worded questionnaires to measure challenge, commitment, and control. | More specific scales, such as Maddi's (1997) Personal Value Survey, have addressed some of the issues with the original questionnaires. | However, issues like low internal reliability of new self-report measures have not yet been fully resolved. |

Real-world application of hardiness training…

| Maddi *et al.*'s (1998) training programmes have been used to increase self-confidence and a sense of control. | Hardiness training is more effective than relaxation / meditation and placebo / social support in increasing job satisfaction and decreasing self-reported illness. | Hardiness training programmes have been used in business, education and military training. |

Low hardiness or negative affectivity…

| High NA individuals are more likely to report distress and dissatisfaction, dwell more on their failures, and focus on negative aspects of themselves and the world. | These characteristics correlate reasonably well with low hardiness levels. | This suggests that hardy individuals might simply be those people who are low in NA. |

Locus of control (LOC) may be the key factor in hardiness…

| Kim *et al.* (1997) found that children with internal LOC showed less stress when their parents divorced. | In addition, Cohen *et al.* (1993) found that people who felt their lives were uncontrollable were twice as likely to develop colds as those who felt in control. | This relates to Rotter's (1966) theory of locus of control: high internal LOC individuals are less disrupted by stress. |

 # APPLY

AO2: An example

SCENARIO Lydia and Silas are being interviewed for a company which wants to recruit 'hardy' employees. Lydia says she works better on her own, whereas Silas says that in a team his colleagues 'would be there to help if things went wrong'. Lydia explains that, 'After my family, my job is the most important thing in my life', while Silas says, 'There are more important things in life than work.' Finally, when asked about the stresses of high-pressure work, Lydia claims she 'relishes' the challenge, whereas Silas asks whether there is private health insurance.

Using your knowledge of the hardy personality, which candidate appears to be more hardy, and why? **(4 marks)**

ANSWER *Lydia shows characteristics of control (working better on her own), commitment (the job is really important to her) and challenge (relishing it), so she is a hardy personality. Silas shows the opposite: low control (depending on colleagues to rescue him if things go wrong), low commitment (there are more important things...) and low challenge (he seems to think about getting ill when he is asked about high-pressure work), so he would score low on hardiness overall, and would be more at risk of getting ill or leaving as he wouldn't be able to cope with the pressure. They should appoint Lydia.*

AO2: Research methods

In a study investigating hardiness and absenteeism from work, a researcher classified 100 participants as either being low or high scorers on a measure of the three Cs, and whether their absence from work either was or wasn't a cause for concern for the company. The researcher hypothesised that there would be an association between scores on the three Cs and whether the company was concerned or not about the employees' absenteeism. The results are shown in the table below.

	High score on the three Cs	Low score on the three Cs
Absence a cause for concern	6	42
Absence not a cause for concern	39	12

a. **Is the researcher's hypothesis directional or non-directional? Explain your answer. (2 marks)**

b. **Write a suitable null hypothesis for this study. (2 marks)**

c. **At what level of measurement is the data in this study? (1 mark)**

d. **Suggest a suitable statistical test that could be used to analyse the data in this study. (1 mark)**

e. **A questionnaire was used to measure the three Cs. Explain one disadvantage of using a questionnaire in this study. (2 marks)**

f. **Participants were led to believe that the questionnaire they completed was part of their annual appraisal. Identify one ethical issue this study raises, and explain how it could be dealt with. (3 marks)**

AO2: One for you to try

Two college lecturers were discussing their jobs. One of them said: 'I've been here 10 years teaching my subject and next year they want me to teach a subject I've never taught before. It's outrageous! Where I work you don't get a choice in which classes you teach, you just have to teach the classes you've been given. We've got an open day coming up, but if the management think I'm going to give up my Saturday morning to go into work, they've got another thing coming.' His colleague replied: 'You need to change! I love working at my college and I'm happy to teach more than I have to. I want our college to be the best! It's great the way I'm allowed to just get on with my job, and not feel that people are watching me all the time. If they wanted me to teach a new course, I'd jump at the opportunity!'

Using your knowledge of hardiness, identify which lecturer appears to be most hardy and explain why using the three Cs. (8 marks)

 ## How do I answer... longer (16-mark) application questions?

Let's imagine a longer version of the question we explored in **AO2: An example**. The scenario is exactly the same but the question is:

> **Discuss hardiness in relation to stress, referring to Lydia and Silas in your answer. (16 marks)**

The AO1 and AO3 material for this question is on the opposite page.

- For the AO1, include all the AO1 points (6 marks).
- For the AO2, link to the scenario (just as you would for the 4-mark version), explaining explicitly how Lydia and Silas fit the criteria for hardiness (4 marks).
- AO3 discussion: as extended answers are marked holistically, the final two points can be used as supporting evidence. You can then go on to evaluate the methodology (AO3 points 1 and 3), and discuss real-world applications of hardiness training (point 2). Three effective AO3 points will be plenty for this (6 marks).
- Plan how you would structure this answer.
  > It is often more efficient to link AO2 to AO1 as you go along, and interweave your AO3 points with your AO1, so you don't have to repeat yourself.
  > For example, you could link Lydia and Silas in to the first AO1 point; and when you describe Kobasa's research (AO1 point 2) you could evaluate the methodology (AO3 points 1 and 3) before moving on to describe hardiness training.
  > Using appropriate linking words, such as 'However' and 'In addition', at the start of each paragraph will also help to make a cohesive and fluent essay that is more likely to get a Level 4 mark.

REVIEW

Write an essay plan for the **AO2: One for you to try** question above, thinking carefully about the order of points and how you will link them. Then try writing this in 20 minutes. If you couldn't finish it in the time, this means you are not writing concisely enough or you are having to think too much. Keep reviewing the material until you know it well and can write a well-balanced essay in 20 minutes.

RECAP

AO1 Description

- **Benzodiazepines (BZs)** are anti-anxiety drugs, e.g. *Librium, Diazepam*. BZs reduce stress by slowing down central nervous system activity and inducing feelings of relaxation.

  > They enhance the activity of GABA, a neurotransmitter that quietens neural activity by increasing the flow of chloride ions into the post-synaptic neuron, which makes it harder for neurons to be stimulated by other neurotransmitters.

  > BZs also reduce the activity of serotonin, a neurotransmitter that has an arousing effect in the brain.

- **Beta blockers (BBs)** target the sympathetic nervous system. BBs bind to beta-receptors in the heart and other organs, and reduce adrenaline and noradrenaline's effects.

  > Heart rate, blood pressure, breathing rate, and sweating are kept at a normal level, and the person feels calmer and less anxious without the brain or alertness being affected.

  > BBs have been used to reduce 'stage fright', and in sports where hand—eye co-ordination is important. However, their use is banned by the International Olympics Committee.

AO3 Evaluation/Discussion

Randomised controlled trials (RCTs) test effectiveness of drug therapies…

Drug therapies are tested against placebos, and BZs and BBs have both been found to be effective.	Lockwood (1989) found that BBs were effective in reducing stress in a study of musicians. The drugs also seemed to increase their confidence and performance.	*Kahn et al. (1986) found that BZs were significantly more effective than a placebo for the treatment of anxiety and stress.*

Drug therapies are easy to use and work quickly…

Drugs require users to do nothing other than remember to take their medication.	In contrast, psychological therapies require time, effort and motivation if they are to be effective.	*Therefore, it isn't surprising that some people prefer drug therapies to manage their stress.*

Addiction and side effects are problems with BZs…

People who take BZs show marked withdrawal symptoms when the drugs are discontinued.	BZs also produce increased agitation or panic and aggressiveness. Cognitive side effects include memory impairment.	*These issues suggest that BZs are not an appropriate way of treating 'everyday stress'.*

Treating the symptoms rather than the underlying problem…

Although drugs are effective, stress reduction occurs only for as long as the drug is being taken.	In contrast, psychological methods aim to address the source of the stress and not just the symptoms it produces.	*This means that psychological treatments may give better long-term outcomes.*

APPLY

AO2: An example

SCENARIO Rosanne is a music student who has started experiencing extreme anxiety when she is preparing for a concert. She shakes, sweats and feels sick.

Explain how possible biological treatments could help Rosanne. **(6 marks)**

ANSWER *If Rosanne is anxious just before a concert, beta blockers could help her. They reduce the effect of adrenaline and noradrenaline on her target organs, so she would not feel her heart beating faster, her palms sweating or the sick feeling. This would help her get through the performance without shaking. Alternatively, if she has developed generalised anxiety that is affecting her preparation some time before the performance, she may benefit from benzodiazepines (BZs), which target the central nervous system. They enhance the action of GABA, dampening down the activity of the brain, and this will make Rosanne feel calmer. She could use these for a few weeks to help her get over her performance anxiety.*

AO2: One for you to try

Chris had always suffered from 'nerves'. When he was told he had an interview for a university place, he knew he'd need to be at his best, but he also knew that the stress and anxiety he'd experience would affect how well he did. His brother advised him to tell his doctor and ask him to prescribe some drugs. However, when he told his mother he was going to do that she got very angry with him and said she wouldn't be happy if he did that.

Using your knowledge of drug therapies, what would your advice be to Chris? (6 marks)

AO2: Research methods

A randomised controlled trial (RCT) is a study in which people are allocated at random to receive one of several clinical interventions. One of these interventions is the standard of comparison or control. The control may be a standard practice, a placebo (sugar pill), or no intervention at all. RCTs seek to measure and compare the outcomes after the participants receive the interventions. Because the outcomes are measured, RCTs are quantitative studies.

a. **Explain what is meant by the terms 'demand characteristics' and 'investigator effects', and why RCTs help to overcome these. (6 marks)**

b. **Write a consent form suitable to give participants in a randomised controlled trial of beta blockers for use in stress. (6 marks)**

How do I answer... selection (multiple choice) questions?

Q1: Which **two** of the following statements are true about beta blockers? Tick **two** boxes. **(1 mark)**

A They prevent adrenaline from having a strong effect. ☐

B They reduce serotonin activity. ☐

C They enhance the action of dopamine. ☐

D They increase the flow of chloride ions into post-synaptic neurons. ☐

E They are also used in the treatment of coronary heart disease. ☐

Q2: Which **two** of the following statements are true about benzodiazepine anti-anxiety drugs? Tick **two** boxes. **(1 mark)**

A They target the sympathetic nervous system.

B They block sites which are normally activated by adrenaline.

C They enhance the action of GABA.

D They bind to receptors in the cells of the heart and other organs.

E They target the central nervous system.

In these examples, you are asked to pick **two** correct answers in each case. Take care to read the instruction carefully, as you could easily assume you were after one correct answer, and then you would miss 50 per cent of the marks available for this question!

Follow the general advice on answering questions like these:

- Read the question very carefully. Is it asking you to pick the statement that matches (as here) or the 'odd one out' that doesn't match? Are you looking for **one** or **two**?
- Make life easier by crossing out any that are obviously not going to be the correct answer given the specific demands of the question.
- Check each answer option rather than just choosing the first one that seems right without considering all the other answers – this is a way of checking you've read the question properly and understood the statements being made in the answer.

Applying this to **Q1**, we cross out **D** as this relates to the effect of BZs in the brain. We can then cross out **B** and **C** as BBs work on adrenaline receptors rather than interactions with other neurotransmitters. This leaves **A** and **E** – check you are happy with those answers, then write them in the answer book.

For **Q2**, we can delete **D** immediately, as BZs have their effect in the brain – answer **D** would have been correct for BBs. Similarly, answer **B** applies to BBs rather than BZs. This leaves **A**, **C** and **E**, but **A** and **E** can't both be correct. Which **two** would you write in your answer book now?

REVIEW

You will need to be able to write short answers using the AO1 content, which means you must be familiar with how to express the action of each drug using correct biopsychological terminology. Write 2-, 4- and 6-mark answers to a question about each type of drug, being sure you know the similarities and differences between the way they work and the relevant evaluation points too. Then try to do this again from memory. Read your answers aloud to see if they are clear and make sense, then score yourself on how many of the key terms you managed to include.

Managing and coping with stress: Stress inoculation therapy

AO1 Description

- **Stress inoculation therapy** (SIT) aims to change how people think about stressors. SIT is a form of cognitive behavioural therapy (CBT) developed by Meichenbaum (1985) specifically to manage stress.

1 Conceptualisation: The therapist and client investigate the client's sources of stress.

> The client is taught to see perceived threats as problems to be solved, to break down global stressors to specific components that can be coped with, and to recognise the maladaptive strategies they use to deal with stress and what can be changed about these.

2 Skill acquisition, rehearsal, and consolidation: Coping skills are taught and rehearsed in the clinic using imagery, modelling, and role play. After this, they are gradually rehearsed in real life.

> These skills match the client's preferred coping method and include positive thinking, time management, and self-statements such as: 'Relax – you're in control. Take a slow breath.'

3 Application and follow-through: Finally, the client applies the coping skills in increasingly stressful situations.

> It is important for the client to learn to anticipate situations where it may be difficult to apply the skills and rehearse coping responses.

AO3 Evaluation / Discussion

SIT is effective in treating a variety of stressors…

The therapy has also been successfully applied to academic stress, the stress of public speaking, and anxiety reduction in people with phobias.	In addition, Jay and Elliott (1990) found SIT reduced the stress experienced by parents whose children were undergoing medical procedures.	This suggests that SIT is a useful psychological alternative to biological approaches to managing stress.

The hello–goodbye effect…

Therapies such as SIT depend on subjective reports from the people who undertake them.	People might exaggerate their problems in order to receive SIT ('hello') and minimise them afterwards to please the therapist ('goodbye').	This means that assessing SIT's effectiveness can be difficult.

Preparation for future stressors…

SIT isn't just a one-off treatment for current stress, unlike biological treatments.	Skills acquisition provides people with skills and confidence to deal with stressors in the future.	SIT not only addresses underlying problems, but also offers a way of approaching future difficulties.

SIT may be unnecessarily complex…

SIT can be time-consuming and requires high motivation and cognitive effort, so may not be suitable for everyone.	However, SIT might be effective just because people learn to relax, which reduces activity in the sympathetic nervous system.	This means that it might be possible to simplify SIT without reducing its overall effectiveness.

APPLY

AO2: An example

SCENARIO Jade is very anxious about starting university. She has been at a small school since she was five, and tends to avoid busy places like shopping centres, as they make her feel stressed.

Explain how a psychologist might use stress inoculation therapy to treat Jade. **(6 marks)**

ANSWER *In the conceptualisation phase, the psychologist would encourage Jade to talk about her worries, and how she copes with stress currently. She would identify maladaptive behaviours like avoiding shopping centres. Jade would start to reconceptualise her problem by breaking it down into parts, like meeting new people, going to lectures and finding her way round the campus. Next, the psychologist would teach Jade coping skills like positive self-statements, 'Relax – you're in control' or 'You can develop a plan to deal with it', and will help Jade to imagine how she can use these at university in different stressful situations. She could also use role play to practise meeting new people, or how to go into a lecture theatre and choose a seat. Finally, in the application stage Jade will rehearse her new skills in real life, maybe by going to a shopping centre, and get follow-up once she starts university to help her generalise the skills.*

AO2: Research methods

A doctor's surgery sent out a feedback survey to patients who had received three types of treatment for stress: SIT, beta blockers and benzodiazepines. They asked the patients 'Do you feel better now than you did before treatment, or not?' Out of 40 patients who had received SIT, 24 felt better now. All but one patient who received beta blockers (a total of 24) felt better, and half of the 16 patients who received benzodiazepines felt better.

a. **What type of question was used during the feedback survey? (1 mark)**

b. **Write a question that could be used in this survey that is likely to produce qualitative data. (2 marks)**

c. **What percentage of patients receiving SIT felt better now than before treatment? (2 marks)**

d. **Draw a contingency table of these results. (3 marks)**

e. **What statistical test could be used to analyse these results? Give reasons for your answer. (3 marks)**

f. **Patients who were taking two treatments at the same time, such as SIT and beta blockers, were excluded from the statistical analysis. Why is this? (2 marks)**

g. **The results of the statistical test were found to be significant at $p<0.05$. Explain this statement. (2 marks)**

h. **What can the doctor's surgery conclude about the three treatments? (3 marks)**

AO2: One for you to try

Our nervous student, Chris, listened to what you told him about the strengths and weaknesses of drug therapy as a treatment for stress. He can't make up his mind about whether to go to his doctor or not, and wonders if there are any other therapies available. He has heard about SIT, and wonders if it might be an alternative to drug therapy.

Compare drug therapy and SIT as treatments for stress. What would your advice be to Chris? (6 marks)

How do I answer... evaluation only questions (AO3)?

Evaluation questions come in all sorts of shapes and sizes. Terms like 'evaluate', 'discuss', 'explain', 'criticism', 'strength' and 'limitation' all indicate that AO3 is required. The AO3 material for these questions is on the opposite page. Let's look at some examples:

Q1: Give **one** criticism of Stress inoculation therapy. **(2 marks)**

Remembering that 'criticisms' can be either negative or positive (so research support would count as a 'positive' criticism), you could choose any one of the AO3 points opposite as your material for **Q1**. For 2 marks, you could use the lead-in phrase (e.g. 'SIT may be unnecessarily complex…), followed by the material in the first two columns (i.e. the main critical claim and its expansion).

Q2: Evaluate the effectiveness of SIT. **(4 marks)**

Q2 requires a little more elaboration than **Q1** but this time you should start with the first evaluation point. You could then use **one** of points 2, 3 or 4 to give a more balanced evaluation.

Q3: Evaluate SIT and compare with **one** other approach to managing stress. **(6 marks)**

For **Q3**, you would take the same approach as for **Q2**, but this time using **two** of the AO3 points. Elaborate them fully and make sure you explain whether your point is a strength (positive evaluation) or limitation (negative evaluation) of the theory. As you are asked to compare with another approach, it would make sense to use point 3 and briefly elaborate 'biological treatments' by explaining about benzodiazepines and beta blockers (just one sentence on these) so that you can make an effective contrast.

REVIEW

Make a summary table of features and evaluation points relating to drug treatments and SITs. Try to do this without looking at the information on the opposite page. As you decide what the features (rows of your table) will be, you will be recalling the types of evaluation point. This could be very helpful for 'distinguish' questions, or for comparison as part of a discussion of one of the treatments. Then fill in the table from memory, to practise recall of both topics. And repeat.

RECAP

AO1 Description

- In **biofeedback**, a person learns to exert voluntary control over involuntary (autonomic) behaviours. Biofeedback combines biological (physiological activity) and psychological (operant conditioning) approaches.

- The four processes in biofeedback are:

  > **Learning relaxation techniques** These reduce sympathetic nervous system activity and activate parasympathetic activity. Since adrenaline and noradrenaline are no longer produced, stress symptoms are reduced.

  > **Feedback** Aspects of sympathetic activity (e.g. sweating) are measured by machines (e.g. skin conductance response), while the person relaxes. The machines give feedback about biological activity using light or sound. Other measures include EEG (heart rate), EEG (brain activity) and EMG (muscle tension).

  > **Operant conditioning** Lowering physiological activity is rewarding and reinforces the behaviour that caused it. Because it is reinforcing, the behaviour becomes more likely to be repeated.

  > **Transfer** The newly acquired learning is applied to the real world whenever stressors are encountered.

- Biofeedback was first demonstrated by Miller and DiCara (1967) who paralysed 24 rats. They rewarded half by stimulating brain 'pleasure centres' when their heart rates slowed, and the other half when their heart rates speeded up. Unconscious learning reinforced the heart rate changes.

- Biofeedback has been used to treat PTSD, a disorder that sometimes develops when a person experiences a traumatic event.

AO3 Evaluation/Discussion

Research evidence for effectiveness…

| Bradley (1995) found that biofeedback users had significantly fewer tension headaches than people using relaxation alone. | Additionally, Lemaire *et al.* (2011) found that doctors reported less stress after using biofeedback daily for a one-month period. | These findings suggest that biofeedback can be successful at managing the negative effects of stress. |

The operant conditioning component may be irrelevant…

| Relaxation itself reduces sympathetic nervous system activity; the presence of specialised equipment might make people believe the technique will be effective. | DiCara's results were 'lost' and may have been fabricated. Replications have been unsuccessful. | It seems that relaxation is the key factor, and operant conditioning may be irrelevant. Benefits may result from a placebo effect. |

Advantages in comparison to other methods…

| Biofeedback, unlike drugs, is not invasive, and can be used when drugs or SIT would be inappropriate (e.g. with children). | Whereas drugs treat symptoms, biofeedback tackles problems and symptoms, offering a long-lasting way of managing stress. | This means that biofeedback is a useful alternative when other methods cannot be used. |

Limitations of biofeedback…

| It is a relatively lengthy treatment, typically lasting more than a month, and requires expensive specialist equipment. | In addition, it requires effort from the person undertaking it, and supervision from trained staff. | This means that alternative approaches may be more useful as cost, time and effort may make biofeedback unsuitable. |

APPLY

AO2: An example

SCENARIO Darius is a soldier who has been suffering from PTSD for three years as a result of horrific experiences serving in the Iraq War. He presents with extreme anxiety attacks, flashbacks and nightmares. He has asked his doctor for drugs to help him, but his doctor would like him to try biofeedback first.

Explain why Darius's doctor is recommending biofeedback treatment for Darius. **(4 marks)**

ANSWER *Darius has a long-term stress disorder, so long-term drug use could lead to dependency or addiction. Biofeedback, however, is non-invasive so would not cause withdrawal symptoms, unlike drugs which could have side effects while they are being taken, and withdrawal symptoms when stopped. Darius's doctor wants him to avoid these unpleasant effects of drugs, and hopes that biofeedback could be just as effective. It would reduce the activity of Darius's sympathetic nervous system, so that his anxiety symptoms don't cause the physiological symptoms of heart racing, breathlessness, sweating, etc., and this would help him to feel more relaxed.*

AO2: Research methods

A researcher wanted to see if the high levels of sympathetic nervous system activity seen in PTSD sufferers could be reduced by biofeedback training. A hundred military personnel were randomly allocated to either an experimental group (who received biofeedback training) or a control group (who received no training). The physiological activity of all of the participants was measured before the study began. After the study was over, physiological activity was measured again. The results of the study are shown in the table below.

	Experimental group (Biofeedback training)	Control group (No biofeedback training)
Number showing a decrease in physiological activity	36	18
Number showing no change or an increase in physiological activity	14	32

a. **What percentage of participants showed a decrease in physiological activity overall? (2 marks)**

b. **State a suitable hypothesis for this study (3 marks)**

c. **Using the data in the table above, explain what the findings show. (4 marks)**

d. **Which statistical test could be used to analyse these findings? Explain your choice. (3 marks)**

e. **The researchers found the results to be significant at $p < 0.05$. Why did they choose this significance level? (2 marks)**

AO2: One for you to try

Chris now knows about a biological approach to managing stress (drugs) and a psychological approach (SIT). He is still undecided about which therapy he should use, so asks you if there is any form of therapy which combines biological and psychological processes. You describe what is involved in biofeedback to him, and he seems to be impressed by its potential. However, he really can't decide which of the three to choose.

Compare the three options, and explain what advice you would give to Chris. (6 marks)

How do I answer... longer (16-mark) questions?

The difference between the following two questions lies in how you approach the AO3 evaluation/ discussion. The AO1 and AO3 material for these questions is on the opposite page.

> **Q1:** Outline and evaluate biofeedback as a way of managing and coping with stress. **(16 marks)**

In **Q1**, the nominal mark division for AO1 (outline) and AO3 (evaluation) is 6 marks for AO1 and 10 marks for AO3. You could aim to include the first six AO1 points, which explain the theory and use important key terms, then use the Miller and DiCara study to show where the theory originated. For the AO3 content, you should include all four of the AO3 points.

> **Q2:** Discuss the usefulness of biofeedback in managing and coping with stress. **(16 marks)**

Q2 uses the command word 'discuss', so it requires AO3 that is a bit more 'discursive', e.g. looking at applications, implications, counter-evidence etc. We have tried to make some of our AO3 points 'discursive' to accommodate this. You will need to link points together to make a logical argument. For example, explain the research evidence (point 1) then evaluate it (point 2). Give an advantage (point 3) then link to a limitation (point 4), using 'However' at the start of your paragraph. You could expand point 3 slightly by adding a sentence about drugs only treating symptoms. If you use all these points in full you would have an excellent discussion.

REVIEW

Now you have covered three types of treatment (drugs, SIT and biofeedback), make a table to summarise key points about each of them. Use this to select points to answer different types of question: 2-, 4- or 6-mark 'outline' questions, 4-mark 'distinguish' questions, 4- or 6- mark 'evaluate' questions, or 16-mark questions on each treatment. Remember you can always include comparison with other treatments in the discussion for any one treatment, as long as you don't go too far down the route of evaluating the treatment you're using as a comparison. Keep focused on the question.

Gender differences in coping with stress

AO1 Description

- **Physiological differences** There are similarities in how men and women respond to stress, including increased adrenaline, noradrenaline, cortisol, and oxytocin.

- There are also important differences. For example, testosterone levels increase in men when confronted with a stressor.

- Testosterone dampens oxytocin, a hormone that promotes bonding feelings. So, while men respond to stress by becoming aggressive, women 'tend' (to their offspring) and 'befriend' (other group members for mutual defence) because their oxytocin is unsuppressed.

- Taylor *et al.* (2000) propose that **tend-and-befriend** is a more adaptive response for women because of differential parental investment in the offspring; such behaviour maximises their own, and their offspring's, survival chances.

- **Psychological differences** It has been claimed that men adopt a **problem-focused** (PF) and women an **emotion-focused** (EF) coping style in response to stressors (Peterson *et al.*, 2006). PF coping involves tackling the problem itself, whereas EF coping involves tackling the symptoms of stress, such as the anxiety that accompanies it.

- These coping differences may occur because men and women typically face different kinds of stressor. Men identify relationship, finance and work-related events as most stressful, whereas women identify family and health-related issues. The former require PF and the latter EF strategies (Matud, 2004).

OXYTOCIN

TEND AND BEFRIEND

TESTOSTERONE

FIGHT OR FLIGHT

AO3 Evaluation/Discussion

Females do not simply 'tend-and-befriend'…

Females behave aggressively in situations requiring defence, such as threats to their offspring.	Also, female animals whose offspring are mobile shortly after birth flee rather than stay huddled together.	*This shows that females adopt a variety of strategies to defend against stressors, rather than only 'tending and befriending'.*

Lack of research support for a gender difference in coping focus…

Hamilton and Fagot (1988) found no differences in coping styles used by male and female undergraduates.	Other research (e.g. Peterson *et al.*, 2006) has found that some men use EF rather than PF coping.	*This means that the simple division of men as users of PF, and women as EF, coping styles is far too simplistic.*

Methodological issues of self-report…

Men and women may differ in their willingness to reveal the emotional side of their coping.	Women may be more willing to report their emotional difficulties than men are.	*This means that reported differences in coping style may be a reflection of social desirability responding.*

Changing roles and lives of men and women…

It has been argued that men experience more job-related stress, but that may be because women were historically doing less stressful jobs.	Frankenhauser (1986) found that females in non-traditional gender roles (e.g. lawyers, bus drivers, engineers) had higher levels of stress hormones than women in traditional roles.	*This suggests that male stress may be a consequence of the activities they traditionally engaged in rather than any inherent differences in coping styles between men and women.*

APPLY

A02: An example

SCENARIO Sally and Jack work in the same council parking office. It is a stressful job, as they have to deal with a large number of difficult, and often abusive, telephone calls from people who are clearly unhappy about having received a parking ticket.

Using your knowledge of gender differences in coping with stress, explain how Sally and Jack are likely to cope with the specific stressors associated with their work role. **(4 marks)**

ANSWER *Sally and Jack are dealing with the same work-related stressors, but they may use different strategies. Peterson found that women tend to use more emotion-focused coping, to try to reduce their emotional response, so Sally may eat chocolate or talk to a friend when she is stressed – women are also more likely than men to use social support to deal with stress. Peterson found that men often use problem-focused coping, so Jack may try to pass difficult calls onto a manager or distance himself by refusing to engage. However, men also sometimes use emotion-focused coping.*

A02: Research methods

A researcher asked men and women to complete a survey about ways in which they dealt with stress. They were given 20 statements and asked to pick one option from a 4 point Likert scale.

1 = I usually don't do this at all

2 = I usually do this a little bit

3 = I usually do this a medium amount

4 = I usually do this a lot

Example statements include:

11. I discuss my feelings with someone.

12. I use alcohol or drugs to make myself feel better.

13. I concentrate my efforts on doing something about it.

a. **Suggest a statement which would relate to 'Problem focused' coping, and a statement to 'Emotion focused' coping. (2 marks)**

b. **What type of data will this scale collect? (1 marks)**

c. **Which statistical test would be suitable to analyse the difference between men's and women's coping styles? Explain your choice. (3 marks)**

d. **Explain what is meant by validity, and why self-report scales may lack validity. (4 marks)**

e. **How could the researcher assess the reliability of this scale? (3 marks)**

f. **The researcher decides to use another research method to gather data about men's and women's coping styles, in order to assess the validity of this self-report data. Suggest a suitable research method, and how it could be used in this study. (4 marks)**

A02: One for you to try

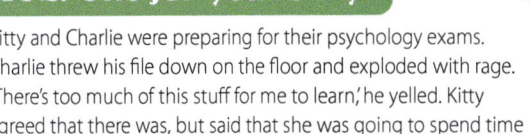

Kitty and Charlie were preparing for their psychology exams. Charlie threw his file down on the floor and exploded with rage. 'There's too much of this stuff for me to learn,' he yelled. Kitty agreed that there was, but said that she was going to spend time with her friends, and probably have an evening at the cinema.

Using your knowledge of gender differences in coping with stress, explain Kitty and Charlie's different reactions to the stress of revising for exams. (6 marks)

How do I answer... methodological questions?

Q1: Self-report scales have been used in many areas of stress research, including stress and Illness, life changes, daily hassles, workplace stress, hardiness, gender differences in coping with stress.

Discuss the validity of self-report measures of stress, referring to at least **two** of the areas above in your answer. **(8 marks)**

This question is focused on a particular research method, which is very commonly used in stress research. You could use AO3 evaluation points from any of the topics mentioned in the stem, so look through this Revision Guide to see how we evaluated the self-report data in each case.

You would bring in issues such as social desirability, and we mentioned on p.134–35 (Workplace stress) that interviews might give more valid data. Making a suggestion for how to improve the validity would be a useful part of your discussion. Similarly, contrasting the subjective nature of self-report data with more objective measures like skin conductance (see p.136) would also be interesting.

For this question, your AO1 would be description of the relevant self-report scales and AO3 would be discussion about validity issues and how to deal with them.

REVIEW

Checking back through all the topics in this chapter, looking for a particular term, such as 'self-report', will help you to gain an overview of the whole Stress topic. It would also be excellent to produce a large mind-map on a huge piece of paper, such as some leftover wallpaper, to link all the topics together. This will prepare you for more synoptic questions where you have to draw on information from more than one topic, either from a methodological angle (like the **How do I answer...?** example on this page) or in a discussion question with a double focus (see the next spread).

 **RECAP**

AO1 Description

- Social support is the help we receive from people during stressful times.
- Nabi *et al.*'s (2013) Facebook research suggests that perceptions of social support are directly correlated with the number of friends we have, and with lower levels of stress and less physical illness.
- Types of social support:
  > **Instrumental support** is when direct aid and material sources are offered. The focus is on doing something, such as providing money, and is a problem-focused approach.
  > **Emotional support** involves focusing on the anxiety a person is feeling, and trying to reduce it. This includes listening or offering advice, and is an emotion-focused approach.
  > **Esteem support** involves increasing a person's sense of self-worth so that they can feel more confident about coping with both instrumental and emotional issues. Typically, this involves someone in a close relationship making a person feel better about themselves.

- The buffering hypothesis proposes that social support protects people from stress because it helps them to think about stress differently. This kind of support is instrumental, because it is problem-focused.
- Social support also has direct physiological effects on the activity of the autonomic nervous system, increasing relaxation.

AO3 Evaluation / Discussion

Research evidence for the effectiveness of social support…

Kamarck *et al.* (1990) studied participants attempting a stressful mental task either alone or with a close same-sex friend for company.	Those attempting the task with a friend showed lower physiological reactions (e.g. heart rate) compared with those attempting the task alone.	*This shows that social support can have a direct physiological effect and lower activity of the autonomic nervous system.*

Gender and cultural differences in types of social support…

Lucknow *et al.* (1998) found that women are more likely than men to use emotional social support, and men are more likely to use instrumental social support.	In addition, Bailey and Dua (1999) found that participants from individualistic cultures (e.g. Anglo-Australian) preferred instrumental social support, whereas those from collectivist cultures (e.g. Asian) use emotional support more.	*Therefore, cultural differences, and differences between social norms for men and women, affect the strategies people use.*

Pets can also provide support and reduce stress…

Allen (2003) found that pets were beneficial in reducing children's blood pressure and cardiovascular risks in the elderly.	Even talking to pets can be more effective than talking to people in reducing stress.	*This suggests that we should value our pets, as much as we value our friends, as forms of support in coping with stress.*

Social support may vary in quality and importance…

Kobasa *et al.* (1985) found that social support was much less important than hardiness in reducing stress levels.	Kiecolt-Glaser and Newton (2001) found that social support was not always beneficial when friendships or relationships were strained.	*This suggests that the benefits of social support depend on the quality of the relationship and may be less important than personality factors like hardiness.*

APPLY

AO2: An example

SCENARIO Some universities provide a 'puppy room' for students to cuddle puppies during exam periods.

How might the puppy room help students during their exam period? **(4 marks)**

ANSWER *Students would be stressed during exams, and cuddling puppies could reduce stress by helping to calm down the sympathetic nervous system. Cuddling produces oxytocin, which is associated with a 'tend-and-befriend' response rather than a 'fight-or-flight' response, so the students will feel calmer. Students can talk to the pets and will not experience any strain in these relationships, whereas other students may also be stressed at exam time and could make things worse. Being with the puppies helps the student not to feel alone, at a time when their friends may be unavailable because they are busy revising.*

AO2: Research methods

A student researcher measured 'perceived social support' in 13 members of her psychology class who had Facebook accounts. As in Nabi *et al.* (2013), perceived social support was measured using the 12-item Multidimensional Scale of Perceived Social Support devised by Zimet *et al.* (1988). This includes statements such as 'My family really tries to help me', which are rated on a 7-point scale. Participants were also asked how many Facebook friends they had. The student then plotted the data on a scattergram, which is shown below.

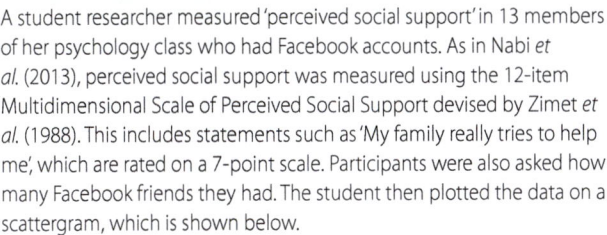

a. **The student was basing her study on Nabi *et al.*'s study. Explain why she used a directional hypothesis. (2 marks)**

b. **What kind of correlation does the scattergram show? (1 mark)**

c. **The student wanted to use Pearson's *r* to determine whether the correlation was significant. Identify two criteria for using a parametric test of correlation. (2 marks)**

d. **What test of correlation could the researcher have used if the criteria for using Pearson's test were not met? (1 mark)**

e. **The researcher set her significance level at *p*<0.05. She found a correlation of .30. Use the table of critical values below to decide whether the correlation is significant. (3 marks)**

Level of significance for a one-tailed test	0.05	0.01
Level of significance for a two-tailed test	0.10	0.02
df = N -2		
11	.476	.553
12	.475	.532
13	.441	.514

Observed value of *r* must be EQUAL TO or GREATER THAN the critical value in this table for significance to be shown.

AO2: One for you to try

Bruce, from Australia, and Ravi, from India, were about to take their psychology exam. Lou-Anne, from America, and Steve, from England, joined them in the cafeteria. All four students were nervous. 'What we need is help from other people to calm us down,' said Bruce. 'You mean social support?' said Steve. 'Yes, but there are different types of social support,' said Ravi. 'I think we'll differ in the kind of support we prefer,' said Lou-Anne.

Using your knowledge of gender and culture differences in social support, identify the different kinds of social support each student is likely to have sought. (4 marks)

How do I answer... synoptic questions?

Synoptic questions require you to link together information from more than one topic. For example:

> Discuss gender differences in relation to the role of social support in coping with stress. **(8 marks)**

- Take some time to underline or highlight key terms in the question, and think. Jot down a quick plan, and think about how many AO1 and AO3 points you will need.
- This example is going to need 3 marks of AO1 and 5 of AO3, and you will hopefully think straight away about the 'Gender...' AO3 point from this spread (research by Lucknow *et al.*). You could then go on to explain what instrumental and emotional social support mean (two AO1 points), with examples of each.
- These link into problem-focused and emotion-focused coping, which appear on the previous spread, 'Gender differences...' (AO1 point 5). You could elaborate using the final point from the 'Gender differences' AO1, which you could use as discussion here. Finally, the second or third AO3 point from the 'Gender differences...' spread would give you another paragraph of AO3.
- The lesson here is: don't be afraid to bring in material from related topics if it is relevant. Be brave, but keep focused!

REVIEW

Now you have finished revising this chapter, it is time for a revision audit. Make a table like this, and tick the 'Got it!' columns when you feel you have mastered the AO1 and AO3 components of each topic.

TOPIC	Got it!			Got it!	
	AO1	AO3		AO1	AO3
The physiology of stress			The role of stress in illness		
Life changes			Daily hassles		
Workplace stress			Measuring stress		
Personality			Hardiness		
Drug therapies			SIT		
Biofeedback					
Gender differences			Social support		

Neural and hormonal influences

 **RECAP**

AO1 Description

Neural influences

- **The limbic system** coordinates behaviours that satisfy motivational and emotional urges, such as aggression and fear. Two key structures in the limbic system that are associated with aggression are the amygdala and the hippocampus.

- **The amygdala** is responsible for evaluating the emotional importance of sensory information and prompting an appropriate response. If certain areas of the amygdala are stimulated, an animal responds with aggression.

- **The hippocampus** is involved with the formation of long-term memories, allowing an animal to compare the conditions of a current threat with similar past experiences. Impaired hippocampal function prevents the nervous system from putting things into context, and so may cause the amygdala to respond inappropriately to sensory stimuli, resulting in aggression.

- **Serotonin** typically inhibits the firing of the amygdala. Low levels of serotonin remove this inhibitory effect, so individuals are less able to control impulsive and aggressive behaviour. As a result, when the amygdala is stimulated by external events, it becomes more active, causing the person to act on their impulses, making aggression more likely.

Hormonal influences

- **Testosterone** The male sex hormone which is thought to influence aggression from young adulthood onwards due to its action on brain areas involved in controlling aggression.

  > Sapolsky (1998) described how removing the source of testosterone in different species typically resulted in much lower levels of aggression. Subsequently reinstating normal testosterone levels with injections of synthetic testosterone led to a return of aggressive behaviour.

  > Evidence for the testosterone-aggression link comes from various sources. Men are generally more aggressive than women (Archer, 2009), and have much higher concentrations of testosterone than women. Dabbs *et al.* (1987) measured salivary testosterone in violent and non-violent criminals. Those with the highest testosterone levels had a history of primarily violent crimes, whereas those with the lowest levels had committed only non-violent crimes.

  > Carré and Olmstead (2015) claim that testosterone concentrations are not static, but fluctuate rapidly in the context of changes to the social environment. Changes in testosterone levels appear to influence aggressive behaviour by increasing amygdala reactivity during the processing of social threat.

AO3 Evaluation/Discussion

Neural influences

Evidence for the role of the amygdala in aggression…

Pardini *et al.* (2014) found that reduced amygdala volume can predict the development of severe and persistent aggression.	They carried out a longitudinal study of male participants from childhood to adulthood. Fifty-six participants with varying histories of violence had a brain MRI at age 26. Those with lower amygdala volumes exhibited higher levels of aggression and violence.	*This suggests that lower amygdala volume compromises the ability to evaluate the emotional importance of sensory information and makes a violent response more likely.*

Evidence for the role of the hippocampus in aggression…

Raine *et al.* (2004) provided support for the role of the hippocampus in aggressive behaviour.	They studied two groups of violent criminals: one group who had acted impulsively and the others who were 'cold calculating criminals'. For individuals in the former group, their hippocampus volume in the two hemispheres of the brain differed in size.	*This asymmetry impairs the ability of the hippocampus and the amygdala to work together, so emotional information is not processed correctly, leading to inappropriate verbal and physical responses.*

Hormonal influences

Inconsistent evidence…

Despite many studies showing a positive relationship between testosterone and aggression, other studies find no relationship.	Positive correlations have been reported between levels of testosterone and self-reported levels of aggression among prison inmates (Albert *et al.*, 1994). On the other hand, no correlation was found between testosterone levels and actual violent behaviour among male inmates in prison.	*This suggests that the relationship between testosterone and aggression in humans remains unclear.*

Aggression or dominance?…

Mazur (1985) suggests that we should distinguish between aggression and dominance, and claims that aggression is just one form of dominance behaviour.	The influence of testosterone on dominance is expressed in varied and subtle ways. Eisenegger *et al.* (2011) found that testosterone could make women act 'nicer' rather than more aggressively depending on the situation.	*This supports the idea that, rather than directly increasing aggression, testosterone promotes status-seeking behaviour, of which aggression is one type.*

 **APPLY**

AO2: An example

SCENARIO Rhodri is a man in his early sixties. He has always been active and hates the thought of getting older. He is told he has low testosterone levels so decides to try having testosterone injections. A worrying side effect is that he finds himself feeling more aggressive and recently got into a fight at a local pub.

Explain what is happening to Rhodri. **(3 marks)**

ANSWER *Testosterone influences aggression because of its action in brain areas controlling aggressive behaviour. Because Rhodri has recently started having testosterone injections, this could explain his increased feelings of aggression and his increased levels of aggression. Testosterone also increases amygdala reactivity in the processing of social threat, so he might have misinterpreted the ambiguous actions of someone in the pub, leading to a fight with them.*

AO2: One for you to try

In 1848 Phineas Gage was working as a foreman during the construction of a new railroad in Vermont, USA. On one occasion, while clearing rocks for the railroad, Gage was using a tamping iron to compact explosives into the rock. However, the iron rod struck the rock, creating a spark that ignited the explosives, sending the rod up through Gage's skull, and exiting through the top of his head. Although he recovered from his injuries, Gage's personality changed after the accident, with reports suggesting that the formerly mild-mannered and friendly man had been transformed into someone who was moody, violently quarrelsome and displaying fits of temper. The accident, as well as destroying a large part of his frontal cortex, had also damaged the connections between the frontal cortex to the limbic system.

Using your knowledge of neural influences on aggressive behaviour, explain why Gage's behaviour changed so dramatically after the accident. (4 marks)

AO2: Research methods

A researcher was interested in studying the effects of testosterone on the brain's threat response in males. She placed an advertisement in a local newspaper inviting healthy young men to take part in the study. The 16 participants were randomly allocated to either a control condition or an experimental condition. The control group participants were given a placebo, while the experimental group participants were given testosterone. The researchers found that, compared with the control group, the experimental group participants showed increased reactivity of the amygdala when they viewed angry facial expressions.

a. **Name the sampling method used by the researcher. (1 mark)**

b. **Outline one limitation of using this sampling method in the study above. (2 marks)**

c. **Why were the participants randomly allocated to the control and experimental groups? (2 marks)**

d. **Identify a statistical test that could have been used to analyse the results. Give two reasons for choosing this test. (3 marks)**

How do I answer... research methods questions?

Questions requiring research methods knowledge can appear in any section of any paper in the AS or A Level exams. They could include any aspect of research methods, data analysis or ethical issues. Doing well in research methods questions is as much a case of thinking clearly and using common sense as it is regurgitating knowledge. Let's look at the example questions in **AO2: Research methods** (below left):

a. You are asked to identify the sampling method used in the study. This is a straightforward identification so no detail other than the name is necessary.

b. These questions will sometimes be set within the context provided by the scenario, but in this case, it is a straightforward 'limitation' question. So, identify a limitation and say why this is problematic for this sampling method.

c. For this question you need to be aware of why random allocation is important and then apply this reason to the context of this study.

d. There is a very useful test choice chart on p.24 of the Year 2 Student Book. Practise using this chart until it becomes second nature. As there is no mention of matching taking place and the researchers are looking for a 'difference' (level of amygdala activity) between the two groups, either an 'independent *t*-test' or a 'Mann-Whitney test' would be appropriate.

 REVIEW

You should be able to use the material on this spread to answer any question on the topic of neural and hormonal influences on aggression. This means being able to write 3-mark (75 words approx.), 4-mark (100 words) and 6-mark (150 words) descriptions of (each of) neural influences on aggression and hormonal neural influences on aggression. You should be able to write one AO3 point (75 words approx.) for each of these three topics and four AO3 points overall. Throughout this chapter we show you how to use this sort of material flexibly to answer all the different types of questions you might be asked. The more you practise using different parts of the same material in response to different questions, the more effective you will be in the exam.

Genetic factors in aggression

RECAP

AO1 Description

- **Twin studies** A study using adult twin pairs found that nearly 50 per cent of the variance in direct aggressive behaviour (i.e. aggression towards others) could be attributed to genetic factors (Coccaro *et al.*, 1997).

- **Adoption studies** A study of over 14,000 adoptions found that a significant number of adopted boys with criminal convictions had biological parents with convictions for criminal violence (Hutchings and Mednick, 1975).

- **Research on genetic factors in aggression** A meta-analysis of twin and adoption studies (Miles and Carey, 1997) found a strong genetic influence in aggression. Both genes and family environment were influential in determining aggression in youth, but at later ages the influence of rearing environment decreased and the influence of genes increased.

  > A meta-analysis by Rhee and Waldman (2002) concluded that although aggressive anti-social behaviour was largely a product of genetic contributions, the influence of other factors affected their expression.

- **MAOA: A gene for aggression?** A gene responsible for producing the enzyme MAOA is associated with aggressive behaviour. MAOA regulates the metabolism of serotonin in the brain, and low levels of serotonin are associated with impulsive and aggressive behaviour.

  > Caspi *et al.* (2002) discovered a variant of the gene associated with low levels of MAOA (MAOA-L). Those with this variant were significantly more likely to grow up to exhibit anti-social behaviour but only if they had been maltreated as children. Children with the MAOA-L variant who were not maltreated did not display anti-social behaviour.

Left: Twins Ronnie and Reggie Kray – sentenced to life imprisonment in March 1969 for gangland murders.

AO3 Evaluation / Discussion

Problems of sampling…

It is difficult to draw meaningful conclusions from studies that have focused exclusively on individuals convicted of violent crime.	Convictions for violent crime are relatively few compared to the vast number of violent attacks by individuals that never result in a conviction. They therefore represent just a small minority of those regularly involved in aggressive behaviour.	*This might explain why so many studies have found little or no evidence of heritability for violence.*

Difficulties of determining the role of genetic factors…

It is difficult to establish genetic contributions to aggressive behaviour for the following reasons:	As well as genetic factors, there are many non-genetic (i.e. environmental) influences on the manifestation of aggressive behaviour. These influences may interact with each other. Genetic factors may affect which environmental factors have an influence, and vice versa (gene–environment interaction).	*This highlights the problem of identifying the specific contribution of genetic factors to aggressive behaviour.*

Evidence for the influence of the MAOA gene…

A Finnish study has added research support that the MAOA gene is implicated in severe violent behaviours.	Tiihonen *et al.* (2015) studied prisoners, revealing that the MAOA-L variant, in combination with another gene (CDH13), was associated with extremely violent behaviour. There was no substantial evidence for either of these genes among non-violent offenders, indicating that this combination of genes was specific for violent offending only.	*However, although these genes may make it harder for some people to control violent urges, they do not predetermine violent behaviour.*

The MAOA gene might explain gender differences in aggressive behaviour…

An advantage of MAOA gene research is that it offers an explanation for the uneven rates of violence for males and females.	Niehoff (2014) suggests this is a consequence of the differential genetic vulnerability that males and females have to the MAOA gene. The MAOA gene is linked to the X chromosome. Women have two X chromosomes, whereas men have only one, and are therefore more likely to be affected.	*This could explain why males typically show more aggressive behaviour than females.*

APPLY

AO2: An example

SCENARIO Carl is in prison for repeated assault charges. While in prison he meets a relative who is also in prison for the same kind of offences. Carl never knew his biological family because he was adopted as a baby due to physical abuse from his parents. The relative tells him that Carl's biological father was also 'doing time' at another prison, and proceeds to tell him of the violent history of all his biological relatives.

With reference to Carl, outline and evaluate the genetic explanations of aggression. **(16 marks)**

ANSWER **An extract showing how you could address the AO2 requirements of this question:** *Carl's aggressive tendencies can be explained in terms of the genetics of aggression. For example, a study by Hutchings and Mednick (1975) found that a significant number of adopted boys with criminal convictions also had biological parents with convictions for criminal violence. It is also possible that members of Carl's biological family share the MAOA-L variant of the MAOA gene. Individuals with this variant have been found to be significantly more likely to grow up to exhibit anti-social behaviour if they had been maltreated as children (Caspi et al., 2002), which is consistent with the reason for Carl's adoption...*

AO2: Research methods

Twin studies assess the role of genetic factors by using the *concordance rate*. This is defined as the probability that a second twin will display a behaviour given that the first twin already displays it. To calculate the concordance rate, we find the number of twin pairs who both display a behaviour and divide it by the total number of twins we have studied.

A student conducted a very simple, small-scale study on twin pairs in his school. He found five pairs of MZ twins and five pairs of DZ twins. The first twin in each of the pairs had been rated by his peers as aggressive. He asked one of his friends to observe the other twins and decide whether they were 'aggressive' or 'not aggressive'. The results are shown below:

MZ twin pair no.	First twin	Second twin	DZ twin pair no.	First twin	Second twin
1	Aggressive	Aggressive	1	Aggressive	Not aggressive
2	Aggressive	Aggressive	2	Aggressive	Aggressive
3	Aggressive	Not aggressive	3	Aggressive	Aggressive
4	Aggressive	Not aggressive	4	Aggressive	Not aggressive
5	Aggressive	Aggressive	5	Aggressive	Not aggressive

a. **Calculate the concordance rate for the MZ twins. (2 marks)**
b. **Calculate the concordance rate for the DZ twins. (2 marks)**
c. **What do the concordance rates for the MZ and DZ twins suggest about the role played by genetic factors in aggression? (3 marks)**

AO2: One for you to try

Sara had read a really unusual report in a newspaper. She told her friend Maia: 'A guy called Freeman May had a grandfather who was really aggressive. The grandfather used to beat both his wife and children with a belt. One of his sons, Landon May, was so aggressive he actually murdered a woman. The really strange thing is that his son ended up on death row in the same prison as him after he murdered one of his friend's parents. It just goes to prove: some people really are natural born killers'.

Maia wasn't convinced: 'Well, you might be right, but it's very difficult to work out what is a product of our genetic inheritance.'

Suggest three reasons Maia could have given to Sara as to why it is difficult to determine the role played by genetic factors in aggression. (6 marks)

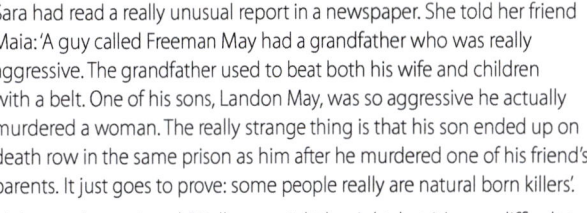

How do I answer... (AO1 + AO3) questions?

1. The command word 'discuss' can indicate AO1+AO3 or AO3 only. In **Q1** below, the addition of the word 'briefly' tells you that this is the former, requiring a brief outline of the role of the MAOA gene and a brief evaluation of this gene's influence.

2. Plan how much you should write for each. In mixed AO1 + AO3 questions up to 6 marks, the division is half and half.

3. Decide *what* to write.

> **Q1:** Briefly discuss the role of the MAOA gene in aggression. **(4 marks)**

For **Q1**, you would use the fifth AO1 point, together with an abridged version of the third AO3 point.

> **Q2:** Outline and evaluate genetic explanations of aggression. **(6 marks)**

For **Q2**, the AO1 requirement would be met by the three AO1 points. They would give a good 3-mark overview as required by the question. For the AO3 content you could use either the second AO3 point or abridged versions of the first and second AO3 points.

> **Q3:** Outline and evaluate findings from research into genetic explanations of aggression. **(6 marks)**

Bearing in mind that research findings can be used as AO1 for **Q3** or as an explanation of research support, we sometimes need a bit of detective work to find 3 marks' worth that we can use as AO1. The fact that research findings might appear in an AO3 section is irrelevant because we would only be using a statement of the findings from a study rather than using it to make a critical point.

REVIEW

One way of making sure you understand all the different aspects of genetic explanations of aggression is to do a bit of 'revision accounting'. When you feel you have mastered these different aspects, you have earned a ✓ in the 'Got it!' column. This list might include:

TOPIC	Got it!			Got it!	
	AO1	AO3		AO1	AO3
Twin studies (AO1)			Problems of sampling (AO3)		

The ethological explanation of aggression

RECAP

AO1 Description

- **Innate releasing mechanisms (IRMs)** An IRM receives its input from sensory recognition circuits that are stimulated by the presence of a very specific stimulus (the sign stimulus) in the environment.
  - > The IRM then communicates with motor control circuits to activate (i.e. release) the Fixed Action Pattern associated with that sign stimulus.

- **Fixed action patterns (FAPs)** All members of the same species have a repertoire of stereotyped behaviours which do not require learning, i.e. they are innate, and are the same in all conspecifics.
  - > FAPs are produced by a neural mechanism (the innate releasing mechanism), which is triggered by a sign stimulus.
- **Ritualistic aggression** Not all aggressive behaviour involves fighting but may be ritualised in the form of threat displays. These displays are important because they help individuals assess their relative strength before escalating a conflict, making costly and dangerous physical aggression less likely to occur.
  - > Gardner and Heider (1968) described how the Dani of New Guinea engaged in highly ritualised patterns of intergroup hostility.
- **Wolves and doves** Some species (e.g. wolves) have evolved natural weapons (e.g. strong jaws) that make them effective hunters. Such species have instinctive inhibitions that prevent them using these weapons against members of their own species. Non-hunting species (such as doves) have no such natural weapons, and therefore have not developed the same inhibitions against hurting their own kind.
  - > Lorenz believed that humans are more like doves than wolves. We do not have powerful natural weapons, and thus have had no need to develop strong instinctive inhibitions against killing one another.

AO3 Evaluation / Discussion

Criticisms of an 'instinctive' view of aggression…

Lehrman (1953) believed Lorenz underestimated the role of environmental factors in the development of species-typical aggressive behaviour patterns.	These environmental factors, largely the result of learning and experience, interact with innate factors in complex ways. Nowadays the term 'fixed action pattern' has been replaced by the term 'behaviour pattern' to reflect the fact that these are not simply innate and can be modified by experience.	*This suggests that patterns of aggressive behaviour are not as fixed as Lorenz claimed.*

Do humans have fixed action patterns for aggression?…

Because the environment in which humans exist changes so rapidly, Eibl-Eibesfeldt suggests FAPs such as aggression are no longer adaptive in modern times.	The flexibility of human behaviour and the ability to respond to an ever-changing environment has proved more effective than the production of stereotypical, fixed patterns of behaviour.	*This suggests that, although non-human species may respond aggressively to specific sign stimuli, human behaviour is far more varied and less predictable.*

The benefits of ritualised aggression…

The main advantage of ritualised aggression is that it prevents conflicts escalating into potentially dangerous physical aggression.	Chagnon (1992) describes how, among the Yanomamö people, chest pounding and club fighting contests can settle a conflict short of more extreme violence. Hoebel (1967) found that, among Inuit Eskimos, song duels are used to settle grudges and disputes.	*This shows that, even in violent cultures such as the Yanomamö, rituals have the effect of reducing actual aggression and preventing injury to, or death of, the combatants.*

Killing conspecifics is not that rare…

A problem for the ethological explanation concerns the claim that predator species have instinctive inhibitions that prevent them using their natural weapons against members of their own species.	This is not borne out by evidence. In some predator species, the killing of conspecifics is more systematic than accidental. Male lions will kill off the cubs of other males, and male chimpanzees will routinely kill members of another group.	*This casts doubts on the claim that much of animal aggression is ritualistic rather than real.*

 APPLY

AO2: An example

SCENARIO On television, a presenter lives with different tribes in the Amazonian rainforest. One tribe in particular is renowned for its violent behaviour, particularly when members of other tribes come into their territory. However, the presenter is at pains to point out that much of this is ritualistic, in the form of war dances and threat displays, rather than actual violence.

How might this form of behaviour be explained in terms of the ethological explanation of aggression? **(3 marks)**

ANSWER *This explanation claims that species have a repertoire of stereotyped fixed action patterns that occur in specific situations and are triggered by a sign stimulus. For the humans in this tribe, the ritualistic displays might be the fixed action pattern to the sign stimulus of enemies entering their territory. These threat displays are intended to make opponents back down without actual fighting. Anthropologists have found evidence of such ritualised aggression in tribal warfare in human cultures.*

AO2: Research methods

A researcher investigated how aggressively a pair of male and female fish behaved under different living conditions. In one condition, the the pair were kept together but in isolation from other fish. In the second condition, they lived with other fish in a communal tank. In the third condition, the fish were kept behind a glass screen that allowed them to see the fish in the other section of the tank. The number of aggressive behaviours seen is shown in the table below:

	Living in isolation	Living in a community	Living behind glass
Average frequency of chasing attacks by both fish	47	9	17

a. **Draw a suitably labelled bar chart of the data in the above table. (4 marks)**

b. **What is the main conclusion that can be drawn from the findings of this study? (2 marks)**

c. **How could the concept of action specific energy be used to explain the aggression that was seen when the fish lived in isolation? (3 marks)**

AO2: One for you to try

Tom was telling Duncan about a TV programme he'd recently seen. In it, two rival groups regularly met at a prearranged battleground and then used bows to fire arrows at each other. However, the arrows had no flights on them, so where the arrow landed was a matter of luck.

'For a culture steeped in the knowledge and experience of birds, and who know the importance of feathers, they must be pretty stupid not to use feathers to make their arrows fly true,' said Tom. 'Not at all,' said Duncan. 'Thanks for telling me that. You've just given me a brilliant AO3 point for a question on the ethological explanation of aggression.'

What AO3 point do you think Duncan was going to make from the description Tom had given him? (4 marks)

How do I answer... description only (AO1) questions?

There is a fairly simple formula in answering description only questions. For 2 marks, say two things, for 3 marks say three things and so on.

Work through the sample questions below, using the advice that follows them. The AO1 and AO3 material for these questions is on the opposite page.

> **Q1:** Briefly explain what is meant by an innate releasing mechanism. **(2 marks)**

Use the **two** AO1 points associated with innate releasing mechanisms.

> **Q2:** Describe the role of fixed action patters and innate releasing mechanisms in aggression. **(4 marks)**

For a 4-mark question, you should aim for about 100–120 words. You would use the two AO1 points associated with fixed action patterns from the opposite page *plus* the material you used in response to **Q1**.

> **Q3:** Outline evolutionary explanations of aggression. **(6 marks)**

Use the last four AO1 points on the opposite page.

This approach adds an appropriate level of detail to each answer and gives the examiner a useful way of discriminating between your answer and one that would be worth fewer than the maximum marks for that question.

REVIEW

In order to feel comfortable with this topic you should practise using the material in all the different ways that might be assessed in your exam.

1. We have shown you how to answer 2-mark questions about innate releasing mechanisms and fixed action patterns, but what could you add to these descriptions to make each worth 3 marks?

2. Write an essay plan showing how you would use the material on this spread to answer an 8-mark extended writing question for the ethological explanation of aggression. Remember, this means 3 marks' worth of AO1 and 5 marks' worth of AO3.

3. Write an essay plan showing how you would use the material on this spread to answer a 16-mark extended writing question for the ethological explanation of aggression.

Evolutionary explanations of human aggression

AO1 Description

- Aggression is a strategy that would have been effective for solving a number of adaptive problems among early humans (e.g. gaining resources or eliminating male rivals for females). Solving these problems enhanced the survival and reproductive success of the individual and, as a result, this strategy would have spread through the gene pool.

- **Sexual competition** Those individuals who used aggression successfully against competitors would have been more successful in acquiring mates and so more likely to pass on their genes to offspring.

  > This would have led to the development of a genetically transmitted tendency for males to be aggressive towards other males.

  > Puts (2010) argues that various male traits imply that competition with other males did take place among ancestral males. Men are far more aggressive than women, and are far more likely to die violently (Buss, 2005).

- **Sexual jealousy** Men are always at risk of cuckoldry, the reproductive cost that might be inflicted on a man as a result of his partner's infidelity. The adaptive functions of sexual jealousy would have been to deter a mate from sexual infidelity, minimising the risk of cuckoldry.

  > Buss (1988) suggests that males have a number of strategies that have evolved specifically for the purpose of keeping a mate.

  > These include the use of violence to prevent a female partner from straying. Studies of battered women have shown that women cite extreme jealousy on the part of their partners as the key cause of the violence directed towards them (Dobash and Dobash, 1984).

AO3 Evaluation/Discussion

Gender differences in aggression may be better explained by socialisation…

Prinz (2012) argues that these may be the product of different socialisation experiences rather than evolved differences.

For example, during childhood, girls learn that they are less powerful than boys. This may lead them to adopt other more social forms of aggression (i.e. behaviours designed to harm another person's social status or self-esteem) rather than physical aggression.

This casts doubt on the claim that males alone have evolved to be aggressive, as females have simply developed a different form of aggressive behaviour.

Aggressive behaviour may not always be adaptive…

One problem with seeing aggressive behaviour as an effective strategy is that it can result in social ostracism, injury or even death in extreme cases.

However, Duntley and Buss (2004) point out that, for our ancestors, the benefits of aggression must have outweighed the costs on average.

If this is the case, then natural selection would favour the evolution of aggressive behaviours, eventually making them fundamental components of human nature.

Support for the link between aggression and status…

The claim that increased aggression confers greater status is supported by anthropological evidence (Daly and Wilson, 1988).

This is also evident in modern industrialised societies, where the most violent gang members often have the highest status among their peers (Campbell, 1993). Males also display a heightened sensitivity to perceived affronts to their status and reputation, with many acts of male-on-male violence resulting from these (Buss, 2005).

This suggests that aggression is an important way of gaining status among males, and also a consequence of threats to that status.

Limitations of evolutionary explanations of aggression…

Evolutionary explanations of aggression fail to explain the astonishing levels of cruelty that are often found in human conflicts yet are not evident among non-human species.

For example, they do not explain the wide-scale slaughter of whole groups, as was evident in the Rwandan genocide in 1994. Nor do they tell us why humans torture or mutilate their opponents when they no longer pose a threat.

Anthropological evidence (e.g. Watson, 1973) suggests that this may be more a consequence of de-individuation effects than of evolutionary adaptations.

APPLY

AO2: An example

SCENARIO

Petra is preparing an assignment on domestic violence against women for her general studies project. *What aspects of the evolutionary explanation of aggression might Petra incorporate into her report?* **(4 marks)**

ANSWER

A problem for early males would have been to avoid cuckoldry, the reproductive cost as a result of his partner's infidelity. Sexual jealousy would have arisen as a consequence of this threat. Buss (1988) suggests that sexual jealousy might have led to the use of violence to prevent a partner from straying. If successful, this reaction would have become widespread in the gene pool because males who were successful would have been better able to pass on their own genes. In similar situations nowadays, when a male suspects his partner of infidelity, he might use violence against her to avoid the costs of cuckoldry.

AO2: Research methods

A researcher studied 10 members of a gang well known for its aggression. Each gang member was rated by his peers in terms of how violent they were. The researcher also asked each gang member to rate themselves and the others in terms of how much status each had in the gang's hierarchy (1 = highest, 10 = lowest). The researcher then ranked each gang member in terms of the two variables. It was predicted that there would be a positive correlation between how violent the gang members were and their status within the gang. The results are shown in the table below.

Gang member	Ranking on the violence measure	Ranking on the status measure
A	3	6
B	4	7
C	1	1
D	8	8
E	10	9
F	7	4
G	9	5
H	5	3
I	2	2
J	6	10

a. **State a null hypothesis for this investigation. (3 marks)**

b. **Identify if the hypothesis was directional or non-directional. Explain your answer. (3 marks)**

c. **Give two reasons why Spearman's *rho* was used to analyse the data. (2 marks)**

d. **The calculated value for Spearman's *rho* is .61. Is the correlation between the two variables significant at $p < 0.05$? Explain your answer. Use the table on p.31 of the Year 2 Student Book to help you. (3 marks)**

e. **The researcher concluded that aggression causes gang members to have a higher status within the gang. Why is this conclusion not justified? (3 marks)**

AO2: One for you to try

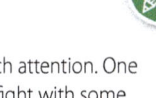

Nicholas liked Denise, but Denise never paid him much attention. One day, when they were out together, Nicholas picked a fight with some other men who had done nothing to provoke him. 'How can she resist me now?' he thought. 'What an idiot,' thought Denise.

What does the above scenario suggest about evolutionary explanations of aggression? (4 marks)

How do I answer... shorter (8-mark) essay questions?

Not all essays follow the 12- or 16-mark format. Some have a slightly lower tariff. Of these lower tariff essay questions, the 8-marker is the most common. It does help to know what you are dealing with, however, as they are not always straightforward.

Q1: Outline and evaluate evolutionary explanations for human aggression. **(8 marks)**

Although you might believe that **Q1** would be worth 4 marks for AO1 and 4 for AO3, this is actually half of a 16-mark essay question, so there is a similar split of marks, i.e. 3 marks for AO1 and 5 marks for AO3 (instead of the 6- and 10-mark split for a 16-mark question). You would be aiming for 75–90 words of AO1 and 125–150 words of AO3. This would mean AO1 points 1, 2 and 4 and any **two** of the AO3 points.

Q2: Angie had been married to Dale for just over two years. Dale was very jealous of her speaking to other men and had once embarrassed her by coming into her work and threatening one of her colleagues that he suspected of having an affair with her. When they were together he would constantly belittle her, calling her 'flat-chested' and telling her she had a 'big backside'. She would often find him looking through her Facebook pages and he would challenge her over any male friends who appeared on her account. On one occasion he had told her that if he ever caught her with another man he would kill her and him.

With reference to Angie and Dale, discuss evolutionary explanations for human aggression. **(8 marks)**

Q2 includes a scenario. This is an indication that there is an additional AO2 requirement in the question. AO2 marks tend to be 'stolen' from the AO3 allocation, so this question would be 3 marks of AO1 (first three points), 3 marks of AO3 (one complete AO3 point) *and* 2 marks' worth of AO2 (about 50 words). The Angie and Dale scenario could be explained through reference to sexual jealousy and the threat of cuckoldry. A consequence of sexual jealousy, as shown by Dale's behaviour, is that males use strategies such as belittling their partner's looks and threatening violence to stop them straying.

REVIEW

Simply reading material is not the most effective way of learning it properly. Using the material on the opposite page, try writing plans for 3-, 4- and 6-mark 'outline' questions on evolutionary explanations for human aggression plus plans for 8- and 16-mark essay questions.

Test yourself on the key points of these explanations by covering up your plans and writing them out again.

Spaced practice is also very effective: come back to the same topic tomorrow and start your revision by seeing how many of the points you can remember before you look at your essay plan.

The frustration–aggression hypothesis

RECAP

A01 Description

- Dollard *et al.* (1939) argued that aggression was the result of frustration. Frustration leads to the arousal of an aggressive drive, which leads to aggressive behaviour, consequently relieving the aggressive urges (catharsis).

- Frustration increases when our motivation to achieve a goal is strong, when we expect gratification, and when there is nothing we can do about it. Brown *et al.* (2001) found an increase in hostile attitudes towards the French as a result of passengers' frustration when their ferry was blocked by protesting French fishermen.

- **Justified and unjustified frustration** Pastore (1952) distinguished between unjustified (e.g. a bus not stopping at a bus stop) and justified (e.g. a bus showing an 'out of service' sign not stopping at a bus stop) frustration. He argued that it was mainly unjustified frustration that produces anger and aggression.

- **Displaced aggression** When it is inappropriate to behave aggressively towards the source of frustration, aggressiveness towards it is inhibited but may be displaced onto someone or something else.

- **Revised frustration–aggression hypothesis** Berkowitz (1989) argued that frustration is only one of many different types of unpleasant experience that can lead to aggression. These experiences create negative feelings in the individual and it is these, rather than the frustration, that triggers aggressive behaviour.

  > Anything that interferes with our ability to reach an anticipated goal is experienced as an unpleasant experience, which may produce anger. The nature of the frustrating event is less important than how negative is the resulting effect.

A03 Evaluation / Discussion

Aggression is not an automatic consequence of frustration…

Social learning theorists have argued that aggressive behaviour is only one possible response to frustration.	Frustration produces only generalised arousal in the individual, whereas social learning determines how that arousal will influence an individual's behaviour. They may respond aggressively if it has been effective for them before or if they have observed it being effective in others.	*Rather than frustration always leading to aggression, an individual learns to produce aggressive actions and also learns the circumstances under which they are likely to be successful.*

Lack of research support for the central claims…

Critics of the frustration–aggression hypothesis claimed that many of its predictions simply had no support, either in research or in real life.	The concept of catharsis, that aggression reduces arousal so that people are less likely to be aggressive, has not been supported by research. Bushman (2002) found that aggressive behaviour kept aggressive thoughts and angry feelings active in memory and made people more rather than less angry and aggressive.	*Bushman's research directly contradicts the claims that catharsis reduces aggression.*

Not all aggression arises from frustration…

A problem for the frustration–aggression hypothesis is that not all aggression arises from frustration.	In a study of baseball games, Reifman *et al.* (1991) found that, as temperatures increased, so did the likelihood that pitchers would display aggressive behaviour towards the batters, with balls often thrown at 90mph directed at the batter's head.	*This does, however, offer some support for the revised frustration–aggression hypothesis in that extreme temperatures, as with frustration, are aversive stimuli that tend to make people angry.*

Real-world application: Sports violence…

Priks (2010) provided evidence for the frustration–aggression hypothesis in a study of violent behaviour among Swedish football fans.	He used teams' performance as a measure of frustration and the number of objects (missiles, etc.) thrown onto the pitch as a measure of aggression. When a team performed worse than their fans expected, more things were thrown onto the pitch and the fans were more likely to fight with opposition supporters.	*Supporters became more aggressive when expectations of good performance were frustrated, thus supporting the frustration–aggression hypothesis.*

 **APPLY**

AO2: An example

SCENARIO The TV news carries a report of protesters blocking major roads and access routes to airports by chaining themselves together across the roads. This leads to aggressive outbursts aimed at the protesters from travellers and other road users.

With reference to these incidents, outline and evaluate the frustration–aggression explanation of aggression. **(16 marks)**

ANSWER An extract showing how you could address the AO2 requirements of this question: *Dollard et al. (1939) claimed that frustration leads to the arousal of an aggressive drive, which then leads to aggressive behaviour. Frustration increases when our motivation to achieve a particular goal is very strong and when there is nothing we can do about it. Because the protesters prevented people from completing their journeys, this was experienced as frustration. Many people would have been prevented from catching flights – therefore their frustration would have been very strong. Pastore (1952) distinguished between justified and unjustified frustration, arguing it was mainly the latter that produces anger and aggression. Many road users expressed their anger against the protesters, suggesting that they perceived this as unjustified frustration...*

AO2: Research methods

A researcher conducted a field experiment to test the frustration–aggression hypothesis. A male research assistant was instructed to push into a queue waiting to be served at a busy ticket office. In one condition, the assistant pushed in front of the person who was second in line. In another condition, the assistant pushed in front of the person who was twelfth in line. The research assistant did this 10 times in each condition. The researcher assumed that how close a person is to reaching their goal has a strong effect on how much frustration they experience. She predicted that people who were second in line would feel more aggressive than those who were twelfth in line. After each person had bought their ticket, they were asked to rate how aggressive they felt towards the research assistant on a 7-point scale (1 = not at all aggressive, 7 = extremely aggressive). The mean ratings are shown in the table below.

	Second in line	Twelfth in line
Mean rating	5.9	2.4

a. **Identify if the hypothesis was directional or non-directional. Explain your answer. (3 marks)**

b. **Outline one strength and one limitation of conducting field experiments in psychology. (4 marks)**

c. **Name a non-parametric statistical test that could have been used to analyse the data. Give two reasons for choosing this test. (3 marks)**

d. **The researcher wrote a report of her investigation and submitted it to a peer-reviewed journal. Explain what is meant by peer review. (2 marks)**

e. **Write a suitable abstract for this investigation. You should make reference to an aim/hypothesis, method, results, and conclusion in your answer. (6 marks)**

AO2: One for you to try

In a study conducted by Mallick and McCandless (1966), one group of children were prevented by a confederate, who directed sarcastic comments towards them, from completing a series of simple tasks for monetary reward (the frustration group). The confederate did not prevent a second group of children from completing the tasks (the control group). When the children were given the opportunity to behave aggressively towards the confederate, the group that were frustrated were significantly more aggressive.

Mallick and McCandless concluded that the results offered clear support for the view that frustration causes aggression. However, there is a potentially confounding variable in this study. Identify the variable and explain how it might affect the validity of the results. (4 marks)

How do I answer... essay questions with an AO2 component?

This type of question has three distinct components, an AO1 descriptive component, an AO3 evaluative component and an AO2 application component. Such questions are essentially the same as a straightforward essay (see p.159) *but*, for a 16-mark question, 4 of the marks available are used to assess your ability to explain the scenario outlined in the question using the material you are discussing. These marks are always taken from the AO3 allocation, so there are still 6 marks for AO1, but now the AO3 component drops from 10 marks to 6 marks with the remaining 4 marks for AO2.

Let's look at the scenario and question in **AO2: An example** on the left.

For 4 marks' worth of AO2, you should aim to write approximately 100–120 words explaining the scenario (in this case, an explanation of travellers' aggressive behaviour) using the psychological material on this spread.

In the scenario above, there are references to how frustration leads to the arousal of an aggressive drive, which then leads to aggressive behaviour. This is followed by an explanation of the frustration experienced as a result of the protesters' actions and why this might have led to aggressive outbursts from the travellers. A second bit of psychology is Pastore's distinction between 'justified' and 'unjustified' frustration. In the context of the scenario, many of the travellers would have perceived this as the latter, hence would be more likely to expressive themselves aggressively.

Remember that, first and foremost, this is an essay on the frustration–aggression explanation of aggression, but you should not ignore the AO2 content, which is not as difficult as you might think!

REVIEW

Understanding the different processes and aspects of frustration–aggression (including the revised frustration–aggression theory) can be tricky. There are a few things that you can do to help you with this.

1. Try explaining these to someone else (or even the dog, cat or teddy bear who won't be critical or snigger while you are doing it!).

2. Go back and read your notes again and then explain each in even more detail until you think Rover, Fang or Teddy would (had they *really* been listening) have a good understanding of both processes.

3. Try writing (and answering) a few of your own exam questions on this topic to consolidate this understanding.

Social learning theory

AO1 Description

- Social learning theory (SLT) suggests that we learn by observing others. We learn the specifics of aggressive behaviour (e.g. the forms it takes and the targets towards which it is directed).

- **Observation** Children primarily learn their aggressive responses through observation – watching the behaviour of role models and then imitating that behaviour.

- **Vicarious reinforcement** Children observe and learn about the consequences of aggressive behaviour by watching others. By observing the consequences of aggressive behaviour in others, a child learns something about what is considered appropriate (and effective).

- **Mental representation** For social learning to take place, the child must form mental representations of events in their social environment. These represent possible rewards and punishments for their aggressive behaviour in terms of expectancies of future outcomes.

- **Maintenance through direct experience** If a child is rewarded for an aggressive behaviour (e.g. bullying), they are likely to repeat the same action in similar situations in the future.

- **Self-efficacy expectancies** Children develop confidence in their ability to carry out the necessary aggressive actions. If previous attempts to use aggression have been unsuccessful, they develop a lower sense of self-efficacy in their ability to use aggression to resolve conflicts.

Bandura *et al.* (1961)

- **PROCEDURE** Participants were male and female children aged three to five years. Half saw adult models displaying distinctive physically aggressive acts towards a Bobo doll and half saw models that were non-aggressive towards the doll.

  > Following exposure to the model, children were frustrated by being shown attractive toys which they were not allowed to play with. They were then taken to a room where, among other toys, there was a Bobo doll.

- **FINDINGS** Children in the aggression condition reproduced a good deal of physically and verbally aggressive behaviour resembling that of the model. Children in the non-aggressive group exhibited virtually no aggression towards the doll.

  > Boys reproduced more imitative physical aggression than girls, but they did not differ in their imitation of verbal aggression.

AO3 Evaluation / Discussion

Lack of realism in research…

There are significant methodological problems with Bandura's Bobo doll studies.	For example, a doll is not a living person, and does not retaliate when hit. This raises questions about whether these studies tell us much about the imitation of aggression towards other human beings (who of course may well retaliate).	Children watched a film of an adult hitting a live clown. They later imitated these same aggressive behaviours, suggesting imitation of aggressive behaviour is also likely towards other human beings.

Research support for social learning theory…

Gee and Leith (2007) supported the SLT explanation of aggression with a study of ice hockey players.	They analysed penalty records from 200 games of the National Hockey League (NHL), believing that players born in North America would have been exposed to more aggressive models on television when young compared to players born in Europe.	In line with these predictions, players born in North America were much more likely to be penalised for aggressive play and fighting than players born in other countries.

Explaining inconsistencies in aggressive behaviour…

A strength of SLT is that it can explain inconsistencies in an individual's use of aggressive behaviour.	SLT would explain the fact that males would act aggressively in some situations but not others in terms of the consequences of acting aggressively in the respective situations.	As a result, this means that we can predict whether or not aggression is likely in a particular situation by knowing its likely consequences.

The consequences of social learning…

If aggressive behaviour can be learned through social learning, this raises concerns about the widespread availability of aggressive models in young people's lives.	ACT Against Violence is an intervention programme that aims to educate parents and others about the dangers of providing aggressive role models and to encourage parents to provide more positive role models instead.	Parents demonstrated increases in positive parenting and discontinuation of physical punishment, showing that social learning can be used to decrease aggressive behaviour (Weymouth and Howe, 2011).

APPLY

AO2: An example

SCENARIO Kelly has noticed that since her three-year-old son has started preschool he has become a lot more aggressive in his behaviour towards other children.

Explain this change in behaviour in terms of the social learning theory of aggression. **(4 marks)**

ANSWER *Children primarily learn their aggressive responses through observation, watching the behaviour of role models with whom they identify and then imitating that behaviour. Kelly's son may have learned by observing and imitating the aggressive behaviour of the older children. By observing the consequences of their behaviour, he would have learned what is appropriate behaviour in that situation. He might have seen other children getting what they wanted by being aggressive, so would have learned through vicarious reinforcement.*

AO2: Research methods

An evaluation of the ACT Against Violence intervention programme measured violence prevention skills and prosocial parenting practices in a sample of 339 parents drawn from communities of Spanish-speaking and English-speaking populations from cities across the US. Participants completed measures assessing various parenting skills and practices. These included their violence prevention skills (e.g. 'I pay attention to what I say and do in front of my child') and their prosocial parenting practices (e.g. 'When my child misbehaves I…'). They completed these measures *before* the intervention programme and then again after the programme, to measure their internalisation of the intervention programme's messages. Some of the results are summarised below.

	Pre-intervention mean score	Post-intervention mean score	Significance level
VIOLENCE PREVENTION SKILLS (Spanish speakers)	38.05	42.08	<0.05
(English speakers)	39.49	41.02	<0.05
PROSOCIAL PARENTING PRACTICES (Spanish speakers)	33.03	39.25	<0.05
(English speakers)	33.19	34.28	<0.05

a. **Construct a directional hypothesis for violence prevention skills among the English-speaking sample. (3 marks)**

b. **Do the Spanish or English speakers show the greatest improvement after the intervention programme? Explain your answer. (3 marks)**

c. **The significance level achieved in all four cases was <0.05. Explain what this means. (2 marks)**

d. **If the researchers decided to only accept their hypothesis at the <0.01 significance level, would this increase the chances of a Type I or a Type II error? Explain your answer. (3 marks)**

AO2: One for you to try

The American Psychological Association-sponsored intervention programme ACT Against Violence aims to educate parents about the dangers of providing aggressive role models for their children and to encourage parents to provide more positive role models instead.

Using your knowledge of the social learning theory explanation of aggression, explain why such a programme might be necessary and what message it would try to get across to parents. (4 marks)

How do I answer… evaluation only (AO3) questions?

Evaluation questions also come in all sorts of shapes and sizes. Terms like 'evaluate', 'discuss', 'explain', 'criticism', strength' and 'limitation' all indicate that AO3 is required. The AO3 material for these questions is on the opposite page. Let's look at some examples:

> **Q1:** Give **one** criticism of the social learning theory explanation of aggression. **(2 marks)**

> **Q2:** Explain **one** limitation of the social learning theory explanation of aggression. **(3 marks)**

> **Q3:** Evaluate the social learning theory explanation of aggression. **(6 marks)**

Remembering that 'criticisms' can be either negative or positive (so research support would count as a 'positive' criticism), you could choose any one of the AO3 points opposite as your material for **Q1**. For 2 marks, you could use the lead-in phrase (e.g. 'There is research support for social learning theory… '), followed by the material in the last two columns (i.e. what Gee and Leith did in their research and what they found).

Q2 requires a little more elaboration than **Q1** but this time you are restricted to something that limits the value of self-disclosure as an explanation of attraction. For example, you might choose to use the second one ('There is a lack of realism in SLT research… ') with material from all three columns being used to access the 3 marks on offer.

For **Q3**, you would take the same approach as for **Q2**, but this time using **two** of the AO3 points. Don't try to use more than two; it would make your treatment of them too superficial.

REVIEW

Simply reading material is not the most effective way of learning it properly. So, using the material on the opposite page, try writing plans for 3-, 4- and 6-mark 'outline' questions on the social learning theory explanation of aggression plus plans for 8- and 16-mark essay questions.

Test yourself on the key points of this explanation by covering up your plans and writing them out again. It's useful to have a supply of cheap paper for this, as the more times you practise retrieving the information, the better you will remember it.

Spaced practice is also very effective: come back to the same topic tomorrow and start your revision by seeing how many of the points you can remember before you look at your essay plan.

De-individuation

AO1 Description

- **The nature of de-individuation** The psychological state of de-individuation is aroused when individuals join crowds or large groups. Zimbardo believed that being in a large group gave people a 'cloak of anonymity' that diminished any personal consequences for their actions.
  - > Factors that contribute to this state of de-individuation include anonymity (e.g. wearing a uniform) and altered consciousness due to drugs or alcohol.

- **The process of de-individuation** People normally refrain from acting in an aggressive manner partly because there are social norms inhibiting such 'uncivilised' behaviour and partly because they are easily identifiable.
  - > Being anonymous (and therefore effectively unaccountable) in a crowd has the psychological consequence of reducing inner restraints and increasing behaviours that are usually inhibited.
  - > Conditions that increase anonymity also minimise concerns about evaluation by others, and so weaken the normal barriers to anti-social behaviour that are based on guilt or shame.

- **Research on de-individuation** Zimbardo et al.'s Stanford prison study (1972) found that 'guards' who wore mirrored sunglasses to increase their de-individuated state acted aggressively towards participants who were in the role of prisoners. Other researchers have found that wearing mirrored sunglasses makes people feel greater anonymity, which in turn increases the experience of de-individuation (Zhong, 2010).

Zimbardo (1969)

- **PROCEDURE** Groups of four female undergraduates delivered electric shocks to another student to 'aid learning'. Half of the participants wore bulky lab coats and hoods that hid their faces, sat in separate cubicles and were never referred to by name.
  - > The other participants wore their normal clothes, were given large name tags to wear and were introduced to each other by name. They were also able to see each other when seated at the shock machines.

- **FINDINGS** Participants in the de-individuation condition (i.e. hooded and no name tags) were more likely to press a button that they believed would give shocks to a 'victim' in another room. They held the shock button down for twice as long as did identifiable participants.
  - > This led to the suggestion that anonymity, a key component of the de-individuation process, increased aggressiveness.

AO3 Evaluation / Discussion

Gender differences in de-individuation effects…

Cannavale *et al.* (1970) found that male and females responded differently under de-individuation conditions.	An increase in aggression was obtained only in all-male groups and not in all-female groups. This was also the finding of Diener *et al.* (1973), who found greater disinhibition of aggression in de-individuated males than in de-individuated females.	One reason for these gender differences is that males respond to provocation in more extreme ways than do females and these tendencies are magnified under de-individuation conditions (Eagly, 2013).

Anonymity and de-individuation…

Rehm *et al.* (1987) provided support for the de-individuation concept with an investigation of aggressive behaviour in sport.	They observed 30 games of handball in German schools. One team in each game wore the same orange shirts, while the other team wore their own different-coloured shirts. The researchers found that the uniformed teams showed significantly more aggressive acts during the game than did the teams without uniforms.	The results support the claim that de-individuation through increased anonymity leads to more aggressive acts.

Inconclusive support for de-individuation…

A meta-analysis of de-individuation studies (Postmes and Spears, 1998) concluded that there is insufficient support for the major claims of de-individuation theory.	Anti-social behaviour was not more common in large groups and anonymous settings. Rather, they found that de-individuation increases people's responsiveness to situational norms. This can lead to aggression, but also to increased prosocial behaviour.	This shows that evidence for de-individuation theory is mixed, and that de-individuation doesn't always lead to aggressive behaviour.

Real-world application: The baiting crowd…

Mann (1981) used the concept of de-individuation to explain the 'baiting crowd' and suicide jumpers.	Mann analysed newspaper reports of suicide leaps. In 10 of the 21 cases, the crowd had urged the potential suicide jumper to jump. These incidents mostly occurred at night, when the crowd was large and some distance from the jumper. These features were likely to produce a state of de-individuation in crowd members.	This study lends support to the notion of the anonymous crowd as a de-individuated 'mob'.

APPLY

AO2: An example

SCENARIO In his cultural history class, Connor learns about the violence in Northern Ireland in the 1980s and 1990s. In one incident, a large group of masked youths took to the streets of Belfast at night and threw petrol bombs and bricks at the security forces.

With reference to this incident, outline and evaluate the de-individuation explanation of aggression. **(16 marks)**

ANSWER **An extract showing how you could address the AO2 requirements of this question:** *A state of de-individuation arises when individuals join crowds or large groups, giving them a 'cloak of anonymity' that diminishes any personal consequences for their actions. This incident describes how the 'large group' of youths were 'masked' and the incident took place 'at night'. These are factors associated with de-individuation. In large groups there is a diminished fear of negative evaluation of actions and a reduced sense of guilt. Research has shown that individuals who believe their identities are unknown are more likely to behave aggressively. This would explain why these youths felt safe to act violently towards the security forces, because their identity was hidden by their masks...*

AO2: Research methods

The table below shows the results obtained by Watson (1973) in his study of the extent to which warriors in 23 societies changed their appearance prior to going to war and the extent to which they killed, tortured, or mutilated their victims.

	Did not change their appearance	Changed their appearance
Low levels of killing, torture, and mutilation	7	3
High levels of killing, torture, and mutilation	1	12

The data in the table above could be analysed using a 2×2 Chi-Squared test. Calculate the value of Chi-Squared using the step-by-step procedure on p.32 of the Year 2 Student Book. [Note: you would never be asked to work out the value of Chi-Squared in an exam, but it's good to practise!]

a. State a non-directional hypothesis for Watson's study. (2 marks)

b. Is the value of Chi-Squared significant at $p < 0.05$? Use the table on p.32 of the Year 2 Student Book to explain your answer. (3 marks)

c. State a conclusion based on the outcome of the statistical test. (2 marks)

AO2: One for you to try

In the trial of the Sharpeville Six in South Africa, the accused were convicted of the mob murder of the deputy mayor after a protest march against rent rises turned violent. During the trial, Graham Tyson, a South African psychologist called as an expert witness, suggested that it was highly probable that de-individuation had taken place, leading to diminished responsibility among the individual members of the mob.

Explain why Tyson might have believed it was 'highly probable' that de-individuation had taken place for members of the Sharpeville Six. (6 marks)

How do I answer... application (AO2) questions?

Let's look again at the scenario of the Sharpeville Six in **AO2: One for you to try** above.

One way of answering questions such as this is to remember the 'say one thing for 1 mark' and 'say four things for 4 marks' strategy.

1. **Find a bit of appropriate psychology,** e.g. 'The psychological state of de-individuation is aroused when individuals join crowds or large groups.'

2. **Use this to explain some aspect of the scenario,** e.g. 'The Sharpeville Six were part of a much larger group of protesters who were on a march against rent rises when the murder took place.'

3. **Find a second bit of psychology,** e.g. 'Zimbardo believed that being in a large group gave people a "cloak of anonymity" that diminished any personal consequences for their actions.'

4. **Use this to explain the scenario,** e.g. 'Tyson suggested that individuals within the mob had acted as they did, not out of a motivation to commit murder but as a consequence of de-individuation.'

REVIEW

Craik and Lockhart (1972) proposed a theory of memory called the 'levels of processing model'. This model claimed that the more that information is elaborated, the more likely we will be able to access that information later on. There are many different ways of elaborating material, so let's try one.

Take a large sheet of paper (A3 works well here) and construct a mind-map so that all your material on the de-individuation explanation of aggression is linked together in a wonderfully visual way. This serves several purposes: (1) It *elaborates* the material, making it more memorable; (2) The act of constructing the mind-map counts as *revision*, again making it more likely you can recall in an exam; and (3) You have a visual image of the material, which, for many people, is a much easier way of remembering complex material.

*Tip: There is a wealth of useful revision videos on the Internet – take a look for some on mind-map construction.

Institutional aggression in prisons

 **RECAP**

AOI Description

Situational explanation: The deprivation model

- **Institutional aggression** is the product of the stressful conditions of the prison itself (Paterline and Peterson, 1999).

- Deprivations linked to an increase in violence include the loss of: liberty, autonomy and security. Some inmates cope by withdrawing through seclusion in their cell, others through violence against other prisoners or staff.

- Violence in prison is frequently a way of surviving the risk of exploitation (Kimmet and Martin, 2002). They found that most violent situations in prisons were related to the need for respect or a way of expressing loyalty.

- **The role of prison characteristics** Cooke et al. (2008) argue that 'violent prisoners are only violent in certain circumstances, for example:

  > **Overcrowding** A government report in 2014 attributed the record rates of murder, suicide and assaults to the increased overcrowding in British prisons.

  > **High temperatures and noise** predispose inmates to aggressive behaviour. Griffitt and Veitch (1971) found that a combination of high temperature and high population density produced more negative emotions among inmates.

Dispositional explanation: The importation model

- Irwin and Cressey (1962) claim that inmates bring with them to prison their violent pasts and draw on their experiences in an environment where toughness and physical exploitation are important survival skills.

- **Cultural belief systems** such as 'the code of the street' define how some individuals behave once in prison, particularly when this code relates to membership of violent gangs.

- **Gang membership** A study of prisons in the US (Drury and DeLisi, 2011) found that individuals who had been members of gangs prior to imprisonment were far more likely to commit an assault.

- **The role of dispositional characteristics** relating to aggressive behaviour in prison including:

  > **Anger, anti-social personality style and impulsivity** Wang and Diamond (1999) found that these three individual characteristics were stronger predictors of institutional aggression than ethnicity and type of offence committed.

  > **Low self-control** DeLisi et al. (2003) found that low self-control, particularly the tendency to lose one's temper easily, was a significant predictor of aggressive behaviour before and during incarceration.

AO3 Evaluation / Discussion

The dispositional explanation
Research support for the importation model

| Mears *et al.* (2013) tested claims that inmate behaviour stems from cultural belief systems that they bring with them into prison. | Their findings supported the argument that a 'code of the street' belief system affects inmate violence. This effect is particularly pronounced among inmates who were involved in gangs prior to imprisonment. | *Mears et al. conclude that, in prisons, the 'code of the street' is likely to involve violence as a way of commanding respect.* |

Challenges to the importation model...

| Evidence from DeLisi *et al.* (2004) challenges the claim that pre-prison gang membership predicts violence while in prison. | Inmates with prior street gang involvement were no more likely than other inmates to engage in prison violence. Neither street gang nor prison gang membership significantly predicted involvement in prison violence. | *This can be explained by the fact that violent gang members tend to be isolated from the general inmate population, therefore greatly restricting their opportunities for violence.* |

The situational explanation
Research support for the deprivation model...

| Research supports the claim that peer violence is a response to the deprivation experienced in institutional cultures, such as prisons. | McCorkle *et al.* (1995) found that situational factors such as overcrowding and lack of privacy significantly influenced inmate violence. Prisons with inmates involved in educational or vocational programmes had lower incidence of violence. | *This suggests that depriving inmates of meaningful activity increases the likelihood of violent behaviour.* |

Challenges to the deprivation model...

| The link between situational factors and institutional aggression is challenged by the findings of Harer and Steffensmeier (1996). | They collected data from 58 prisons in the US. They included importation variables (e.g. criminal history) and deprivation variables (e.g. staff-to-prisoner ratio) and tested which of these predicted the likelihood of aggressive behaviour. | *Age and criminal history were the only significant predictors of violence, whereas none of the deprivation variables were significant in this respect.* |

⚙ APPLY

AO2: An example

SCENARIO *Using insights from the dispositional explanation of prison violence, consider what steps might be taken to minimise institutional aggression in prisons.* **(4 marks)**

ANSWER *Drury and DeLisi (2011) found that individuals who had been members of gangs prior to imprisonment were significantly more likely to engage in violence while in prison. Prisoners might be screened for gang membership when entering prison, and any members of violent street gangs could be kept in special units where their contact with other prisoners is minimised. Other dispositional characteristics that have been found to relate to aggressive behaviour in prison include anger and low levels of self-control (DeLisi et al., 2003). Prisoners could be given anger management sessions and be taught self-control to minimise the likelihood of them getting into fights with other prisoners.*

AO2: Research methods

Psychologists carried out case studies of six individuals who had been members of violent gangs prior to being sent to prison. These six individuals were studied for the first six months of their prison sentence, with researchers having access to video material showing their interactions with other prisoners and with staff. Researchers also carried out regular unstructured interviews with the individuals and with prison staff.

a. **Briefly explain one strength and one limitation of using case studies to investigate the dispositional explanation of institutional aggression. (4 marks)**

b. **Briefly explain what is meant by an 'unstructured interview' and give one strength of using unstructured interviews in this investigation. (4 marks)**

c. **Suggest one open question that the researchers might use in interviews with the six individuals. (1 mark)**

d. **Identify one ethical issue that might arise in this study and explain what the researchers might do about it. (3 marks)**

AO2: One for you to try

Under the heading 'Prisoners live in luxury', a national newspaper reported the following:

'Dozens of photos uploaded to Facebook show prisoners boasting of a cushy prison lifestyle with access to TVs showing Champion's League football, gaming consoles and gyms, while eating food that includes curries, kebabs, birthday cakes and crisps.'

The article attracted the following comment from a reader:

'Send them to Penal Colony 43 in Siberia, −40C and no luxuries there.'

Linz burst out laughing at this comment. 'Why are you laughing?' said Fay. 'It's exactly what should happen to people who are put in prison.' 'Don't be ridiculous,' said Linz. 'There's actually a very good reason for prisoners having access to all that stuff.'

Using your knowledge of research into institutional aggression in prison, explain what the 'very good reason' might be. (3 marks)

🐾 How do I answer... 'Distinguish between' questions?

Explain the difference between dispositional and situational explanations of institutional aggression. **(3 marks)**

There are some fairly simple rules for answering this sort of question. If you are asked to 'distinguish between…', 'compare…' or 'explain the difference between…', then these rules apply:

1. Don't just *describe* the two things you are being asked to distinguish between.

2. Pick some characteristic that applies to both but which is different for each and point that out (e.g. how each explains institutional aggression). For example, 'Dispositional explanations claim that inmates bring with them to prison their violent pasts and draw on these experiences while in prison.' 'Situational explanations claim that institutional aggression is the product of the stressful conditions of the prison itself, and in response to these conditions, inmates act more aggressively.'

3. Use words like 'whereas', 'however' and 'on the other hand' to point out this difference. That gives us 'Dispositional explanations claim that inmates bring with them to prison their violent pasts and draw on these experiences while in prison. On the other hand, situational explanations claim that institutional aggression is the product of the stressful conditions of the prison itself, and in response to these conditions, inmates act more aggressively.'

4. Don't be too ambitious; one point of difference is usually enough.

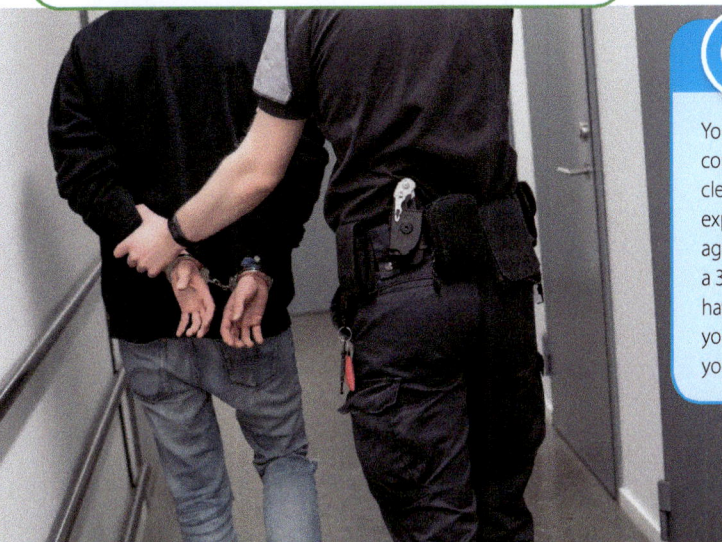

🔄 REVIEW

You need to be able to answer questions with different mark allocations concisely while using enough detail to explain these two explanations clearly. Practise answering 3-, 4- and 6-mark AO1 questions on dispositional explanations and the same for situational explanations of institutional aggression. You should spend about a minute and a quarter per mark, so for a 3-mark question you have just under 4 minutes, for a 4-mark question you have 5 minutes and for a 6-mark question you have 10 minutes. Make sure you allow time to plan logical answers. You could use a timer to make sure you keep to time.

Media influences on aggression

RECAP

AO1 Description

Violent films and TV

- **Laboratory and field experiments** A consistent finding is that those who watch violent scenes display more aggressive behaviour and have more aggressive thoughts or aggressive emotions than those who do not.
  - › Compared with children who viewed a non-violent film, 5- to 6-year-olds who watched a violent film were subsequently rated much higher on measures of physical aggression (Bjorkqvist, 1985).
- **Longitudinal studies** Huesmann *et al.* (2003) studied children between the ages of 6 and 10, and then again 15 years later. Habitual early exposure to TV violence was predictive of later adult aggression.
  - › This relationship persisted even when the possible effects of socioeconomic status, intelligence and any differences in parenting styles were controlled.
- **Meta-analyses** Bushman and Huesmann (2006) found significant effect sizes for exposure to media violence on aggressive behaviours, aggressive thoughts, angry feelings and arousal levels.
  - › Short-term effects of violent media were greater for adults than for children. Long-term effects were greater for children than for adults.

Violent computer games

- Interactive violence in video games has the potential to exert even more influence than TV violence, where the viewer plays a more passive role (Porter and Starcevic, 2007).
- **Experimental studies** Lab experiments have found short-term increases in hostile feelings and aggressive behaviour following violent game play compared to non-violent game play (Gentile and Stone, 2005).
  - › Anderson and Dill (2000) found that participants blasted their opponents with white noise for longer after playing a violent game, compared to those who played a slow-paced puzzle game.

- **Longitudinal studies** surveyed children at two points during the school year. Children with higher exposure to violent video games became more verbally and physically aggressive and less prosocial (Anderson *et al.*, 2007).
  - › Adachi and Willoughby (2013) suggest that the link found between violent video games and aggression may be due to the competitive nature of the games, rather than any violence.

Greitemeyer and Mügge (2014)

- **PROCEDURE** Greitemeyer and Mügge carried out a meta-analysis of 98 studies, involving nearly 37,000 participants.
  - › The researchers were interested in how playing violent video games influenced aggressive and prosocial behaviour as well as aggressive and prosocial cognitions and emotions.
- **FINDINGS** The researchers found a small average effect size in these studies, i.e. violent video game use was linked to an increase in aggressive outcomes and a decrease in prosocial outcomes.
  - › Prosocial games showed the opposite effect – they were linked to a reduction in aggressive behaviour and an increase in prosocial, cooperative behaviour.

AO3 Evaluation/Discussion

Media violence research: Overstating the case…

A 'statistically significant' relationship between media violence and violent behaviour may be an overstatement.	Studies that found a relationship between the two typically report small effect sizes. Very few have measured aggression against another person.	*When aggression towards another person or violent crime is the measure of aggression, the relationship is close to zero (Ferguson and Kilburn, 2009).*

Failure to consider other causal variables…

Many studies fail to account for other variables that might explain both aggressive behaviour and a preference for violent games.	Ferguson *et al.* (2009) claim that much of the research on computer game violence has failed to control for variables known to influence aggressive behaviour, e.g. family violence.	*These other risk factors, as opposed to exposure to media violence, may be the primary cause of aggressive behaviour.*

Problems with research on the effects of computer games…

In experiments, researchers must use alternatives that have no relation to real-life aggression or that only measure short-term effects.	These alternative 'measures' include administering noise blasts to another participant.	*However, participants may be exposed to other forms of media violence during a study, so the effect from violent video games alone is uncertain.*

Game difficulty rather than content may lead to aggression…

Przybylski *et al.* (2014) suggest aggressive behaviour may be linked to a player's experiences of failure and frustration during a game.	They found that it was not the violent storyline or imagery, but the lack of mastery and difficulty players had in completing the game, that led to frustration and aggression.	*The researchers suggest that even non-violent games can leave players feeling aggressive if they are poorly designed or too difficult.*

APPLY

AO2: An example

SCENARIO Toby loves nothing better than an evening in, playing *Call of duty*. When his parents suggest he might like to do something 'more healthy' he becomes abusive towards them and they observe he is a lot less friendly and helpful to other members of the family.

Consider whether Toby's parents might be right in blaming violent computer games for his aggressive behaviour. **(4 marks)**

ANSWER *Research by Greitemeyer and Mügge (2014) concluded that violent video game use was linked to an increase in aggressive outcomes and a decrease in prosocial outcomes. This is consistent with the observation that Toby was becoming more aggressive after playing them and displaying lower levels of prosocial behaviour towards other members of his family. However, Przybylski et al. (2014) found it was the difficulty players had in completing the game that led to frustration and aggression, so Toby's aggression might be more to do with his inability to master the game than being the victim of its violent storyline.*

AO2: Research methods

Bushman and Anderson (2002) randomly assigned participants to play either a violent (e.g. *Duke Nukem*) or a non-violent (e.g. *Austin Powers*) computer game for 20 minutes. The participants then read a story, and were asked to list 20 thoughts, feelings, and actions about how they would respond if they were the character in the story. One of the stories was about 'Todd':

Todd was on his way home from work one evening when he had to brake quickly for an amber light. The person in the car behind him must have thought Todd was going to jump the light because he crashed into the back of Todd's car, causing a lot of damage to both vehicles. Fortunately, there were no injuries. Todd got out of his car and surveyed the damage. He then walked over to the other car.

The researchers found that participants used responses like 'Call the guy an idiot' and 'This guy's dead meat', although the extent to which these phrases were used depended on whether they had played a violent or non-violent game, as shown in the bar chart below:

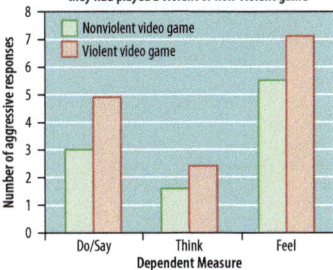

A graph to show the number of aggressive thoughts, feelings and actions of the participants listed and whether they had played a violent or non-violent game

a. **What is the main conclusion that can be drawn from this study? (3 marks)**

b. **Identify one non-parametric statistical test that could be used to determine whether the 'violent' and 'non-violent' groups differ in terms of the number of aggressive responses they used? (1 mark)**

c. **Give two reasons for selecting this test. (2 marks)**

AO2: One for you to try

Sasha has three brothers. She was watching Zak, the second oldest, playing *Carmageddon*, a particularly violent computer game. As he played, he got more and more aggressive. Joel, the oldest brother was playing *Super hexagon,* which is not violent, but very difficult to progress further than the lowest stages. Much to Sasha's surprise, Joel behaved even more aggressively than Zak when he played this game. Her youngest brother, Adam, who was six, loves to watch *The Simpsons,* particularly the *Itchy and Scratchy* cartoons. He laughs out loud whenever the mouse blows the cat up or cuts him up with a bacon slicer. Sasha is amazed that Adam doesn't show any violent tendencies in his own play.

Using your knowledge of media influences on aggression, explain why Sasha's three brothers behave as they do. (6 marks)

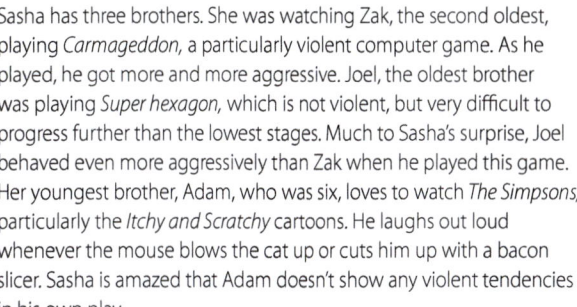

How do I answer... longer (16-mark) questions?

For a 16-mark essay question, the command words might require you to 'outline (or describe) and evaluate…'. Alternatively, a question might ask you to 'discuss' media influences on aggression. Whilst all of these instructions indicate that you should include both AO1 and AO3 in your answer, the 'discuss' command word requires you to go a little further than just writing about strengths and/or limitations.

> **Q1: Discuss media influences on aggression. (16 marks)**

The nominal mark division for AO1 and AO3 in this question is 6 marks for the former and 10 marks for the latter. You could aim to include the six AO1 points to cover the 'outline' component of this question. For the AO3 content, you should include all four of the AO3 points.

The command word 'discuss' requires AO3 that is a bit more 'discursive', e.g. looking at applications, implications, counter-evidence, etc. We have tried to make some of our AO3 points 'discursive' to accommodate this.

> **Q2: Discuss media influences on aggression, including the influence of violent computer games. (16 marks)**

This question requires you to include the influence of violent computer games in your answer. The whole essay doesn't have to be about violent computer games, but they have to be included. In fact, you could construct an answer to *this* question and use it for both questions. You would choose six of the AO1 points. These could be the first and fifth AO1 points under the 'Violent films and TV' heading, the second and fourth points under the 'Violent computer games' heading, and the first and third points from the key study. You would include the same four AO3 points as for the previous question.

REVIEW

Write an essay plan for the first of the two essay questions in **How do I answer…?** above. Think carefully about what you will include and the level of detail for each point. Then try writing this essay in 20 minutes. If you couldn't finish it in the time, this means you are not writing concisely enough or you are having to think too much. Keep reviewing the material until you know it well and can write a well-balanced essay in 20 minutes. Then, repeat this whole process for the second of the two essays in the **How do I answer…?**

Explanations of media influences

AO1 Description

- **Desensitisation** Anxiety about violence inhibits its use. Media violence may lead to aggressive behaviour by removing this anxiety. The more violence a child watches, the more they perceive it as 'normal', and the more likely they are to engage in it.
  - > Desensitised individuals feel less sympathy for the victims of violence and they have fewer negative attitudes towards violence, both of which would increase the likelihood of aggressive responses in real life.
- **Disinhibition** Exposure to violent media can legitimise the use of violence by the individual in their own lives because it undermines the social sanctions that usually inhibit such behaviour.

  - > Prolonged exposure to media violence gives the message that violence is an acceptable part of everyday life. When violence is justified or unpunished on television, the viewer's guilt or concern about consequences is also reduced.
- **Cognitive priming** When people are constantly exposed to violent media, this activates thoughts about violence, which then activate other aggressive thoughts through their association in memory pathways.
  - > Frequent activation through prolonged exposure to violent media may result in a lowered activation threshold for aggressive thoughts, allowing them to be accessed more readily and so used to process and interpret information.

AO3 Evaluation / Discussion

Research support for desensitisation…

Carnagey et al. (2007) provided evidence for the claim that playing violent computer games produces physiological desensitisation.	Participants played a violent or non-violent video game and watched a 10-minute film clip with scenes of real-life violence. Those who had played the violent game had a lower heart rate while viewing the real-life violence.	*This demonstrated a physiological desensitisation to violence, as predicted by this explanation.*

The good and bad of desensitisation…

Desensitisation can be adaptive for some individuals, e.g. making troops more effective in combat.	However, desensitisation to violence may also be detrimental for society. Bushman and Anderson (2009) suggest that it reduces helping others in distress.	*This suggests that people exposed to media violence become 'comfortably numb' to the suffering of others and are consequently less helpful.*

The disinhibition effect depends on other factors…

The likelihood of disinhibition occurring is determined by different factors, some relating to the viewers, and some to the context media is viewed.	Younger children are more likely to be affected as they are drawn into violent episodes without considering the consequences (Collins, 1989). The disinhibition effect is stronger if children are punished by parents (Heath et al., 1989).	*This demonstrates that the relationship between media violence and disinhibition is mediated by individual and social characteristics.*

Negative consequences make disinhibition less likely…

Disinhibition is less likely in situations where viewers are also exposed to the negative consequences of violent behaviour.	Goranson (1969) showed a film of a boxing match where there were either no apparent consequences or the loser took a beating. Participants in the first condition were more likely to behave aggressively after viewing.	*This suggests disinhibition is more likely in violent media where any negative consequences are not made apparent to viewers.*

Research support for cognitive priming…

Bushman (1998) provided support for the cognitive priming explanation in a study of psychology students.	Participants who watched a violent film had quicker reaction times to aggressive words than those who watched a non-violent film. Video content did not influence reaction times to nonaggressive words.	*This supports the cognitive priming explanation. Violence in the media primes aggressive thoughts in memory, making them more accessible to viewers.*

Priming is less likely with less realistic media…

Film or game realism is an important factor in the relationship between violent media and the priming of aggressive thoughts (Atkin, 1983).	Higher levels of aggression resulted from more realistic violence. Fictional violence may not have the same priming effects as in games with more realistic violence.	*This suggests that exposure to more realistic and intense forms of aggression influences the types and intensity of activated thoughts.*

APPLY

AO2: An example

SCENARIO

After Toby has been playing violent computer games, he finds that he no longer seems to be bothered about watching scenes of devastation and war on television. Whereas it used to make him very anxious and upset. Also, when he sees a younger child being bullied in the street, he just walks by unbothered.

Using your knowledge of 'desensitisation', 'disinhibition' and 'cognitive priming', explain which one best fits Toby's behaviour. **(3 marks)**

ANSWER

Desensitisation best fit's Toby's behaviour as media violence removes anxiety about aggression by representing it as 'normal'. Desensitised individuals are less likely to notice violence in real life and feel less sympathy for the victims of violence (Mullin and Linz, 1995). This would explain why Toby is no longer anxious or upset when he watches violence on the TV, and why he no longer appears to feel sympathy for the younger children who are being bullied in his street.

AO2: One for you to try

Emily had read about a study in which young adults played either a violent or non-violent video game for 25 minutes. After the game, the participants had been asked to look at neutral pictures, such as a man on a bike, or violent pictures, such as a man with a gun. The researchers had found that when shown a violent image, those who had played the violent game showed a smaller brain response than those who had played the non-violent game. Emily could not understand why these findings were important.

Using your knowledge of desensitisation, explain why these findings are important. (4 marks)

AO2: Research methods

In Goranson's (1969) study, participants were shown a film of a boxing match. For one group, the loser was depicted as dying. The other group saw no apparent consequences. Afterwards, participants undertook another task in which their aggressiveness was measured by the intensity of electric shocks they were willing to deliver to another person (who happened to be a confederate) using the Buss-Durkee 'aggression machine' technique.

Outline one ethical issue that arises using this method of measuring aggression, and explain one way in which this issue could be dealt with. (4 marks)

Desensitisation

How do I answer... selection (multiple choice) questions?

> Which **one** of the following applies to the desensitisation explanation of media influences? **(1 mark)**
>
> A Violence on television legitimises the use of violence by individuals in their own lives.
>
> B Violence on television activates other thoughts or ideas about violence.
>
> C Violence on television makes viewers more anxious when they encounter real-life violence.
>
> D Violence on television removes viewers' anxiety about violent behaviour in their own lives.

Usually these questions require you to pick out the **one** statement that is correct, matches or defines a concept or idea. They may also (on occasion) ask you to pick out the **one** statement that is *incorrect or does not* match or define a concept or idea.

Although these are generally worth only 1 mark, getting them correct is still important because that 1 mark can be the difference between one grade and another. So, some general advice on answering these:

- Read the question very carefully. Is it asking you to pick the statement that matches (as here) or the 'odd one out' that doesn't match?
- Make life easier by crossing out any that are obviously *not* going to be the correct answer given the specific demands of the question.
- Applying this to the question above we cross out **B** because that is describing the cognitive priming explanation. Alternative **A** is referring to the disinhibition explanation so that leaves **C** and **D**. The answer is **D** because it suggests that violence on TV removes our anxiety about violence in our own lives (i.e. it *desensitises* us).

REVIEW

In this final Review section of this chapter, it is time for some more 'revision accounting'. You should make a table like this with all 10 topics from this chapter on aggression. When you feel you have mastered the AO1 and AO3 components of these and can cope with any of the different types of question that we have covered in the **How do I answer...?** sections, you will have earned a tick in the 'Got it!' column.

TOPIC	Got it!			Got it!	
	AO1	AO3		AO1	AO3
Neural and hormonal influences	✓		Social learning theory		
Genetic factors in aggression			De-individuation		
The ethological explanation of aggression			Institutional aggression in prison		
Evolutionary explanations of human aggression			Media influences on aggression		
The frustration–aggression hypothesis			Explanations of media influences		

Offender profiling: The top-down approach

RECAP

AO1 Description

- **The top-down approach** is a way of narrowing down potential suspects by creating a profile of the most likely offender. There are six stages:

  1. **Profiling inputs** Data is collected including a detailed description of the crime scene, the crime, and background information about the victim. Possible suspects must not be considered, to avoid bias.

  2. **Decision process models** The profiler organises the data into patterns, considering issues such as murder type (mass, spree or serial), time and location.

  3. **Crime assessment** The crime is classified as being committed by an organised or disorganised type of offender.

     > **Organised**: planned, targeted victim, violent fantasies may be acted out. The offender is usually intelligent, socially and sexually competent.

     > **Disorganised**: unplanned, random selection of victim. The offender usually leaves evidence at the crime scene like blood, semen, fingerprints and the weapon.

  4. **Criminal profile** Hypotheses about the offender's background, habits and beliefs are used to work out a strategy for the investigation.

  5. **Crime assessment** People matching the profile are evaluated.

  6. **Apprehension** If a suspect is caught, the process is reviewed to check that conclusions at each stage were valid.

AO3 Evaluation/Discussion

How useful is the method?...

The approach was developed by the FBI to solve bizarre and extreme murder cases.	Copson (1995) questioned 184 US police officers; 82 per cent said the technique was useful and 90 per cent said they would use it again.	It can offer investigators a different perspective, which can help prevent wrongful conviction.

The basis of the method is flawed...

The method is based on interviews with 37 dangerous sexual killers.	These individuals may be highly manipulative and unreliable, and may have a different approach to 'typical' killers.	This means the classification of criminals using this data may not be generalisable.

Top-down profiling could mislead investigations...

Top-down analysis is not evidence-based, and has been dismissed by courts as 'junk science'; ambiguous descriptions could fit many individuals.	In addition, smart offenders could deliberately try to deceive profilers by providing misleading clues.	So police and courts must take care not to be convinced by the believability of profiles that appear to be a good match.

A false dichotomy...

Turvey (1999) suggests that the dichotomy between organised and disorganised is false as it is more likely to be a continuum rather than two distinct categories.	Canter et al. (2004) analysed murders committed by 100 US serial killers. They found a number of subsets of organised-type crimes and little evidence for disorganised types.	This suggests that having two distinct categories is not the best approach.

APPLY

AO2: An example

SCENARIO A psychologist was analysing police reports of a range of crime scenes. Based on the reports, she categorised the offenders as either organised or disorganised.

Explain the common features found in the crimes of organised types of offender and the common features found in those of disorganised types of offender. **(3 marks)**

ANSWER *The crime scenes of disorganised offenders would contain clues such as blood, semen and fingerprints. It is likely the offender selected the victim at random and would have shown little engagement with the victim. Organised offenders would have planned their crime and targeted a specific victim. They may have hidden any weapons and transported the body from the scene.*

AO2: One for you to try

Luke works as a psychiatrist in a high-security prison, and wants to collect some data to test the hypothesis that serial killers can be divided into two groups, organised or disorganised. He decides to carry out semi-structured interviews of convicted serial killers, and to analyse these along with the court transcripts and police reports relating to the crimes.

a. **Explain how Luke could analyse the content of the interview transcripts and other materials to test this hypothesis. (4 marks)**

b. **Explain why there might be discrepancies between the different sources? (3 marks)**

AO2: Research methods

A study (Alison *et al.,* 2001) investigated whether police officers were prepared to perceive offender profiles as accurate descriptions of offenders. Group A were given a description of the real offender, and Group B were given a fabricated account of an offender with very different characteristics. They were both told that the offender had confessed when he was caught. Both were given the same profile, and asked to rate it for accuracy on a 7-point Likert scale (1 = very inaccurate, 7 = very accurate). The mean accuracy ratings are shown in the table.

	Group A (genuine offender)	Group B (fabricated offender)
Mean accuracy rating	5.3	5.3
Standard deviation	0.89	1.3

a. **What do the results show about accuracy ratings of the profile by the two groups? (3 marks)**

b. **What can you conclude from these findings about the usefulness of offender profiles? (3 marks)**

c. **The median scores for each group were 6. What does this tell you about the distribution of scores? (3 marks)**

How do I answer... application (AO2) questions?

Saga and Henrik are investigating a series of murders in Malmö and Copenhagen which seem to have some common features, such as the bodies being staged after death to look like artworks in a gallery. How could the investigators make use of top-down profiling techniques to help them locate and apprehend the murderer? **(6 marks)**

One way of answering questions such as this is to remember the 'say one thing for 1 mark' and 'say four things for 4 marks' strategy. So, for a 6-mark question we could say six things.

1. Find a bit of appropriate psychology, e.g. 'In top-down profiling, investigators should collect all details of the crimes and scenes, no matter how trivial and look for patterns using intuition and experience.'

2. Use this to explain some aspect of the scenario, e.g. 'Saga and Henrik should collect every detail of all the crimes, and look for patterns, such as the staging of the bodies.'

3. Find a second bit of psychology, e.g. 'Then the offender should be classified as organised or disorganised.'

4. Use this to explain the scenario, e.g. 'This murderer is likely to be an organised type, as the bodies were staged after death.'

5. Find a third bit of psychology, e.g. 'Finally they should construct a profile of the offender and use it to assess the crimes, reconsidering the profile as new evidence or suspects emerge.'

6. Use this to explain the scenario, e.g. 'Saga and Henrik will use their experience and intuition to help them, but try not to get fixed on a particular suspect and miss other possible explanations. A profile might suggest the likely background, habits and beliefs of the offender and will help them develop a strategy for catching the offender.'

REVIEW

Being able to describe something concisely, while maintaining accuracy, is not as easy as it sounds. On the opposite page, we have stripped down the descriptive detail you will find in the Year 2 Student Book to give you some guidance about how to do just that. Let's now play around with that content to make it a bit more familiar.

1. Write two different 6-mark 'describe' or 'outline' questions on the AO1 content.

2. Next think of four different short answer (2- to 3-mark) questions.

3. Finally, and possibly the hardest, write a multiple choice question.

After you've written the questions, you should write the mark schemes. This will make you think hard about which points you would include in different length answers.

You could pair up with a study buddy and each write questions like these for different topics, then swap.

173

Offender profiling: The bottom-up approach

RECAP

A01 Description

Investigative psychology

- This data-driven approach was developed by David Canter. Three features are:
  - > Interpersonal coherence assumes that people are consistent in their behaviour, so there will be correlations between the crime and their everyday life, although there may be changes over time.
  - > Forensic awareness: rapists who conceal fingerprints often have a previous conviction for burglary.
  - > Smallest space analysis: a statistical technique which explores correlations between crime scene details and offender characteristics from large numbers of similar cases. This can identify themes or categories of offender, such as instrumental opportunistic, instrumental cognitive or expressive impulsive murderers.

Geographical profiling

- This analyses locations and connections between crime scenes.
- **Circle theory** Canter also proposed that offenders commit crimes within an imaginary circle.
  - > Marauders commit crimes within a defined radius of their home.
  - > Commuters travel to another area to commit crimes.
- **Criminal geographic targeting (CGT)** is a computerised system developed by Rossmo. The formula uses data about time, distance and movement, and produces a map called a 'jeopardy surface', showing likely closeness to the offender's residence.

A03 Evaluation/Discussion

Issues/Debates
Scientific reductionism

Scientific basis of the bottom-up approach…

| This approach appears more scientific because it uses statistical analysis of objective data from offenders. | However, it doesn't include data from unsolved crimes. Also, some of the underlying assumptions and formulae may be incorrect. | *This means that bottom-up approaches have the potential to be objective and systematic, but in practice are biased.* |

Circle theory has limitations…

| Canter and Larkin (1993) studied 45 sexual assaults, and found 91 per cent of offenders were marauders and the rest were commuters. | However, in cities people's ranges may not be circular due to transport links. | *Circle theory can be useful for narrowing down searches, but could lead police to look in the wrong place.* |

Lack of value in geographical profiling…

| The geographic approach can help prioritise house-to-house searches or DNA testing. | However, geographic profiling is limited to spatial behaviour. It ignores personality characteristics, so it is unable to distinguish between multiple offenders in an area. | *So there may not be any advantage over the traditional method of sticking pins in a map to see where a group of crimes were committed.* |

Offender profiling should be used with caution…

| Profiling can help police narrow down the field of possibilities. The danger lies in being restricted by profiling. | In the murder of Rachel Nickell, a psychologist's profile led to the wrong suspect, as the actual murderer was taller than described in the profile. | *This can lead to police wasting time trying to convict the wrong person, or even wrongful convictions.* |

 **APPLY**

A02: An example

SCENARIO A team of police officers were using a geographical profile to investigate a spate of muggings in their local community.

What should they consider regarding the usefulness of the profile for their investigation? **(3 marks)**

ANSWER *The police should remember that while a geographical profile can help identify possible areas to conduct house-to-house enquiries, they should not eliminate other locations if they do not fit the profile. The offender's home base may not be in the centre of the circle and elements of the landscape may not necessarily form a circle. While previous police investigations have found geographical profiling useful – 75 per cent of officers stated it was of use (Copson, 1995) – it often does not lead to identification of the actual offender.*

A02: Research methods

Criminal geographic targeting (CGT) can be used to locate the residence of a criminal by analysing the locations of crime sites. The graph below shows the relationship between the number of crime sites available for analysis and the 'hit percentage' produced by this model. The lower the hit percentage, the more successful the model.

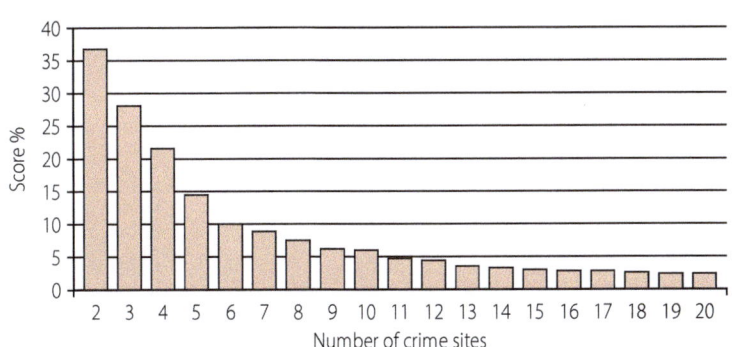

a. **How many crime locations are required to produce hit percentages of less than 10 per cent? (1 mark)**

b. **What can we conclude from this about the validity of the CGT model? (2 marks)**

c. **This model assumes that the offender is not a commuter. Explain what this means. (2 marks)**

A02: One for you to try

Saga and Henrik have decided to take a more scientific approach to their investigation in Malmö and Copenhagen (see previous spread).

How could the investigators make use of bottom-up profiling techniques? (6 marks)

 How do I answer... 'Distinguish between' questions?

Q1: Distinguish between the methods used in top-down and bottom-up offender profiling. **(2 marks)**

Q2: Compare the research basis of top-down and bottom-up offender profiling. **(2 marks)**

If you are asked to explain the difference between top-down and bottom-up offender profiling, you need to give direct comparisons between aspects of each; for example, their assumptions, what information is needed at the start of the profiling, how the profile is developed. **Q1** and **Q2** ask for more specific comparisons, so this helps you to keep focused. In any case, don't just describe one and then the other.

1 Identify the point of comparison.

2 Explain the position of each type of profiling in relation to that point.

3 Link it with 'whereas'.

For example, for **Q1**, 'Top-down profiling relies on the experience and intuition of the profiler, whereas bottom-up profiling makes predictions based on empirical data.'

For **Q2**, 'Top-down profiling is based on FBI interviews with 37 imprisoned serial killers, whereas bottom-up profiling used data from court and police records of hundreds of prisoners.'

REVIEW

To prepare for 'distinguish' questions, and to organise your notes graphically so they are more memorable, make a comparison table for top-down and bottom-up processing. You should include these aspects, with a row for each, so that you can use them for direct comparisons in 'distinguish' questions as well as for evaluation of each separately:

Developed by… Starts with… Research basis… How the profile is developed… Assumptions… Usefulness… Criticisms…

Biological explanations of offending behaviour: A historical approach

AO1 Description

Neanderthal man, based on 40,000-year-old remains

Atavistic form

- Lombroso (1876) proposed that offenders possess similar physical characteristics to lower primates, such as a large jaw and excessively long arms. They are throwbacks to an earlier stage of evolution, which causes them to become criminals.

- Lombroso gathered empirical evidence from post-mortem examinations of over 50,000 criminals and measurements of the faces of living criminals. In a study of 383 convicted Italian criminals, he found that 21 per cent had just one atavistic feature and 43 per cent had at least five.

- He linked specific features to different crimes, like an aquiline nose in murderers, and produced an atlas of criminal types, identifying three types:

  > Born criminals: the atavistic type.

  > Insane criminals: mentally ill.

  > Criminaloids: offenders whose mental characteristics predisposed them to criminal behaviour under the right circumstances.

- Later, Lombroso recognised that inherited atavistic form (nature) interacts with environment (nurture).

Somatotypes

- Sheldon (1949) linked body types to temperaments:

  > Mesomorphs (athletic, active and assertive).

  > Ectomorphs (tall and thin, restrained and nervous).

  > Endomorphs (round, relaxed and sociable).

- He studied 200 young adults, concluding that delinquents tended to be mesomorphs.

AO3 Evaluation / Discussion

Contribution to the science of criminology…

Lombroso based his theories on empirical observation, but didn't compare prisoners with non-prisoners, so there was no control group.	Goring (1913) compared 3,000 convicts with non-convicts, and the only difference was that convicts were slightly smaller.	Although Lombroso's methods and conclusions can be criticised, he did raise the possibility of scientific studies of the criminal mind.

A deterministic theory…

In Lombroso's theory, criminality is outside the control of the individual; it's caused largely by biological factors.	Before this, criminals were believed to have a free choice to commit crimes and should be deterred by harsh punishments.	Lombroso believed that biology and environment may remove free will, so criminals should be treated humanely.

The theory is gender-biased as Lombroso believed women are less evolved than men…

Issues/Debates
Gender bias

Lombroso didn't study women directly, but believed that women are naturally passive, low in intelligence and maternal; unlikely therefore to become criminals.	He also believed that those women who did become criminals had masculine traits which would be beneficial in a man but made women 'monsters'.	These androcentric views were fairly typical in the nineteenth century and were not developed from empirical evidence.

Link between personality type and criminality…

Although the theory of atavistic form has been rejected, we still try to identify criminal types, for example, using Eysenck's theory of personality types.	In addition, research into genetic causes of criminality implies that some people have an innate disposition to commit crimes.	So Lombroso's later ideas, of an interaction between biological and environmental factors, have similarities with current theories.

⚙ APPLY

AO2: An example

SCENARIO Sally enjoys books about famous cases and true-life crime documentaries. She explained to her friend that criminals have a 'look' about them and claims she could probably predict people with criminal tendencies just by observing their appearance.

With reference to Sally's comments, discuss the historical approach to explaining offender behaviour. **(16 marks)**

ANSWER **An extract showing how you could address the AO2 requirements of this question:** *By stating that criminals have a 'look', Sally could be seen to support the atavistic form which claims criminals are 'throwbacks' to lower primates. The physical traits Sally may look for when trying to predict possible criminals include unusually sized ears, a chin that either recedes or is excessively long, and exaggerated cheekbones. In his study of 383 convicted criminals, Lombroso found 43 per cent had five or more atavistic traits, which may explain why Sally feels criminals have a 'look' about them. However, because Lombroso did not study non-prisoners we cannot be certain these features are not also found in non-criminal populations...*

AO2: Research methods

a. **Identify strengths and limitations of Lombroso's research methods. (4 marks)**

b. **Overall, how scientific was his approach to collecting data? (2 marks)**

c. **Why were there problems with the validity of his conclusions? (3 marks)**

↻ REVIEW

In order to feel comfortable with this topic you should practise using the material in all the different ways that might be assessed in your exam.

1. Try constructing 3-, 4- and 6-mark descriptions of Lombroso's theory of atavistic form.

2. Write an essay plan showing how you would use the material on this spread to answer a 16-mark extended writing question, then highlight which points you would include in an 8-mark version of the question.

AO2: One for you to try

Count Dracula by Bram Stoker contains this description of Dracula, a murderous vampire:

'His face was a strong, a very strong, aquiline, with high bridge of the thin nose and peculiarly arched nostrils… His eyebrows were very massive, almost meeting over the nose, and with bushy hair that seemed to curl in its own profusion. The mouth, so far as I could see it under the heavy moustache, was fixed and rather cruel-looking, with peculiarly sharp white teeth. These protruded over the lips… his ears were pale, and at the tops extremely pointed. The chin was broad and strong… his hands… were rather coarse, broad, with squat fingers. Strange to say, there were hairs in the centre of the palm.'

How does this description fit the theory of atavistic form? (6 marks)

🐾 How do I answer... evaluation only questions (AO3)?

Like the description only questions on the next spread, evaluation questions come in all sorts of shapes and sizes. Terms like 'evaluate', 'discuss', 'explain', 'criticism', 'strength' and 'limitation' all indicate that AO3 is required. The AO3 material for these questions is on the opposite page. Let's look at some examples:

Q1: Give **one** criticism of the theory of atavistic form. **(4 marks)**

Because 'criticisms' can be either negative or positive (research support would count as a 'positive' criticism), you could choose any one of the AO3 points as your material. For 2 marks, you could use the lead-in phrase (e.g. 'The theory is deterministic… '), followed by the material in the first two columns (i.e. the main critical claim and its expansion).

Q2: Explain why the theory of atavistic form can be considered gender biased. **(3 marks)**

This question requires a little more elaboration, but this time you are restricted to the third AO3 evaluation point, relating to gender bias, with material from all three columns being used to access all 3 of the marks on offer.

Q3: Evaluate the historical approach to explaining crime (atavistic form). **(6 marks)**

You would take the same approach as for **Q2**, but this time using two of the AO3 points. Elaborate them fully and make sure you explain whether your point is a strength (positive evaluation) or limitation (negative evaluation) of the theory.

Biological explanations of offending behaviour: Genetic and neural

RECAP

A01 Description

Genetic explanations

- Genes may predispose individuals to criminal behaviour.
- A faulty MAOA gene was found by Brunner *et al.* (1993) in 28 violent males in a Dutch family.
- Tiihonen *et al.* (2015) estimated that 5–10 per cent of violent crime in Finland is caused by abnormal MAOA or CDH13 genes.
- Caspi *et al.* (2002) found that 12 per cent of men with low MAOA expression had experienced childhood maltreatment, but were responsible for 44 per cent of violent convictions.
- Environmental factors 'switch' genes on or off. This is an **epigenetic** effect, changing the phenotype but not the genotype.

Neural explanations

- Differences in brain structures may be innate or acquired. Sixty per cent of US prisoners have had a brain injury, compared with 8.5 per cent of the general population (Harmon, 2012).
- Raine (2004) reviewed 71 brain imaging studies, showing that violent criminals have reduced functioning in the pre-frontal cortex, an area associated with control of impulses.
- Raine *et al.* (1997) found that murderers had abnormalities in their amygdala, an area of the limbic system linked to emotion and motivation.
- **Neurotransmitter differences:**
  - > When serotonin levels are low, the pre-frontal cortex is unable to inhibit impulsive aggressive urges. Dopamine hyperactivity may enhance this effect.
  - > High noradrenaline is associated with sympathetic nervous system activation: the fight-or-flight response.

A03 Evaluation / Discussion

Issues/Debates
Nature–nurture

Research support from twin and adoption studies…

Raine (1993) reviewed research on the delinquent behaviour of twins, and found 52 per cent concordance rate for MZ twins (with identical DNA) and 21 per cent for DZ twins (with 50 per cent of the same genes).

In addition, Mednick *et al.*'s (1987) study of 14,000 adoptees found that 15 per cent of boys adopted by a criminal family became criminals themselves, compared to 20 per cent with biological parents who were criminals.

Taken together, these findings suggest that inherited factors are marginally more significant than environmental influences.

Non-violent crimes are more difficult to link to biological explanations…

There is evidence from twin studies (e.g. Blonigen *et al.*, 2005) that the personality trait of psychopathy is inherited, which causes lack of empathy, increasing the likelihood that the psychopath will commit crimes.

However, offending behaviour includes a broad range of behaviours such as fraud, drug use and bigamy, and Findlay (2011) points out that crime is a social construction.

This suggests that it is hard to explain such a range of behaviours simply in terms of genetics and their interaction with the environment.

Biological explanations are deterministic…

Issues/Debates
Biological determinism

An issue with genetic explanations is how far they can be used to excuse offending behaviour, as they imply that a person may be unable to control their criminal urges.

Lawyers have argued that it is hard for some men with genetic predispositions and adverse experiences to avoid criminal violence.

However, not everyone with the defective gene in Tiihonen's study became an offender, and Caspi's study supports a diathesis-stress model.

Real-world applications…

One potential benefit of research on neural abnormalities is that it could lead to possible methods of treatment.

If low levels of serotonin are related to increased aggressiveness in criminals, then prisoners could be given diets (e.g. avoiding artificial sweeteners) that would enhance their serotonin levels and decrease their aggression.

This suggests that drugs or changes in diet could help some individuals, particularly if they also have mental health issues.

 **APPLY**

AO2: An example

SCENARIO Jake has been excluded from school a number of times for aggressive behaviour. The headmaster remembers teaching Jake's father and uncle who, in his opinion, were 'nothing but trouble'. His experiences with Jake's family have led him to conclude that some people are born with criminal tendencies.

With reference to the headmaster's experiences, discuss biological explanations of offending behaviour. **(4 marks)**

ANSWER *Jake's family has a history of offending behaviour which has led his headmaster to suggest that the cause of Jake's aggression originates from within him. He could be referring to genetic explanations as Jake and his first-degree (father) and second-degree (uncle) relatives also show criminal behaviour. This claim is supported by Brunner et al. who found male members of a Dutch family who had a history of impulsive and criminal behaviour shared a gene that lead to abnormally low levels of MAOA. MAOA regulates metabolism of serotonin which, in low levels, is associated with aggressive behaviour.*

AO2: Research methods

1. Twin studies have shown higher concordance rates for delinquent behaviour in monozygotic twins than dizygotic twins. For example, 52 per cent concordance for MZ and 21 per cent for DZ.

   a. **What can you conclude from this about genetic causes of delinquency? (3 marks)**

   b. **A criticism of these studies is that there is an assumption that MZ and DZ twins only differ in their genetics. Why might this assumption not be correct? (2 marks)**

   c. **Why might the classification of twins as MZ or DZ have been inaccurate in early studies? How might this problem be avoided using modern techniques? (2 marks)**

2. Adoption studies aim to separate out the effect of genes and the environment, by comparing adopted children's criminal behaviour with that of their biological and adopted parents. The assumption is that similarities with biological parents are due to heredity, while similarities with adoptive parents are caused by environmental influences.

   a. **One criticism of adoption studies is that children are not all adopted at birth. Explain how this might affect the findings of the studies. (3 marks)**

   b. **Adoption agencies often try to match children and adoptive parents on key characteristics. Explain how this might affect the validity of conclusions of these studies. (3 marks)**

   c. **Outline how the adoption process might itself influence outcomes for children. Consider the effect of attachments to caregivers. (2 marks)**

AO2: One for you to try

Alana has discovered that her estranged lover, the father of her son, has been arrested for murder. In his trial, his lawyer presents evidence that he has two genes, variants of MAOA and CHD13, which together make it very difficult for him to resist violent behaviour. Alana is very worried that her son, Alan, will also become a murderer.

Use your knowledge of research into genetic explanations of offending behaviour to examine this possibility. (6 marks)

How do I answer... description only questions (AO1)?

There is a fairly simple formula for answering description only questions. For 2 marks, say two things, for 3 marks say three things, and so on. This is how you would tackle the sample questions below. The AO1 material for these questions is on the opposite page.

This approach adds an appropriate level of detail to each answer while keeping it within the time restriction of 1 ¼ minutes per mark. It also gives the examiner a useful way of discriminating between your answer and one that would be worth fewer than the maximum marks for that question.

> **Q1:** Briefly describe genetic explanations of criminal behaviour. (2 marks)

Use the first two points under the AO1 heading, 'Genetic explanations'.

> **Q2:** Briefly outline how genes and neurotransmitters can explain criminal behaviour. (3 marks)

Use three AO1 points, such as two from 'genetic explanations' and one from 'neurotransmitter differences'. You must touch on both types of explanation in your answer because of the word 'and' in the question.

> **Q3:** Explain the role of biological factors such as genes and brain differences in criminal behaviour. (4 marks)

Use four points, which can be from any part of the AO1 material, as you are given the choice this time.

> **Q4:** Outline research into genetic and neural explanations of criminal behaviour. (6 marks)

Use six AO1 points. Choosing points that are clearly findings of research is a good way to answer this question, although any knowledge of genes and neurotransmitters on this page does come from research. Again, you must include some information about genes and some about neural factors (brain structures or neurotransmitters).

REVIEW

You need to be able to answer questions with different mark allocations concisely while also including enough detail to explain the concept clearly. Practise answering the questions above, spending about a minute and a quarter per mark, e.g. 5 minutes for a 4-mark question, 10 minutes for a 6-mark question. Make sure you allow time to plan logical answers.

1. Practise recalling the material in the AO1 points opposite.

2. Practise writing the full answer, setting a timer to make sure you use the time available.

3. Check your answer is clear and logical, and has relevant key terms in each point.

Psychological explanations of offending behaviour: Eysenck's theory

RECAP

AO1 Description

Eysenck's theory of the criminal personality

- Character traits cluster along three normally distributed dimensions:
  > Extraversion–introversion.
  > Neuroticism–stability.
  > Psychoticism–normality.
- Eysenck (1982) claimed each trait has a **biological basis** and 67 per cent of the variance for the traits is due to genetic factors.
  > **Extraversion** is related to cortical arousal level. Extraverts seek external stimulation to increase arousal. Introverts are innately over-aroused and seek to avoid stimulation.
  > **Neuroticism** relates to reactivity in the sympathetic nervous system. A neurotic person is unstable and gets easily upset. A stable personality has a less reactive nervous system and is calm under pressure.
  > **Psychoticism** is related to higher testosterone levels, so men are more likely to be at this end of the spectrum.
  > **Link to criminal behaviour** Extraverts seek more arousal and therefore engage in dangerous activities. Neurotics are unstable and may overreact to situations of threat. Psychotic individuals are aggressive and lack empathy.
- Criminality develops from an interaction between innate traits and environmental factors such as conditioning. People who are high in extraversion and neuroticism are less easily conditioned, and do not learn to avoid anti-social behaviour.

I'm having a moral dilemma. Should I be treacherous or devious?

AO3 Evaluation / Discussion

Twin studies support a genetic basis to personality types...

Issues/Debates
Nature–nurture

Zuckerman (1987) found a +.52 correlation for neuroticism in MZ twins but only .24 for DZ twins. For extraversion, MZ twins had +.51 and DZ had +.12 correlation, and results for psychoticism were similar.

However, a correlation of +.50 means that about 40 per cent of variance in this trait is due to genes. In addition, the figures may be artificially high as MZ twins tend to be treated more similarly than DZ twins.

This indicates that genetic factors are involved in personality traits, as MZ twins have higher concordances than DZ, but the correlation is not as high as Eysenck suggested.

Personality may not be consistent...

However, many psychologists support a situational perspective; someone may be calm and relaxed at home but neurotic at work.

Mischel and Peake (1982) asked family, friends and strangers to rate 63 students in a variety of situations and found almost no correlation between traits displayed.

This shows that the notion of a fixed criminal personality is flawed, as people behave differently in different situations.

Personality tests may lack validity...

Personality tests depend on self-reported data. People may tend towards socially desirable answers, so their answers may not be truthful. Lie scales are included to try to eliminate dishonest responders.

In addition, the Eysenck Personality Questionnaire (EPQ) consists of forced-choice items, such as 'Are you a worrier?', which must be answered with 'yes' or 'no' – there is no option for 'sometimes'.

This means the findings of the EPQ may not represent reality.

Personality and criminal behaviour...

Criminals score higher for the personality traits of extraversion and psychoticism than non-criminals.

Dunlop et al. (2012) found that these traits, and high scores on the lie scale, were good predictors of delinquency. However, participants were students and their friends, and only minor offences were assessed.

So there is some support for a link between personality traits and criminal behaviour, but it is inconsistent and limited.

APPLY

AO2: An example

SCENARIO Jharred's job as a prison guard involves managing a range of different people currently serving custodial sentences. He believes that, while their age and backgrounds may differ, the people in his care all share similar personality characteristics; they are often aggressive and lack empathy.

With reference to Jharred's views, briefly outline Eysenck's theory of the criminal personality. **(4 marks)**

ANSWER *Eysenck's personality theory suggests those high in extraversion, neuroticism and psychoticism may be more likely to engage in criminal activities than those high in introversion, stability and normality. Extraverts' search for stimulation may lead them to partake in dangerous activities while a raised level of testosterone may lead to the aggressive, anti-social actions of someone who lacks the ability to empathise with others. Jharred seems to be describing psychoticism, suggesting that as well as a lack of empathy and aggression, the prisoners in his charge may also show traits of egocentricism, impulsivity and a lack of concern about others' welfare. Jharred's comments reflect Eysenck's view that there is a biological basis to personality as he states 'regardless of age and background', suggesting personality is innate.*

AO2: One for you to try

Luca is an energetic, lively teenager who loves climbing over fences and walls. At school he is the class clown, and is getting into trouble because he can't seem to sit still, and responds rudely to teachers who ask him to calm down. However, he often feels anxious, particularly when he is alone.

How might Luca score on the Eysenck Personality Questionnaire, and how does this relate to his anti-social behaviour? (6 marks)

AO2: Research methods

The Eysenck Personality Questionnaire (EPQ) is one of the best-known psychological tests. A number of shorter versions have been developed including the EPQ-BV ('BV' stands for brief version). Sato (2005) assessed this new scale in terms of test–retest reliability and concurrent validity.

a. **Explain how test–retest reliability can be assessed. (3 marks)**

b. **If the reliability was low, explain how this could be improved. (2 marks)**

c. **Explain what is meant by 'concurrent validity'. (1 mark)**

d. **Concurrent validity was calculated by comparing the current scale and the original scale. A figure of .88 was produced. Explain what this value means in the context of concurrent validity. (2 marks)**

e. **Name one other method that could be used to assess the validity of a questionnaire or psychological test and explain how it could be used here. (3 marks)**

f. **Describe two factors that threaten the validity of psychological tests such as the EPQ. (4 marks)**

How do I answer... research methods questions?

Questions requiring research methods knowledge can appear in any section of any paper in the AS or A Level exams. They could include any aspect of research methods, data analysis or ethical issues. Let's look at the AO2: Research methods questions below:

a. For 3 marks, you must explain three steps you would take in order to assess test–retest reliability, including a suggestion of what a 'reliable' correlation coefficient would be. But do not stray into 'how to improve' as this is the next question.

b. Give one way to improve reliability and elaborate this.

c. You will need to know the definitions of face, concurrent, ecological and temporal validity as these are specifically named in the specification. See Research methods (Chapter 1 in this Revision Guide) if you need to revise the definitions.

d. Another 2-marker, so you need some elaboration beyond just saying that there is a strong correlation (between what and what?). What does this tell you?

e. Now you need to recall and explain another type of validity that would be relevant for this particular type of research. For 3 marks, you need to name it and explain, and elaborate your explanation.

f. You need to give two different issues. First will be the issue of social desirability bias in self-report questionnaires. To elaborate, explain how this affects the validity of the measure. Second is the issue of forced choice answers, and again explain how this affects validity.

REVIEW

Graphic organisers include mind-maps, flow charts, tables and charts, and there is good evidence that using these helps you to learn. Making concepts visual can give them a structure, which works well with the cognitive links and schemas used in memory. This topic lends itself to becoming a diagram, as Eysenck described three dimensions of personality:

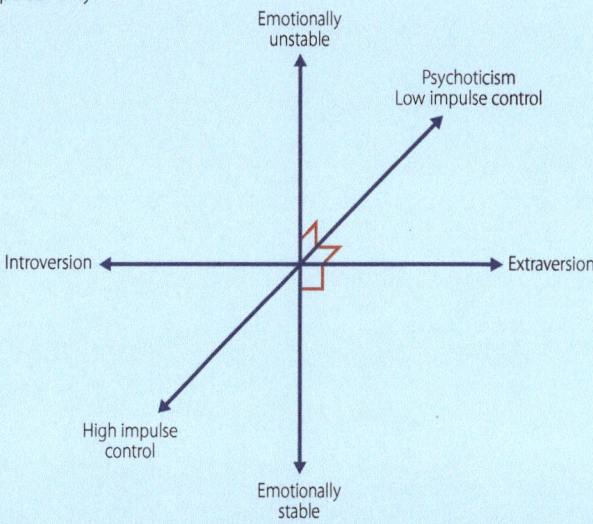

Try to imagine this in 3-D. Then add on key points about Eysenck's theory of the biological basis of these traits (arousal), and the links to criminal behaviour. This will make you a mind-map.

Psychological explanations of offending behaviour: Cognitive

 **RECAP**

A01 Description

Cognitive distortions

- Irrational or inaccurate thinking which can allow an offender to rationalise their behaviour.
- **Hostile attribution bias** is a negative interpretation of events, attributing malicious intentions to other people's behaviour. For example, if someone smiles you perceive them as mocking.
- **Minimalisation** is underplaying the consequences of an action to reduce negative emotions such as guilt. For example, a burglar may think that stealing from a wealthy family doesn't affect them.

Level of moral reasoning

- In England and Wales the 'age of criminal responsibility', when children are considered to be able to understand principles of right and wrong, is 10 years old.
- Kohlberg (1969) interviewed men and boys about the reasons for their moral decisions. He constructed a cognitive developmental theory, describing three stages in the development of moral reasoning:
  - > **Pre-conventional level** Children under 10 years old accept the rules of authority and judge actions by their consequences. Criminals are likely to be at this level, believing that breaking the law is justified if the rewards outweigh the risks of punishment.
  - > **Conventional level** Most adults believe that conformity to social rules is desirable, as it maintains social order and positive relationships. They may break the law in order to protect a family member.
  - > **Post-conventional level** Ten per cent of adults reach this stage, defining morality by abstract moral principles rather than compliance to norms.

A03 Evaluation / Discussion

Cognitive distortions
Research support for hostile attribution bias…

Schönenberg and Aiste (2014) showed emotionally ambiguous pictures to violent offenders in prison.	The pictures showed varying intensities of angry, happy and fearful emotions. Offenders were more likely than matched controls to interpret pictures as expressing aggression.	*This suggests that misinterpretation of facial expressions may at least partly explain aggressive-impulsive behaviour in susceptible individuals.*

Research support for minimalisation…

Kennedy and Grubin (1992) found that sex offenders' accounts of their crimes often downplayed their behaviour.	For example, the offenders suggested that the victim's behaviour contributed in some way to the crime, or simply denied that a crime had been committed.	*This supports the idea that this kind of cognitive distortion may underlie offending behaviour.*

Real-world applications…

Cognitive explanations can be used in treatment of offenders, using cognitive behavioural therapy (CBT).	Heller *et al.* (2013) used CBT to reduce cognitive distortions in disadvantaged young men in Chicago. Participants had a 44 per cent reduction in arrests compared to a control group.	*This suggests that CBT can be effective in helping to reduce judgement and decision-making errors, and thus reduce crime.*

Level of moral reasoning
Research support for levels of moral reasoning…

Issues/Debates
Gender bias

Research supports a universal sequence of stages.	For example, Gudjonsson and Sigurdsson (2007) found that 38 per cent of male juvenile offenders did not consider the consequences of their actions, suggesting they were at Kohlberg's pre-conventional level of moral reasoning.	*In addition, Chen and Howitt (2007) found, in Taiwanese male adolescent offenders, that those with more advanced reasoning were less likely to be involved in violent crimes.*

Limitations of Kohlberg's theory…

Kohlberg's theory concerns moral thinking rather than behaviour. Also, Kohlberg's theory was based on research in men and boys, so is gender biased.	Krebs and Denton (2005) found that people are motivated by factors like financial gain and only use moral principles to justify behaviour retrospectively.	*So the theory is limited in its ability to explain causes of offending behaviour, and particularly in relation to women.*

⚙ APPLY

AO2: An example

SCENARIO David has served a number of short-term prison sentences for theft. He claims his crimes are not serious as he only targets wealthy properties and never takes any items that could belong to children or that may have sentimental value such as jewellery. He argues any items he steals can easily be replaced as they will be covered by home insurance.

Using your knowledge of cognitive distortions, explain David's offending behaviour. **(4 marks)**

ANSWER *Cognitive distortions are a form of irrational thinking. In this case David has twisted the reality of his crimes so that they no longer represent the actual truth: David is underplaying his offending behaviour, which allows him to rationalise it. He has minimalised the impact his burglaries have on victims by justifying his choice of items to steal (no children's items or those with sentimental value) and the families he targets (wealthy households who are able to replace the items he takes). This helps David accept the consequences of his behaviour and reduces any negative feelings he may experience, e.g. guilt.*

AO2: Research methods ✏

1. In 1983 an article was published in volume 48 of the journal Monographs of the Society for Research in Child Development, nos. 1–2. The article was by A Colby, L Kohlberg, J Gibbs and M Lieberman and it was titled 'A longitudinal study of moral judgement'.

   Write a reference for this article, suitable for publication in the references section of a scientific journal. (2 marks)

2. An article called 'Patterns of denial in sex offenders' was written by HG Kennedy and DH Grubin, and published in 1992 in the journal Psychological Medicine, which is published by Cambridge University Press in Cambridge, UK. The article appeared in pages 191-6 of volume 22, issue 1.

   Write a reference for this article, suitable for publication in the references section of a scientific journal. (2 marks)

AO2: One for you to try ✏

In his investigation of levels of moral reasoning in young males, Kohlberg used scenarios such as this:

> Heinz's wife was dying from a particular type of cancer. Doctors said a new drug might save her. The drug had been discovered by a local chemist and Heinz tried desperately to buy some, but the chemist was charging ten times the money it cost to make the drug and this was much more than Heinz could afford. Heinz could only raise half the money, even after help from family and friends. He explained to the chemist that his wife was dying and asked if he could have the drug cheaper or pay the rest of the money later. The chemist refused, saying that he had discovered the drug and was going to make money from it. The husband was desperate to save his wife, so later that night he broke into the chemist's and stole the drug.

Then Kohlberg asked: 'Should Heinz have stolen the drug?'

a. **How would a person at each level of moral reasoning have answered? (6 marks)**

b. **What issues of validity might there be with this research? (3 marks)**

🐾 How do I answer... unexpected questions?

Don't be shocked if an unexpected question comes up, such as the referencing questions in **AO2: Research methods** on the left. Just have a go, and try to use your general knowledge of research methods, which you have gained during your course.

You probably know that the author's surname comes first, then the date and title of the article, and this would get you 1 mark. In a reference for a journal article, you then need the journal name, followed by the volume, issue number and pages in the journal. There are specific rules about italics and punctuation, but it is not worth trying to learn these for your A Level exam.

You should also be familiar with a reference for a book, which is slightly different. The authors' names and initials are first, then the date in brackets, followed by the title of the book. Then comes the place of publication and the publisher's name.

Q2 is trying to mislead you by giving you the information about the publisher, which is not needed for a journal article reference.

🔄 REVIEW

As you are probably aware, simply reading material is not the most effective way of learning it properly. So, using the material on the opposite page, try writing plans for 3-, 4- and 6-mark 'outline' questions on cognitive explanations plus plans for 8- and 16-mark essay questions.

Test yourself on the key points of cognitive explanations of criminal behaviour by covering up your plans and writing them out again. It's useful to have a supply of cheap paper for this, as the more times you practise retrieving the information, the better you will remember it.

Spaced practice is also very effective: come back to the same topic tomorrow and start your revision by seeing how many of the points you can remember before you look at your essay plan.

Psychological explanations of offending behaviour: Differential association

RECAP

AO1 Description

- Sutherland (1939) proposed that offending behaviour can be explained entirely by social learning.
- **What is learned?** A child learns attitudes towards crime, and which crimes are acceptable or desirable, as well as methods of committing crimes.
- **Who is it learned from?** Family, peers and the local community may model criminal behaviour or may show acceptance of deviant attitudes.
- **How is it learned?** Sutherland did not specify this, but it is likely to be direct reinforcement (operant conditioning), and observation; if role models are successful this provides vicarious reinforcement. Social norms are also involved.

- **Nine key principles:**
  1. Criminal behaviour is learned rather than inherited...
  2. (through **association** with...
  3. (intimate personal groups.
  4. Techniques and attitudes are learned.
  5. Learning is directional – for or against crime.
  6. If favourable attitudes outweigh unfavourable ones, then a person becomes an offender.
  7. Learning experiences (differential associations) vary in frequency and intensity.
  8. Criminal behaviour is learned through the same processes as any other behaviour.
  9. General 'need' (e.g. for money) is not a sufficient explanation for crime because not everyone with those needs turns to crime.

Some crime involves learning complex skills from others

AO3 Evaluation/Discussion

This theory made a major contribution to changing people's views...

| In this theory, crime could be explained in terms of people's social experiences, rather than labelling them as 'mad' or 'bad'. | Sutherland also introduced the concept of 'white collar crimes', committed by middle-class, respectable people, e.g. fraud or copyright infringements. | *This has important applications, as we can try to change social learning environments, whereas genes cannot be changed.* |

Issues/Debates
Ethical implications, socially sensitive research

Supporting evidence from family studies and peer group studies...

| Osborne and West (1979) found that 40 per cent of sons of fathers with a criminal conviction had committed a crime before age 18, compared to 13 per cent of sons of non-criminal fathers. | In addition, Akers *et al.* (1979) surveyed 2,500 US adolescents, finding that peers were the greatest influence on drinking and drug-taking. | *Family studies can't separate out the effects of genes and environment, but peer studies show that young people are influenced by their peers, supporting differential association theory.* |

Methodological issues...

| An issue with this research is that it is correlational, so it is possible that offenders seek out other offenders, rather than being influenced by them. | Some critics also argue that the theory is untestable because of the interaction between learned and inherited factors, and it is unclear what ratio of favourable to unfavourable influences would tip the balance. | *This means that we cannot conclude cause and effect, and we cannot test the theory experimentally, so its validity is unclear.* |

Issues/Debates
Determinism

The role of biological factors...

| This explanation ignores biological factors. | There is clear evidence that biological factors are also important in the development of anti-social and violent behaviour. There may be innate genetic factors or early experiences which affect brain development. | *This means that a diathesis-stress model may offer a better account by combining social factors with biological predispositions.* |

Issues/Debates
Biological and environmental determinism

APPLY

AO2: An example

SCENARIO Gemma's friends regularly use pirate sites to download music and films. They know it is illegal but can't really see the harm as everyone seems to be doing it. Gemma has recently begun using the sites herself.

How would differential association theory explain Gemma's behaviour? **(4 marks)**

ANSWER *As people in Gemma's social network condone the use of illegal sharing sites she sees the crime as acceptable within her circle of friends and so is likely to want to access music and films in this way too. She states, 'her friends regularly use pirate sites', which suggests the intensity and frequency of the learning experiences are sufficient to influence her own behaviour. Gemma has learned from her peers techniques that enable her to access films and music without purchasing them herself. Her peers are role models who have been successfully using these sites without consequence, increasing the likelihood Gemma will also imitate their actions.*

AO2: One for you to try

Lauren's mother and father divorced and Lauren and her mother had to move to the rough part of town to find cheaper accommodation. Initially Lauren found it difficult to make friends but then started hanging out with the 'bad girls' in the neighbourhood, many of whom have been excluded from school. Lauren's behaviour seems to go from bad to worse, and the visits from the police soon started after she was found to be selling stolen property at school.

How can we explain Lauren's behaviour in terms of differential association theory? (6 marks)

AO2: Research methods

A researcher is investigating sixth form students' use of tobacco and e-cigarettes, and whether they are influenced by their friends in their smoking or vaping activities. He wants to give students a questionnaire, as he hopes the anonymity will encourage them to be honest about their behaviour and motivations. He wishes to collect quantitative and qualitative data.

a. **Write a question suitable to collect quantitative data in this study. (2 marks)**

b. **Write a question which would collect qualitative data in this study. (2 marks)**

c. **Write a brief consent form which the researcher could give to participants before they complete the questionnaire. Your consent form should:**
   - Explain what participants are going to be asked to do.
   - Refer to relevant ethical issues.
   - Be in an appropriate format. **(6 marks)**

How do I answer... shorter (8-mark) essay questions?

Not all essays follow the 12- or 16-mark format. Some have a slightly lower tariff. Of these lower tariff essay questions, the 8-marker is the most common. It does help to know what you are dealing with, however, as they are not always straightforward. The AO1 and AO3 material for these questions is on the opposite page.

Q1: Outline and evaluate differential association as an explanation of offending behaviour. **(8 marks)**

Although you might think that this question would be worth 4 marks for AO1 and 4 for AO3, this is actually half of a 16-mark essay question, so there is a similar split of marks, i.e. 3 marks for AO1 and 5 marks for AO3 (instead of the 6- and 10-mark split for a 16-mark question).

Q2: There has been a recent outbreak of vandalism at a secondary school, including graffiti on walls inside and outside the building, and damage to property at weekends. The headteacher believes there are a group of pupils in Year 10 who are a bad influence on others in the year group, and wishes to exclude these pupils from the school.

Discuss the differential association explanation of criminal behaviour, and suggest what advice you could give to the head teacher. **(8 marks)**

This question includes a scenario that is referred back to in the question. This is an indication that there is an additional AO2 requirement. AO2 marks tend to be 'stolen' from the AO3 allocation, so there are 3 marks of AO1 (first three points), 3 marks of AO3 *and* 2 marks' worth of AO2. The scenario is about young people, so the second AO3 point would be most relevant, and it would look impressive to link this point to the scenario too. For example:

'Peer groups are important influences in young people's behaviour, as Akers found in his survey of US adolescents, so the headteacher can remove the offending young people from the school to stop this bad influence spreading.'

You can take this to a higher level by referring to the methodological issues with this research too:

'However, the research is correlational which means that we can't conclude cause and effect: it could be that young people who are already enjoying damaging property are seeking out friends who want to do the same at weekends.'

REVIEW

Practise remembering Sutherland's nine key principles by completing the sentences from memory, then check against the list on the opposite page. Practise several times until you can remember them fluently, then come back to them at the beginning of your next revision session to practise retrieval.

Criminal behaviour is...

(How?)

(Who?)

(What?)

Learning is...

If... then...

Learning experiences vary in...

The learning processes are...

General 'need' is not...

Psychological explanations of offending behaviour: Psychodynamic

RECAP

AO1 Description

- **Maternal deprivation theory** Bowlby (1951) was a Freudian psychiatrist. He proposed that prolonged separations between a mother and child would have long-term emotional consequences.

- There was most risk if the separation was before the age of about two-and-a-half years and there was no substitute mother-person, with continuing risk up to age five years. The long-term consequence is **affectionless psychopathy**; lack of empathy, shame or sense of responsibility.

- Bowlby (1944) studied 44 delinquent children attending his clinic. Thirty-nine per cent of all thieves, and 12 out of 14 classified as affectionless, had experienced frequent separations.

- **The superego** In Freud's psychoanalytic theory, the id operates according to the pleasure principle, and the superego is a moral compass, causing guilt when rules are broken. The ego acts as the reality principle and mediates between the id and superego.

  > A child whose parent is absent develops a weak superego, and acts impulsively to gratify the id.

  > A child with a strict parent develops a harsh superego, with excessive guilt and anxiety.

  > A child with a criminal parent will identify with them and adopt the same deviant superego.

- Committing crime and receiving punishment may relieve these feelings.

AO3 Evaluation / Discussion

Real-world application of Bowlby's theory…

It is difficult to treat emotional problems in adolescent delinquents, and much better to prevent them by avoiding early separations.	Bowlby, with the Robertsons (1952), demonstrated that children could cope with separations from parents as long as alternative emotional care was provided.	Social policies and childcare provision have been influenced enormously by Bowlby's work on attachment and maternal deprivation.

However, the research does not allow causal conclusions…

There could be other explanations of the association between separation and emotional problems, such as the effect of disrupted home life.	Separation was not manipulated by the researcher, so it is even possible that the child's affectionless personality caused the separations in some cases, as the mother could not cope.	This means Bowlby's 44 thieves study should be used with caution to support his theory.

Freud's theory is gender biased…

Issues/Debates
Gender bias

Freud proposed that women develop a weaker superego than men. This alpha-biased theory devalues women and is not supported by evidence.	This is partly because Freud believed there was little reason for anyone to identify with a woman, because of her lower status, so girls' identification with their mother was weaker.	If Freud's views were correct, women should be more likely to become criminals than men. This is not the case.

Complex set of factors…

There are many factors that interact to cause offending, including: family history of criminality; risk-taking personality; low school attainment; poverty; poor parenting.	These were the most important risk factors at age 8–10 for later offending, as identified by Farrington *et al.* (2009), in a 40-year longitudinal study in London.	This shows that a combined approach (biological, personality, cognitive and psychodynamic) can give a fuller picture of the causes of offending.

⚙ APPLY

AO2: An example

SCENARIO A psychologist was interested in researching the life experiences of prisoners prior to their offending. He identified a number of individuals who had experienced periods of time when they were separated from their primary caregivers. Further interviews revealed many prisoners had a tendency to act in impulsive ways and showed little regard for others.

With reference to the above scenario, describe and evaluate psychodynamic explanations of offending behaviour. **(16 marks)**

ANSWER **An extract showing how you could address the AO2 requirements of this question:** *Bowlby's 44 juvenile thieves study suggests prolonged mother–infant separation leads to long-term emotional consequences. Thirty-nine per cent of the thieves had experienced early separations compared to a control group, none of whom had experienced separations. The psychologist in the scenario seems to have found similar evidence. The scenario also suggests that offenders show affectionless psychopathy (identified by Bowlby), as it mentions they 'showed little regard for others'. The psychologist may also have identified some prisoners with a weak superego: 'a tendency to act in impulsive ways'. Freud suggests that, during the phallic stage, failure to identify with a same-sex parent (possibly because of separations experienced) can lead to the development of a weak superego. Therefore, these individuals have little control over their anti-social behaviour...*

AO2: Research methods

Bowlby's study of 44 thieves at a London clinic included a comparison group of 44 adolescents who had been referred to the clinic for emotional issues but had not yet committed any crime.

a. **What sort of sampling did Bowlby use? What are the limitations of this type of sample? (3 marks)**

b. **Bowlby diagnosed some as having affectionless psychopathy. He also carried out the clinical interviews to collect data about separations, and knew which young people had committed thefts and which had not. Explain how this could affect his findings. (3 marks)**

c. **The number of separations experienced was measured by asking the young people to remember their early childhood. Explain how measuring it like this might affect validity? (3 marks)**

AO2: One for you to try

A prison researcher works in a high-security prison for violent offenders. He has been observing male prisoners interacting with their visiting children, and concluded that they are often harsh and lacking in displays of warmth and affection towards their children. He wonders whether this is because of their own experience of harsh, authoritarian parenting.

Using your knowledge of psychodynamic explanations of offending behaviour, explain how the prisoners' own experience as children could have put their offending behaviour before their relationship with their own children. (6 marks)

🐾 How do I answer... description and evaluation (AO1 + AO3) questions?

1 Recognise what you need to do. Two different command words – e.g. 'outline' (an AO1 term) – and 'evaluate' (an AO3 term) – is a clue that this is a mixed AO1 + AO3 question.

2 Plan how much to write for the AO1 and AO3 parts. In mixed AO1 + AO3 questions up to 6 marks, the division is half and half (it is different with mark totals higher than this as we will see on p.191).

3 Decide what to write. Look at the examples below. (The AO1 and AO3 material for these questions is on the opposite page.)

Q1: Briefly outline a psychodynamic explanation of crime and give **one** criticism of research into psychodynamic explanations. **(4 marks)**

Use the first two AO1 points and one AO3 point.

Q2: Outline and evaluate the maternal deprivation theory of criminal behaviour. **(6 marks)**

The AO1 requirement would be met by the first three AO1 points for 'maternal deprivation theory'. They would give a good 3-mark overview as required by the question. For the AO3 content you might use one complete AO3 point, or two briefer ones. The first point is relevant to Bowlby's theory, and you could make it more interesting by using the methodological evaluation of the second point. Keep it brief though; the lead-in and first column would be enough.

Q3: Outline and discuss findings from research into psychodynamic explanations of offending. **(6 marks)**

Although 'discuss' is more commonly used as an AO1 + AO3 term in its own right, in **Q3** it is being used just as an AO3 term. You have a number of ways to answer this, but whichever route you take, there should be about 75–90 words of AO1 and 75–90 words of AO3. This time you should use the findings associated with research into psychodynamic explanations (Bowlby's 44 thieves study is useful for this) and again AO3 points 1 and 2 would be most relevant.

🔄 REVIEW

Compare the four psychological explanations by making a table, with a column for each (Eysenck's, cognitive, differential association, psychodynamic). Your rows could include: Key assumptions; link to criminal behaviour; applications; research support; criticisms.

Dealing with offending behaviour: Custodial sentencing and recidivism

RECAP

AO1 Description

- In the UK in 2015, about 150 people were in prison per 100,000 population. The prison population has doubled in 20 years.
- **Recidivism** means reoffending after being punished for an offence. Within a year of release, 46 per cent of adults and 67 per cent of under-18-year-olds are reconvicted. The cost to the economy is £9.5 billion per year.

- **Custodial sentencing** requires an offender to be held in a prison or secure psychiatric hospital. Aims include:
  - > **To protect the public – incapacitation** Necessary with violent offenders or psychopaths.
  - > **To punish an offender and prevent recidivism** A behaviourist approach, aiming to decrease the likelihood of the behaviour being repeated.
  - > **To deter others** A social learning approach, learning from the consequences of others' behaviour.
  - > **To atone for wrongdoing – retribution** The offender should pay for what they have done.
  - > **To rehabilitate offenders** Therapy or education is provided to prevent further criminal behaviour.
- **Psychological effects of custodial sentencing**
  - > **De-individuation** is the loss of individual identity, leading to increased aggression.
  - > **Depression, self-harm and suicide** Offenders may feel hopeless and helpless. Young men are at highest risk of suicide in the first 24 hours of imprisonment.
  - > **Overcrowding and lack of privacy** Twenty-five per cent of prisoners are in overcrowded accommodation, with two people in a cell designed for one. This causes stress, aggression and illness.
  - > **Effects on the family** Parents in prison experience guilt and separation anxiety, and their children suffer financially and psychologically.

AO3 Evaluation/Discussion

Punishment is ineffective as a deterrent...

At least 50 per cent of the prison population reoffend within a year of release, and even severe punishments do not work as deterrents; murder rates in US states with the death penalty are no lower than in those without it.	This may because of the long gap between offending and sentencing, so the offender sees the sentence as a punishment for being caught. Evidence shows that cautions are more effective deterrents than arrests (Klein *et al.*, 1977).	*This means punishment does not work, as offenders may learn that they should avoid being caught.*

Incapacitation, retribution and rehabilitation are limited in their benefits...

Incapacitation only applies to a small number of dangerous prisoners; rehabilitative therapy cannot be forced on someone; and retribution can be better achieved in other ways.	Restorative justice offers the chance for offenders to make amends to victims, while changing their attitudes to offending. Non-custodial sentences, such as community service, fines or electronic monitoring, avoid the psychological problems of imprisonment.	*This means that many of the aims of custodial sentencing could be better achieved by non-custodial sentencing.*

Prison may even increase reoffending...

Sutherland's differential association theory suggests that spending time with criminals will normalise pro-criminal attitudes and provide learning opportunities for future criminal activity.	Restorative justice offers the chance for offenders to make amends to victims, while changing their attitudes to offending. Non-custodial sentences, such as community service, fines or electronic monitoring, avoid the psychological problems of imprisonment.	*So imprisonment may reinforce pro-criminal attitudes and encourage increased criminal behaviour on release.*

Individual differences in recidivism...

Custodial sentences may be more effective with some offenders than others.	Home Office statistics show that young people are more likely to reoffend, and those committing theft or burglary are twice as likely to reoffend as drug or sex offenders.	*Thus, sentencing should be targeted in different ways with different groups of offenders.*

APPLY

AO2: An example

SCENARIO Ian, a father of two young children, has received numerous cautions and fines for driving offences. He was recently arrested for speeding and driving a car without an MOT or insurance. His court case is soon and he is worried the magistrate will give him a custodial sentence.

What psychological effects might Ian experience if he is sent to prison?
(4 marks)

ANSWER *Prisons face increasing pressure from a growing prison population. In 2012, the Ministry of Justice reported 25 per cent of prisoners are in overcrowded accommodation. This means Ian may have to share a cell which could have a negative impact on him psychologically. Ian may feel helplessness on entering prison and hopeless about his future, both of which could lead to depression. He may also be at risk of self-harming behaviour. Newton (1980) reported that self-harming was becoming part of inmate culture so Ian may conform and engage in the behaviour. Ian may also feel guilt and separation anxiety as contact with his family would be greatly reduced.*

AO2: Research methods

Women only represent 5 per cent of the prison population, but their characteristics differ from male prisoners, as shown in the table below.

Social characteristics of male and female prisoners		
Characteristic	Men	Women
Have experienced emotional, physical or sexual abuse	27%	53%
Committed their offence in order to support the drug use of someone else	22%	48%
Serving a prison sentence for a non-violent offence	71%	81%
Have no previous convictions	12%	26%
Have spent time in local authority care	24%	31%
Have symptoms indicative of psychosis	15%	25%
Have attempted suicide at some point	21%	46%

a. **In October 2015 there were 3,948 female prisoners. How many of these had committed their offence in order to support the drug use of someone else? (1 mark)**

b. **What percentage of female prisoners were serving sentences for violent crimes? (1 mark)**

c. **Using data from the table, describe the psychological differences between male and female prisoners. (3 marks)**

AO2: One for you to try

Brigitte had a difficult childhood with an alcoholic mother, and was taken into care at age 13. As a teenager she was cautioned by the police for shoplifting to fund her drug habit, but managed to get work in a hotel when she was 17 and kept on the right side of the law. She started medication for depression and anxiety, which she still takes. When she was 22 she fell in love with Ethan, who was good to her, and treated her to new clothes and foreign holidays, but turned out to be a drug dealer. Brigitte and Ethan now have a 13-month-old baby. After a police raid, Brigitte was arrested and has been found guilty of supplying heroin in her local city.

What factors should the judge consider in deciding whether to give Brigitte a custodial sentence for her crime? (6 marks)

How do I answer... longer (16-mark) application questions?

Q1: A group of policymakers were holding discussions about the penal system, as they were concerned that recidivism rates were too high and prisoners may be suffering psychologically from their time in prison. They started by considering the aims of custodial sentencing, and whether those aims are being met currently. They then discussed alternative ways of dealing with offending behaviour.

Discuss the aims of custodial sentencing, and suggest an alternative way of dealing with offending behaviour which the policymakers could consider. **(16 marks)**

If the question was simply 'Discuss custodial sentencing', you would need 6 marks of AO1 and 10 marks of AO3. However, this question includes a stem to refer to, so you still need 6 marks of AO1, but you will now need to include 4 marks' worth of AO2 application and just 6 marks of AO3 discussion. (The AO1 and AO3 material for this question is on the opposite page.)

- For the AO1, you should include all the aims listed in our AO1 section, with brief descriptions of each. You should also explain recidivism.

- For your AO2 section, you need to make links with the scenario. You could refer here to the psychological effects of custodial sentencing on the prisoner, and evidence about recidivism rates.

- Your AO3 will then be two of our AO3 points, and a brief comparison with an alternative way of dealing with offending, such as restorative justice. For example, you could use the second AO3 point for restorative justice to show how these programmes have better results in reducing reoffending. Don't get distracted onto describing restorative justice in detail, however, as there won't be any credit for this.

REVIEW

There are two lists of points to remember in this topic. You could make flash cards or use an app to keep testing yourself on your recall of these. Summarise them in single words:

Aims: Incapacitation, Punishment, Deterrence, Retribution, Rehabilitation.

Effects: De-individuation, Depression, Overcrowding, Separation.

Recite them to yourself as lists until they trip off your tongue, and then recite them more slowly, allowing yourself time to mentally elaborate the concepts.

Dealing with offending behaviour: Behaviour modification in custody

AO1 Description

Token economy

- **Behavioural modification is based on operant conditioning.**
- Prisoners are rewarded with tokens when they perform desirable behaviours, such as obeying orders. These can be exchanged for treats like cigarettes, food or TV time.
- This **reinforcement** increases the likelihood that the behaviour will be repeated (**operant conditioning**).
- The treats are primary reinforcers and the tokens become secondary reinforcers through **association** (classical conditioning).
- Target behaviours and rewards must be clearly defined in advance, with a hierarchy of rewards for different behaviours.
- **Punishment** can also be used by removing tokens for undesirable behaviour.
- **Shaping** works progressively towards longer-term objectives and more complex behaviours.

Operant conditioning

Hobbs and Holt (1976)

- **PROCEDURE** A token economy was introduced into a school for delinquent boys to try to reduce inappropriate social behaviour.
  - > One hundred and twenty-five boys were observed in four cottages over 14 months. One was a control group with no tokens. Two supervisors observed each boy and recorded behaviours in six categories such as following instructions or completing chores. Boys were told daily how many tokens they had earned, and exchanged them weekly for treats, or saved them for off-campus activities.
- **FINDINGS** Social behaviours increased by an average of 27 per cent in boys who were included in the programme, with no increase in the control group, showing the effectiveness of token economy in improving behaviour.

AO3 Evaluation / Discussion

Token economy can be effective…

It is easy to implement, providing a means of controlling unmanageable behaviour and improving the prison environment for staff and prisoners, without needing input from psychologists.

For it to work well, the token economy needs careful pre-planning and consistent application by staff. Bassett and Blanchard (1977) rescued a failing token economy system by improving consistency.

This means that, as long as the token economy is clear and consistent, it can provide a simple and cost-effective way of improving prison life.

It is less successful in prisons than in other contexts…

It was used widely and was effective in US prisons in the 1970s, increasing socially acceptable behaviours and reducing crime (Milan and McKee, 1976).

However, good results did not persist, and use in the UK was limited to young offenders' institutes. It has been very successful in some special schools for young people with behavioural difficulties or autism.

Token economy has fallen out of favour in prisons, but is still used successfully elsewhere.

Short- versus long-term goals…

In the short term, a token economy can improve behaviour in the prison environment, but may not affect offenders when they return to their natural environment.

This is because a token economy only has short-term effects while the rewards are available, and once they cease the stimulus-response link is extinguished.

This suggests that token economies give the illusion of changing behaviour but don't actually have a lasting effect.

Ethical issues…

Token economy systems can violate human rights as individuals are being manipulated, not always with their agreement.

This can be overcome by agreeing procedures and goals between prisoners and staff. However, it is unethical to make basic needs (food or visiting rights) dependent on tokens, or to take away tokens as a punishment.

These ethical issues contributed to the loss of popularity of token systems in prisons.

 # APPLY

AO2: An example

SCENARIO Just after his 16th birthday, Aaron was arrested for knife crime and given a custodial sentence of six months. Initially Aaron's behaviour at the secure centre was very challenging but staff's use of behavioural modification strategies improved his behaviour and, they hoped, reduced his risk of reoffending.

With reference to Aaron, describe and evaluate the use of behavioural modification in custody as a means of dealing with offender behaviour.
(16 marks)

ANSWER **An extract showing how you could address the AO2 requirements of this question:** *The secure centre could use a token economy system to encourage Aaron to adopt desirable behaviour, e.g. if he made his bed on a daily basis and stood in line in the canteen he'd receive tokens. The tokens are a secondary reinforcer as they can be redeemed for chocolate and cigarettes (primary reinforcers). This system may modify Aaron's behaviour as Cohen and Filipcjak (1971) found juvenile delinquents who had been trained with a token economy system were less likely to reoffend. However, to maintain Aaron's good behaviour, staff must remain consistent in the way they award tokens...*

AO2: Research methods

In the study by Hobbs and Holt, data was gathered by recording behaviour on a daily chart. Two supervisors recorded each boy's behaviour in five categories, such as following rules, following instructions and walking in a straight line. The boys' behaviour was compared before and after they were awarded tokens.

a. **Identify the independent and dependent variables. (2 marks)**

b. **Explain why this study might be classed as a natural experiment. (2 marks)**

Two supervisors recorded the behaviour for each boy.

c. **Why were two supervisors used? (2 marks)**

Reliability was calculated by comparing the observations of each boy by the two supervisors. Calculations of reliability ranged from 70–100 per cent.

d. **How could the reliability be improved in this study? (2 marks)**

e. **After the research programme finished, the token economy programme gradually deteriorated. Suggest why this might be. (2 marks)**

f. **Hobbs and Holt comment that there is no evidence to show whether behaviours learned at the school were transferred to real life when the boys left. Using your knowledge of operant conditioning, explain why the boys were unlikely to continue these behaviours after release from the programme. (4 marks)**

AO2: One for you to try

Mrs Cole is the headteacher at a school for teenagers with behavioural difficulties who have been excluded from mainstream school. She wants to try a token economy system to improve the young people's behaviour.

Using your knowledge of token economy systems, what recommendations can you make to Mrs Cole about how to set this up, and what benefits might there be for her school? (6 marks)

How do I answer... longer (16-mark) questions?

The difference between the following two questions lies in how you approach the AO3 evaluation/ discussion. The AO1 and AO3 material for these questions is on the opposite page.

Q1: Outline and evaluate behaviour modification in custody as a way of dealing with offending behaviour. **(16 marks)**

In **Q1**, the nominal mark division for AO1 (outline) and AO3 (evaluation) is 6 marks for AO1 and 10 marks for AO3. You could aim to include the first six AO1 points, which explain the theory and use important key terms, then use the Hobbs and Holt study as an example. For the AO3 content, you should include all four of the AO3 points.

Q2: Discuss the usefulness of behaviour modification in dealing with offending behaviour. **(16 marks)**

Q2 uses the command word 'discuss', so it requires AO3 that is a bit more 'discursive', e.g. looking at applications, implications, counter-evidence etc. We have tried to make some of our AO3 points 'discursive' to accommodate this. For example, the second AO3 point includes a 'however', which links some evidence with some counter-evidence, and reaches a conclusion about the application of token economy. Points 3 and 4 are also discursive, as they discuss the usefulness of the application of token economy, and ethical issues associated with it. If you use all these points in full you would have an excellent discussion.

REVIEW

As this topic is about application of psychological principles to modifying behaviour, it is very suitable for application type questions as well as straightforward 'outline and evaluate' or 'discuss' questions. Practise the examples in **AO2: One for you to try** and **AO2: Research methods** and check your answers against the answer section at the back of this book. Test yourself on your explanations of classical and operant conditioning and check you are using all the key terms correctly. Are you clearly explaining the psychology, and clearly linking it to the scenario? See tips on **How do I answer... application (AO2) questions** on p.175.

Dealing with offending behaviour: Anger management

RECAP

AO1 Description

- Anger management programmes use a cognitive approach to reduce aggression in prisons as well as rehabilitating offenders and reducing recidivism.
- Novaco (2011) identified three aims of anger management programmes:
  > Cognitive restructuring – greater self-awareness and control of angry thoughts.
  > Regulation of arousal – control of the physiological state of anger.
  > Behavioural strategies – problem-solving, strategic withdrawal and assertiveness.

- **Stress inoculation therapy** (SIT) A CBT model developed by Novaco (1975), used with groups in prison or on probation.
  1. Cognitive preparation: learning about anger and analysing their own patterns of anger.
  2. Skill acquisition: learning skills like self-regulation, cognitive flexibility and relaxation, and how to resolve conflicts assertively without getting angry.
  3. Application training: applying skills in role play with feedback from group members, then in real-world settings.
- **Example 1** Ireland (2004) compared baseline and post-treatment assessments for 50 young offenders who had 12 hours of anger management therapy. They were assessed by self-report and by prison officers. She found significant improvements in this group, with no change in an untreated control group.
- **Example 2** Trimble *et al.* (2015) studied 105 offenders on probation. They had nine two-hour anger management sessions, which significantly reduced the anger the offenders experienced or expressed compared to pre-treatment scores.

AO3 Evaluation/Discussion

Anger management programmes have mixed success…

Taylor and Novaco (2006) report 75 per cent improvement rates based on six meta-analyses of general anger management programmes.	However, findings of studies with offenders are inconsistent; meta-analyses show only moderate benefits of anger management programmes (Howells *et al.,* 2005).	This means it is difficult to draw clear conclusions about the effectiveness of anger management programmes for offenders.

Problems with research…

The studies are difficult to compare as some are brief and intense, and some last for years; some are run by psychologists, and others by prison staff.	Also, anger is assessed through self-report or observations by prison staff, both of which are subject to bias. Prisoners often want to be helpful in showing that the therapy worked; the 'hello–goodbye effect'.	This means that meta-analyses are not comparing like with like, so findings are inconsistent and may be invalid.

High dropout rate from anger management programmes…

Many offenders drop out of the programmes, maybe because they find it difficult to talk about their thoughts and feelings, and to make the effort to change their attitudes and behaviours.	It helps to measure 'readiness to change' before the start of a programme. Drama-based courses are a useful alternative, less reliant on verbal ability.	This way programmes can be focussed on the offenders who will complete the course and benefit most from it.

Anger and aggression…

Anger management programmes assume that treating anger will reduce aggression and violent crime.	However, Loza and Loza-Fanous (1999) found no difference between violent and non-violent offenders' anger levels. This may be because violent offenders mask their anger.	Howells et al. (2005) concluded that much violence can take place without anger being a prominent feature.

 **APPLY**

A02: An example

SCENARIO Shelly has a number of convictions for anti-social behaviour including a recent conviction for physically attacking someone in a pub when she thought they had deliberately bumped into her. While serving a custodial sentence Shelly is offered the opportunity to participate in an anger management programme.

What might prison officers tell Shelly about the programme? . **(4 marks)**

ANSWER *Prison officers could tell Shelly the programme will be a form of CBT which aims to change her maladaptive thoughts that led to aggressive behaviour. The programme will involve three steps. First, Shelly will learn about anger and she will identify her own anger patterns and situations that provoke anger such as thinking people are deliberately disrespecting her. Second, she will be taught skills to manage her anger, e.g. self-reflection, relaxation. Finally, Shelly will role-play these skills such as recreating the scene in the pub to practise alternative ways to behave. She will later apply these to real-life situations.*

A02: Research methods

A secure training centre for young offenders aged 12–17 has been running 10-week anger management classes. The summary table below shows how self-report anger ratings changed over the 10-week period in 17 young people who took this programme.

Group	Anger ratings decreased	Anger ratings increased	Anger ratings stayed the same
Completed programme	14	2	1
Control group	8	6	5

A sign test can be used to test the significance of the data.

a. **What is the calculated value of the sign test statistic 'S' for the group who completed the programme? Explain your answer. (2 marks)**

Table of critical values of S

Level of significance for a one-tailed test	0.05	0.01
Level of significance for a two-tailed test	0.10	0.02
N		
15	3	3
16	4	3
17	4	4
18	5	4

b. **A directional hypothesis was used. Using the table of critical values of 'S' above, state whether the findings of the study are significant at $p < 0.05$. Explain your answer. (2 marks)**

c. **The control group consisted of young people who have signed up for this course but are currently on a waiting list. Why was this a suitable control group? (2 marks)**

d. **What conclusions can you draw from the results of the control group? (3 marks)**

e. **How might the validity of the anger ratings be criticised? (2 marks)**

A02: One for you to try

Dexter frequently gets into fights when he goes out to town for the evening and has a bit of a reputation in the bars and clubs around town as a 'hard man'. After he is arrested for fighting yet again, the magistrate decides that Dexter has 'anger issues' and recommends that he take part in anger management treatment.

Suggest an appropriate anger management programme suitable for Dexter and explain how this treatment would proceed. (6 marks)

 **How do I answer... questions on consent and debriefing?**

Q1: Write a consent form suitable to give to young offenders in the **A02: Research methods** question. **(6 marks)**

A consent form could contain:

- An explanation of the general purpose of the research.
- The aim of the 10-week anger management course.
- Details about what the course will involve: time commitment, what will take place in sessions, homework tasks.
- No pressure to take part.
- They can withdraw at any time.
- They can ask the course leader, researcher or prison officers questions at any time.
- Any personal information they share in the course will be confidential.
- A question: do you agree to take part?
- A space for the young offender to sign the form.

Q2: Write a debriefing statement which researchers could read to young offenders at the end of the research. **(6 marks)**

A debriefing statement could include:

- Thanks for taking part.
- Explain full purpose of research and the two conditions.
- All data will be confidential and kept secure and anonymous.
- Right to withdraw data.
- Offer further support.
- Do you have any questions?

 REVIEW

A good way to remember a process, such as Stress Inoculation Therapy, is to role-play it. Pretend you are the therapist, and find a willing client (friend, family member, pet or teddy bear). First explain the aims of anger management, then work through the three stages with them. You won't know enough to be able to do this properly, and you're not qualified to either (consider ethical issues here!) but you can probably help them identify when they become angry, practise a bit of relaxation with them and make suggestions for how they can apply their relaxation skills in real-world settings.

Dealing with offending behaviour: Restorative justice programmes

 **RECAP**

AO1 Description

- Restorative justice enables offenders to repair the harm they have done, often by meeting with victims and a mediator, or by letter.

- **Aims of restorative justice:**

  > **Rehabilitation of offenders** The victim explains the impact of the crime. The offender can understand the victim's perspective, and take responsibility. This should affect their future behaviour.

  > **Atonement for wrongdoing** Offenders may offer compensation (money or community service) and show their remorse. The victim can express their distress; this helps the offender develop empathy.

  > **Victim's perspective** The victim feels less powerless, as they have a voice. They may understand the offender's story better, reducing their sense of victimisation.

- **A theory of restorative justice** Wachtel and McCold (2003) propose that the focus should be on restoring relationships, rather than punishment. Three stakeholders must be involved for fully restorative justice; the victim seeking reparation, the offender taking responsibility, and the community aiming to maintain a healthy society.

- Peace circles have been set up in communities with high crime levels, supporting victims and welcoming offenders into the circle to enable mutual understanding. A 'talking piece' is passed round to allow each person to talk without interruption. A 'keeper' helps to maintain an atmosphere of respect and develop constructive solutions.

AO3 Evaluation/Discussion

Success from the victim's perspective…

Victims find restorative justice beneficial, and this is supported by evidence from the UK Restorative Justice Council (2015).	85 per cent of victims were satisfied after face-to-face meetings with offenders. Dignan (2005) found that victims were more satisfied by this process than when cases go through court.	*This research shows that, for a large range of crimes, from theft to violent crime, restorative justice benefits victims.*

Reoffending rates are reduced…

Sherman and Strang (2007) reviewed 20 studies of face-to-face meetings in three countries, and found reduced reoffending in all cases.	One study found an 11 per cent reoffending rate compared to 37 per cent in matched controls who served prison sentences.	*This shows that restorative justice is also successful in its aim of reducing crime rates.*

Restorative justice also has other advantages…

It is much less expensive than custodial sentencing and reduces exposure to criminal attitudes in prison.	It also promotes offender accountability: facing a victim may still be sufficiently unpleasant to act as a punishment and a deterrent to future crime.	*Overall, restorative justice meets many of the aims of custodial sentences while also addressing the needs of victims.*

Ethical issues…

We should consider possible harmful effects on the victim and the offender.	One concern is whether the victim may feel worse afterwards. Also, sometimes the victims can abuse their position of power over the offender, who may be young or vulnerable.	*So restorative justice programmes must be carefully managed to ensure benefit to both victim and offender.*

 **APPLY**

AO2: An example

SCENARIO A small group of adolescents has been causing trouble on Selina's housing estate. Over a period of months their anti-social behaviour escalated, leading to one of them pushing Selina over on her way home from the shops and kicking her shopping into the road. Police have asked Selina if she would be willing to meet with the young person who committed the offence.

Describe and evaluate restorative justice programmes with reference to Selina's experience. **(16 marks)**

ANSWER An extract showing how you could address the AO2 requirements of this question: *Restorative justice would involve Selina meeting with the young person who pushed her over to discuss the offence. This would help Selina reduce her sense of victimisation as she would no longer feel powerless. She may also gain a greater understanding of the young person's actions and maybe see that she wasn't specifically targeted. However, the process should be carefully managed to avoid Selina trying to shame the offender as the offender is younger than her. By meeting Selina, the young person may come to understand the effects of their actions and develop empathy for Selina and other residents of the housing estate. This may reduce the possibility of further anti-social behaviour...*

AO2: One for you to try

Nick's twin brother was murdered in a local park by a 16-year-old called Craig who lost control of his temper while beating him up to try and get his credit card PIN number. Craig was arrested and sent to prison. Sixteen years later, Nick took the opportunity to meet Craig for restorative justice when Craig applied for parole. Nick said later that, 'Restorative justice helped me understand that all people can make a serious mistake in their life and be given a second chance – even murderers, even the murderer of my twin brother.'

What was the purpose of this meeting, and how could it benefit Craig and Nick? (4 marks)

AO2: Research methods

A survey was carried out by the Restorative Justice Council in March 2016, to find out what restorative justice programmes were being offered in different parts of the UK.

- 215 organisations were providing restorative justice services.
- 193 offered face-to-face victim/offender meetings.
- 132 providers reported that they had delivered a total of 2,638 face-to-face interventions.
- 96 providers reported they had facilitated letter exchanges in a total of 2,179 cases.
- 90 providers reported they had facilitated shuttle mediation in a total of 2,124 cases.

a. **What percentage of organisations were offering face-to-face victim/offender meetings? (2 marks)**

b. **What percentage facilitated letter exchanges? (2 marks)**

c. **What was the average number of face-to-face interventions per provider? (2 marks)**

 ## How do I answer... comparison questions?

Q1: Outline the aims of restorative justice programmes, and compare them with at least **one** other way of dealing with offending behaviour. **(16 marks)**

You could be asked to outline one approach or intervention (A), then compare it with another (B). The comparison becomes your AO3. Beware: you will not get any marks for evaluating A by itself. The normal evaluation points are not relevant, unless you can use them as a direct comparison with aspects of B. You also get no marks for outlining B. The AO1 and AO3 material for these questions is on the opposite page.

Read the question carefully, and plan your answer:

- Outline the aims of restorative justice (RJ) (6 marks available). Use the first AO1 point, the three relating to aims of RJ, and the point about Wachtel and McCold's theory.
- Select another intervention which you can compare directly, for example Behaviour Modification in Custody (BM) But DO NOT outline this one.
- DO NOT go straight for normal AO3 evaluation points for RJ or BM.
- Make comparison points between RJ and BM based on basic assumptions and aims.
- You need to be clear how the approaches differ in relation to a specific point, using 'whereas', just as you do when answering 'distinguish' questions (see p.177).
- You need four effective AO3 points for 16 marks.

In **Q1** the instruction was to compare with 'at least one other way...' so you could also make comparisons with anger management if you like. Stick to the aims still, rather than the process or research evidence.

Q2: Discuss the effectiveness of restorative justice programmes, comparing them with other ways of dealing with offending behaviour. **(16 marks)**

This is a slightly different comparison question, as you can now use AO3 points relating to RJ alone, as well as bringing in comparison with BM and anger management. Notice you are asked to compare with other ways (plural), so you must refer to both of these. Also, this question is focused on the effectiveness, not just the aims, although 'effectiveness' refers to how well they achieve their aims, so you can also include these.

 ## REVIEW

In this final Review section of this chapter, it is time for some more 'revision accounting'. You should make a table like this with all 13 topics from this chapter. When you feel you have mastered the AO1 and AO3 components of these and can cope with any of the different types of question that we have covered in the **How do I answer...?** sections, you will have earned a √ in the 'Got it!' column.

TOPIC	Got it!			Got it!	
	AO1	AO3		AO1	AO3
Defining/measuring					
Top down profiling			Bottom up		
Atavistic form			Genetic and neural		
Eysenck			Cognitive		

Describing addiction

RECAP

A01 Description

Physical dependence

- **Physical dependence** can occur with the long-term use of many drugs. Many different types of drug can lead to physical dependence if abused.

- People who are physically dependent on a particular substance need to take the drug in order to feel 'normal'.

- Physical dependence can be demonstrated by the presence of unpleasant physical symptoms referred to as **withdrawal syndrome** if the person suddenly abstains from the drug.

- Physical dependence is often accompanied by increased tolerance to the drug, in that the user requires increased doses in order to obtain the desired effect.

Psychological dependence

- **Psychological dependence** occurs when a drug becomes a central part of an individual's thoughts, emotions and activities, resulting in a strong urge to use the drug.

- A craving is an intense desire to repeat the experience associated with a particular drug or activity. If the individual attempts to abstain from the drug or activity, they experience intense cravings.

  > The individual may feel unable to cope without a particular substance or activity, and the desire to use it again becomes so intense that it takes over their thinking completely.

- People commonly experience differences between what they think and what they feel, the outcomes of two different information-processing systems.

  > The rational system is conscious, analytical and relatively emotion-free. Using this system, we are able to work out the right and appropriate way to behave.

  > The experiential system is preconscious, automatic and strongly associated with emotion. It drives us to behave in a particular way based largely on how that makes us feel. Acting irrationally means that the experiential system has taken priority over the rational system.

Tolerance

- When drugs are used for a long time, **tolerance** can develop, so an individual no longer responds to the drug in the same way. Larger and larger doses are needed in order to feel the same effects as before.

- Tolerance may occur because enzymes responsible for metabolising the drug do this more efficiently over time, resulting in reduced concentrations in the blood, making the effect weaker.

- A second way is that prolonged drug use leads to changes in receptor density, reducing the response to the normal dose of the drug.

- The final way is learned tolerance, which means that a user will experience reduced drug effects because they have learned to function normally when under the influence of the drug.

Withdrawal syndrome

- If taking a drug is discontinued, withdrawal symptoms can occur. These include increased anxiety, irritability and headaches. The individual may then take the drug again to relieve these symptoms.

- Withdrawal symptoms occur because the body is attempting to deal with the absence of a drug's effects.

- During the acute withdrawal stage, the physical cravings that the addict experiences are intense and persistent, as the body has yet to adjust to the loss of the drug it had become used to for so long.

- The post-acute withdrawal stage is characterised by emotional and psychological turmoil as addicts experience alternating periods of dysfunction and near-normality as the brain slowly reorganises and rebalances itself.

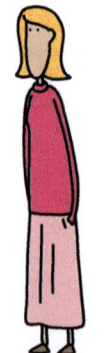

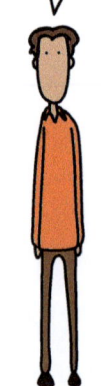

APPLY

AO2: An example

SCENARIO Ash got into heroin when he was just 17 and now spends all his money chasing his next fix. He used to be able to manage with just the occasional injection, but now needs higher and higher doses to get the same effect. He has tried to quit but feels anxious without his daily fix, and loses patience with those around him. He becomes desperate for the drug again to feel better.

With reference to withdrawal syndrome and tolerance, explain what is happening to Ash. **(4 marks)**

ANSWER *Over time, drug users no longer respond to a drug in the same way, so larger and larger doses are needed in order to feel the same effects as before (tolerance). It is possible that enzymes in Ash's body metabolise the heroin more efficiently over time, making the effect of the drug weaker. If taking heroin is discontinued, withdrawal symptoms would occur. These include increased anxiety and irritability, which describes how Ash feels without heroin. Physical cravings are intense without the drug, as the body has yet to adjust to the loss. He would need to take heroin again to relieve these symptoms.*

AO2: One for you to try

When she is at work, Elaine drinks at least eight cups of coffee a day. If she goes more than an hour without a coffee, she starts to feel nauseous and anxious and has to get another cup as soon as possible. She claims that she now needs this much coffee in order to feel the effect and stay awake.

Using your knowledge of dependence, tolerance and withdrawal symptoms, explain the example of addiction described above. (5 marks)

How do I answer... description only (AO1) questions?

There is a fairly simple formula in answering description only questions. For 2 marks, say two things, for 3 marks say three things and so on. This approach adds an appropriate level of detail to each answer and gives the examiner a useful way of discriminating between your answer and one that would be worth fewer than the maximum marks for that question. Work through the sample questions below, using the advice that follows them. The AO1 and AO3 material for these questions is on the opposite page.

Q1: Briefly explain what is meant by physical dependence. **(2 marks)**

Use any **two** of the AO1 points associated with 'physical dependence' from the opposite page.

Q2: Outline the nature of drug tolerance in the context of addiction. **(3 marks)**

For a 3-mark question, you should aim for about 75 words. You would use the first three AO1 points associated with 'tolerance' (if this was for 4 marks, you could use all four points).

Q3: Explain withdrawal symptoms in the context of addiction. **(4 marks)**

Use all **four** of the AO1 points associated with 'withdrawal symptoms'.

Q4: Explain psychological dependence in the context of addiction. **(6 marks)**

Use all **six** of the AO1 points associated with 'psychological dependence'.

AO2: Research methods

Researchers collected data relating to the experience of withdrawal symptoms in people giving up smoking. From the examples below, identify whether each is an example of nominal, ordinal or interval data. **(1 mark each)**

a. **Researchers counted the number of males and females experiencing each of the symptoms of anxiety, irritability and headaches.**

b. **Individuals placed these three withdrawal symptoms in rank order of how troublesome they found them.**

c. **Researchers measured individual's reaction time (in milliseconds) before and after giving up smoking.**

d. **Each individual rated their anxiety when not smoking on a scale from 1 to 10.**

REVIEW

You should be able to use the material on this spread to answer any question on the topic of 'describing addiction'. This means being able to write 2-mark (50 words approx.), 3-mark (75 words approx.) and 4-mark (100 words) descriptions of (each of) physical dependence, psychological dependence, tolerance and withdrawal symptoms. We have added a 6-mark example for the most substantive topic – psychological dependence. This should be about 150 words in length. There is no AO3 content for this topic as it is about your ability to describe addiction, rather than evaluate it in any way. Throughout this chapter we show you how to use this sort of material flexibly to answer all the different types of questions you might be asked. The more you practise using different parts of the same material in response to different questions, the more effective you will be in the exam.

 **RECAP**

AOI Description

Genetics

- **Genetic vulnerability** Slutske *et al.* (2010) found that monozygotic twins had a higher rate of both twins being pathological gamblers (if one twin was a pathological gambler) than did dizygotic twins.
    > The likelihood of becoming addicted to nicotine was influenced primarily by genetic factors (Vink *et al.*, 2005).
- **The dopamine receptor gene** Individuals vulnerable to drug addiction have abnormally low levels of dopamine and a decreased ability to activate dopamine receptors in the reward centre of the brain.
    > A variant of the dopamine receptor gene associated with decreased dopamine receptor availability occurred with a much higher frequency in DNA samples of alcoholics compared to non-alcoholics (Sinha *et al.*, 2000).

Stress

- **Self-medication** This proposes that some individuals use different forms of pathological behaviour (e.g. alcohol) to 'treat' psychological symptoms they experience because of everyday stressors in their life.
    > Stress is one of the strongest predictors of increased drug cravings (Sinha *et al.*, 2000).
- **Traumatic stress** Robins *et al.* (1974) found that, 20 per cent of US soldiers in the Vietnam War developed physical or psychological dependence for heroin during their time in Vietnam.
    > Kessler *et al.* (1995) found that, among men with a history of PTSD, 34 per cent reported drug abuse or dependence at some point in their lives, compared to 15 per cent of men without PTSD. For women, the figure was 27 per cent, compared to 8 per cent.

Personality

- Impulsivity contributes to a wide range of addictive behaviours such as alcohol abuse, gambling and polysubstance use (Krueger *et al.*, 1998).
- **The addiction-prone personality (APP)** Barnes *et al.* (2005) found that personality was a significant predictor of 'heavy' marijuana use. Studies using the APP scale have shown that personality differences can discriminate drug addicts from non-addicts.
- **Addiction and personality disorders** Verhheul *et al.* (1995) found that the overall prevalence of personality disorders was 44 per cent in alcoholics, 70 per cent for cocaine addicts.

AO3 Evaluation / Discussion

Genetics

Gender differences in genetic vulnerability to addiction…

Research with women shows inconsistent findings regarding the role of genetic factors in alcohol addiction (McGue, 1997).	Only two of four adoption studies have reported a significant correlation between alcoholism in female adoptees and their biological parents.	*This suggests that genetic factors may be less important in the development of alcoholism in women than in men.*

Genetics and the diathesis-stress model…

An advantage of genetic explanations is that they can explain why some people develop addictive behaviour, yet others who have the same experiences do not.	The A1 variant of the dopamine-receptor gene has been found to be associated with cocaine dependence (Noble *et al.*, 1993) and nicotine dependence (Connor *et al.*, 2007).	*This suggests individuals who inherit this variant are more vulnerable to addictive behaviour because of low levels of dopamine and the increase in dopamine possible with drugs.*

Stress

If stress leads to addiction, coping can lead to abstinence….

Individuals who develop effective coping strategies for stress should have less of a need for addictive behaviour.	Matheny and Weatherman (1998) found a strong relationship between participants' use of stress coping resources and their ability to maintain abstinence from smoking.	*This suggests that stress management techniques would be an effective strategy in predicting abstinence maintenance.*

The role of stress varies by type of addiction…

A limitation of stress explanations is that the relationship between stress and addiction varies according to the type of addiction.	Arévalo *et al.* (2008) found evidence of an association between stress and illicit drug use, but not between stress and alcohol addiction.	*The researchers suggest a limitation of this study is its reliance on self-report measures, which are vulnerable to social desirability effects.*

 **APPLY**

AO2: An example

SCENARIO Ryan returned from a tour of duty in Iraq in 2015, but since then he has found it difficult to hold down a job because of substance abuse. When he started taking drugs in order to deal with the traumatic memories of combat, his wife left him. He then started drinking as well and his addiction worsened.

Explain Ryan's behaviour in terms of the relationship between stress and addiction. **(4 marks)**

ANSWER *Ryan is dealing with the traumatic stress of his tour of duty in Iraq by using drugs. Support for this claim comes from Robins et al. (1974), who found that 20 per cent of US soldiers returning from the Vietnam War had developed dependence for heroin during their time in Vietnam.*
The self-medication explanation proposes that some individuals deal with stressful events in their life by engaging in behaviours that make them feel better or forget the stress. Ryan's use of alcohol appears to have been a way of him dealing with another stressful event in his life: the breakdown of his marriage.

AO2: Research methods

A psychologist wanted to investigate the link between impulsivity and alcohol addiction. She tested 10 participants who were alcoholics (Group A) and 10 participants with no addictive behaviour (Group B). Each participant was given a questionnaire that measured impulsivity. The scores are shown in the table below.

Table 1: Impulsivity scores for 10 alcoholic and 10 non-alcoholic participants.

Group A (Addicted to alcohol)	Score on impulsivity questionnaire	Group B (No addictive behaviour)	Score on impulsivity questionnaire
1	65	1	16
2	69	2	18
3	70	3	25
4	75	4	24
5	66	5	26
6	62	6	21
7	71	7	18
8	63	8	17
9	72	9	19
10	66	10	14

a. **Calculate the mean impulsivity score for each of the two groups. Show your calculations. (4 marks)**

b. **Why was the mean used rather than the median/mode? (2 marks)**

c. **Sketch a fully labelled graph for the results displayed in Table 1. (4 marks)**

 **REVIEW**

Make sure you understand all the aspects of risk factors (genetics, stress and personality) on addiction by doing some 'revision accounting'. Draw up a table and tick off each aspect when you have mastered it.

AO2: One for you to try

Chris comes from a family of smokers; both of his parents smoke and so does his younger brother Adam. Chris began smoking at an early age and now he is in his twenties. He has tried to stop and is finding it very difficult, especially when his job as a teacher is particularly stressful.

Using your knowledge of risk factors, outline two risk factors relevant to Chris's behaviour. (4 marks)

How do I answer... description and evaluation (AO1 + AO3) questions?

Q1: Briefly discuss the role of genetics as a risk factor for addiction. **(4 marks)**

Q2: Outline and evaluate the role of stress as a risk factor for addiction. **(6 marks)**

Q3: Outline and evaluate findings from research into personality as a risk factor for addiction. **(6 marks)**

1 The key to answering mixed AO1 + AO3 questions is recognising that this is what you are being asked to do! The command word 'discuss' can indicate AO1+AO3 or AO3 only. In **Q1**, the addition of the word 'briefly' tells you that this is the former, requiring a brief outline of the role of genetics in addiction and a brief evaluative point.

2 Plan how much you should write for each. In mixed AO1 + AO3 questions up to 6 marks, the division is half and half (it is different with mark totals higher than this as we will see on p.213).

3 Decide *what* to write. If you have followed the advice in the previous spreads, this should be easy to work out. The AO1 and AO3 material for these questions is on the opposite page.

- For **Q1**, this would mean using the first two AO1 points, together with an abridged version of either the first or second AO3 point.

- For **Q2**, the AO1 requirement would be met by the first three AO1 points for 'Stress' opposite. They would give a good 3-mark overview as required by the question. For the AO3 content you could use either the first or second AO3 point or abridged versions of both of these AO3 points.

- For **Q3** we have included this type of question to show how sometimes you need to be creative in the material you use in response to a question. Bearing in mind that research findings can be used as AO1 or as an explanation of research support, we sometimes (but not in this particular case) need a bit of detective work to find 3-marks worth that we can use as AO1. The fact that research findings might appear in an AO3 section is irrelevant because we would only be using a statement of the findings from a study rather than using it to make a critical point.

Risk factors: Family influences and peers

RECAP

A01 Description

Family influences

- Social learning theory (Bandura, 1977) claims that behaviours are learned through the observation of those people with whom a person has the most social contact.

- Reith and Dobbie (2011) found that gambling knowledge and behaviour was passed on through the routines of everyday life. Individuals watched and heard family members doing and talking about their gambling and eventually joining in with it.

- **Parental influences** Parents exert influence on their offspring's addictive behaviour in two main ways. First, they provide social models for their offspring, for example, adolescents with substance-abusing parents are more likely to engage in substance abuse themselves (Biederman *et al.,* 2000).

  - > A second route of parental influence is via their style of parenting. Authoritative parents show warmth but also exert appropriate control.

  - > This form of parenting is associated with the shaping of psychological resilience and lowered levels of substance abuse (Fletcher *et al.* 1995).

Where'd you get the idea it's ok to smoke?

The role of peers

- **Peer pressure** Peers exert their influence by introducing individuals to risky behaviours or pressuring them to take part and to continue to do so.

  - > Social identity theory (Tajfel and Turner, 1986) suggests that a significant part of an individual's self-concept is formed as a result of the groups of which they are a part. As it is essential to be associated with these ingroups in order to be socially accepted, this makes individuals more likely to adopt their behaviours.

- **Social networks** Among adolescents, smokers tend to befriend smokers, and non-smokers befriend other non-smokers (Eiser *et al.,* 1991) – therefore, social networks often comprise of individuals with similar habits.

  - > Latkin *et al.* (2004) found that the probability of drug abuse was related to the number of members within an individual's social network who used drugs. In this way, members of social networks represent drug abuse as a positive and socially acceptable experience.

A03 Evaluation / Discussion

Family influences

Support for the role of family influences…

Evidence supports the importance of family influences on substance abuse and addictive behaviour.	Bahr *et al.* (2005) found that adolescents with parents who were tolerant of substance use were more likely to interact with peers who smoked, drank or used illicit drugs.	*These findings suggest that family and peer influences are not independent of each other, but tolerant parental attitudes make it more likely that adolescents seek out peers that endorse substance abuse.*

Intervention studies tend to ignore sibling influences…

Most attempts at family intervention relating to substance use in adolescence target only parents rather than siblings.	Interventions targeted only at the adolescent user or their parents could be undermined by sibling influences. Older siblings are more likely to be engaged in substance use behaviours than their younger siblings, and so more likely to be the main source of influence for them.	*Feinberg et al. (2012) claim that failure to address sibling influences is therefore likely to hinder efforts to reduce early substance use.*

The role of peers

Support for peer influences through social media…

Research on social media supports the claim that peer influences are an important influence on addictive behaviour.	After exposure to peers' Facebook profiles that portrayed alcohol use, teenagers reported a greater willingness to use alcohol, more positive feelings towards it and lower perceptions of its negative consequences (Litt and Stock, 2011).	*Litt and Stock's research suggests that exposure to social media alters adolescents' normative perceptions and other alcohol-related risk cognitions.*

Real-world application: reducing peer influences…

Adolescent alcohol abuse has become a major public health concern.	A longitudinal study (Pitkänen *et al.,* 2005) found that early onset of drinking was a significant risk factor for alcohol dependence in adulthood. This is because adolescent behaviour is influenced by misperceptions of drinking behaviour among peers.	*As overestimations of alcohol use in peers cause an increase in their own drinking, correcting misperceptions should result in a decrease in the problem behaviour and lessen the likelihood of later alcohol abuse.*

APPLY

AO2: An example

SCENARIO Casey has been using drugs since he was 14. In the early years, he smoked cannabis with his friends, most of whom used drugs on a regular basis. Now, at the age of just 23, he is addicted to class A drugs such as cocaine and heroin.

Explain Casey's addictive behaviour in terms of peer influences. **(4 marks)**

ANSWER *Social identity theory suggests that an individual's self-concept is formed as a result of the groups of which they are a part. In order to be accepted by his peers, Casey would be more likely to adopt their behaviours. Latkin et al. (2004) found that the probability of drug abuse was related to the number of peers within an individual's social network who used drugs. Most of Casey's peer group already used drugs on a regular basis, which explains why he began experimenting with drugs, and why he is now addicted to class A drugs as his peer groups change.*

AO2: Research methods

The Reith and Dobbie study mentioned opposite used a variety of recruitment techniques to obtain their sample. For example, they approached adult individuals in casinos, bingo halls and betting shops. They also recruited individuals from Gamblers Anonymous, as well as advertising in a local newspaper and displaying posters in local community venues. During the interviews, respondents were encouraged to tell their 'gambling story', accounts of how they began to gamble and how their gambling developed over time. Throughout this process, interviewers were dealing with retrospective accounts of respondents' childhood and early years.

a. **Identify the type of sampling method used in this study? (1 mark)**

b. **Give one limitation of this type of sampling method as used in this study. (2 marks)**

c. **The researchers collected qualitative data in this study. Explain one strength of using qualitative data in this study. (3 marks)**

d. **This study (Beginning gambling: The role of social networks and environment) was carried out by Gerda Reith and Fiona Dobbie and published on pages 483–493 in Issue 6 of Volume 19 of the journal *Addiction Research and Theory* in 2011. Construct an appropriate scientific reference for this study. (3 marks)**

AO2: One for you to try

Tola is 17 years old and has recently started smoking. Most of her friends smoke and she believes that smoking will help her to fit in with the group of popular girls at school, who also smoke. Furthermore, Tola has recently told her parents that she regularly smokes and they believe that she is beyond their help and refuse to get involved.

Use your knowledge of risk factors (family influences and peers) and discuss how family and peers are contributing to Tola's addiction. (4 marks)

How do I answer... research methods questions?

Questions requiring research methods knowledge can appear in any section of any paper in the AS or A Level exams. They could include any aspect of research methods, data analysis or ethical issues. Doing well in research methods questions is as much a case of thinking clearly and using common sense as it is regurgitating knowledge. Let's look at the example questions in **AO2: Research methods** on the left:

a. You are asked to identify the sampling method used in the study. This is a straightforward identification so no detail other than the name is necessary. Although part of the sample in the stimulus material comprises volunteers, overall this would be an 'opportunity sample'.

b. These questions will sometimes be set within the context provided by the scenario, but in this case, it is a straightforward 'limitation' question. So, identify a limitation and say why this is problematic for this sampling method. For example, you could point out that 'an opportunity sample is inevitably biased because those who happen to be available at the time may not be representative of the population under study'.

c. For this question you need to explain why qualitative data was advantageous given what the researchers were trying to find out. Think – respondents told their 'gambling story' rather than attempting to quantify their experiences, so qualitative data provides a much richer and more detailed description of gamblers' lives.

d. Referencing is definitely an art form, and something that even academics get wrong on occasion. **Surname** followed by **initials**, then the **date** in **brackets**. Next comes the **paper title**, followed by the **journal name**, then the **volume number** with the **Issue number** in brackets. Finally, put the **page numbers**.

REVIEW

In order to feel comfortable with this topic you should practise using the material in all the different ways that might be assessed in your exam. For example:

1. Can you write 3-, 4- and 6-mark descriptions of family influences on addictive behaviour? Can you do the same for peer influences?

2. Write an essay plan showing how you would use the material on this spread to answer an 8-mark extended writing question for family influences on addictive behaviour. Remember, this means 3 marks' worth of AO1 and 5 marks' worth of AO3.

3. Do the same for peer influences on addictive behaviour.

4. Write an essay plan showing how you would use the material on this spread to answer a 16-mark extended writing question for family influences on addictive behaviour.

5. Do the same for peer influences on addictive behaviour.

Explanations for nicotine addiction: Brain neurochemistry

 **RECAP**

AO1 Description

- **Nicotine** When inhaled through cigarette smoke, nicotine has a range of different effects, including decreased irritability, increased alertness and even improved cognitive functioning.

    > Because smokers are often in a state of mild nicotine withdrawal, smoking a cigarette allows the nicotine level in the body to return to normal.

- **Dopamine and the brain's reward pathways** Nicotine becomes addictive because it activates areas of the brain that regulate feelings of pleasure, i.e. the 'reward pathways' of the brain.

    > Nicotine attaches to neurons in the ventral tegmental area (VTA), triggering release of dopamine in the nucleus accumbens (NAc).

    > Nicotine also stimulates release of glutamate, triggering additional release of dopamine, producing pleasure and a desire to repeat the behaviours that led to it.

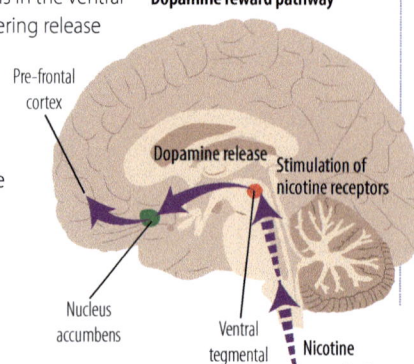

Dopamine reward pathway

Pre-frontal cortex

Dopamine release

Stimulation of nicotine receptors

Nucleus accumbens

Ventral tegmental area

Nicotine enters brain

- **Glutamate, GABA and MAO** Nicotine causes glutamate to speed up dopamine release, and prevents GABA from slowing it down after dopamine levels have been raised. This results in an increase in dopamine and an amplification of the rewarding properties of nicotine.

    > Cigarette smoke contains a substance that blocks the action of monoamine oxidase (MAO). MAO is responsible for breaking down dopamine after it has had its effects. Blocking MAO results in even higher dopamine levels, strengthening the smoking habit by maintaining the feelings of pleasure.

- **The development of nicotine addiction** Continued activation of the dopamine-enhancing neurons changes their sensitivity to nicotine, resulting in tolerance, dependence and ultimately addiction.

    > The brain quickly becomes sensitised to nicotine, enabling a nicotine-dependent state to develop. This state is associated with significant withdrawal symptoms when the smoker attempts to abstain from smoking.

AO3 Evaluation / Discussion

Support for the nicotine–dopamine link...

Support for the link between nicotine and dopamine comes from research on the effects of an epilepsy drug (GVG).	Paterson and Markou (2002) found that GVG reduces the surge of dopamine in the NAc that occurs after taking nicotine. This reduces the addictive tendencies of nicotine and other drugs that boost the brain levels of dopamine.	*By counteracting any pleasurable experiences that may be gained by the increase in dopamine, this offers an alternative way of treating nicotine addiction.*

Support for the role of glutamate and GABA...

The role of glutamate and GABA in nicotine addiction is supported by a study of nicotine dependent rats (D'Souza and Markou, 2013).	Blocking transmission of glutamate resulted in a decrease in nicotine intake and nicotine seeking in the animals. Nicotine intake and nicotine seeking also decreased when GABA neurotransmission was enhanced.	*This shows that by blocking glutamate the dopamine-releasing effects of nicotine were decreased, making it less rewarding. Enhancement of GABA reduced its inhibitory effect, decreasing the pleasurable effects of nicotine.*

Nicotine and Parkinson's disease...

Further support for the link between nicotine and dopamine comes from the treatment of patients with Parkinson's disease (PD).	Fagerström *et al.* (1994) treated two elderly PD patients with nicotine gum and patches. They found significant changes in symptoms that were attributed to the increased levels of dopamine caused by the nicotine administration.	*This suggests that nicotine may have a neuroprotective function against the development of PD and may also be beneficial in its treatment.*

Nicotine affects men and women differently...

Cosgrove *et al.* (2014) used (PET) scans to demonstrate changing levels of dopamine in males and females when smoking.	In women, there was a strong dopamine effect in the dorsal putamen, whereas men only had moderate to low activation in this area. Men had a strong activation effect in the ventral striatum, whereas women were only mildly affected.	*This supports the claim that men and women smoke for different reasons – men for the nicotine effect itself, and women to relieve stress and manage mood.*

APPLY

AO2: An example

SCENARIO   Tim is trying to give up smoking but finds that he has to sneak a cigarette several times a day. He claims it 'gives him a buzz' and that he finds it hard to give up.

With reference to Tim, outline and evaluate the relationship between brain neurochemistry and nicotine addiction. **(16 marks)**

ANSWER   **An extract showing how you could address the AO2 requirements of this question:** *Nicotine, the main active ingredient of tobacco, activates the 'reward pathways' of the brain. It attaches to neurons in the ventral tegmental area, which trigger a release of dopamine in the nucleus accumbens. This would explain the 'buzz' that Tim experiences when he smokes, and why he finds it difficult to give this up. Tim admits he smokes several times a day. This is because the effects of nicotine disappear within a few minutes, so he needs to smoke frequently to continue the intake of nicotine throughout the day in order to get the dopamine 'rush' he appears to crave...*

AO2: One for you to try

Paige starting smoking when she was 15. She thought it made her look 'cool', and she would always accept cigarettes when out with her friends. When Paige started going out with Ian, an avid non-smoker, she decided to stop smoking, but was amazed to discover it was a lot harder than she thought it was going to be.

Using your knowledge of brain neurochemistry explanations of nicotine addiction, explain why Paige found it so difficult to give up smoking. (4 marks)

AO2: Research methods

Researchers recruited a sample of 18 smokers and 18 non-smokers, matched for age and general health. They used brain imaging techniques to measure glutamate levels in the thalamus, an area of the brain rich in nicotine receptors.

a. **Suggest an appropriate statistical test that the researchers might have used for this first part of the study. Give reasons for your choice of test. (3 marks)**

The mean glutamate levels did not differ between the two groups. However, within the smoking group, 'glutamate levels were negatively correlated with self-reports of the number of cigarettes smoked over the last 30 days'.

b. **Suggest an appropriate statistical test that the researchers might have used for this second part of the study. Give reasons for your choice of test. (3 marks)**

c. **Explain what is meant by '... glutamate levels were negatively correlated with self-reports of the number of cigarettes smoked over the last 30 days. (2 marks)**

How do I answer... shorter (8-mark) essay questions?

Not all essays follow the 12- or 16-mark format. Some have a slightly lower tariff. Of these lower tariff essay questions, the 8-marker is the most common. It does help to know what you are dealing with, however, as they are not always straightforward. The AO1 and AO3 material for these questions is on the opposite page.

> **Q1:** Outline and evaluate explanations for nicotine addiction based on brain neurochemistry. **(8 marks)**

Although you might believe that this question would be worth 4 marks for AO1 and 4 for AO3, this is actually half of a 16-mark essay question, so there is a similar split of marks, i.e. 3 marks for AO1 and 5 marks for AO3 (instead of the 6- and 10-mark split for a 16-mark question). So, you would be aiming for 75–90 words of AO1 and about 125–150 words of AO3. This would mean AO1 points one, two and four and any **two** of the AO3 points.

> **Q2:** Gerry has been smoking for many years. When he gets up in the morning, he finds it very difficult to get going until he has had his first cigarette of the day. His wife finds him irritable and bad-tempered until he has had a cigarette, and he is certainly more relaxed after it.
>
> Outline and evaluate brain neurochemistry explanations of nicotine addiction. Make reference to Gerry in your answer. **(8 marks)**

A scenario that is referred back to in the question indicates that there is an additional AO2 requirement. AO2 marks tend to be 'stolen' from the AO3 allocation, so this question would be 3 marks of AO1 (first three points), 3 marks of AO3 (one complete AO3 point) and 2 marks' worth of AO2 (about 50 words). The Gerry scenario could be explained through reference to him being in a state of mild nicotine withdrawal when he first wakes. Smoking his first cigarette allows the nicotine level in his body to return to normal, removing the withdrawal symptom of irritability, and making him more relaxed.

REVIEW

Simply reading material is not the most effective way of learning it properly. So, using the material on the opposite page, try writing plans for 3-, 4- and 6-mark 'outline' questions on neurochemistry explanations for nicotine addiction plus plans for 8- and 16-mark essay questions.

Test yourself on the key points of these explanations by covering up your plans and writing them out again. It's useful to have a supply of cheap paper for this, as the more times you practise retrieving the information, the better you will remember it.

Spaced practice is also very effective: come back to the same topic tomorrow and start your revision by seeing how many of the points you can remember before you look at your essay plan.

Explanations for nicotine addiction: Learning theory

AO1 Description

- **Initiation** Social learning theory explanations propose that young people begin smoking as a consequence of social models they have around them who smoke (Kandel and Wu, 1995).

  > Addictive substances and activities are immediately rewarding, which explains why people get 'hooked' on nicotine very quickly after starting to smoke.

  > Inhaled nicotine enters the circulation rapidly and enters the brain within seconds. As a result, the individual feels a sudden 'rush', which reinforces the activity that produced it.

- **Maintenance** Smoking becomes an established behaviour because of its positive consequences. Not being able to smoke makes people irritable, and smoking provides them with relief (negative reinforcement).

  > People maintain their smoking habit to avoid withdrawal symptoms, which can occur if they abstain. These increase the craving for another cigarette and relief from the withdrawal symptoms.

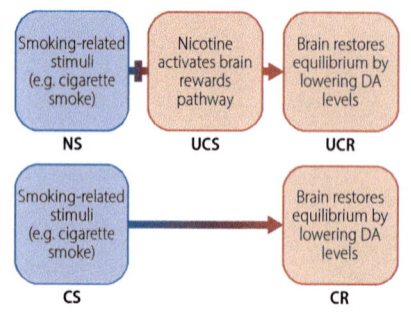

- **Relapse: Cue reactivity** The person comes to associate specific situations or environmental factors (smoking-related cues) with the rewarding effects of nicotine. These cues often trigger relapse.

  > Nicotine activates brain reward pathways, increasing the release of dopamine. This leads to a conditioned association between the sensory aspects of smoking (smell of the smoke, etc.) and the reinforcing effects of nicotine.

  > This 'nicotine effect' acts as an unconditioned stimulus (UCS). The brain responds by attempting to lower dopamine levels back to normal (UCR). Anything associated with nicotine input (e.g. cigarette smoke) changes from being a neutral stimulus (NS) to a conditioned stimulus (CS), capable of activating the same conditioned response (CR).

  > This occurs even in the absence of the UCS because the brain's response in the absence of nicotine means that dopamine levels are lowered below the optimum level. This is experienced as withdrawal symptoms, and the person is motivated to smoke again in order to feel better.

AO3 Evaluation/Discussion

Support for social learning explanations of smoking initiation...

The claims of social learning influences on the development of smoking have been supported by research evidence.

Peer group influences have been found to be the primary influence for adolescents who experiment with smoking (DiBlasio and Benda, 1993). Those adolescents who smoked were more likely to 'hang out' with other adolescents who also smoked.

The researchers concluded that connectedness to parents tended to decrease the odds of experimental smoking, while connectedness to friends who smoked increased the odds.

Support for the role of cue reactivity...

Wiers *et al.* (2013) provided support for the importance of classically conditioned cues in nicotine cravings.

Heavy smokers showed a significant approach bias towards smoking-related cues compared to non-smokers and those who had been abstinent for five years. The extent of this bias was positively correlated with the extent of their craving.

This was not the case for ex-smokers or non-smokers, confirming that smoking cues play a significant role in nicotine addiction.

Gender differences in patterns of nicotine addiction...

A limitation of learning theory explanations of nicotine addiction is that they fail to acknowledge the fact that it follows a different pattern in men and women.

Lopez *et al.* (1994) found that women start smoking later than men, and that there are gender-related differences in relation to both the development and context of smoking behaviour. Women also experience withdrawal effects sooner and have a harder time giving up the habit.

These findings suggest that these gender differences may be usefully applied to smoking cessation interventions.

Implications for treatment...

A treatment is based on the idea that the cues associated with smoking are an important factor in the maintenance of that habit.

Cue exposure therapy (CET) presents the cues without the opportunity to engage in smoking. This leads to stimulus discrimination, as without the reinforcement provided by the actual nicotine, the association between the cue and smoking is extinguished.

The effectiveness of this approach was demonstrated by Unrod et al. (2014), with CET resulting in a progressive decline in cue-provoked craving.

APPLY

AO2: An example

SCENARIO Most of Harry's friends smoke cigarettes. Harry used to smoke and finds it difficult on nights out with his friends, because when they light up it makes him want to smoke again.

With reference to Harry, outline and evaluate the learning theory explanation of nicotine addiction. **(4 marks)**

ANSWER *When people smoke cigarettes, nicotine increases the release of dopamine in the brain. When Harry is out with his friends and they start to smoke, the smoking-related cues of their cigarettes (e.g. the smell of the cigarette smoke) act as conditioned stimuli that, for Harry, predict the coming of nicotine. These cues are capable of producing the same conditioned response as nicotine, i.e. Harry's brain acts to lower dopamine levels back to normal. However, because Harry isn't actually smoking, this means that his dopamine levels are lowered below the optimum level and so Harry feels the urge to smoke again in order to feel better.*

AO2: Research methods

In the Unrod *et al.* study described in the final AO3 point opposite, researchers recruited cigarette smokers from the community to examine the effectiveness of cue exposure therapy for the treatment of nicotine addiction.

After the study was approved by the university ethics review board, 159 participants provided informed consent. The study comprised an intensive four weeks of treatment, with multiple sessions, each lasting approximately 75 minutes. Of these 159 participants, only 100 completed their treatment sessions.

a. **Suggest what sampling technique the researchers might have been using in this study, and give one limitation of this technique. (3 marks)**

b. **Why is it important that a study be passed by an ethical review board before being carried out? (2 marks)**

c. **"Of these 159 participants, only 100 completed their treatment sessions." Explain how this might affect the validity of any conclusions that might be drawn from this study. (3 marks)**

AO2: One for you to try

Nico has recently given up smoking, but is really struggling. When he used to smoke, he had to stand outside the front of his work building. Now he has given up, every time he leaves work, especially after a stressful day, he has an overwhelming urge to smoke.

Using your knowledge of learning theory, explain why Nico is finding it hard to resist the urge to smoke. (4 marks)

How do I answer... essay questions with an AO2 component?

This type of question has three distinct components, an AO1 descriptive component, an AO3 evaluative component and an AO2 application component. Such questions are essentially the same as a straightforward essay (see p.213) *but*, for a 16-mark question, 4 of the marks available are used to assess your ability to explain the scenario outlined in the question using the material you are discussing. These marks are always taken from the AO3 allocation, so there are still 6 marks for AO1, but now the AO3 component drops from 10 marks to 6 marks with the remaining 4 marks for AO2.

Let's look again at **AO2: An example** on this page. The AO1 and AO3 material for this question is on the opposite page. This scenario could be built into a 16-mark essay, where it might look like this:

> **Q1:** Most of Harry's friends smoke cigarettes. Harry used to smoke and finds it difficult on nights out with his friends, because when they light up it makes him want to smoke again.
>
> Discuss the learning theory explanation of nicotine addiction. Make reference to Harry in your answer. **(16 marks)**

You should start by planning the substantive part of your essay. Remember, for this type of question, you need 6 mark' worth of AO1 plus 6 marks' worth of AO3 (either two complete AO3 points or three abridged points). For 4 marks' worth of AO2, you should aim to write approximately 100–120 words explaining the scenario (in this case, Harry's desire to smoke) using the same material as before.

One last point concerns the 'discuss' command word, which requires you to engage with your AO3 rather than just state strengths and/or limitations. Including the final AO3 point (implications for treatment) would add that 'discursive' element to your answer.

REVIEW

Understanding the different processes and aspects of learning theory explanations of nicotine addiction (including cue reactivity) can be tricky. There are a few things that you can do to help you with this.

1. Try explaining these to someone else (or even the dog, cat or teddy bear who won't be critical or snigger while you are doing it!).

2. Go back and read your notes again and then explain each in even more detail until you think Rover, Fang or Teddy would (had they really been listening) have a good understanding of both processes.

3. Try writing (and answering) a few of your own exam questions on this topic to consolidate this understanding.

Explanations for gambling addiction: Learning theory

RECAP

A01 Description

- Griffiths (2009) argues that gamblers become addicted because of the physiological rewards (e.g. a buzz from winning), psychological rewards (e.g. the near miss), as well as financial rewards if they win.

- **Partial reinforcement** With a partial reinforcement schedule, wins follow some bets, but not all. This means that gambling behaviours are much slower to extinguish because of the uncertainty of reinforcement.

  > **Variable reinforcement** Gambling machines use one particular type of partial reinforcement, variable-ratio reinforcement, with wins occurring after an unpredictable number of responses. The average ratio of wins to losses is set, but when they occur is unpredictable. It is the unpredictability of these rewards that keeps people gambling.

- **Gambling and its rewards: The 'big win' hypothesis** Pathological gamblers often report having a 'big win' early in their gambling career. They continue to gamble because of a desire to repeat that early 'peak experience' (Aasved, 2003).

  > **The 'near miss'** Gambling can provide reinforcement even in the absence of a win. Near misses or losses that are 'close' to being wins create a brief period of excitement and thrill that encourage further gambling (Reid, 1986).

  > **The gambling environment** The casino itself is experienced as reinforcing. Flashing lights, ringing bells and the sound of coins tumbling out of the fruit machines are all exciting for the gambler.

A03 Evaluation/Discussion

Learning theory can't explain all forms of gambling…

A problem for explanations based on operant conditioning is that it is difficult to apply the same principles to all forms of gambling.	Some forms of gambling have a short time period between the behaviour and the consequence (e.g. scratch cards), whereas others (such as sports betting) have a much longer period between bet and outcome.	This suggests that the latter form of gambling has less to do with conditioning and more to do with the skill of the individual.

Fails to explain why only some people become addicted…

There are problems with explaining pathological gambling solely as a product of its reinforcing properties.	For example, although many people gamble at some time during their lives and experience the reinforcements associated with this behaviour, relatively few become addicts.	This suggests, therefore, that there are other factors involved in the transition from gambling behaviour to gambling addiction.

Support for the influence of partial reinforcement…

Horsley et al. (2012) showed that partial reinforcement is fundamentally important to the persistence of gambling, particularly among high-frequency gamblers.	After partial reinforcement, high-frequency gamblers continued to respond on a gambling simulation for longer compared to low-frequency gamblers despite the lack of further reinforcement.	The researchers concluded that this may be a result of increased dopamine function in this type of gambler, making them more likely to continue gambling, even in the absence of reinforcement.

Reinforcement schedules may lead to irrational beliefs…

There is support for the claim that an early big win can lead to persistence in gambling behaviour.	Sharpe (2002) claimed that the placement of wins early in the gaming experience may lead to irrational beliefs about gaming machine reinforcement schedules, e.g. the illusion that they can control the outcomes and possess the skill necessary to win.	A consequence of this is that overestimation of the chances to win and an underestimation of the possible losses encourage persistent gambling.

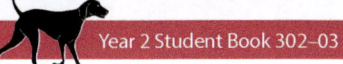

 APPLY

A02: An example

SCENARIO Matt and Gareth like nothing more than going to the casino to gamble on the fruit machines. Although neither seems to come away in profit at the end of the evening, they do experience the occasional win. Gareth admits part of the attraction is the whole casino experience.

Using learning theory explanations of gambling addiction, explain why Matt and Gareth continue to visit the casino to gamble, even though they end up losing. **(4 marks)**

ANSWER *The use of variable reinforcement, where only a proportion of a player's responses are rewarded, has wins occurring after an unpredictable number of responses. It is the unpredictability of these wins that keeps Matt and Gareth gambling. They win 'occasionally', which is providing variable reinforcement, maintaining their gambling behaviour. Gareth admits that part of the attraction is the 'whole casino experience', which suggests that they are experiencing the casino itself as reinforcing. For example, flashing lights and ringing bells are likely to produce exhilaration for the gambler, which is why Matt and Gareth are driven to return to that environment again and again.*

A02: Research methods

Griffiths (1993) carried out a case study of an 18-year-old ('David') to gain a greater understanding of fruit machine addiction. Data was collected through interviews with David and his mother. During these interviews, David explained that although winning money was the first thing that attracted him to playing fruit machines, this gradually converted to light, sounds and excitement.

a. **Briefly explain what is meant by a 'case study'. (2 marks)**

b. **Explain one strength and one limitation of case studies as a method of investigation. (4 marks)**

c. **Explain David's responses in terms of what you know about learning theory explanations of gambling addiction. (3 marks)**

A02: One for you to try

Sally is on holiday in Monte Carlo and can't resist a flutter on the slot machines in the casino. She tells her friends it is just a bit of fun and she will stop after a few euros. She is delighted when she puts her first euro in the machine that she immediately wins €10. She wins another €20 on her second play. Her friends tell her to quit while she is ahead, but she is grinning wildly and is no longer listening to them and continues to play until, 20 minutes later, she has lost nearly €100.

Using your knowledge of the learning theory approach, explain why Sally has continued to gamble, even though she was losing all her money. (4 marks)

How do I answer... evaluation only (A03) questions?

Evaluation questions also come in all sorts of shapes and sizes. Terms like 'evaluate', 'discuss', 'explain', 'criticism', 'strength' and 'limitation' all indicate that AO3 is required. The AO3 material for these questions is on the opposite page. Let's look at some examples:

> **Q1:** Give **one** criticism of learning theory explanations of gambling addiction. **(2 marks)**

Remembering that 'criticisms' can be either negative or positive (so research support would count as a 'positive' criticism), you could choose any one of the AO3 points as your material for **Q1**. For 2 marks, you could use the lead-in phrase (e.g. 'Learning theory can't explain all forms of gambling... '), followed by the material in the last two columns (i.e. what Gee and Leith did in their research and what they found).

> **Q2:** Explain **one** limitation of learning theory explanations of gambling addiction. **(3 marks)**

Q2 requires a little more elaboration than **Q1**, but this time you are restricted to something that limits the value of self-disclosure as an explanation of attraction. For example, you could again use the first AO3 point or you might choose to use the second one ('Fails to explain why only some people become addicted... ') with material from all three columns being used to access the 3 marks on offer.

> **Q3:** Evaluate learning theory explanations of gambling addiction. **(6 marks)**

For **Q3**, you would take the same approach as with **Q2**, but this time using two of the AO3 points. Don't try to use more than two; it would make your treatment of them too superficial.

⟳ REVIEW

Simply reading material is not the most effective way of learning it properly. So, using the material on the opposite page, try writing plans for 3-, 4- and 6-mark 'outline' questions on learning theory explanations of gambling addiction plus plans for 8- and 16-mark essay questions.

Test yourself on the key points of these explanations by covering up your plans and writing them out again. It's useful to have a supply of cheap paper for this, as the more times you practise retrieving the information, the better you will remember it.

Spaced practice is also very effective: come back to the same topic tomorrow and start your revision by seeing how many of the points you can remember before you look at your essay plan.

Explanations for gambling addiction: Cognitive theory

 **RECAP**

AO1 Description

- **The role of cognitive biases** Irrational beliefs and distorted thinking patterns contribute to the development and maintenance of problem gambling.

- **The gambler's fallacy** is the belief that completely random events such as a coin toss are somehow influenced by recent events, e.g. a gambler might believe that runs of a particular outcome will be balanced out by the opposite outcome.

- **Illusions of control** Pathological gamblers may also show an exaggerated self-confidence in their ability to 'beat the system' and influence chance. Success is attributed to their personal ability or skill, and failure attributed to bad luck.

- **The 'near miss' bias** Near misses occur when an unsuccessful outcome is close to a win. As a consequence of these, the gambler may feel that he is 'not constantly losing but constantly nearly winning' (Griffiths, 1991).

- **The recall bias** Pathological gamblers have a tendency to remember and overestimate wins while forgetting about and underestimating losses (Blanco *et al.*, 2000). Consequently, a string of losses does not act as a disincentive for future gambling.

Cognitive bias in fruit machine gambling (Griffiths, 1994)

- **PROCEDURE** Griffiths compared 30 regular gamblers (who played fruit machines more than once a week) with 30 non-regular gamblers, who played less than once a month. Each individual was given £3 to spend playing a fruit machine in the arcade.

  > Griffiths was interested in the gamblers' verbalisations as they played the machine, assuming that this would give some insight into the particular cognitive biases that were operating at the time.

- **FINDINGS** Regular gamblers believed they were more skilful than they actually were. They were more likely to make irrational statements during play such as 'Putting only a quid in bluffs the machine', an example of the 'illusion of control' bias.

  > Interviews with the participants revealed that whereas the majority of the non-regular gamblers believed playing the game was 'mostly chance', most of the regular gamblers believed success was either due to skill or equally chance and skill.

  > Regular gamblers explained away their losses by seeing 'near misses' as 'near wins', something that justified their continuation. One third of the regular gamblers continued playing until they had lost all their money, whereas only two of the non-regular gamblers did so.

AO3 Evaluation / Discussion

Research support for the role of cognitive biases...

There is a great deal of evidence demonstrating the presence of high rates of cognitive biases in populations of problem gamblers.	Ladouceur *et al.* (2002) found that up to 80 per cent of gambling-related verbalisations made by problem gamblers would be classified as irrational. Research with recreational gamblers has not found the same high degree of cognitive biases.	This supports the claim that irrational beliefs are what sustains the gambling habit and makes people more vulnerable to developing a gambling addiction.

Implications for treatment...

An implication of the cognitive explanation of gambling addiction is that cognitive behavioural therapy (CBT) might be helpful in reducing that addiction.	CBT could be used to correct cognitive biases, which in turn would reduce the motivation to gamble. Echeburúa *et al.* (1996) found that CBT was effective in preventing relapse in gamblers who played slot machines.	The researchers did acknowledge, however, that slot machine pathological gamblers may not be totally representative of the larger population of problem gamblers.

Irrational thinking varies with type of gambling...

Lund (2011) argues that some types of gambling are more likely to encourage cognitive biases and other irrational beliefs.	Lund found that increased frequency of gambling was related to increased cognitive biases, but this effect was more likely in gamblers who preferred gambling machines and Internet gambling than those who engaged in sports betting and horse racing.	Lund concluded that illusions of control are important factors in the development of cognitive biases, which in turn can lead to gambling addiction.

Awareness does not decrease susceptibility to cognitive bias...

Research suggests that possessing relevant knowledge does not make people less susceptible to cognitive distortions.	Benhsain and Ladouceur (2004) administered a gambling-related cognition scale to two groups of university students: one group trained in statistics and the other in a non-statistical field. They found no difference between the two groups in their susceptibility to irrational gambling-related cognitions.	This suggests that, when pathological gamblers gamble, irrational beliefs (e.g. being able to control outcomes) override more objective considerations.

APPLY

AO2: An example

SCENARIO Tom and Saif spend a lot of time playing the fruit machines. Tom is convinced that he is a skilled gambler and can 'play the system' to beat the machines. Saif has lost a lot of money in recent weeks, but only seems to remember the (relatively) few times he has won.

With reference to Tom and Saif's behaviour, outline and evaluate cognitive biases in gambling addiction. **(16 marks)**

ANSWER **An extract showing how you could address the AO2 requirements of this question:** *Tom is displaying the illusion of control in that he shows an exaggerated self-confidence in his ability to influence chance. Tom is a regular gambler, and Griffiths (1994) found that most regular gamblers who played fruit machines believed their success was due to skill rather than chance. Saif is displaying the recall bias: the tendency to remember and overestimate wins while forgetting about or underestimating losses (Blanco et al., 2000). This is demonstrated by the fact that although overall he is losing money, he tends to overestimate the number of times he has won relative to the number of times he has lost...*

AO2: Research methods

Mark Griffiths' study (The role of cognitive bias and skill in fruit machine gambling – Griffiths, 1994) was carried out to increase understanding of the cognitive processes and behaviour of persistent fruit machine gamblers. The study used a quasi-experiment and independent group design, involving a volunteer sample of 30 regular gamblers and 30 non-regular gamblers.

a. **Outline a suitable directional hypothesis for this study. (3 marks)**

b. **Explain what is meant by a 'quasi-experimental independent groups' design, and identify what it is about this study that would make it 'quasi-experimental.' (3 marks)**

c. **Outline one limitation of an independent groups design in this study. (2 marks)**

d. **The study used a volunteer sample. Explain one limitation of this type of sampling method. (2 marks)**

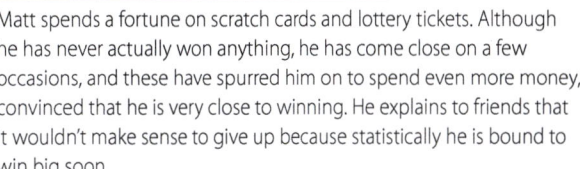

AO2: One for you to try

Matt spends a fortune on scratch cards and lottery tickets. Although he has never actually won anything, he has come close on a few occasions, and these have spurred him on to spend even more money, convinced that he is very close to winning. He explains to friends that it wouldn't make sense to give up because statistically he is bound to win big soon.

Explain the cognitive biases that Matt is displaying. (4 marks)

How do I answer... application (AO2) questions?

Let's look again at the Matt scenario in **AO2: One for you to try** above.

One way of answering questions such as this is to remember the 'say one thing for 1 mark' and 'say four things for 4 marks' strategy.

1 **Find a bit of appropriate psychology,** e.g. 'The "near-miss bias" occurs when an unsuccessful outcome is close to a win. As a consequence of these, the gambler may feel that he is not constantly losing but constantly nearly winning.'

2 **Use this to explain some aspect of the scenario,** e.g. 'Matt has come close to winning on a few occasions, and these have spurred him on to spend even more money, convinced that he is very close to winning.'

3 **Find a second bit of psychology,** e.g. 'The gambler's fallacy is the belief that random events are influenced by recent events, e.g. a gambler might believe that runs of a particular outcome will be balanced out by the opposite outcome.'

4 **Use this to explain the scenario,** e.g. 'Matt explains to friends that it wouldn't make sense to give up because statistically he is bound to win big soon.'

REVIEW

Craik and Lockhart (1972) proposed a theory of memory called the 'levels of processing model'. This model claimed that the more that information is elaborated, the more likely we will be able to access that information later on. There are many different ways of elaborating material, so let's try one.

Take a large sheet of paper (A3 works well here) and construct a mind-map so that all your material on cognitive explanations for gambling addiction is linked together in a wonderfully visual way. This serves several purposes: (1) It *elaborates* the material, making it more memorable; (2) The act of constructing the mind-map counts as *revision*, again making it more likely you can recall in an exam; and (3) You have a *visual* image of the material, which, for many people, is a much easier way of remembering complex material.

*Tip: There is a wealth of useful revision videos on the Internet – take a look for some on mind-map construction.

RECAP

AO1 Description

- **Drug therapy** Drugs interact with receptors or enzymes in the brain to reduce cravings for a drug or the desire to engage in a particular behaviour.

- **Nicotine replacement therapy (NRT)** works by gradually releasing nicotine into the bloodstream at lower levels than in a cigarette and without the harmful chemicals found in cigarette smoke. This helps the individual control their cravings for a cigarette and helps to prevent relapse.

- **Drug treatments**
  Bupropion reduces a person's craving for tobacco and helps with withdrawal symptoms. Bupropion works by inhibiting the reuptake of dopamine and is effective as a smoking cessation drug (Hughes *et al.*, 2004).

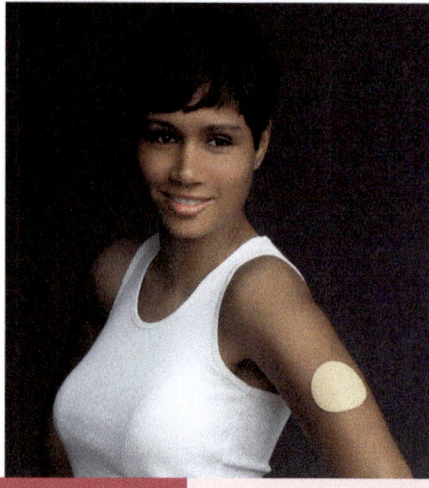

- **Drug treatments for gambling addiction**
  Antidepressants reduce the urges and cravings to gamble and can also reduce the symptoms of depression or anxiety that may trigger continued gambling.

- **Heroin addiction and methadone** Methadone mimics the effects of heroin but is less addictive. A drug abuser is prescribed gradually increasing amounts of methadone to increase tolerance to the drug. The dose is then slowly decreased until they no longer need either methadone or heroin.

- **Opioid antagonists** Opioid antagonists bind to opioid receptors in the body, blocking these receptors. This prevents the individual experiencing the rewarding response they associate with a particular substance or behaviour.

- **Antidepressants** Gamblers treated with SSRIs show significant improvements in their gambling behaviour compared to a control group. As many gamblers report gambling as a response to stressors in their life, reducing the symptoms associated with these stressors (e.g. depression) lessens the urge to gamble.

AO3 Evaluation / Discussion

Support for the effectiveness of nicotine replacement therapy…

Stead *et al.* (2012) investigated the effectiveness of nicotine replacement therapy compared to placebo in the treatment of nicotine addiction.	Their meta-analysis of 150 trials found that all the different types of NRT (e.g. patch, gum) were effective in helping people kick their nicotine habit, and 70 per cent more effective than a placebo.	The effectiveness of NRT was independent of any additional support provided to the individual, suggesting that quitting was a consequence of the NRT treatment alone.

Lack of blinding in NRT studies…

In NRT trials, patients receiving nicotine can recognise the sensation and those receiving a placebo feel the withdrawal effects of no nicotine.	Mooney *et al.* (2004) found that, of 73 double-blind NRT trials, only 17 had asked participants whether they believed they were using a real NRT device or a placebo. Two thirds of those in the placebo condition were 'confident' they had not received the real nicotine.	This lack of blinding means that conclusions about the effectiveness of NRT are more uncertain than has been claimed.

Opioid antagonists can make fun activities seem 'uninspiring'…

A problem with the use of opioid antagonists is that they work by blocking the brain's reward system.	This mechanism is a general one and, by stopping the brain from releasing dopamine (which makes the activity feel good), it could cause some patients to lose pleasure in other areas of life while they are on the drug.	This tendency to make fun activities seem 'uninspiring' is a downside of opioid antagonists, and one reason why some individuals choose not to continue with their treatment.

Methodological issues in drug therapies for gambling addiction…

The validity of conclusions from drug therapy research is compromised by methodological limitations of this research.	Blaszczynski and Nower (2007) claim that research studies are characterised by small sample sizes and high dropout rates. Many studies fail to include control groups or randomly assign gamblers to different treatment conditions.	Moreover, they argue, research has generally failed to address the impact of co-morbidity on treatment response, which makes it difficult to draw conclusions about the influence of drug therapies alone.

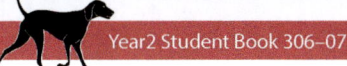
 **APPLY**

AO2: An example

SCENARIO Sabrina is trying to fight her nicotine addiction. She admits she simply lacks willpower to deal with her cravings, so seeks help from her doctor. He suggests that drug therapies might be the best form of treatment for her.

Explain one advantage and one problem for Sabrina using drug therapies for her nicotine addiction. **(4 marks)**

ANSWER *Drugs such as bupropion inhibit the reuptake of dopamine and are believed to be effective in reducing the craving for tobacco and help with any withdrawal symptoms. This would be a significant advantage for Sabrina as she admits lacking the willpower to deal with her nicotine cravings. A problem with the use of drugs such as bupropion is that their effectiveness in the treatment of nicotine addiction is inconclusive. For example, only in a minority of studies have patients been unaware of whether they were receiving the drug or a placebo, which means that conclusions about the effectiveness of drug treatments are more uncertain than Sabrina's doctor believes.*

AO2: Research methods

a. A meta-analysis of nicotine replacement therapy (NRT) versus placebo studies (Mooney *et al.*, 2004) concluded that the majority of double-blind NRT trials were not truly 'blind', because the patients receiving nicotine recognised the sensation and the ones receiving a placebo felt the withdrawal effects of no nicotine.

   (i) **What is meant by 'double-blind' in the context of this study? (2 marks)**

   (ii) **How might this 'lack of blinding' have impacted on the results? (2 marks)**

b. One specific concern identified by the researchers was the different rates of attrition (i.e. the rate of participant dropout) for those in the placebo group compared to those in the NRT group.

   (i) **Suggest one reason why participants in the placebo condition were more likely to drop out compared to those in the NRT condition. (1 mark)**

   (ii) **How might the different attrition rates for the two groups have impacted on the validity of any conclusions drawn from the study? (2 marks)**

AO2: One for you to try

You are employed by the NHS to use your knowledge of psychology to produce a short booklet explaining the different treatments available for smoking addiction. This requires a brief explanation of how each treatment works and a statement of its effectiveness and any 'side effects' that patients might experience.

Construct an appropriate 150-word explanation of drug treatments of smoking addiction in the manner outlined above. (6 marks)

 How do I answer... longer (16-mark) questions?

For a 16-mark essay question, the command words might require you to 'outline (or describe) and evaluate… '. Alternatively, a question might ask you to 'discuss the use of drug therapy as a way of reducing addiction'. Whilst all of these instructions indicate that you should include both AO1 and AO3 in your answer, the 'discuss' command word requires you to go a little further than just writing about strengths and/or limitations. Let's look at these different types of question as they might appear in the context of the interactionist approach. The AO1 and AO3 material for these questions is on the opposite page.

> **Q1:** Outline and evaluate the use of drug therapy as a way of reducing addiction. **(16 marks)**

The nominal mark division for AO1 and AO3 in this question is 6 marks for the former and 10 marks for the latter. You could aim to include the seven AO1 points to cover the AO1 component of this question. For the AO3 content, you should include all four of the AO3 points.

> **Q2:** Jack has tried to give up smoking and is now getting desperate. His GP has suggested using a course of drugs coupled with nicotine replacement therapy.
>
> Discuss the use of drug therapy as a way of reducing addiction. Explain why a drug therapy coupled with nicotine replacement therapy might be a good way of treating Jack's smoking addiction. **(16 marks)**

In this question, the mark division is slightly different to **Q1**. The number of marks allocated to AO1 remains the same (6 marks), but the number of marks allocated to AO3 drops from 10 to 6, with the missing 4 marks being 'diverted' to the AO2 component.

The command word 'discuss' requires AO3 that is a bit more 'discursive', e.g. looking at applications, implications, counter-evidence, etc. We have tried to make some of our AO3 points 'discursive' to accommodate this. For example, the second AO3 point is 'discursive' because it discusses how the lack of blinding in NRT studies means that conclusions about its effectiveness are more uncertain than has been claimed.

 REVIEW

You will need to be able to answer questions with different mark allocations concisely but keeping enough detail to describe these two explanations clearly. Practise answering 3-, 4- and 6-mark AO1 questions on drug treatments for the reduction of addiction. You should spend about a minute and a quarter per mark, so for a 3-mark question you have just under 4 minutes, for a 4-mark question you have 5 minutes and for a 6-mark question you have 10 minutes. Make sure you allow time to plan your answers, to make sure you write them in a logical way. You could use a timer to make sure you keep to time.

Reducing addiction: Behavioural interventions

AO1 Description

- Behavioural therapies try to change a person's motivation to engage in behaviours such as smoking or gambling.

- **Aversion therapy** The aim of aversion therapy is to decrease or eliminate the undesirable behaviours associated with addiction by associating them with unpleasant or uncomfortable sensations.

  > Aversion therapy is based on the principles of classical conditioning – an individual learns to associate an aversive stimulus (something that causes a strong feeling of dislike or disgust) with an action they had previously enjoyed.

  > During aversion therapy, the patient is asked to engage in the behaviour while at the same time being exposed to something unpleasant such as a drug that makes them nauseous or even mild electric shocks.

  > Once the behaviour becomes associated with the unpleasant stimulus, it will begin to decrease in frequency or stop entirely.

- **Covert sensitisation** Involves eliminating an unwanted behaviour by creating an association between the behaviour and an unpleasant stimulus or consequence.

  > Once this association is firmly established, engaging in the behaviour is no longer appealing for the individual. Covert sensitisation works very similarly to aversion therapy, but with one major difference – the unpleasant stimulus is only imagined by the individual.

  > Rather than experiencing actual physical consequences such as an electric shock, the consequences are instead pictured in the person's mind. By associating unpleasant sensations with the undesirable behaviour, this leads to decreased desire and avoidance of the situation in the future.

AO3 Evaluation/Discussion

Research support for aversion therapy...

Smith and Frawley (1993) demonstrated the effectiveness of aversion therapy in patients being treated for alcoholism.	Contact was made a minimum of 12 months after completion of aversion therapy treatment. Of those contacted, 65 per cent were totally abstinent from alcohol at this point. The 12-month abstinence rate for cocaine was 83.7 per cent.	*This study provides research support for the claim that aversion therapy eliminates the urges to drink or use drugs.*

Ethical problems with aversion therapy...

Although aversion therapy has been shown to be effective in reducing addictive behaviour, there are ethical concerns surrounding its use.	There are problems concerning patient acceptance and some forms of aversion therapy use drugs that cause extremely uncomfortable consequences, including nausea and vomiting.	*These effects can lead to poor compliance with treatment and high dropout rates, which decreases the potential positive impact of this type of treatment.*

Support for covert sensitisation...

Kraft and Kraft (2005) provided support for the effectiveness of covert sensitisation in treating different addictive behaviours.	They treated a patient with a chocolate addiction, eliminating her cravings for chocolate in just four sessions. Kraft and Kraft concluded that covert sensitisation was a rapid and effective form of treatment for the elimination of cravings associated with unwanted behaviour.	*Although not all patients respond to this form of treatment, Kraft and Kraft claim it is effective in 90 per cent of cases.*

Problems with behaviour modification of addiction...

Behaviour modification therapies share a common problem in that they focus only on the learned aspect of addictive behaviours.	Addictions are often highly complex in the reasons for their development – therefore, failure to address the underlying issues that led to the addiction in the first place may mean the treatment is doomed to failure.	*A consequence of only treating the symptoms is that it leaves individuals at risk of developing another addiction even if the addiction being treated is eliminated.*

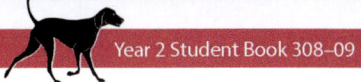

⚙️ APPLY

AO2: An example

 **SCENARIO** Rosa is desperate to kick her addiction to cigarettes so decides to undergo covert sensitisation after talking to her psychologist friend.

Explain how covert sensitisation might be used in the treatment of Rosa's nicotine addiction. **(4 marks)**

ANSWER *Covert sensitisation would involve Rosa imagining herself engaging in behaviours associated with smoking (e.g. lighting a cigarette, taking a drag on it) and then imagining a very unpleasant consequence (e.g. experiencing intense feelings of nausea and vomiting all over the floor). These consequences must be vivid enough so that Rosa experiences feelings of considerable discomfort or anxiety when she imagines herself smoking a cigarette. By consistently associating smoking and its unpleasant consequence over and over in her mind, she should eventually lose the desire to smoke and avoid cigarettes in the future.*

AO2: Research methods

Smith and Frawley (1993) studied a sample of 600 patients being treated for alcoholism using aversion therapy at three addiction treatment hospitals in the US. Seventy-five of these patients were also being treated for cocaine dependence. Contact was made a minimum of 12 months after completion of treatment. Of the patients contacted, 65 per cent were totally abstinent from alcohol at this point.

a. 'Seventy-five of these patients were also being treated for cocaine dependence'. Express this as a percentage of the total sample size. (2 marks)

b. 'Of the patients contacted, 65 per cent were totally abstinent from alcohol'. Which of the following fractions relates to 65%? (1 mark)

   (i)   1/11
   (ii) 13/20
   (iii) 16/25

c. Round (up or down) 66.5 to an appropriate whole number. (1 mark)

d. Round up each of the following. (1 mark each)

   (i)   43.753 to one decimal place
   (ii) 101.2648 to two decimal places
   (iii) 7.12852 to three decimal places

e. What is 8.5291 rounded to 1 significant figure, then to 2 significant figures? (1 mark each)

AO2: One for you to try

Tim's gambling habit has been getting worse. He used to have the odd flutter on major horse races such as the Grand National and the Derby, but now he spends most of his time (and money) checking form and placing bets, either online or in the local betting shop. He has tried to stop but seems incapable of giving up his addictive behaviour.

Explain how aversion therapy might be used in the treatment of Tim's gambling addiction. (4 marks)

🐾 How do I answer... 'Distinguish between' questions?

Explain the difference between aversion therapy and covert sensitisation. (3 marks)

There are some fairly simple rules for answering this sort of question. If you are asked to 'distinguish between…', 'compare…' or 'explain the difference between…', then these rules apply:

1 Don't just *describe* the two things you are being asked to distinguish between.

2 Pick some characteristic that applies to both but which is different for each and point that out (e.g. how each associates a particular behaviour with unpleasant or uncomfortable sensations). For example, 'During aversion therapy, the patient is asked to engage in the behaviour while at the same time being exposed to something unpleasant.' In covert sensitisation, rather than experiencing actual physical consequences, the consequences are instead pictured in the person's mind.'

3 Use words like 'whereas', 'however', 'on the other hand' to point out this difference. That gives us, 'During aversion therapy, the patient is asked to engage in the behaviour while at the same time being exposed to something unpleasant, whereas in covert sensitisation, rather than experiencing actual physical consequences, the consequences are instead pictured in the person's mind.'

4 Don't be too ambitious; one point of difference is usually enough.

🔄 REVIEW

Write an essay plan for the essay question:

Discuss behavioural interventions for reducing addiction. (16 marks)

Think carefully about what you will include and the level of detail for each point. Then try writing this essay in 20 minutes. If you couldn't finish it in the time, this means you are not writing concisely enough or you are having to think too much. Keep reviewing the material until you know it well and can write a well-balanced essay in 20 minutes.

Reducing addiction: Cognitive behavioural therapy

AO1 Description

- **Cognitive behavioural therapy (CBT)** is based on the idea that addictive behaviours are maintained by the person's thoughts about these behaviours.

- The main goal of CBT is to help people change the way they think about their addiction, and to learn new ways of coping more effectively with the circumstances that led to these behaviours in the past.

- **CBT and gambling addiction** CBT can be used to help gamblers identify the triggers to their problem behaviour, challenge their irrational thinking and find better ways to cope with the feelings and urges that prompt a gambling episode.

- **How CBT works in the reduction of addiction** CBT helps individuals develop more constructive ways of thinking and behaving. Follow-up sessions aim to stop people relapsing back into the problem behaviour.

  > **Identifying and correcting cognitive biases** CBT involves identifying and changing cognitive distortions about the problem behaviour. Clients being treated for gambling addiction are not always aware of the cognitive biases on which they base their decisions. The therapist can educate clients about the nature of cognitive biases and that gambling outcomes are determined by chance.

  > **Changing behaviour** After the individual begins to think differently about their problem behaviour, they are encouraged to practise these changes in their daily life. For example, gamblers may be asked to visit a casino and refrain from betting.

  > **Relapse prevention** involves learning to identify and avoid those risky situations that can trigger feelings or thoughts that can lead to relapse to the particular problem behaviour.

AO3 Evaluation/Discussion

Supporting evidence for the role of CBT in treating addiction...

CBT has been effective in the treatment of a number of different addictions.

Magill and Ray (2009), in a meta-analysis, found CBT to be effective in reducing both alcohol and illicit drug addiction. In the treatment of gambling addiction, CBT has been successfully applied in both individual and group settings.

In the treatment of gambling addiction, CBT may be even more effective than referral to Gamblers Anonymous (Petry et al., 2006) and drug therapy (Ravindran et al., 2006).

Advantages of CBT as a treatment for addiction...

There are a number of advantages associated with CBT in this context.

Addicts frequently suffer from negative thought patterns that contribute to feelings of helplessness. The development of more positive ways of thinking means they no longer feel overwhelmed by everyday circumstances and are less likely to engage in addictive behaviours in order to cope.

A consequence of this is that individuals are more confident in their ability to resist pressures to engage in activities that created the addiction.

Irrational thinking or irrational environment?...

A problem in using CBT alone is that there is an overemphasis on an individual's irrational thinking rather than acknowledging the stressful environment that perpetuates their addictive behaviour.

These stressful environments (e.g. an unhappy marriage) exist beyond the therapeutic setting and so continue to produce and reinforce problem behaviours once the therapy has finished.

This suggests that CBT can be effective only as part of a wider form of intervention that also addresses the social environment in which addiction occurs.

Making the transition from use to non-use...

McHugh et al. (2010) suggest a challenge to the success of CBT is the shift in lifestyle associated with use, relative to non-use.

Among those who have long histories of substance abuse, their 'fit' to society is with others with similar problems, and this may vary dramatically from mainstream culture. As well as giving up their addictive behaviour, they must also make the transition to a culture where they have few skills and resources.

This can make the individual ambivalent about change, and the reduction of addictive behaviour more difficult.

APPLY

AO2: An example

SCENARIO Despite his losses, Arno is convinced that he has the skills to make his living in the casino. Even when he tries to give up the casino he finds he can't pass a betting shop without going in to place a bet.

Explain why cognitive behavioural therapy would be an appropriate method of treatment for Arno. **(4 marks)**

ANSWER *CBT would be appropriate for Arno because he is not aware that believing he can influence chance is an example of irrational thinking. He can be educated about cognitive biases and how gambling outcomes in the casino are determined by chance. He can also be asked how effective his strategy has been over time, and as he has lost money this would challenge his view that it is about skill. CBT incorporates relapse prevention techniques, so Arno would be taught to identify and avoid risky situations (e.g. casinos or betting shops) that might lead him to gamble again. This could be as simple as changing his route so he no longer walks past betting shops.*

AO2: One for you to try

Gareth has been recommended to sign up for a course of cognitive behavioural therapy because of his problem gambling. He spends over £200 a week playing slot machines in pubs, casinos, and even online.

Explain how cognitive behavioural therapy could be used to help Gareth reduce his gambling addiction. (4 marks)

AO2: Research methods

A study by Budney *et al.* (2006) studied 90 adults seeking treatment for marijuana dependence at an outpatient clinic in the US. These adults were randomly assigned to one of three treatment groups – CBT, monetary vouchers, or both CBT and vouchers. Each time a participant in the vouchers-only or combination treatment submitted a marijuana negative urine sample, he or she received a voucher worth $1.50; a second consecutive negative sample earned $3.00, a third $4.50, and so on.

The participants were assessed immediately after treatment and then every three months for one year. The percentage of participants who were completely abstinent from marijuana immediately after treatment, 6 months after and 12 months after treatment were as follows:

Months after treatment	0	6	12
CBT	31	13	23
Vouchers	40	24	17
CBT + vouchers	43	33	38

a. **Draw a fully labelled bar chart to represent the data in the table. (4 marks)**

b. **Draw *two* conclusions from this bar chart. (4 marks)**

c. **Explain why it was important to 'randomly assign' participants to the different treatment groups. (2 marks)**

How do I answer... draw a graph...' questions?

From time to time (as in question **a** on the right), you could be asked draw a suitable graph or chart to represent a set of data. Sometimes the type of graph required is identified for you (as in question **a**), and at other times you are required to identify an appropriate graph or chart and draw it.

The term 'fully-labelled' is important in these questions, as this means the mark-scheme will have identified the specific features that will earn marks. Usually marks are given for drawing an appropriate graph or chart (in question **a**) the examiner would be looking to see that you have actually drawn a bar chart rather than a histogram, scattergram or some other non-appropriate alternative. Second, they would be looking to see if you had properly titled the bar chart. This should be a simple statement that

tells the reader what they are looking at. For question **a**, this might say… **'Percentage of participants abstinent from marijuana after 0, 6 and 12 months'.** Next, the examiner would be checking whether you have labelled your axes correctly. For question **a**, the Y (or vertical) axis would be labelled %, and the X (or horizontal) axis would indicate the three times periods, **0 months, 6 months, 12 months.** Finally, as this is a 4-mark question, you would include a key (usually to the side of the bar chart) indicating which condition is which. For question **a**, this would indicate which bar(s) represents which condition, i.e. **CBT, Vouchers, CBT + Vouchers.**

REVIEW

Questions such as the **AO2: One for you to try** above are subtly different from other AO1 questions on the nature of CBT as a way of reducing addiction. This one asks you to explain 'how' CBT could be used, in other words what would actually happen during therapy – what would Gareth be required to do? To prepare for the different types of AO1 question in this area (and in the other ways of reducing addiction), you should

practice answering 2-, 3-, 4- and 6-mark descriptions of the *nature* of CBT but also 2-, 3-, 4- and 6-mark descriptions of what happens during therapy. Remember also that if you are asked to apply it to a particular scenario, then you must do that. You must also be able to outline (describe, explain, etc.) CBT as it is used in the treatment of addiction, not CBT as a treatment for any other form of behaviour.

The theory of planned behaviour

AO1 Description

- An individual's decision to engage in a particular behaviour can be directly predicted by their intention to engage in that behaviour. Intention is a function of three factors:
  - > **Behavioural attitude** reflects an individual's personal views towards a behaviour such as gambling or smoking. They are more likely to hold a favourable attitude if they believe that engaging in that behaviour will lead to positive outcomes.
  - > **Subjective norms** are a product of an individual's subjective awareness of social norms relating to that behaviour. They reflect what we believe significant others feel is the right thing to do, as well as perceptions of what others are actually doing.
  - > **Perceived behavioural control** refers to the extent to which an individual believes they can actually give up an addictive behaviour. An individual with higher perceived behavioural control is likely to try harder and to persevere for longer.

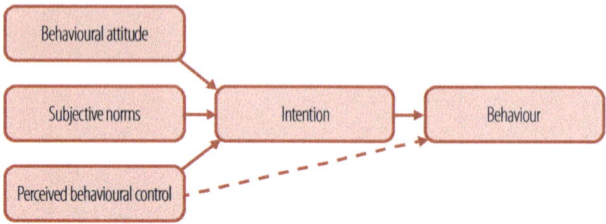

- **Using the TPB to reduce addiction**
  The TPB can be used as a means to understand prevention and treatment.
  - > **Changing behavioural attitude** The US Office of National Drug Control Policy (2005) aimed to create a different attitude among teenagers towards the effect of marijuana use.
  - > **Changing subjective norms** Anti-drug campaigns often seek to give adolescents actual data about the percentage of people engaging in risky behaviour. This is done in order to change subjective norms.
  - > **Perceived behavioural control** Godin *et al.* (2002) examined the extent to which the TPB could explain outcomes in adults intending to give up smoking. The researchers found that perceived behavioural control was the most important predictor of ultimate behaviour.

AO3 Evaluation / Discussion

The TPB is too rational…

A limitation of the TPB is that it fails to take into account emotions or other irrational determinants of human behaviour.	When asked about attitudes and intention, people might find it impossible to anticipate the strong desires and emotions that compel their behaviour in real life.	*The presence of strong emotions might explain why people sometimes act irrationally by failing to carry out an intended behaviour (e.g. stop drinking) even when it is in their best interest to do so.*

The TPB ignores other factors…

Aside from emotion, there are many other influential factors that are ignored by the TPB.	An element that is missing from the TPB is motivation. Klag (2006) found that recovery was consistently more successful in individuals who had themselves decided to give up rather than in people who were coerced in some way to change their addictive behaviour.	*Self-determination theory, according to Klag, is preferable to the TPB because it emphasises the importance of self-motivation in recovery.*

Methodological issues with the TPB…

Questionnaires may be poor representations of the attitudes and intentions that eventually exist in the behavioural situation.	A smoker may express an intention to give up when completing a questionnaire. However, their actual behaviour may differ when they find themselves in a group of smokers with all the associated sights and smells of smoking.	*This suggests that, when a habit develops, the behaviour is likely to be under the control of stimulus cues, thus making intentions expressed on questionnaires poor predictors of actual behaviour.*

Predicts intention rather than behaviour change…

Armitage and Conner's (2001) meta-analysis found that this model was successful in predicting intention to change rather than actual behavioural change.	This pattern of results is typically found in the prediction of health behaviours that involve the adoption of difficult behavioural change, such as stopping using drugs of abuse or eating a healthy diet.	*This suggests that the TPB is primarily an account of intention formation rather than specifying the processes involved in translating the intention into action.*

 **APPLY**

AO2: An example

SCENARIO  Sophie's parents are both psychologists and decide to use the theory of planned behaviour to change Sophie's digital addiction.

Explain how they might use this theory to reduce Sophie's reliance on digital technology. **(4 marks)**

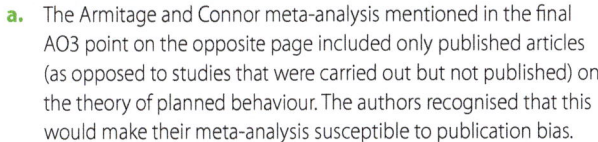 *They could start by changing her attitude to digital technology, e.g. by providing evidence of how a reduction in digital use can make life less stressful. They could then alter the subjective norm for this behaviour. Sophie might believe that others regard spending a lot of time on the Internet and checking Facebook as a good thing, but her parents may have evidence to challenge this belief. Finally, Sophie may lack confidence that she could actually reduce her reliance on digital technology (i.e. a lack of perceived behavioural control). Her parents could arrange for Sophie to have counselling to increase her self-efficacy and, as a result, her intention to overcome her digital addiction.*

AO2: Research methods

a. The Armitage and Connor meta-analysis mentioned in the final AO3 point on the opposite page included only published articles (as opposed to studies that were carried out but not published) on the theory of planned behaviour. The authors recognised that this would make their meta-analysis susceptible to publication bias.

Explain what is meant by publication bias and why it might impact on any conclusions that might be drawn from this study. (3 marks)

b. The researchers discovered that the relationship between Theory of Planned Behaviour variables and intention to change an addictive behaviour was stronger in studies where behaviour was measured by self-report as compared with studies where behaviour was observed directly.

Explain the implications of this finding for any conclusions drawn from the meta-analysis. (3 marks)

c. The researchers concluded that this model was successful in predicting intention and behaviour with regards to addictive behaviour.

Consider possible implications for the economy of Armitage and Conner's meta-analysis. (3 marks)

AO2: One for you to try

After trying cognitive behavioural therapy to reduce his gambling addiction, which he did not get on well with, Gareth asks his friend Radha, who teaches psychology, if she could help him.

Explain how Radha could use the theory of planned behaviour to reduce Gareth's gambling addiction. (6 marks)

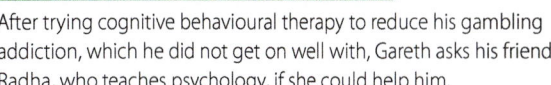 **How do I answer... selection (multiple choice) questions?**

> Which **one** of the following describes the three components of the theory of planned behaviour? **(1 mark)**
>
> A Genetic predisposition, subjective norm, behavioural inhibition.
>
> B Behavioural attitude, subjective norm, perceived behavioural control.
>
> C Genetic predisposition, social norms, behavioural inhibition.
>
> D Behavioural attitude, social norms, perceived behavioural control.

Usually these questions require you to pick out the one statement that is correct, matches or defines a concept or idea. They may also (on occasion) ask you to pick out the one statement that is incorrect or does not match or define a concept or idea.

Although these are generally worth only 1 mark, getting them correct is still important because that 1 mark can be the difference between one grade and another. Follow the general advice on answering questions like these:

- Read the question very carefully. Is it asking you to pick the statement that matches (as here) or the 'odd one out' that doesn't match?
- Make life easier by crossing out any that are obviously not going to be the correct answer given the specific demands of the question.

Applying this to the question above we cross out **A** and **C** because the theory of planned behaviour has nothing to do with genetics. The difference between **B** and **D** is the difference between 'subjective norms' and 'social norms'. These concepts are very similar, so it pays to know the specific wording of the model (in this case it is 'subjective norm' so the correct answer is **B**).

REVIEW

What else could be asked about this topic? Generating different questions can help you process the information and be ready to use it in different ways. You might also practise answering these questions, or at least construct answer plans for each. All of this is what Craik and Lockhart (see p.165) refer to as 'elaborated processing'. The more you process material, in all sorts of different ways, the more memorable it becomes.

Prochaska's six-stage model of behaviour change

RECAP

AO1 Description

- **An overview of the model** Stage theories emphasise the gradual nature of change, and assume a transition through a fixed series of discrete stages.

- **The six stages of change** The first three of the stages represent variations in a person's intention to change ('pre-action'). The latter three stages are all 'post-action' stages and represent the duration of the change.

  > **Stage 1: Precontemplation** Individuals currently have no intention to change their behaviour in the near future. They may be unaware that their behaviour is becoming problematic and may only seek help because of pressure from others.

  > **Stage 2: Contemplation** The person may be aware that a problem exists but has yet to make a commitment to doing anything about it.

  > **Stage 3: Preparation** This stage combines intention to change with actual behavioural change. Individuals who are prepared to change their problem behaviour report small behavioural changes.

  > **Stage 4: Action** Individuals modify their behaviour in order to overcome their problems. This involves the most overt behavioural changes and requires considerable commitment.

  > **Stage 5: Maintenance** The individual works to consolidate gains attained during the previous stage. Individuals in this stage have stayed free of the addictive behaviour for a period of six months or more.

  > **Stage 6: Termination** The individual is no longer tempted to revert to the former behaviour and is completely confident that they are able to maintain the change.

- **The processes of change** Prochaska *et al.* (1992) describe activities that help individuals move from one stage to the next. Movement from the precontemplation stage to the contemplation stage may involve the use of consciousness raising (e.g. learning new facts that would support the behaviour change) and environmental re-evaluation (e.g. realising the negative impact their behaviour has on others).

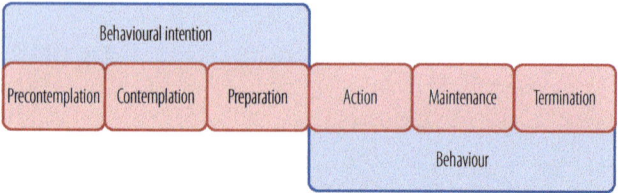

AO3 Evaluation / Discussion

Usefulness of the model…

The stage model suggests that the most effective strategy in reducing addiction is determined by the individual's current stage. → Women in the first stage of change were most resistant to engaging in positive health behaviour during pregnancy, whereas pregnant women further along the cycle of change were more convinced about the health risks of smoking during pregnancy (Haslam and Draper, 2000). → *This suggests that interventions need to be tailored to an individual's stage of change to maximise their effectiveness.*

Evidence does not always demonstrate behavioural outcomes…

There is a paucity of empirical studies that have used behavioural outcomes as a way of measuring the usefulness of this model. → Much of the evidence has tended to focus on what Whitelaw *et al.* (2000) refer to as 'softer' indications of effectiveness, such as stage progression within the model, rather than actual behaviour change. → *Whitelaw et al. conclude that the popularity of the model has 'little to do with its scientific support', as the strength of the evidence base tends to be overstated.*

Design weaknesses in supporting studies…

Whitelaw *et al.* (2000) claim that few studies have included all the characteristics associated with a robust experimental design. → Some studies have not used control groups (e.g. Marcus *et al.*, 1996), whereas others have used a variety of interventions as part of any treatment. For example, Steptoe *et al.* (1999) used nicotine replacement therapy alongside behavioural counselling. → *As a result, it becomes difficult to disentangle the specific effects of a 'stages of change' approach from the more generalised effects of intervention.*

Research fails to support the effectiveness of the model…

Recent research that does employ a robust experimental protocol has cast doubts on the effectiveness of staged intervention. → Baumann *et al.* (2015) randomly allocated problem drinkers to either an experimental group, who received an intervention tailored to their motivational stage, or a control group, who received minimal intervention only. Very few participants subsequently gave up drinking completely (2 per cent). → *As there was no significant difference in beneficial effects between the staged intervention group and the control group, this suggests that the advantages of Prochaska's model may be overstated.*

APPLY

AO2: An example

SCENARIO Prochaska's six-stage model is a useful approach to treatment because it suggests that the most effective strategy to use in reducing nicotine addiction is determined by the current stage the individual is in.

With reference to this claim, discuss Prochaska's 'stages of change' model in the treatment of addiction. **(16 marks)**

ANSWER **An extract showing how you could address the AO2 requirements of this question:** *There is support for the claim that the success of intervention is linked to the person's current stage in Haslam and Draper's study of women smoking during pregnancy. Women further along the cycle of change were more likely to consider the dangers of smoking while pregnant. Research has also shown that the current stage of an individual dictates the type of process that is likely to make intervention effective. For example, movement from the precontemplation stage to the contemplation stage could involve consciousness raising, where the individual learns new facts and ideas that support their attempts to give up their nicotine addiction...*

AO2: One for you to try

A researcher is investigating Prochaska's six-stage model of behaviour change. She interviews people attending a smoking cessation clinic. She asks them various questions about their smoking habits and, from their responses, she carries out a thematic analysis to see if the same stages identified by Prochaska emerged in her sample.

From the sample responses below, identify which stage of Prochaska's model each of these respondents would be in. (1 mark each)

(i) *Respondent A* - "I do want to kick the habit and have managed to cut down a little."

(ii) *Respondent B* - "I never thought I'd be able to live without my cigarettes, but now I just think of it as a filthy habit and I can't stand to even be in the company of other smokers. "

(iii) *Respondent C* - "I'm only here because my doctor told me I had to come because of my health. Mind you, he should send himself, I see him smoking when he's in the pub! I can't see myself ever giving up."

(iv) *Respondent D* - "I've finally managed to stop completely, although the temptation is still there. It's so hard, particularly when my friends all smoke."

AO2: Research methods

Using the research study in **AO2: One for you to try**, answer the following questions.

a. **Explain what is meant by thematic analysis and outline one strength of using thematic analysis in this study. (4 marks)**

b. **Is the data that would emerge from this study quantitative or qualitative? Explain your answer. (2 marks)**

c. **The researcher took her sample from people attending a smoking cessation clinic. Explain one limitation of using this sample to draw conclusions about the different stages of smoking addiction. (3 marks)**

d. **Identify one possible ethical issue that might arise in this study and explain how this might be overcome. (3 marks)**

How do I show... clear and coherent organisation?

"The answer is clear, coherent and focused" (AQA marking criteria Top Level)

In this last **How do I answer... ?** section, we concentrate on an often-ignored part of essay writing – organisation. Once you have mastered the content and know when to use it and how much of it to use, we still have to present this material in way that demonstrates that we actually understand not only the content, but also its relevance in the context of the question.

1 Have a clear plan for your answer rather than presenting a rambling account. For example, faced with a question that asks you to 'Describe and evaluate **two** interventions for reducing addiction' you might choose Prochaska's six-stage model and CBT. In that case you could organise your answer as follows:

Prochaska model AO1	CBT for addiction AO1
AO3 Strength	AO3 Strength
AO3 Limitation	AO3 Limitation

2 Have a logical flow to your material. By presenting your material in a logical and structured manner (perhaps using the plan above or something similar), this will ensure that what you are writing makes sense as a response to the question.

3 Finally, make the AO1 and AO3 clear for the examiner *and* for yourself. Skilled essay writers may like to mix together AO1 and AO3 in the same paragraph (or even in the same sentence), but it really is easier to separate them into distinct chunks, adding descriptive detail to expand your descriptive content and elaborating your AO3 content in the way we have shown you throughout this book.

REVIEW

In this final Review section of this chapter, it is time for some more 'revision accounting'. You should make a table like this with all 12 topics from this chapter on Addiction. When you feel you have mastered the AO1 and AO3 components of these and can cope with any of the different types of question that we have covered in the **How do I answer... ?** sections, you will have earned a ✓ in the 'Got it!' column.

TOPIC	Got it!			Got it!	
	AO1	AO3		AO1	AO3
Physical and psychological dependence	✓		Explanations for gambling addiction: Cognitive theory		
Risk factors: Genetics, stress and personality			Reducing addiction: Drug therapy		

Appendix: The examinations

There are three examinations that make up your A Level in psychology – Papers 1, 2 and 3. Each paper is worth 33.3% of your A Level marks and you will have two hours to complete each paper. We have covered all of the content for Paper 1 (Introductory topics in psychology) and all of the content for Paper 2 (Psychology in context) – except Research Methods – in *The Complete Companions* Year 1 and AS Revision Guide.

The A level examination

Paper 1 (7182/1) Introductory topics in psychology

Paper 1 contains four sections, each worth 24 marks. You must answer all questions. The content of the four sections is as below:

Section A: Social influence

Section B: Memory

Section C: Attachment

Section D: Psychopathology

Paper 2 (7182/2) Psychology in context

Paper 2 contains three sections, two worth 24 marks each, and the third, Research methods, worth 48 marks. You must answer all questions. The content of the three sections is as follows:

Section A: Approaches in psychology

Section B: Biopsychology

Section C: Research methods

Paper 3 (7182/3) Issues and options in psychology

You will have two hours to answer questions on this paper.

The paper is divided into four sections, each worth 24 marks. Section A is compulsory. For Sections B–D, you choose one topic (e.g. for Section C, you answer questions on EITHER Schizophrenia OR Eating behaviour OR Stress).

The content of the four sections is as below:

Section A: Issues and debates in psychology

Section B: Relationships

Gender

Cognition and development

Section C: Schizophrenia

Eating behaviour

Stress

Section D: Aggression

Forensic psychology

Addiction

Assessment objectives

The examinations assesses three separate skills, known as **assessment objectives**. These are as follows:

AO1 (description of knowledge)
AO2 (application of knowledge)
AO3 (evaluation/discussion of knowledge)

We look further at these three assessment objectives, how you can master them and how they are examined on the next few pages. In practice, the differences between these three skills can be quite subtle, as it is a case of what you *do* with material that makes it AO1, AO2 or AO3 rather than any inherent properties of the material itself. Let's look at a (completely fictional) example from a galaxy far, far away.

Now let's look at how this material can be used as a way of responding to three very different types of question. Note that the underlying material is more or less the same in all three cases, but it has been 'tweaked' so that it is being used in either a descriptive (AO1), application (AO2) or evaluative (AO3) way.

An AO1 question

Outline the findings of one psychological study of de-individuation as an explanation of aggression. **(4 marks)**

'Snoke (2016) found that factors that increase de-individuation also tend to increase aggression. He found that galactic stormtroopers behaved far more aggressively when invading other planets if they were all wearing the same military uniform rather than when they were wearing their own civilian clothes. He also found that stormtroopers were more aggressive when patrolling in large groups than when they patrolled on their own.'

An AO2 question

Ground stewards at Grimsby United have been instructed to ban fans wearing masks and face paint and anything else that increases their anonymity. The football club believe that this will decrease violence on the terraces. Using your knowledge of de-individuation as an explanation of aggression, explain why this is likely to be the case. **(3 marks)**

'Grimsby officials believe that anonymity as a result of masks and face painting will de-individuate fans, and so would increase aggression, as it did with the galactic stormtroopers studied by Snoke (2016). Snoke found that when stormtroopers were wearing the same uniform and helmets covering their faces, they acted more aggressively. The officials at Grimsby believe that if they ban masks and face paints then de-individuation will be less likely therefore avoiding aggression.'

An AO3 question

Explain one critical point concerning the relationship between de-individuation and aggression. **(3 marks)**

'The claim that there is a relationship between de-individuation and aggression is supported by research by Snoke (2016). He found that galactic stormtroopers behaved far more aggressively when invading other planets if they were all wearing the same military uniform rather than when they were wearing their own civilian clothes. He also found that stormtroopers were more aggressive when patrolling in large groups than when they patrolled on their own. This supports the claim that factors that increase de-individuation also tend to increase aggression.'

Training yourself to be an examiner

Throughout this book we offer you suggestions as to how to structure material for the most effective exam answers, but there is another skill that will help you understand exactly why it is necessary to do this. Knowing what the examiner is looking for and why they award marks is vital. Therefore, over the next few pages, we'll train you to be an examiner, so you can mark your own answers. We'll start with AO1.

Step 1

We have summarised the main skills an examiner looks for in the table at the bottom of the page. First, we need to determine whether the answer is **accurate** (as it is in the case of the two answers below). Next, we look at the amount of **detail**. Is it overly brief and superficial or has the candidate fleshed out their answer with appropriate elaboration? The term 'appropriate' is important because not all detail adds to the quality of the answer.

Training task 1

Outline biological explanations of schizophrenia. **(6 marks)**

Answer 1

The first biological explanation is genetic factors. Twin studies are used where researchers compare identical and non-identical twins. Identical twins are genetically identical whereas non-identical twins only share 50% of their genes. Studies with twins have shown a strong genetic influence because identical twins that are schizophrenic are more likely to have a twin who is also schizophrenic. The second biological explanation is the dopamine hypothesis. This claims that schizophrenia is caused by too much activity in the brain, which leads to the abnormalities experienced by schizophrenics. A third explanation is neural correlates. This refers to the different parts of the brain that are associated with schizophrenia. For example, schizophrenics have been found to have reduced brain matter and enlarged ventricles compared to non-schizophrenics. These enlarged ventricles show that the schizophrenic has lost important brain matter.

Answer 2

Genetic explanations claim that schizophrenia is inherited biologically. Twin and family studies have shown that the closer the degree of genetic similarity with a schizophrenic patient, the greater the risk of developing the disorder. Adoption studies such as Tienari et al. (2000) have found that adopted children are more likely to develop schizophrenia if a biological parent has the disorder than if an adoptive parent has.
The dopamine hypothesis claims that schizophrenia is a consequence of dopamine receptors in the mesolimbic pathway of the brain firing too easily or too often. Drugs that block this dopamine activity also tend to reduce positive symptoms, such as hallucinations and delusions, suggesting that these symptoms are caused by excess dopamine activity. The revised dopamine hypothesis claims that the negative and cognitive symptoms found in some schizophrenics are caused by a deficit of dopamine in areas of the prefrontal cortex.

Step 2

The next skill we need to assess is how well the answer is **organised**, i.e. does it ramble around the topic in a seemingly illogical way or is it carefully structured and easy to follow? You know yourself from reading textbooks that well organised content is easier to follow and understand.

Finally we need to make a judgement about the use of specialist terminology. Has the candidate used appropriate **psychological terminology** or described the material in more general (and vague) ways?

The verdict

Answer 1 is a Level 2 response. Because the candidate has tried to cram in 3 explanations, detail is sacrificed. Some of this detail is unnecessary and doesn't add much. It is mostly clear and organised with some fairly vague terms so 4 marks.

Answer 2 is a Level 3 response. Given the time available for an answer of this type, this is a very detailed answer. It is well organised (clear, coherent and logically organised). Good use of specialist terminology, so the full 6 marks.

The 'magnet effect'

Mark allocation tables such as the one on this page give information about what an answer at a particular level would look like. However, often an answer does not fit neatly into one level. For example, an answer might be 'mostly clear and organised', but also lacking in detail, so a mix of Level 2 and Level 1 criteria.

An examiner would therefore make a decision about the 'best fit' level (e.g. Level 2), but the actual mark would be drawn in the direction of the lower level (like a magnet), with the result that the examiner would award the lower of the two Level 2 marks (i.e. 3 rather than 2 marks).

Description questions (AO1: 6 mark questions)

Level	Marks	Knowledge	Organisation	Specialist terminology
3	5-6	Generally accurate and well-detailed	Clear and coherent	Used effectively
2	3-4	Evident with some inaccuracies	Mostly clear and organised	Some appropriate use
1	1-2	Limited and lacks detail	Lacks clarity and organisation	Absent or used inappropriately
0	0	No relevant content		

A02

Step 1

First, a candidate must show appropriate psychological content, i.e. they must recognise and describe the appropriate underlying psychology. Second, they must engage with the scenario outlined in the stem, i.e. they must apply their psychological knowledge.

So, the first thing an examiner will be looking for is the **knowledge** shown in response to the stem. Is it **clear** and appropriate, **accurate** and **detailed**?

Training task 2

When schizophrenia patients were given drugs that lowered their dopamine levels, they showed improvement in some symptoms (e.g. hallucinations) but a worsening in others (e.g. cognitive impairment). When the same patients took psychostimulants, which raised dopamine levels, the opposite pattern emerged, with increased hallucinations but reduced cognitive impairment.

Explain how this evidence supports the dopamine hypothesis of schizophrenia. **(4 marks)**

Answer 1

> The dopamine hypothesis claims that schizophrenia is due to an excess of the neurotransmitter dopamine in the brain. Neurons fire too often or too easily. This excess of dopamine activity in the nervous system leads to the positive symptoms of schizophrenia such as hallucinations and delusions. The revised dopamine hypothesis states that low levels of dopamine in areas of the brain such as the prefrontal cortex lead to cognitive impairments such as memory deficits.

Answer 2

> Positive symptoms of schizophrenia (such as hallucinations mentioned above) are caused by an excess of dopamine in mesolimbic pathways in the brain. Drugs that lowered dopamine levels in this study would have blocked dopamine transmission in these areas and so reduced these positive symptoms. Negative symptoms, such as cognitive impairment, are caused by a depletion of dopamine in the mesocortical pathways. Drugs that lowered dopamine levels would have mimicked this depletion and caused cognitive impairments. Reversing this by the use of psychostimulants would have increased positive symptoms and cognitive impairments, which is what was found in this study.

Step 2

The examiner will then look at the **application** of the material. Has it been linked effectively to the stem (i.e. has it been used to address the specific context of the question?)

An examiner will also assess whether the application of the knowledge is **appropriate** (does the knowledge actually explain the context given in the stem material?) and whether the integration of the knowledge is done **effectively** (i.e. is it clear and convincing?)

The verdict

Answer 1 is a Level 1 response. Although the knowledge is clear, accurate and detailed, it is not linked explicitly to the stem material. The 'magnet effect' would pull the answer toward Level 2 due to the answer mentioning hallucinations, but the lack of appropriate and effective application of the knowledge would keep it in Level 1 with 2 marks.

Answer 2 is a Level 2 response. The knowledge is also clear, accurate and detailed but this time there is an appropriate application of this knowledge to the question. So, a glance at the other criteria would tell us it is clear, coherent and makes good use of terminology. We wouldn't expect more for a 4-mark answer, so this would get all 4 marks.

Application questions (AO2: 4 mark questions)

Level	Marks	Knowledge	Application	Organisation	Specialist terminology
2	3-4	Clear, detailed and mostly accurate	Appropriate and effective	Generally coherent	Effective use of terminology
1	1-2	Lacking accuracy and detail	Not always effective	Lacks clarity	Either absent or inappropriate
0	0	No relevant content			

Examiners are canny folk. You can't fool them by a couple of brief throwaway references to the stem material. They'll be looking closely to see if you have *really* engaged with it before they award you a mark in the higher-level band.

Step 1

Evaluation /discussion questions can come in many different forms and with many different tariffs (e.g. 2, 3, 4 or 6 marks), therefore an examiner will adjust what he or she expects in an answer. The question below asks for two evaluative points and effectively offers three marks for each. Therefore, he or she will expect a reasonable amount of clear **detail** and for the point to be made **effectively**.

Training task 3

Explain two strengths and/or limitations of the dopamine hypothesis as an explanation of schizophrenia. **(6 marks)**

Answer 1

Leucht et al. (2013) carried out a meta–analysis of 212 studies that had compared the effectiveness of different antipsychotic drugs (that block dopamine transmission in the brain) against a control group that received a placebo instead of the antipsychotic drugs. They found that the antipsychotic drugs were more effective than the placebo in relieving the positive symptoms of schizophrenia.

Antipsychotic drugs do not alleviate hallucinations and delusions in all schizophrenia patients. Noll (2009) found this is the case in about one–third of the people who have these symptoms. Noll also found that some people who experience hallucinations and delusions actually have normal levels of dopamine.

Answer 2

The dopamine hypothesis is supported by research evidence, e.g. Leucht et al. (2013) carried out a meta–analysis of 212 studies that compared the effectiveness of antipsychotic drugs against a placebo. They found that the antipsychotic drugs were more effective than the placebo in relieving the positive symptoms of schizophrenia. Because antipsychotic drugs block dopamine transmission this supports the claim that excess dopamine activity is a causal factor in schizophrenia.

Noll (2009) provides evidence that challenges the dopamine hypothesis explanation of schizophrenia. He found that antipsychotic drugs do not alleviate hallucinations and delusions in about one–third of the people who have these symptoms. Noll also found that some people who experience hallucinations and delusions actually have normal levels of dopamine. This suggests that dopamine cannot be the sole neurotransmitter involved in schizophrenia.

Step 2

Next, the examiner will look at how well the point is **organised** (does it make sense and is it a **coherent** as a strength or limitation of the topic it refers to?) Does the candidate make it clear why this is a strength or limitation?

Finally the examiner will address the question of **specialist terminology**. They are looking for evidence that a candidate is familiar with the terms that are commonly used within a particular topic, e.g. 'antipsychotic drugs' rather than just 'drugs' and 'placebo' rather than 'something else'.

The verdict

Answer 1 is a Level 1 response worth 2 marks. Working from the bottom level, it includes some detail, but the answer appears to be focused on how effective the treatment is without explaining how it is relevant to the question. It is clear and organised with use of specialist terminology (which pushes it to top of Level 1) but the lack of 'effectiveness' keeps it at Level 1.

Answer 2 is a Level 3 response worth 6 marks. It is a crafted version of Answer 1, but this time with a lead-in phrase that explains the nature of the strength and/or limitation, and a conclusion that explains the significance of the critical point (i.e. making it effective).

Now we've covered the basics of marking, we're going to ramp it up a bit and stick all the constituent parts together in an essay, and even better, you get to mark it!

The question on the next page contains all three components, AO1, AO2 and AO3. In essay questions with this 'additional' AO2 component, AQA nominally assign 6 marks for AO1, 4 for AO2 and 6 for AO3. Although we would not expect the division of content to exactly reflect these weightings, there should be a proportional division that is roughly along these lines.

Using the mark allocation table at the bottom of the next page, try to work out the correct mark for this essay. We've had a go at this as well, and you can find our suggested mark on page 240.

Evaluation questions (AO3: 6 mark questions)

Level	Marks	Evaluation/ discussion	Organisation	Specialist terminology
3	5-6	Clear and effective	Coherent and well-organised	Used effectively
2	3-4	Mostly effective	Mostly clear and organised	Used appropriately
1	1-2	Lacks detail and/or explanation	Poorly organised	Absent or used inappropriately
0	0	No relevant content		

Training task 4

Ben and his friends had gone to a music festival for the weekend. While at the festival, he was persuaded by his friends to take cocaine, a drug that elevates dopamine levels in the brain. Ben reacted badly to the drug. He started hearing voices in his head and was convinced that somebody or something that he was unable to see was following him. His reaction to the drug worried his parents because Ben's elder brother was a diagnosed schizophrenic.

With reference to Ben's psychotic reaction to the drug, discuss biological explanations of schizophrenia. **(16 marks)**

Answer

Genetic explanations claim that schizophrenia is inherited through a person's genes. For example, family studies have shown that schizophrenia is more common among biological relatives of someone with schizophrenia than among people who do not share genes with someone with the disorder. This is why Ben's parents are so concerned because his brother has schizophrenia. Also, adoption studies, e.g. Tienari et al. (2000) have shown that adopted children are more likely to become schizophrenic if their biological parents have schizophrenia than if their adoptive parents have the disorder.

The dopamine hypothesis of schizophrenia claims that the disorder is a consequence of having too much dopamine in certain areas of brain. This excess of dopamine leads to the positive symptoms of schizophrenia, such as the hallucinations and delusions typical of the disorder. Ben has an excess of dopamine in his brain because he has taken cocaine. The revised dopamine hypothesis extends the idea that dopamine is important in schizophrenia by claiming that the cognitive impairments found in schizophrenia are caused by a deficit of dopamine in pathways in the frontal lobes of the brain. Schizophrenia has also been shown to have neural correlates, in that certain parts of the brain, such as the prefrontal cortex, have been found to correlate with schizophrenic behaviour. There is also evidence (Cannon et al., 2014) that schizophrenia is linked to a reduction in grey matter in the brain. Other research has shown that schizophrenics also have a reduction in white matter in pathways between the prefrontal cortex and the hippocampus. It is possible that both Ben and his brother have these deficits, making them more vulnerable to psychoses such as schizophrenia.

A problem for twin studies is that twins, particularly identical twins, are usually treated more similarly than children that are not twins, so it is possible that the greater likelihood of an identical twin becoming schizophrenic if the other twin is schizophrenic is more to do with this rather than any shared genes.

There are also problems for the dopamine hypothesis explanation because antipsychotics, which block dopamine transmission at dopamine receptors do not work with all schizophrenics. Noll (2009) found that about one-third of patients with schizophrenia experienced no reduction in their symptoms when taking antipsychotic medication.

Vita et al. (2012) carried out a meta-analysis of 19 studies, involving over 800 patients with schizophrenia and over 700 healthy controls. They found that the schizophrenic patients had a greater loss of grey matter than did the healthy control group.

Marking notes

Knowledge is (tick one):

Level 4   Level 1

Level 3   Level 0

Level 2

Evaluation is (tick one):

Level 4   Level 1

Level 3   Level 0

Level 2

Application is (tick one):

Level 4   Level 1

Level 3   Level 0

Level 2

Organisation is (tick one):

Level 4   Level 1

Level 3   Level 0

Level 2

Use of specialist terminology (tick one):

Level 4   Level 1

Level 3   Level 0

Level 2

Final level of Answer 1 (Circle one)

4   3   2   1   0

Final mark awarded for Answer 1

Level	Marks	Knowledge	Evaluation	Application	Organisation	Specialist terminology
Essay questions (16 mark questions)						
4	13-16	Accurate and generally well-detailed	Thorough and effective	Appropriate. Links to stem explained	Coherent, well organised	Used effectively
3	9-12	Evident with some occasional inaccuracies	Apparent and mostly effective	Appropriate. Links to knowledge not always explained	Mostly clear and organised	Mostly used effectively
2	5-8	Some knowledge is present. Lacks accuracy in places	Partly effective but mostly descriptive	Application is partial	Lacks clarity and organisation in places	Used inappropriately on occasions
1	1-4	Limited with many inaccuracies	Limited, poorly focused or absent	Application is limited or absent	Lacks clarity and poorly organised	Either absent or used inappropriately
0	0	No relevant content				

Training task 4: A review

When determining a mark for essays such as this, an examiner will make use of a mark allocation table similar to the one on the page opposite. This table contains the different criteria that would describe an answer at the various levels associated with different marks. If you look at this table, you will find references to several different 'skills' associated with an effective answer.

Description - First, the examiner might make a judgement on the descriptive content of the essay or the 'knowledge' skill. In this case they must consider how accurate and detailed is the description of biological explanations of schizophrenia. The examiner would expect at least two explanations (note the plural 'explanations' in the question). Including *more* than two, however, could run the risk of making each explanation less-detailed than it should be.

The answer opposite covers three appropriate explanations, genetic, the dopamine hypothesis and neural correlates. The description is accurate and reasonably well-detailed. It would have been a little more effective to have covered two explanations in greater detail, but this is still '**Accurate and generally well-detailed**' (**Level 4**).

Evaluation - The 'discuss' command indicates the need to evaluate these biological explanations of schizophrenia but to do so in a more discursive way. The evaluative content of this answer is less well-developed than the descriptive content, so would be described as 'apparent' rather than 'thorough'. For the three critical points to be described as 'effective', the answer should include a more discursive treatment of the points being made, perhaps by offering counterpoints, implications of a critical point and so on. The most appropriate descriptor for the evaluative content is therefore '**Apparent and mostly effective**' (**Level 3**).

Application – As this question includes an application component, (Ben's reaction to the drug), the answer must go further than just describing and evaluating biological explanations of schizophrenia. It must also use this knowledge in the context of the stem material. This answer does make some reference to Ben's psychotic reaction, but does not really explain *why* each of these explanations offer any informed insight into Ben's schizophrenic symptoms. This component appears a little speculative, and the lack of explanation would indicate a **Level 2** answer ('**Application is partial**').

Organisation – Some A level psychology essays appear to lack planning or organisation and appear instead as a series of disconnected thoughts and information that may or may not be directly addressing the question set. Well organised answers allow the examiner to follow your train of thought and demonstrate a clear and logical development of your answer to the question. This answer is clear, it covers appropriate material in a logical manner, first describing explanations and then evaluating them. However, the lack of a discursive element and the use of speculation and assertion rather than explanation for the application component means this would be seen as '**Mostly clear and organised**' (**Level 3**).

Specialist terminology – A characteristic of psychology is the special language it uses. Why, for example, do we talk about 'neural correlates' when we just mean 'the brain', and why talk about 'genetic explanations' rather just saying 'parents pass it on to their children'. The answer is 'precision', and that is what is being assessed here. Psychological language is '**used effectively**', which adds authority to the answer, and puts this into **Level 4** for this criterion.

Overall, this is a mixture of Level 4 (Description, Specialist terminology), Level 3 (Evaluation, Organisation) and Level 2 (Application). This mix of levels locates this answer in Level 3 overall. We then need to decide whereabouts in Level 3 we place this particular answer. To do this we use the 'Magnet Effect' (see p223). Is the answer closer to the Level 4 criteria or the Level 2 criteria? This is clearly closer to a Level 4 answer than a Level 2 answer (i.e. 11 or 12), but perhaps not quite at the top.

Final mark: Level 3 (11/16)

Level	Knowledge
4	Accurate and generally well-detailed
3	Evident, with some occasional inaccuracies
2	Some knowledge is present. Lacks accuracy in places
1	Limited, with many inaccuracies
0	No relevant content

Level	Application
4	Thorough and effective
3	Apparent and mostly effective
2	Partly effective but mostly descriptive
1	Limited, poorly focused or absent
0	No relevant content

Level	Evaluation
4	Appropriate. Links to stem explained
3	Appropriate. Links to knowledge not always explained
2	Application is partial
1	Application is limited or absent
0	No relevant content

Level	Organisation
4	Coherent, well organised
3	Mostly clear and organised
2	Lacks clarity and organisation in places
1	Lacks clarity and poorly organised
0	No relevant content

Level	Specialist terminology
4	Used effectively
3	Mostly used effectively
2	Used inappropriately on occasions
1	Either absent or used inappropriately
0	No relevant content

Activities: suggested answers

Chapter 1 Research Methods

Content analysis p.6–7
Three for you to try: 1. (a) For example, females or males with long hair, dancing, using weapons.
(b) Choose which Disney films, choose coding categories by watching one film, watch all the films and tally the occurrences of each coding category.
(c) The decisions about behaviours may be subjective. The categories should be clearly operationalised and examples given, so that different observers can code behaviour in the same way.
(d) People in different cultures may be portrayed with different hairstyles and this may not be gender stereotyping. Categories should be chosen which are not culturally relative, such as height, bicep diameter, length of eyelashes.
(e) Examples would be collected, such as screenshots, to illustrate the categories, instead of counting.
2. B

3. 1D, 2E, 3B, 4A, 5C

Case studies p.8–9
Three for you to try: 1. (a) She could find some secondary published data relating to the questions she was asking teenagers. She could then see if her data matched the findings of previous research. Alternatively, she could send out a questionnaire to teenagers in other youth clubs around the country, and compare results of her group with the others.

(b) Case study advantage: A detailed description of migrants' personal lives will catch people's attention and induce an empathetic response. Disadvantage: The family he chooses may not have interesting stories to tell, or may not speak very good English, or may not be telling the truth. Statistical data advantage: Gives an overview of the migrant situation in Northern France, which is useful for policy makers. Disadvantage: May be biased or incomplete data as aid organisations and police have different political interests in the situation.

2. Researchers should keep checking that HM was happy to continue with tasks and stop if he wasn't. Ask next of kin for consent. Ask other experts to monitor research independently to make sure it wasn't likely to distress HM.

3. C

Reliability p.10–11
Three for you to try: 1. (a) For example: 'How many hours a day do you spend doing your homework?'
(b) 'How do household responsibilities affect your attendance at school?'

2. (a) The scores for 4 out of 5 behaviours are different for the two observers. The scores for observer 1 are higher than observer 2 for most of the behaviours. There are large differences particularly for behaviours D and E.
(b) They could calculate a correlation coefficient, and could test the significance of the correlation.
(c) The behavioural categories may not be clearly operationalised. Observer 1 may be more biased against particular politicians and notice aggressive behaviours more than observer 2.
(d) They could make sure the behavioural categories are clear and independent, without any overlap, and with examplars. They could train the observers to make sure they are consistently interpreting behaviours.

3. 1C, 2A, 3B, 4E, 5D, 6F

Validity p.12–13
Two for you to try: 1. D

2. He could ensure the concurrent validity of these tests by comparing the data obtained by self-report with some more objective measurement of the same behaviour. This could, for example, involve assessment by others (e.g. by tutors) or by observation of their actual behaviour. If these alternative assessments produce similar results to the cognitive and personality tests, then these tests can be seen to be valid.

Ensure the young offenders know their responses will be anonymous and confidential, so they will be more honest, avoiding social desirability bias and improving internal validity. OR Ensure sample of young offenders represents the population, by using random or stratified sampling, so findings can be generalised, improving population validity.

Features of science p.14–15
Two for you to try: 1. No, she should not take it seriously. For example: Scientific theory should be based on empirical research – the quiz is based on stereotypes rather than evidence. Scientific evidence should be objective – the quiz comes up with percentages which sound scientific but are probably based on subjective views of 'typical' male and female responses. Scientific theory should lead to testable hypotheses – the quiz gives a percentage but what does this mean? Which 72% of Rachel's brain is male? This appears untestable, and therefore unfalsifiable, and so lacks scientific validity.

2. A

Probability p.16
Two for you to try: 1. (a) Null: there is no difference between cats and dogs in their puzzle-solving ability. Alternative: Cats solve the puzzle more quickly than dogs. Or a non-directional alternative: Cats and dogs differ in their time taken to solve the puzzle.
(b) Null: Rats and lizards are equally affectionate. Alternative: Lizards demonstrate different numbers and types of affectionate behaviours from rats.

2. (a) Null hypothesis: There is no difference in aggressive behaviour between children who observe aggressive or non-aggressive models. Alternative hypothesis: Children who observe aggressive models will be show more aggressive behaviour than those who observe non-aggressive models.
(b) Null hypothesis: There is no difference in conformity between participants in groups with different numbers of confederates (or different levels of unanimity, or different difficulties of task). Alternative hypothesis: There is a difference…
(c) Null hypothesis: There is no difference in the amount of time the baby monkeys spend on the wire or cloth mothers. Alternative hypothesis: There is a difference…

Statistical tests p.17
One for you to try: A

Tests of correlation p.20
One for you to try: (a) There is a weak positive correlation between the two variables. As openness to experience increases, liking for sci-fi films also increase. There is a broad range of variability of liking for sci-fi films, but less variability of scores for openness to experience.
(b) They are testing for correlation rather than difference, and the data is non-parametric as scores from a Likert scale are ordinal. The data is related as each participant provides two scores.

Chi-squared test p.21
One for you to try: (a)

	Better	Not	**Row totals**
Self help	24	16	40
CBT	23	1	24
Exercise	8	8	16
Column totals	55	25	80

(b) There is an association between the type of treatment (self help, CBT or exercise) and whether patients with mild depression feel better or not. OR There is a difference between proportions of patients feeling better or not depending on the type of treatment given (self help, CBT or exercise).
(c) $(3-1) \times (2-1) = 2 \times 1 = 2$
(d) As the observed value of chi-squared (12.24) is greater than the critical value (4.60) (df = 2, $p<0.05$), there is a significant association between the type of treatment and whether patients feel better or not.

Reporting investigations p.22–23
Two for you to try: 1. D, C, E, H, J, F, B, G, A

2. For example: This study aimed to test whether innate personality characteristics of individuals are the cause of aggressive behaviour in prisons. In a controlled observation, we investigated the behaviour of student volunteers randomly allocated to roles as guards or prisoners in a simulated prison over a 2-week period, and were de-individuated by the use of uniforms, numbers and sunglasses. 'Guards' rapidly took an aggressive role, while 'prisoners' initially tried to resist but were controlled by increasingly harsh psychological means by 'guards'; two 'prisoners' became distressed and were removed early and the observation was aborted after six days. These findings support our hypothesis that situational factors determine behaviour more than innate individual differences. There are implications for the operation of prisons, as guards should be trained to keep order without abusing prisoners.

Chapter 2 Issues and debates in psychology

Gender in psychology: Gender bias p.24–25
One for you to try: Asch's sample only contained men yet his conclusions in relation to conformity are applied to explain conformity of both sexes. This is an example of androcentrism as Asch views the world from a male centred point of view and the findings of his study (based only on males) are used as the standard or norm to explain psychological experiences of both sexes. Furthermore, there is also the possibility of beta bias, as Asch has minimised (ignored) the differences between males and females and assumed there was no need to use female participants, when in fact females may conform differently to males.

Research methods: (a) They could advertise at parent and toddler groups where caregivers meet during the day, asking for parents of young children to contact them, and recruit a volunteer sample.
(b) More mothers than fathers may attend these groups, and it may be harder to recruit men. The researchers could visit different types of groups, or baby clinics at doctor's surgeries, to recruit a more representative sample.

Culture in psychology: Cultural bias p.26-27
One for you to try: Limitation: Mead was judging and assessing the different cultures from a different perspective, for example how she viewed aggressive behaviour was influenced by her own cultural norms and this could have distorted and exaggerated the

differences between the cultures that she was studying. Strength: However, Mead also demonstrates cultural relativism as she immersed herself in the culture which she examined and tried to understand the way in which different cultures/tribes see the world.

Research methods: The participants would not have understood how their data was going to be used, as they would not know about publication of research in scientific journals, so this issue of informed consent is tricky. Mead could have told them what she had written about them, to check they were happy with it, and asked if she could tell other people in her country about them.

Free will and determinism p.28–29

One for you to try: Andrew's behaviour may be the result of environmental determinism (classical and/ or operant conditioning) because he has learned his aggressive behaviour from his older brother who was excluded for hitting another student. Furthermore, Andrew's behaviour may be caused by biological determinism, as an aggressive gene may run in his family, as his older brother is also aggressive.

Research methods: In an experiment, the IV is systematically varied by the researcher in order to measure the effect on the DV. If other variables are properly controlled, this allows the researcher to conclude that the change in the IV has caused the change in the DV – the principle of scientific determinism.

The nature-nurture debate p.30–31

One for you to try: There are different reasons you could suggest here. Firstly, despite having the same genes, Rainbow and CC might have different diets and therefore nurture may be one reasons for the differences found between these two cats. Furthermore, epigenetics may also play a role and CC's life experiences (her diet) may switch on/off a gene for metabolism which causes the differences seen in these two cats.

Research methods: The results appear to support the nature side of the nature–nurture debate. This is because the concordance rate is strong in MZ twins (69%), where there is a greater genetic relatedness (100%). However, the results also highlight the role of nurture, as the concordance rate is not 100% (only 69%).

Holism and reductionism p.32–33

One for you to try: Fred's suggestion relies on operant conditioning, reward and punishment, which is an environmentally reductionist approach. It breaks down behaviours into stimulus (reward) and response (increasing the likelihood of repeating the behaviour). Mary takes a more holistic view, considering different levels of explanation of behaviour such as modelling (seeing Fred tidying), cognitive processes (realising how lucky he is) and social comparison (thinking about other children who don't even have a room).

Research methods: (a) A field experiment
(b) Anxiety improved accuracy of recall in a real-life bank robbery.
(c) Victim / bystander
(d) It might trigger stressful memories by reminding participants of what they had experienced several months before. They should also be assured of confidentiality.
(e) People may pay more attention to real events than to artificial situations in a lab or on a video. Only a low level of anxiety can be induced in a lab due to ethical concerns, whereas real life experiences may have been much more stressful, causing alertness due to the adrenaline response.
(f) Lab experiments control extraneous variables so that all participants see the same event from the same angle and distance. Also they can be replicated.
(g) Variables are controlled to such a degree that the research loses mundane realism and ecological validity as the task becomes over-simplified or artificial.

Idiographic and nomothetic approaches to psychological investigation p.34–35

One for you to try: An idiographic approach focuses on individuals and emphasises uniqueness. The psychologist who conducted a case study on Jack is using an idiographic approach to gather qualitative data, to develop an understanding of Jack's behavioural difficulties. A nomothetic approach seeks to formulate general laws based on the study of groups. The psychologist who examined the entire student population is using a nomothetic approach to gather quantitative data, to develop a theory which can be generalised.

Research methods: (a) Observations of Jack could be analysed by tallying behavioural categories, such as 'physical aggression towards another child', or 'swearing', and turning it into quantitative data, which could be displayed as bar charts. Interviews could be transcribed and analysed using thematic analysis, allowing themes to emerge from the data by reading and re-reading the transcripts, keeping the rich, descriptive nature of this data.
(b) There are many ethical issues that should be considered here, although they need to be suitable for this case study. Informed consent is not suitable, although parental consent is. Privacy should be considered in terms of the interviews, to ensure that Jack and the teachers are in control of the information they provide. Furthermore, confidentiality should also be considered and any data from the observations should be coded to ensure that Jack, the teachers and the other pupils remain anonymous.
(c) Self-report questionnaire, with Likert scales (primary data). Scores by parents or teachers. Mathematical ability scores from test results (secondary data).
(d) They could use inferential statistical testing to see if there is a correlation between mathematical ability and self-confidence. This would be a Spearman's *rho* test of correlation for non-parametric (ordinal level) data as self-confidence will presumably be measured using a self-report Likert scale.
(e) Idiographic research gives a more detailed understanding of an individual's behaviour rather than trying to find general norms of behaviour for a large group of students. It enables many factors to be explored as they interact in one individual, in this case Jack. However, it is very time-consuming to collect in-depth data about one individual and it isn't possible to generalise about other individuals from this one case study. Nomothetic research is more efficient and data can be statistically analysed, so we can see what norms of behaviour are and how unusual particular cases may be. A combination of both approaches gives the fullest understanding.

Ethical implications of research studies and theory p.36–37

One for you to try: Research findings suggest that children at the comprehensive school were not as intelligent as those from independent schools. If published this could have much wider implications for the wider community. The researcher should therefore not identify the type of schools used. A further issue is that of debriefing and protection from psychological harm for those students who were found not to be very intelligent. This would need to be carried out in a sensitive manner and ensure confidentiality and anonymity of all data.

Research methods: (a) Nominal.
(b) Nominal data is an unsophisticated measure. This is because it does not provide any information about each of the participants, it simply places them into one of three categories (not very intelligent, moderately intelligent, not very intelligent). Therefore, we do not know the differences between individual participants.
(c) The scores for the state school are negatively skewed, with the mode higher than the median and mean. This is because there are a few extreme low scores for IQ in

state schools which have a strong effect on the mean. The mode for Independent schools is the same as for state schools, but there is a positive skew, as there are a few extremely high IQ scores in these schools, so the mean is higher than the mode.
(d) Test of difference, IQ scores treated as Interval level, independent groups. Unrelated *t*-test.

Chapter 3 Relationships

Evolutionary explanations for partner preferences p.38–39

One for you to try: According to evolutionary theory, Ashiakia will start dating Tim and not Reuben because Tim has a job, which means that he may have more resources to invest in her and any potential offspring. Furthermore, the resources may also mean that Tim is able to protect Ashiakia and any potential offspring, which makes him a more sensible choice.

Research methods: (a) Males and females emphasise different qualities in their profiles in newspaper personal ads and in what they are looking for in a potential mate.
(b) An opportunity sample. A limitation of this method would be that it could be biased. The type of newspaper would determine the type of individual advertising in the personal ads. For example, in tabloid newspaper ads males and females may act in more sex stereotypical ways, whereas in broadsheet newspapers, with a more professional readership, these differences may be less evident.
(c) An opportunity sample of four newspapers (*Times, Guardian, Daily Mirror* and *Daily Mail*) that include personal ads of males and females looking for partners was used in this study. Male and female advertisers who made reference to their own qualities (e.g. 'young', 'graduate', 'slim' etc.) when advertising for a mate were selected for analysis. Two researchers reviewed each advert as to whether advertisers were offering or looking for resources and whether they were offering or looking for personal characteristics. Coding between the two researchers was checked to ensure inter-rater reliability with only those in agreement contributing to the analysis of gender differences.

Physical attractiveness p.40–41

One for you to try: Evolutionary research suggests that males place a greater emphasis on physical attractiveness and youth, whereas females place a greater emphasis on resources and other factors. According to research in this area (e.g. Buss, 1989) males are interested in characteristics that are a sign of fertility. By having a sun tan, wearing fashionable clothes and changing the colour of her hair from grey to blonde, Lorraine is representing herself as youthful (and therefore more 'fertile') in the eyes of her date. She states that men 'aren't interested in us oldies', which is a reference to males equating physical attractiveness with youth.

Research methods: The results suggest that males place a greater emphasis on physical attractiveness and youth, whereas females place a greater emphasis on resources and other factors. Evolutionary explanations would support this trend, as males are interested in characteristics that are a sign of fertility, whereas females are interested in characteristics like resources, which can be invested in her and her potential offspring.

Self-disclosure p.42–43

One for you to try: Bobby is engaging in a lot of personal disclosure and research suggests that people should only engage in moderate personal self-disclosure in the early stages of a relationship. Chelsea may feel that Bobby discloses information indiscriminately with everyone. Chelsea on the other hand is engaging in neutral self-disclosure and Bobby may not feel like his disclosure is being reciprocated and that she is not interested in him. This would explain why both Chelsea and Bobby do not want to see one another again.

Research methods: Dindia, K., and Allen, M. (1992). Sex differences in self-disclosure: a meta-analysis, *Psychological Bulletin, 112*(1), 106-124.
Ruppel, E., Gross, C., Stoll, A., Peck, B., Allen, M. and Kim, S-Y. (2017). Reflecting on Connecting: Meta-Analysis of Differences Between Computer-Mediated and Face-to-Face Self-Disclosure. *Journal of Computer-Mediated Communication, 22*(1), 18-34.

Attraction: Filter theory p.44–45

One for you to try: The first filter is social demography. Factors such as age, social background and location determine the likelihood of people meeting in the first place. Tommy is drawn to female students in his psychology class, so these are likely to be of the same age and come from the same geographical region.

The second filter is similarity of attitudes. This particularly important at the beginning of a relationship with individuals being attracted to others who share the same attitudes and values. Tommy is drawn to those students who share his passion for Korean Hip Hop music.

The final filter is complementarity of needs, with individuals being attracted to those others meet their needs. Because Tommy likes to impress with his knowledge of Korean Hip Hop, he is particularly drawn to one girl who respects his knowledge of Hip Hop and listens intently when he talks about it.

Research methods: (a) Nominal
(b) A chi-squared test. The data fits the criteria for this test. The level of measurement used in nominal, independent (each individual contributes data to only one cell of the table) and researchers are interested in a possible association between gender and the likelihood of being in a long-distance relationship.
(c) Males and females are equally likely to be in a 'non long-distance' relationship of under 50 miles (20 males, 22 females). However, females are four times more likely (48 females compared to 12 males) to be in a long-distance relationship of greater than 50 miles.

Social exchange theory p.46–47

One for you to try: The social exchange theory of relationships claims that individuals compare their current relationship with alternative and previous relationships. If their current relationship does not match their expectations based on previous relationships, or if a more attractive alternative presents itself, they may terminate the current relationship. Nick finds his relationship with Ekaterina less rewarding than his previous relationship with Ann. Likewise, he considers a relationship with his sister-in-law to be potentially more rewarding than his current relationship, so is tempted to leave.

Research methods: (a) There is a positive correlation between profitability scores in romantic relationships and relationship satisfaction scores.
(b) This was to counterbalance the two questionnaires in order to prevent any systematic order effects from completing one questionnaire before the other.
(c) Yes, the correlation is significant at <0.05. The n value is 24 and the correlation of 0.47 is greater than the critical value of 0.407.
(d) On the basis of this significant correlation, the researcher would conclude that there is a positive relationship between the perceived profitability of outcomes in romantic relationships and relationship satisfaction.

Equity theory p.48–49

One for you to try: According to Schafer and Keith (1980) women often feel under-benefited during the child-rearing years and therefore it is expected that marital satisfaction will dip during this period. This is evident from the fact that Emmanuela did all the chores while the children were growing up while Chris relaxed. However, usually during the empty-nest stage (when children have left home) husbands and wives should perceive their relationship to be equitable.

Now, Emmanuela would expect Chris to take an equal share of the chores, which he has not, and therefore she feels under-benefited, which explains her growing dissatisfaction.

Research methods: (a) Males 12.1 Females 10.7
(b) As the mean satisfaction score for females is lower than it is for males, we can conclude that, among married couples, wives' marital satisfaction is less than husbands' marital satisfaction.
(c) Both males and females appear to show a positive correlation between equity and marital satisfaction. High equity scores are associated with high marital satisfaction scores and low equity scores are associated with low marital satisfaction scores.

The investment model of relationships p.50–51

One for you to try: Commitment is high in partners who have high levels of satisfaction and investment. Wendy is irritated by her boyfriend's lack of interest and his wish to spend time with his mates. As they still live with their parents, neither Wendy nor her boyfriend have invested much in the relationship. Janice has a boyfriend who is very fond of her and they have invested in buying a flat together.

The model also proposes that commitment is low where high quality alternatives exist. As Wendy is attracted to a doctor at her surgery, she would be less committed to her current relationship and more likely to leave.

Research methods: (a) Quantitative data measures behaviour numerically, for example the measurement of a dependent variable (such as a memory score) in an experiment. On the other hand, qualitative data is non-numerical, such as answers to open questions or in material such as letters and photographs.
(b) Qualitative data would be more revealing because of the depth of insight it would give into how investment size, quality of alternatives and satisfaction contributed to satisfaction among respondents.
(c) Tell me about how you might think about your investment in a relationship when making decisions about your commitment to that relationship.
(d) A thematic analysis is a way of grouping qualitative responses of participants into a number of identifiable themes.
(e) The researcher begins by identifying features of the data that appear interesting, for example a number of respondents may mention the importance of relationship satisfaction or being tempted by alternative partners. This data can then be sorted into overarching themes which may identify the importance of the different aspects which contribute to commitment in romantic relationships.

Relationship breakdown p.52–53

One for you to try: The dyadic phase is when one partner expresses their dissatisfaction to the other. Tola has gone through the dyadic phase because she has tried talking to Tamer to explain she was unhappy with the relationship. The social phase is when the dissatisfied partner starts to involve others outside the relationship, seeking their advice and support. Tola has moved to the social phase by talking to Abena, who tells her that 'He was no good for you anyway'.

Research methods: There is a whole range of ethical issues that the research should consider here, including: privacy, confidentiality, right to withdraw, protection from harm, informed consent. One issue the researcher would need to consider is privacy. The participants should control the flow of information that is given during the interview and not feel pressured to answer questions – especially on this sensitive topic. Furthermore, the research should consider protection from harm, as this is an emotional topic. The researchers should let the participant know that at any stage of the experiment they can withdraw.

Virtual relationships in social media p.54–55

One for you to try: There are two factors that could contribute to Dion's improved confidence and success online. Firstly, there is the absence of gates, which are barriers that limit his opportunities as a shy male. Furthermore, he may feel like he can reveal more intimate and personal information online and control the information he provides about himself, which may provide him with an opportunity to 'stretch the truth' in an effort to project a self that is more socially desirable. It is for these reasons why he finds it easier to conduct his relationships online.

Research methods: The aim of this study was to explore the impact of gating features on subsequent attraction. A volunteer sample of thirty-one male and thirty-one female university students engaged in two 20-min meetings with a partner. Results showed that when they interacted in an Internet chat room first and then met face-to-face, it was the initial quality of the interaction that determined subsequent liking. This was not the case when they interacted in person on both occasions. The conclusion from this study was that in face-to-face interactions, it is the more superficial gating features that dominate liking and overwhelm other factors.

Parasocial relationships p.56–57

One for you to try: Margie shows the characteristics of an anxious-ambivalent attachment style. Anxious-ambivalent attachment results in individuals who turn to TV characters as a way of satisfying their unmet relational needs. Margie has never had a serious relationship and so she has formed a parasocial bond with the main character from the soap.
A characteristic of attachment is protest at disruption of the attachment bond. This is evident in Margie's distress when the subject of her parasocial relationship was killed off in a dramatic Christmas special.

Research methods: (a) They might have posted a notice on the social media page for first-year students at the university, asking anybody interested in taking part in the study to get in touch.
(b) A limitation is that the use of social media as a sampling method may bias the sample in some important way. For example, people reliant on social media may be more prone to having parasocial relationships than those who do not rely so much on social media.
(c) The purpose of debriefing is so participants have the chance to air any concerns and so the researcher can make sure there is no lasting impact of participation. The researcher can explain what the study was about and ask if the participant had any concerns. They can then reassure them that their data will be kept confidential, and remind them that they can withdraw their data at any time.
(d) Confidentiality. The researcher could use participant numbers rather than names and ensure that no personal information is taken that might link an individual to their data. This data should be kept in a password protected file on a locked computer.

Chapter 4 Gender

Sex-role stereotypes and androgyny p.58–59

One for you to try: People learn sex-role stereotypes from parents or society. Robin has been protected her/his parents from stereotypes about behaviour and clothes, and therefore enjoys a variety of typically 'boy' and 'girl' toys.

Many people think it is healthy to teach boys and girls stereotyped behaviour. Robin is free to explore all sorts of toys and clothes and play with boys and girls, so according to Bem, Robin will be more psychologically healthy as he/she will grow up more androgynous.

Research methods: (a) Self-report scales are easy to administer and to score, and can be very reliable. The

BSRI has good test-retest reliability, as tested by Bem in the 1980s, who found a correlation of up to .94 over four weeks. However, the scale may lack validity as there can be intervening variables which affect the validity of the scores, and it has been suggested that self-esteem is being measured by the BSRI rather than androgyny. In addition, the items are all oriented the same way (positive = high score) so a positive response bias will affect the total scores for each subscale of femininity and masculinity.
(b) It should be given to the same participants again after a few weeks. Scores can be compared to assess test-retest reliability. A correlation of over 0.8 is considered to be good reliability.
(c) By making sure that items are clear and unambiguous, so they cannot be interpreted in different ways, and by giving the same instructions to participants.

The role of chromosomes and hormones in sex and gender p.60–61

One for you to try: (a) Timmy could have Klinefelter's syndrome, which is XXY.
(b) Timmy is likely to be infertile due to low testosterone.

Research methods: (a) 29 – 8.6 = 20.4
(b) 5-nmol/L is well above the normal range for women so a BTC above 5-nmol/L would indicate some abnormality.
(c) 1.67 x 3 = 5.01-nmol/L so she could be out of the acceptable range. This would mean she would not be allowed to compete as a woman unless she used hormone suppression.

Cognitive explanations of gender development: Kohlberg's theory p.62–63

One for you to try: Pre-operational thinking. Phoenix thinks that as the doll's appearance changes, its gender changes too. This is characteristic of the gender labelling stage of Kohlberg's theory, which is generally age 2–3, so Phoenix's understanding fits what is expected for a child age 3. Some confusion remains during the gender stability stage at age 4–7, as children still go by outward appearances, although they know that gender is stable over time. When they get to the gender constancy stage at about age 6 they understand conservation.

Research methods: (a) Boys: 17/27 = 63%, girls 21/27 = 78%.
(b) Boys: 5, girls: 5.5
(c) Chi-squared, as it is nominal data (categories), test of difference, independent data (males, females, three stages)
(d) The children may have seen boys and girls playing football, so the football question would not be a good measure of adherence to gendered behaviour. There were different numbers of boys and girls in each age group, for example there were eight 2-year-old boys but only four 2-year-old girls, so this is an unrepresentative sample. The children may be answering as they think the researcher expects them to (demand characteristics) or may be in a 'pretend' mode, answering questions based on this rather than what they really think about human gender. Children may see women dressing like men more than they see men dressing like women, so this could affect their answers to the questions.

Cognitive explanations of gender development: Gender schema theory p.64–65

One for you to try: She could provide models, such as real male nurses or female firefighters, or books featuring counter-stereotypical roles that children might then want to imitate, as they will form new mental representations of male and female dress. She could challenge their existing schemas directly, by saying 'we are all going to be superheroes today' or labelling the clothes 'nurses costumes for boys and girls'.

Research methods: (a) Repeated measures
(b) The role portrayed (firefighter, teacher, nurse, chemist) will affect whether children remember the correct gender of the people in the pictures or not.
(c) Gender schemas are resilient so existing schemas (men as firefighters, women as nurses) have caused cognitive distortions (remembering incorrectly) and selective memory (not remembering counter-stereotypical answers).
(d) Adults can suppress stereotypical responses more due to social desirability, and may have encountered more diverse examples, so may have made fewer errors.
(e) Other examples they have seen during the week e.g. books, films. If children experience different films, some may have changed their schemas during the week and others won't have, so the results would be less valid.

Psychodynamic explanations of gender development p.66–67

One for you to try: B

Research methods: (a) For example, Freud's case of Little Hans: can't be generalised, and data collected very subjectively and mostly via Hans' father.
(b) Freud claimed he 'didn't understand women'; alpha bias – women seen as inferior to men.
(c) Findings in case studies are interpreted retrospectively, hypotheses cannot be tested in controlled experiments.
(d) Predictions from the theory are not supported by evidence, e.g. children of same-sex couples develop sexual identities normally.
(e) Data suggests an association between childhood experiences and later sexual behaviour, but this is correlation not causation.

Social learning theory as applied to gender development p.68–69

One for you to try: Children learn from models, and preferentially imitate same-sex models. So if boys see boys taking leading roles in the books, they are more likely to believe they can do the same, whereas girls lack these models in picture books, so may believe leading is not gender-appropriate behaviour for them. Children store mental representations of behaviour they have seen, which will affect them in the future. By self-direction, children internalise gender-appropriate behaviour and actively direct their own behaviour. This means boys may be more likely to take a lead in the future than girls.

Research methods: (a) Skelton, C. (2018), Schooling the Boys: Masculinities and Primary Education. Educating Boys, Learning Gender. (Florence, KY, Taylor and Francis, 2001) pp.47-51.
(b) Tontodonato, P. & Crew, B. (1992). 'Dating violence, social learning theory, and gender: A multivariate analysis.' Violence and victims. 7 (1) pp.3-14.

Cultural and media influences on gender roles p.70–71

AO2: One for you to try (a) 90/2.5 = 36 seconds
(b) 90 × 60 = 5,400 seconds male talking time. 36 × 40 = 1,440 seconds female talking time. 5,400 + 1,440 = 6,840 seconds total student talking time. Percentage female = 1,400/6,840 ×100 = 20.5%
(c) Female time = 1,400 × 3 = 4,200 seconds. Percentage female = 4,200/6,840 × 100 = 61.4%.

Research methods: (a) Decide on a sample, e.g. TV advertisements on ITV over one weekend. Carry out a pilot observation the previous weekend to decide on behavioural categories. Make a tally chart, watch the advertisements, tally the behaviours.

(b)
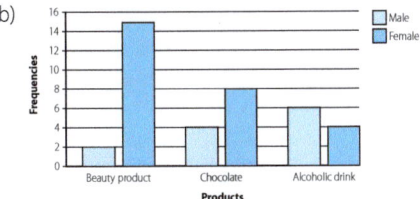

(c) Males are slightly more likely to start a conversation than females, but much more likely to give information than females. Females were shown expressing emotion quite often, whereas males didn't at all. The most common behaviour for males (the mode) was giving information, whereas for females it was expressing emotion.

Atypical gender development p.72–73

One for you to try: Gender stereotypes are societal expectations about 'masculine' and 'feminine' behaviour, which can be explicit or implicit. Carol desperately wanted to be a boy, and felt she was better at 'boys stuff' than her brothers. She still describes herself as 'not girly', i.e. not fitting stereotypes of feminine behaviour, although she became reconciled to being a girl at puberty. Becks similarly 'never felt properly feminine', and even doubted her reproductive function because her personality and height fitted masculine stereotypes rather than feminine. Gender dysphoria is the feeling of discomfort with the assigned gender. Not fitting the stereotypes could make someone feel that they are in the wrong body. And Adam experienced bullying for being a boy with stereotypically feminine attributes. He points out that the stereotypes should be fought, implying that this would help people to be comfortable with a range of personality traits that don't necessarily fit the stereotypes.

Research methods: (a) Interviews with Sam, with questions such as 'describe your experience of taking hormone treatment' to get qualitative data about their experience. Interviews or questionnaires from family members and Sam's doctor to find out longitudinal aspects of the case, such as how Sam liked to dress and play as a young child.
(b) Each case is unique, so it is not possible to generalise about gender dysphoria from one case. However, case studies explore the complex interactions of a number of factors, so the longitudinal and idiographic presentation of the case may shed light on how people's experience of gender can change through childhood and adolescence. This may give rise to useful research questions to be explored with a larger sample of people undergoing gender transition, maybe using questionnaires. But researchers must bear in mind that retrospective data, such as Sam's memory of experiences and feelings many years ago, may be unreliable. And the case study must protect the anonymity and confidentiality of the participant.
(c) The researcher will send the article to the editor of a scientific journal. The editor will send it to experts in the field of gender dysphoria (the peer reviewers) for their comments. They could recommend that the article should be accepted for publication as it is, or with some changes, or rejected outright. The editor will then respond to the author.
(d) Peer review ensures that published research is high quality, with valid research methods and conclusions, and is contributing something important and original to the field of gender dysphoria.

Chapter 5 Cognition and development

Piaget's theory of cognitive development p.74–75

One for you to try: (a) The child has a schema that humans who are bald on the top of their head and have long frizzy ginger hair on the side are 'clowns'. When the child sees someone with that appearance, assimilation occurs. The child incorporates this new information into its existing schema.
(b) Mark could explain to this toddler that Girish is not a clown, even though part of his appearance suggests he is. Girish is not wearing a clown's costume and isn't doing things that make people laugh. The toddler would be able to change his schema to accommodate what a clown is – has funny hair, wears a costume, makes people laugh.

Research methods: (a) The number of children in that group.

(b) Test of difference, interval data (percentages/times), independent groups (different children in each age group): unrelated *t*-test.

(c) The probability of this result arising by chance is less than 1%, so the chance of it being a real effect in the population is at least 99%.

(d) Infants prefer looking at faces to concentric circles at every age, but the difference is greater at 2–6 months than at the younger ages. The differences are significant at each age.

(e) Infants have an innate preferences for faces, showing that there are innate schemas, but the schema develops as the infant gains experience of faces and assimilates more information, so the preference grows stronger with age.

Piaget's stages of intellectual development p.76–77

One for you to try: This activity is based on a study conducted by McGhee (1976). Concrete operational children recognise that it doesn't matter if the pizza is cut into six or eight pieces, the amount of pizza doesn't change. Pre-operational children lack these conservation skills. Thus, the concrete operational child finds what Rona said funny while the six-year-old does not.

Research methods: (a) Nominal level

(b) Chi-squared test. The data are at the nominal level, and the researcher is looking for a difference. Additionally, an independent groups design has been used.

(c) The results indicate that significantly more pre-operational children are able to solve the class inclusion task if it is presented in a different way than usual (i.e. the researcher's hypothesis has been supported). The null hypothesis can be rejected at $p<0.05$.

Vygotsky's theory of cognitive development p.78–79

One for you to try: Scaffolding is how an expert helps a learner through the zone of proximal development. It is a temporary support that aims to help a learner only when necessary, and will be gradually withdrawn as the learner masters the task and is able to work independently. In this case, Beth's mum is the expert and she creates a 'scaffold' to help Beth make cakes. As Beth didn't know how to make cakes at the beginning, Beth's mum had to give her lots of help with things like scales. She also gave more explicit, clear instructions about what she had to do. As Beth mastered the task, she became more successful and so her mother gave fewer explicit instructions and eventually Beth had learned how to make cakes on her own.

Research methods:

(a)

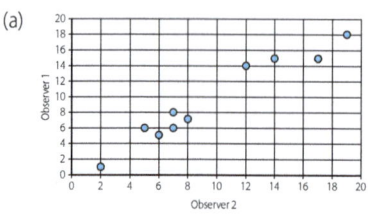

(b) Inter-observer reliability.

(c) Pearson's *r*.

Baillargeon's explanation of early infant abilities p.80–81

One for you to try: This fictitious example illustrates violation of expectation. Violation of expectation research suggests that infants will show surprise when they see an impossible event. In this case, the infant expected to see the lemmings fall off the cliff, so she looked only very briefly. Then, she got bored and stopped looking. However, when Larry the Lucky Lemming remained suspended in mid-air, this violated her expectation (that he was going to fall) and so she looked at it for longer.

Research methods: This is done to avoid the mother unconsciously communicating cues to the infant about how it should react to the stimuli which may affect the results.

The development of social cognition: Selman's theory p.82–83

One for you to try: Frank is 9 years old, so he is at the self-reflective perspective-taking stage. This means he can view his own thoughts and feelings from another person's perspective and recognise that others can do the same. So Frank thinks that the boy's father will not be angry once he realises the boy's perspective, i.e. that he ran down the road to catch a thief (not for fun). Lisa is 13 years old and so she is at the societal perspective-taking stage. This means that her personal decisions are made by referring to social conventions, including the idea that stealing is wrong. This means Lisa understands that the reason the boy's father won't be angry is because the boy wants to catch a thief, since stealing is conventionally wrong in our society.

Research methods: (a) Group A mean: 6.3 Group B mean: 3.3

(b) Group A median: 6.5, Group B median: 3

(c) Group A mode: 5, Group B mode: 3

(d) The standard deviation is a measure of dispersion, and tells us how much variation there is around the mean score. The larger the standard deviation, the more variable performance is. The standard deviations indicate that there is some variability in the performance of both groups, but slightly more in Group A.

(e) Mann-Whitney *U* test (or Unrelated *t*-test).

(f) The researcher is looking for a difference, and an independent groups design has been used. Additionally, the data are at least at the ordinal levels of measurement.

The development of social cognition: Theory of mind p.84–85

One for you to try: Given that ToM usually develops around the age of four, we might expect Kirsty's three- and six-year-old sisters to differ in their responses. If the six-year-old has a ToM, and understands that Dad won't know the tube is full of buttons, she will say 'Smarties'. However, if the three-year-old doesn't have a ToM, she will not be able to put aside her knowledge that the tube does not have Smarties in it, and so will say 'buttons' because she cannot appreciate that Dad has a separate belief to her.

Research methods:

(a)

	Non-autistic children	Autistic children
Successful at the test	23	4
Unsuccessful at the test	4	16

(b)

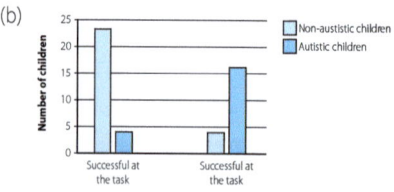

(c) 2 × 2 chi-squared test

(d) The data are at the nominal level, and an independent groups design has been used. Additionally, a difference is being looked for.

(e) A Type I error occurs when the null hypothesis is rejected when it should have been accepted.

(f) Since the significance level was set at $p<0.05$, there is less than 5% chance that a Type I error has been made (falsely rejecting the null hypothesis).

The development of social cognition: The mirror neuron system p.86–87

One for you to try: Your answer to this needs to make reference to mirror neurons (MN). Paresh observed a player being kicked on the knee. When Paresh saw this, mirror neurons reacted, and enabled him to experience the action as if it was happening to him. Presumably, Paresh's observation-response link was 'online' and he repeated the behaviour immediately. This caused his leg to react as though it had been kicked, which caused his pizza to go flying through the air.

Research methods: (a) 12/184 = 6.5%

(b) 39/87 = 44.8%

(c) 12/39 = 30.8%

Chapter 6 Schizophrenia
Classification of schizophrenia p.88–89

One for you to try: Charlotte is showing the negative symptom of speech poverty (alogia). This is characterised by the lessening of speech fluency and productivity. Her confused response, which goes off on a tangent, together with a long pause before Charlotte answers demonstrates the lack of fluency and productivity. Charlotte is also demonstrating the negative symptom of avolition, a reduction of interests and an inability to initiate purposeful behaviour. Charlotte saying she didn't want to do anything shows this characteristic reduction of interests and her admission that she just sat (a lot) shows an ability to initiate purposeful behaviour.

Research methods: (a) The patient is demonstrating positive symptoms of delusions (he is being watched and controlled by the CIA) and auditory hallucinations (commands instructing him to harm friends and family).

(b) This is an example of an idiographic approach because it is a study of a unique individual (the 19-year old male patient) who demonstrates symptoms that are unique to him rather than being general symptoms.

(c) Strength – Because this method provides in-depth insights into the nature of schizophrenia that might be overlooked by other methods. Limitation – it is difficult to generalise from individuals with schizophrenia to others with the disorder. The unique symptoms of one individual may not apply to others.

Reliability and validity in diagnosis and classification p.90–91

One for you to try: Reliability of diagnosis means that clinicians must be able to reach the same conclusions at two different points in time (test–retest reliability), or different clinicians must reach the same conclusions (inter-rater reliability). This does not necessarily indicate that these diagnoses are valid because they may be subject to gender bias, e.g. some diagnostic categories may be biased toward pathologising one gender more than another. There is also the problem of symptom overlap, as many of the symptoms of schizophrenia are also found in other disorders. Therefore, even if clinicians agree on diagnosis, they may still be subject to gender bias and the problem of symptom overlap.

Research methods:

(a)

	Genuinely schizophrenic	Not schizophrenic
Schizophrenia diagnosed	23	14
Schizophrenia not diagnosed	12	12

(b) 35/55 = 64%

(c) 12/35 = 34%

(d) (6/20) x 100 = 30%

Biological explanations for schizophrenia p.92–93

One for you to try: Pearl would be more likely to develop schizophrenia than Jade. Identical twins share the same genes, so because schizophrenia has a strong genetic component, the fact that Ruby has already been diagnosed with schizophrenia, means that Pearl has a 50% of developing the disorder. Amber and Jade are non-identical twins, sharing only half their genes. As a result, Jade is less likely to develop schizophrenia than Pearl.

Research methods: The major issue here would appear to be one of generalisation (using insights from a study of one species to understand another). Boksa (2007) claimed that we will never be able to model the complete disorder of schizophrenia in a rat as there is no such thing as a schizophrenic rat.

Psychological explanations for schizophrenia p.94–95

One for you to try: This is the double-bind theory. According to this theory, Jack receives conflicting messages about his relationship with his mother. She tells him that he is driving her mad and she can't have him living there anymore, but also maintains that he needs her and would not be better off moving to a hostel.

Research methods: (a) High EE is 196/4 = 49%. Low EE is 61/4 = 15.25%.
(b) Relapse is much more likely if participants came from high EE families. All four studies show the same thing, and so the finding is reliable.
(c) High EE is 58-32=26. Low EE is 28-0=28.
(d) The ranges are very similar to the high and low EE participants. This suggests similar variability in relapse rates (even though the means are very different).

Drug therapy p.96–97

One for you to try: A problem with many of the older 'typical' antipsychotics such as quetiapine is that patients experience side-effects, which means they make stop taking the drug.
For example, Tomasz reports that he has problems with sluggishness and believes that the drug has had an adverse effect on his sex life.
A key advantage of atypical antipsychotics is that they are less likely to produce the side-effects associated with typical antipsychotics.
Changing to an atypical antipsychotic may reduce the side-effects Tomasz has reported, which means that he is more likely to continue with his treatment and see a reduction in his symptoms.

Research methods: (a) IV = Antipsychotic drug (A, B, C, and D). DV = Amount of improvement as measured by a 7-point rating scale.
(b) The researcher's colleague's observations might be biased given his familiarity with antipsychotic medication.
(c) We do not know to what extent the schizophrenics would have shown an improvement if they had been given no medication. For example, if there was no improvement whatsoever in those schizophrenics given no medication, then a case could be made for claiming that each drug was to varying degrees 'effective'.
(d) The Mann-Whitney U test could have been used. The researcher is looking for a difference, an independent groups design has been used, and the data are at the ordinal level of measurement.

Cognitive behavioural therapy p.98–99

One for you to try: The aim of CBTp is to identify and correct distorted beliefs. The stimulus material is based on a study reported by Chadwick et al. (1996). They showed a patient video recordings of people talking and asked him to predict what would be said next. In 50 attempts, the patient failed to make any correct predictions, which appeared to be sufficient to change his belief that he did not have this ability after all.

Research methods: One of the things that meta-analysis fails to take into account is a study's quality. In good quality research looking at CBTp's effectiveness, participants are randomly allocated to treatment conditions. However, in many studies participants were not allocated in this way. Therefore, conclusions drawn from meta-analytic studies should be treated with extreme caution.

Family therapy p.100–101

One for you to try: Some schizophrenics live in families characterised by high levels of expressed emotion, e.g. criticism or over-involvement from other family members.
Joe tells Scott that his mother 'is always fussing around me' (an example of over-involvement) and his father is 'always having a go at me' (an example of criticism). Family therapy aims at reducing the level of expressed emotion within the family, as expressed emotion has been found to increase the likelihood of relapse. This would be a suitable form of therapy for Joe and his family as it would encourage family members and Joe to listen to each other and negotiate potential solutions together.

Research methods:

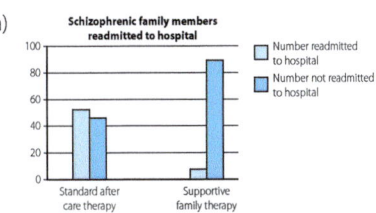

(a)

(b) 2×2 chi-squared. The researcher is looking for a difference and the data are at the nominal level of measurement. Additionally, an independent groups design has been used.
(c) 5%
(d) The calculated value of chi-squared is actually 45.3, and the result is significant beyond the 5% level. The table indicates that significantly fewer schizophrenics are readmitted to hospital following supportive family therapy than standard after care therapy.

Token economy and the management of schizophrenia p.102–103

One for you to try: One reason is that the two new patients would not have been through the preparation for the token economy. An essential part of this technique is that the tokens must first have some value attached to the tokens. This would not have happened with these new patients so they did not associate them with any desired outcomes.
A second reason is that when the token economy was suspended in the evening, appropriate responses would not have been rewarded. Because of this, the responses that were being rewarded with tokens during the day would undergo extinction during the evening. This means that each day they would have to learn the association between responses and tokens all over again.

Research methods: (a) One ethical issue is the lack of informed consent in that permission was given by the NHS trust but not by the patients themselves. They could deal with this by explaining what would happen during the study to the patients and judge from their responses whether they consented to be a part of it.
(b) They could use an independent assessor who was not aware of whether patients had taken part in the token economy trial or antipsychotic medication alone. He or she could then assess their behaviour before the study and again after the study to judge the amount of improvement over the first assessment.

An interactionist approach p.104–105

One for you to try: Adrian has medium biological vulnerability and is experiencing stress. However, he is not schizophrenic. Barry has high biological vulnerability and is experiencing stress. He is schizophrenic. Chris has low biological vulnerability and is experiencing a lot of stress. However, he is not schizophrenic. Dave has moderate biological vulnerability and is experiencing some stress, but he is not schizophrenic. However, subsequent stressors impact on him and Dave develops schizophrenia.

Research methods: The aim of this study was to investigate how genetic factors moderate susceptibility to risks associated with adoptive family functioning.

Women diagnosed with schizophrenia who had one or more of their offspring adopted away were selected for this study. A sample of 145 adopted-away offspring (high-risk) was matched with 158 adoptees without this genetic risk (low-risk). Both groups were assessed after 12 and 21 years.
Fourteen had developed schizophrenia, 11 from the high-risk group and 3 from the low-risk group.
Being reared in a 'healthy' adoptive family had a protective effect even for those at high genetic risk for schizophrenia.

Chapter 7 Eating behaviour
The evolutionary explanation for food preferences p.106–107

One for you to try: Taste aversion is a learned response to eating toxic or poisonous food. Animals avoid eating the food that they associate with the illness.
Alex had associated his sickness with the taste of sushi, a food he had never eaten before. He consequently felt ill whenever he saw or smelt sushi.
The development of taste aversions helped our ancestors to survive because, if they survived eating poisoned food, they would not make the same mistake again.
The result of this conditioned response is long-lasting and, as Alex found, occurs even when other information about the source of the illness is available.

Research methods: (a) Content analysis is a form of indirect observation which involves analysing artefacts produced by people, such as letters, paintings, etc.
(b) They could read through the written material and listen to the tape-recorded material and code the material into themes which describe consistent aspects of the lives and diet of the Pirahã.
(c) Strength – If the sources of the content analysis can be accessed by other researchers then findings can be replicated, increasing their reliability. Limitation – However, other researchers may interpret data differently because of observer bias, which limits its internal validity.

The role of learning in food preference p.108–109

One for you to try: Parents may manipulate the availability of certain foods because of a perceived health gain associated with these foods (e.g. low sugar foods).
The celebrity chef could, through TV programmes, educate parents about healthy and unhealthy foods, so they can modify the eating habits of their children.
The behaviour of same-age peers has an influence on the food preferences of children. Children exposed to peers eating healthy foods were more likely to try these foods themselves.
The chef could use child role models when advertising healthy foods so that children viewing these adverts would acquire new eating habits through social learning.

Research methods: (a) There is a positive correlation between parents' consumption of healthy snacks and their children's consumption of healthy snacks.
(b) Opportunity sample. A limitation of this type of sampling is that the children in these two schools may not be truly representative of children of this age throughout the rest of the UK. This restricts the generalization of any conclusions that might be drawn.
(c) The purpose of the consent form is that parents can read about the study, any risks of participation and how the data will be stored and used. As a result of this information, parents can make an informed decision about whether they and their child should take part.
(d) This tells us that there is a moderate positive relationship between parents' consumption of unhealthy snacks and their children's consumption of unhealthy snacks. Children of parents who consume a lot of unhealthy snacks are more likely to consume a lot of unhealthy snacks themselves.
(e) The probability of the relationship between parents'

consumption of unhealthy snacks and their children's consumption of unhealthy snacks being due to chance is less than the probability of the relationship between parents' consumption of healthy snacks and their children's consumption of healthy snacks being due to chance.

Neural and hormonal mechanisms p.110–111

One for you to try: Leptin decreases appetite when the body has enough stored energy. Leptin is usually produced by fat tissue, where it travels in the bloodstream to the brain, decreasing appetite. As Max has failed to lose weight using other methods, treatment with leptin supplements should mean that more signals are sent to the brain to decrease his appetite and so he should begin to lose weight.

Research methods: (a) Peer review is the process by which psychological research papers, before publication, are subjected to independent scrutiny by other psychologists working in a similar field who consider the research in terms of its validity, significance and originality.
(b) Because leptin treatment helps in the treatment of obesity, this has significant economic implications. Obesity poses a significant health risk to individuals, therefore this has cost implications for the NHS. There is also a significant psychological impact on morbidly obese individuals so the cost of support can also be reduced with leptin treatment.

Biological explanation for anorexia nervosa p.112–113

One for you to try: Kaye (2009) suggests that starvation decreases the serotonin in the brains of anorexia patients, reducing their anxiety. Eileen says that when she starves herself she feels less anxious about things going on in her life. This is a result of her serotonin levels decreasing. When someone with AN begins eating again, serotonin levels rise dramatically, causing extreme anxiety in the individual, and making recovery even more difficult. Eileen reports that this happens to her. When she starts eating again, her serotonin levels rise, as does her anxiety levels and she starves herself once again in an attempt to feel better.

Research methods: (a) The new measuring instrument could be completed twice by the same respondents, 3 months apart. A high positive correlation of scores indicates test-retest reliability.
(b) The new measuring instrument could be administered and marked by two different clinicians. A high positive correlation of scores indicates inter-observer reliability.
(c) Face validity can be assessed either by giving the measure to a group of experts to judge whether the questions are truly representative of the thing being measured.
(d) Concurrent validity can be assessed by comparing scores on the new measure with a previously validated measure on the same topic. People should get similar scores on both measurements.

Family systems theory and anorexia nervosa p.114–115

One for you to try: There are two factors that might have contributed to Demelza's AN. Firstly, she has an enmeshed family, who are overly-involved with each other. For example, her mother insists on knowing everything about her children and will even read their diaries. This over-involvement might have stifled Demelza's ability to cope with everyday stressors and contribute to her AN. Secondly, her father is showing a high degree of control and over protectiveness, which may affect Demelza's belief about the amount of control she has in her own life. Consequently, Demelza may be rebelling against this control by refusing to eat.

Research methods: While there are a range of ethical issues you could outline here, there are some which are more suitable to this particular experiment. For example: The researcher would need to consider

privacy, as this is a particularly sensitive topic involving patients with AN. He/she would need to ensure that the patient and their family members control the flow of information from the interview and do not feel as though they have to answer any particular question(s). Furthermore, the researcher would need to consider confidentiality and ensure that the data and information gathered remains anonymous and could not be traced back to the individual participants. Furthermore, any transcripts from the interviews must be coded or destroyed, following the interview process.

Social learning theory and anorexia nervosa p.116–117

One for you to try: There are two key influences that might be affecting Denise's behaviour. Firstly, she is reading lots of fitness magazines and therefore the media may have an impact on her body image and desire for thinness, especially if she has low self-esteem. Secondly, Denise's behaviour is being positively reinforced by her boyfriend who keeps telling her how great she looks, which will motivate her to continue skipping meals and going to the gym seven days a week.

Research methods: (a) The results suggest that the media has resulted in a decrease in BMI for both males and females, although the effect is larger in females than in males. There is a 2.7 decrease for females, in comparison to a 1.6 decrease for males.
(b) The standard deviation is useful as it shows the variability in the scores. For example, the results reveal the spread of scores in 1998 were much more varied, suggesting that the media does not affect everyone equally.

Cognitive theory and anorexia nervosa p.118–119

One for you to try: Cognitive models emphasise the role of cognitive distortions that lead individuals to develop a negative body image due to comparisons with thin models in the media. Asha is in awe of the slim models that everybody makes a fuss of, and feels depressed about the way she looks compared to the models.
Individuals develop self-defeating habits because of faulty beliefs they have about themselves, e.g. they must be thin for others to like them.
Asha is convinced that she doesn't have friends because she is too fat, and goes on a crash diet so she that will be popular like the models.

Research methods: 1. Time taken for food-related words mean score 3.26. Time taken for non-food words mean score 1.65.

2. The results suggest that patients with AN take longer to solve food-related words in comparison to non-food words, because of their cognitive preoccupations. Their attention is drawn to the food-related word which causes them to take longer when responding in the Stroop test.

Biological explanations for obesity p.120–121

One for you to try: There are two key biological explanations that could support Daniel's view that his weight problem is inherited. Maes et al. (1997) conducted a meta-analysis and found heritability estimates for BMI of 74% in MZ twins and 32% in DZ twins, highlighting a large genetic component. Furthermore, Stunkard et al. (1989) examined 540 adult adoptees. They found a strong relationship between the weight category of adopted individuals and their biological parents, but no significant relationship with their adoptive parents, also suggesting a strong genetic link. These two studies highlight a genetic component with obesity and support Daniel's claim that his weight problem 'is not his fault'.

Research methods: (a) It is important to repeat studies to assess the validity of their findings. If the outcome is the same, this affirms the original results.
(b) The control group does not receive the drug under test, therefore any difference in weight loss between

the experimental and control groups can be attributed to the drug.

Psychological explanations for obesity p.122–123

One for you to try: According to the boundary model, Helen, who is trying to be restrained, may have a higher biological satiety level. Furthermore, once she starts eating she goes through her self-imposed boundary and experiences the 'what the hell effect' and continues to eat the entire bag, before feeling satiated.

Research methods: (a) Matched pairs
(b) Strength – Because participants do not take part in both conditions, there is no danger of order effects (as is the case in a repeated measures design). Limitation – Participants can only be matched on known variables, which means that participants are not matched on other relevant participant variables that might affect the DV.
(c) The Wilcoxon test. This is because the researchers are testing to see if there is a difference between the restrained eating group and the exercise group, the two groups are matched and the data (BMI) is at least ordinal.

Explanations for the success and failure of dieting p.124–125

One for you to try: Jasmine's diets are likely to fail because she is getting bored. According to Redden, people like experiences less the more they repeat them, so as she becomes accustomed to each diet, they're more likely to fail. For a diet to work Jasmine must focus on the particular details of a meal, rather than considering the meal as a whole, this will stop her from getting bored and help her to maintain her diet.

Research methods: (a) The aim was to test whether focusing on specific details of each meal means people get bored less easily. 135 people were given 22 jelly beans, one at a time. As each bean was dispensed, information about it was flashed onto a computer screen. One group saw general information (e.g. 'number 7'), the other group saw specific flavour details (e.g. 'cherry flavour number 7'). Participants got bored with eating beans faster if they saw general information and enjoyed the task more if they saw specific flavour details. This suggests that details of food consumed cuts down on repetitive feelings, making sticking to a diet more likely.
(b) Redden, J.P. (2008). Reducing Satiation: The Role of Categorization Level. *Journal of Consumer Research*, 34(5), 624-634.

Chapter 8 Stress
The physiology of stress p.126–127

One for you to try: Susie's body was responding as if this was a real attack, as her amygdala responded to a terrifying stimulus and sent signals to her hypothalamus. This activated her sympathetic nervous system, which stimulated the release of adrenaline from her adrenal medulla. As adrenaline stimulated the fight or flight response, she felt sick as her digestion was inhibited. She started shaking as her muscles were prepared for running away from zombies. When she remembered the video, the mental images again stimulated the SAM pathway.

Research methods: (a) It is primary data because it has been collected from participants directly (or 'first-hand'), rather than gathered from reports of previous research.
(b) One strength of primary data is that first-hand data can be controlled, whereas secondary data may have been gathered under differing conditions. Other explanations include less peripheral/redundant information, and the fact that the data gathered is more likely to be focused on the purpose of the research.
(c) The scattergram shows a positive correlation. As scores on the adrenaline measure increase, they tend to increase on the perceived stress measure.
(d) Spearman's rank order method or Pearson's *r* method. Both are tests for a correlation between two variables. Spearman's is appropriate to use with

data that are at least ordinal in nature. Pearson's is appropriate when the data are at least interval in nature. (e) Just because two variables are correlated, it does not necessarily mean that a change in one is causing a change in the other (i.e. causality cannot be inferred on the basis of correlation alone).

The role of stress in illness p.128–129

One for you to try: Kirkup and Merrick (2003) propose that losing a home game may lead to anger, frustration, or depression among supporters. All of these are known to increase the risk of heart attacks and strokes. Stroke rates are also known to be higher in association with mental stress, particularly depression. The lack of an effect on women might reflect differences in interest in football between men and women. Kirkup and Merrick say that home defeats are widely accepted to be the worst result for a team. Supporters have lower expectations away from home, but are predisposed to anticipate a victory in a home game. The article on which this activity is based can be found at: http://jech.bmj.com/content/57/6/429.full.

Research methods: (a) The hypothesis was directional. The researcher clearly specified the direction the difference would take ('wounds would take longer to heal').
(b) The researcher was looking for a difference and an independent groups design was used. Additionally, the data are at least at the ordinal level of measurement.
(c) Independent *t*-test.
(d) A Type I error occurs when the null hypothesis is rejected when it should have been accepted (i.e. the researcher concludes that there is a significant difference/correlation when there isn't). We are told that the difference was significant at $p<0.05$, so the probability of a Type I error being made is 5/100 (5%).
(e) The researcher has concluded that caring for relatives is the causal factor affecting wound-healing time. However, we do not know to what extent other consequences of caring for a relative with dementia (such as sleep disturbances) affect the immune system's functioning.

Sources of stress: Life changes p.130–131

One for you to try: Nadia mentions life events which are in the SRRS and are clearly stressful. However, there are other events which are much less stressful, and the scale ignores the stress caused by daily hassles, as well as the impact of positive events. As Munya points out, it is a simplistic scale as it reduces each event to a numerical value, ignoring the different meaning of life events for different individuals. In particular, as students, Munya and Nadia may be living with their parents, making decisions about their futures and experiencing romantic relationships for the first time, and the events in their teenage lives are not accounted for in the SRRS. As Munya also says, the data is retrospectively collected and people may not accurately recall events in the last year. However, Hardt found good reliability of recall for most childhood events so this may not be a problem.

Research methods: (a) There is a positive correlation between scores on the SRRS and estimated number of days taken off through sickness in the previous year.
(b) Internal validity refers to how accurately a test or measuring instrument measures what it says it measures.
(c) Volunteer sampling
(d) One limitation of this sampling method is that the sample is likely to be non-representative, making the findings difficult to generalise.
(e) The study is looking for a correlation, and the data collected is at least at the ordinal level of measurement. Additionally, the test is suitable for pairs of scores, and there is a linear relationship between the scores.
(f) Pearson's *r*
(g) The table for Pearson's *r* can be found on page 31 of the Complete Companion Student Book. For a directional hypothesis (one-tailed), at the $p<0.05$ level, with $N=12$, the tabled value is .475. There is not a

significant correlation between the two variables. With Pearson's *r*, the reported correlation (.27) must be equal to or greater than the appropriate tabled value (.475). Since it isn't, the null hypothesis cannot be rejected.

Sources of stress: Daily hassles p.132–133

One for you to try: Sasha notices a correlation between Liza's health and her college attendance, as Liza often doesn't go to college when she's been moaning. The accumulation of daily hassles in Liza's day may lead to stress, which makes her vulnerable to colds and headaches as well as affecting her sleep. On the other hand, feeling depressed may make Liza report more hassles on Twitter, and also lead to not attending college – it's not possible to know which factor is causal.

Research methods: (a) Content analysis is a method for analysing various kinds of qualitative data. Categories can be established and observations falling into the categories can be counted (qualitative). Alternatively, data can be analysed in terms of its themes (qualitative).
(b) One approach would be to watch some of the recordings from the head-cams and identify instances of instances that could be described as 'hassles'. These could include things like 'finding the canteen has run out of sandwiches', 'having to queue to enrol', and so on. The two researchers would have come to an agreement on what counted as a 'hassle' and then watched the twenty recordings, counting the number of hassles each student experienced.
(c) Two ways in which reliability could be intra-rater reliability (test-retest reliability) and inter-rater reliability. Since there are two researchers watching the recordings, they could content analyse them independently and then compare their observations. If their observations are reliable, then a strong positive correlation should be found.
(d) The prediction is non-directional since the researchers are predicting that that there will be a difference in the number of hassles experienced by males and females without specifying the direction the difference will take.
(e) Mann-Whitney *U* test. It is a test for a difference and can be used with an independent groups design. Additionally, the data is at least at the ordinal level of measurement.
(f) The probability of a Type I error (rejecting the null hypothesis when it is true) is less than 1 in 100, so there is at least a 99% chance that this is a real relationship between the variables.
(g) For a non-directional hypothesis (two-tailed), at the $p<0.02$ level, with $N=10$, the critical value is .648. For males, the observed value (.66) is greater than the critical value, and therefore the correlation is significant. However, for females (.63) it isn't, and therefore the correlation is not significant.

Sources of stress: Workplace stress p.134–135

One for you to try: Homer is experiencing work overload. Because the type of work is too hard for him, it is called *qualitative work overload*.
Moe finds his job too easy, and is experiencing *qualitative work underload*.
Lenny is experiencing work overload. However, he has too much work to do and not enough time to do it. This is called *quantitative work overload*.
Karl doesn't have enough work to do, so he is experiencing *quantitative work underload*. Note that Moe makes reference to 'being his own boss', so he has a high degree of control, which the other three, as employees, might not.

Research methods: 1. (a) Low degree of control mean $= 65/10 = 6.5$. High degree of control mean $= 34/10 = 3.4$.
(b) There is a very low score in the low degree of control group (the rating of 1), which makes the mean artificially low for that group: a negative skew.

(c) Median and mode
(d) Standard deviation (or range)
(e) Unrelated *t*-test
(f) Mann-Whitney *U* test
(g) The rating scale is at least at the ordinal level.

2. The participants were asked about harmful and illegal behaviours. They needed to know that their answers were confidential, but on the other hand the researchers had a responsibility to protect participants from harm, so they should have informed participants about sources of confidential help, such as substance abuse counselling.

Measuring stress: Self-report scales and physiological measures p.136–137

One for you to try: Young children may not be able to express their stress levels verbally, but physiological measures could be used. Non-invasive methods such as a heart rate monitor might be most appropriate. This will measure the stress response as adrenaline causes heart rate to increase. Skin conductance could also be used, although the children may not like having electrodes attached to their fingers.

Research methods: (a) The teaching staff.
(b) $117 \times 3 = 351$. $135 \times 3 = 405$.
(c) $210/405 \times 100 = 51.9\%$
(d) The administrative staff.
(e) Marks would be awarded here for correctly labelled axes, an appropriate title, and an accurate bar chart.
(f) The teaching staff appears to be the most stressed, since they have the highest hassles score and lowest uplifts score. The students appear to be the least stressed, since they have the lowest hassles score and highest uplifts score. The administrative staff are midway between the teachers and students. Other conclusions are possible. For example, the hassles score for the teachers is twice that of the students, and the students have an uplifts score four-and-a-half times that of the administrative staff.

Individual differences in stress: Personality p.138–139

One for you to try: (a) Ben
(b) Oliver
(c) Sanya
(d) Oliver
(e) Sanya
(f) Ben

Research methods: Amongst other things, the findings suggest that Type As are more likely than Type Bs to suffer from some sort of CHD (heart attacks, recurring heart attack, and fatal heart attacks). Type As are nearly three times more likely than Type Bs to suffer fatal heart attacks and over three times more likely than Type Bs to suffer recurring heart attacks. Type As are twice as likely as Type Bs to suffer a single heart attack.

Individual differences in stress: Hardiness p.140–141

AO2: One for you to try: The first lecturer is low in challenge and sees change as a threat ('Next year they want me to teach a subject I've never taught before'). The lecturer is also low in commitment (he is not willing to work outside his contracted hours) and has a low degree of control (he doesn't get a choice in which classes are taught). The second lecturer scores highly on the 3Cs. He would 'jump at the opportunity' to teach a new course (challenge), 'wants the college to be the best' (commitment), and is allowed to 'just get on with my job' (control). The second lecturer is clearly the hardier of the two.

Research methods: (a) Non-directional. It states an association, but does not specify whether a higher or lower score would be associated with greater concern about absence.
(b) There is no association between participants' scores on the 3Cs and the company's concern or otherwise about their absenteeism.
(c) Nominal
(d) A chi-squared test

(e) One disadvantage is social desirability responding (especially given the sensitive nature of the topic being studied!). Participants may give the answer they believe will make them appear in a 'good light'.

(f) Deception, as participants were not told the true purpose of the questionnaire before completing it. This could be dealt with at the end of the study by debriefing participants as to the real purpose of using the questionnaire.

Managing and coping with stress: Drug therapies p.142–143

One for you to try: Chris should ask his doctor about the options of drug treatments. BZs can help reduce CNS activity which will make him feel more relaxed, but BZs cause problems with addiction and side effects, so are not suitable for dealing with stress in an interview situation. His mother is right to be concerned. However, Chris could instead be offered beta blockers which don't have the same problems and can also be very effective, by reducing the effect of adrenaline on the heart and other organs, so Chris would feel less stressed. However, both types of drugs are just addressing symptoms and he should also ask the doctor if CBT is available instead.

Research methods: (a) A demand characteristic is a cue that makes participants unconsciously aware of the aims of a study or helps participants work out what the researcher expects to find. An investigator effect is anything that an investigator does that has an effect on a participant's performance in a study other than what was intended. Clearly, if the participant knows that she has been given the drug that is being investigated, her behaviour is likely to change. Equally, if a researcher knows that the participant has been given the drug her behaviour is likely to change as well. RCTs overcome both of these issues. When neither the participant nor researcher are aware of whether the participant has been given the drug or a placebo, the term 'double blind control' is used.

(b) Please read the following information, and sign at the bottom if you are happy to take part. This research is testing a drug which is thought to help with stress. If you take part, you will be randomly allocated to one of two groups, and you will either receive the active drug or a placebo, to take for two weeks. You will be asked to report your stress levels at hourly intervals and any new physical or psychological symptoms you may experience. We do not expect you to experience any unpleasant symptoms, but you will be able to withdraw from the trial at any time, and you will be monitored by a doctor. Please ask if you have any questions, and sign below if you are happy to take part.

Managing and coping with stress: Stress inoculation therapy p.144–145

One for you to try: The advice given will depend (a) on whether BZs or BBs are chosen, and (b) the weight you assign to each of the strengths/weaknesses. For example, SIT and BBs are both effective, do not lead to biological dependence, and do not have unpleasant side effects. However, SIT requires time/effort whereas BBs do not. BBs are also widely available and relatively inexpensive compared with SIT. SIT addresses the causes of stress whereas BBs do not.

Research methods: (a) Closed question

(b) Describe how you felt during the course of the treatment.

(c) 24/40 = 0.6 = 60%

(d)

	Better	Not better	Total
SIT	24	16	40
BB	23	1	24
BZ	8	8	16
Total	55	15	80

(e) Chi-squared. Independent data at the nominal level, test of difference.

(f) It wouldn't be possible to know which treatment had helped them, and the data would not be independent

as they would be in two categories.

(g) There is less than 5% probability that the results are due to chance. There is at least 95% chance that the results represent a real effect in the population.

(h) Beta blockers were the most effective, as the highest proportion of patients felt better when taking beta blockers, and benzodiazepines were least effective. All three treatments had benefits, as at least half of patients felt better on all three treatments.

Managing and coping with stress: Biofeedback p.146–147

One for you to try: As in the previous chapter, the advice given will depend (a) on whether BZs or BBs are chosen, and (b) the weight you assign to each of the strengths/weaknesses. All three therapies are effective and (if BBs have been chosen) none lead to biological dependence or have unpleasant side effects. However, BBs do not address the causes of stress, which the other two do. BBs do not require time/effort which the other two do. BBs and biofeedback are widely available and relatively inexpensive compared with SIT.

Research methods: (a) (36 + 18) / 100 = 54%

(b) Physiological activity will be decreased in participants receiving biofeedback training compared to those not receiving biofeedback training.

(c) In the experimental group, most participants had a large decrease in physiological activity. In the control group, most participants showed no change or an increase in physiological activity. This shows that the biofeedback training benefited some people in the experimental group.

(d) A test of difference, independent data, nominal level (number of people in each category) – chi-squared.

(e) The 5% significance level balances the risks of Type I errors (where the null hypothesis is rejected when it is actually true) and Type II errors (when the null hypothesis is accepted when it is actually untrue).

Gender differences in coping with stress p.148–149

One for you to try: To summarise, Charlie is showing the typical male response to stress in which adrenaline, noradrenaline and testosterone levels rise, leading to aggression. Kitty, by contrast, is displaying the typical female tend-and-befriend response, possibly as a result of unsuppressed oxytocin production.

Research methods: (a) I concentrate my efforts on doing something about it – PF. I discuss my feelings – EF.

(b) Ordinal level / quantitative

(c) Test of difference, independent groups design, ordinal level data – Mann-Whitney U test.

(d) Validity is the extent to which a test is actually measuring what it aims to test. Self-report scales are subject to demand characteristics and social desirability bias, as participants may answer the way that they think puts them in a good light. For example, men may answer in a way that they think seems masculine, according to stereotypes.

(e) Test-retest reliability: Get the same participants to complete the same scale a few weeks later. If the two sets of results are similar, with a correlation of above 0.8, then the test has good reliability.

(f) They could conduct observations of males and females in stressful meetings, tallying behavioural categories such as 'shouts', 'tries to comfort another person', 'suggests a solution', 'talks about feelings'. The tallies could then be compared with the self-report results.

The role of social support in coping with stress p.150–151

One for you to try: Based on Bailey and Dua's (1999) research, we might expect to find that Bruce (an Australian) would seek instrumental social support, whereas Ravi (an Indian) would seek emotional support. Based on Lucknow et al.'s (1998) research, we might expect Lou-Anne to seek emotional support, while Steve might be expected to seek instrumental support.

However, we don't know to what extent culture and gender interact, so Lou-Anne (as a woman from an individualistic culture) and Ravi (as a man from a collectivist culture) are, perhaps, the more difficult to predict.

Research methods: (a) As it is a replication study, there is previous research indicating the direction of the relationships between the variables.

(b) The scattergram shows a weak positive correlation.

(c) Pearson's r assumes that the data are at the interval level of measurement, the populations are assumed to have a normal distribution, and the variances of the samples are assumed to be the same.

(d) Spearman's rho.

(e) The sample size is 13 and the hypothesis is one-tailed. At the $p<0.05$ level, the tabled value is .484. Since the calculated value (.30) is smaller than the table value, the null hypothesis cannot be rejected. On this occasion, then, the student has failed to replicate Nabi et al.'s findings.

Chapter 9 Aggression

Neural and hormonal influences p.152–153

One for you to try: The amygdala is responsible for evaluating the emotional importance of sensory information and prompting an appropriate response. Gage is reported to have become moody, violently quarrelsome and displaying fits of temper. The accident may well have caused damage to the amygdala, meaning he lost the ability to behave appropriately. The hippocampus compares the conditions of a current threat with similar past experiences. Impaired hippocampal function may cause the amygdala to respond inappropriately to sensory stimuli, resulting in aggression. Gage's accident had damaged the connections between the frontal cortex to the limbic system, impairing the action of the hippocampus.

Research methods: (a) Volunteer sampling

(b) One limitation is that because people self-select, the sample could be biased and the results would be difficult to generalise to the population from which the sample was drawn.

(c) Random allocation is used as a way of trying to distribute participant variables evenly across the two groups (although this cannot be guaranteed, of course).

(d) Mann-Whitney U test (or Unrelated t-test). An independent groups design was used, and the researcher was looking for a difference. Additionally, the data are at least at the ordinal level.

Genetic factors in aggression p.154–155

One for you to try: 1 – Families typically share environments as well as genes so it is difficult to isolate the influence of each on its own. 2 – More than one gene usually contributes to a given behaviour so we may not be aware of all genetic influences. 3 – Genes and environment may interact with each other. Genetic factors may affect which environmental factors have an influence, and vice versa.

Research methods: (a) There are five MZ twin pairs and three are concordant for aggression. Therefore, the concordance rate is 3/5 or 60%.

(b) There are five DZ twin pairs and two are concordant for aggression. Therefore, the concordance rate is 2/5 or 40%.

(c) Both types of twin share environments. However, MZs share all of the genes whereas DZs do not. The higher concordance rate in MZs suggests that genetic factors at least play a role in aggressive behaviour.

The ethological explanation of aggression p.156–157

One for you to try: Unwittingly, Tom has given Duncan an evaluation point about ritualised aggression. The culture in question (actually the Dani of New Guinea) do not lack an ability to use their knowledge in a practical way. What is likely is that they are practising a form of 'arms limitation' (Marsh, 1978); they are well aware that putting flights on to arrows would result in more deaths of rival group members. However, if they use flights, then their opponents will do the same, and more members of their own group will be killed. By 'fighting' in this ritualised way, neither group will suffer as badly as would otherwise be the case.

Research methods:

(a)
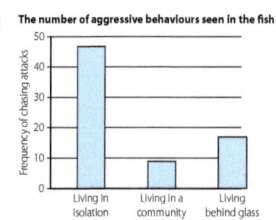

The number of aggressive behaviours seen in the fish

(b) Aggression was lowest when the fish were with other fish in a communal tank, and highest when they were kept in isolation from other fish. An intermediate amount of aggression was seen when the fish were kept behind a glass screen that allowed them to see fish in the other section of the tank.

(c) It is possible that action-specific energy increased in the isolated male. Because this energy needed to be released, the male became aggressive towards the female sharing the tank with him.

Evolutionary explanations of human aggression p.158–159

One for you to try: The scenario suggests that evolutionary explanations of aggression might not be true. Aggressive behaviour may not always be adaptive, and may actually be maladaptive. Rather than being accepted as a mate for behaving aggressively, aggression may lead to a male being rejected as a potential mate. In this case, Nicholas' attempt at behaving aggressively, by starting a fight with other men, has led to him being rejected by Denise. This challenges the claims made by evolutionary explanations that aggressive displays will attract a mate.

Research methods: (a) There will be no positive correlation between how violent gang members are as assessed by self- and peer-ratings and their status within the gang (and any correlation there is reflects the operation of chance factors).
(b) One-tailed. The hypothesis states the direction the correlation will take (positive).
(c) The researcher predicted a correlation and the data are at least at the ordinal level.
(d) The correlation is significant. The tabled value (see page 31 of the Complete Companion book for the Critical Value Table) for a one-tailed test at $p<0.05$ is .564. Since the calculated value (.61) is greater than the table value, the null hypothesis can be rejected.
(e) Just because two variables are correlated, it does not necessarily mean that a change in one causes a change in the other. Just because the more violent the gang members were, the higher their status within the gang, this does not mean that being more violent causes this status increase. Correlations do not permit us to infer causality.

The frustration-aggression hypothesis p.160–161

One for you to try: The confederate directed sarcastic comments towards the children at the same time he frustrated them. It is possible that the comments provoked anger, and it is therefore impossible to determine whether the children in the frustration group later demonstrated greater aggression against the confederate than those in the control group because of his frustrating actions, his comments, or both of these factors.

Research methods: (a) The hypothesis was one-tailed. The researcher specified the direction the difference would take ('People who were second in line would feel more aggressive than those who were twelfth in line.').

(b) One strength is that field experiments tend to have higher external validity (greater 'mundane realism'). One limitation is that field experiments tend to have lower internal validity, since it is more difficult to control extraneous and confounding variables.
(c) Mann-Whitney U test. The researcher is looking for a difference and an independent groups design has been used. Additionally, the data are at the ordinal level at least.
(d) Peer review is the process by which psychological research papers, before publication, are subjected to independent scrutiny by other psychologists working in a similar field who consider the research in terms of its validity, significance and originality.
(e) The aim of this study was to test the frustration–aggression hypothesis. A male research assistant was instructed to push in front of a person who was either second or twelfth in line. This was done ten times in each condition. After each person had bought their ticket, they were asked to rate how aggressive they felt towards the research assistant on a 7-point scale, with a higher value indicating more aggression. The average rating was 5.9 for the second in line group and 2.4 for the twelfth in line group. It was concluded that how close a person is to reaching their goal has a strong effect on how much frustration they experience, and that this is reflected in how aggressive they feel.

Social learning theory p.162–163

One for you to try: Social learning theory suggests that children primarily learn their aggressive responses through observation – i.e. observing the behaviour of role models and then imitating that behaviour. The ACT programme aims to educate parents about the dangers of providing aggressive role models for their children in an attempt to stop children learning aggression by observation. Social learning theory also predicts that positive (non-aggressive) behaviour will be more likely to produce rewards if reproduced by children. Therefore, the programme also encourages parents to provide more positive role models for their children.

Research methods: (a) Participation in the ACT against Violence intervention programme increases violence prevention skills in an English-speaking population in the US.
(b) The Spanish-speaking sample show a greater improvement in violence prevention scores (+4.03 versus +1.53 for the English-speaking sample) and prosocial parenting practices (+6.22 versus +1.09).
(c) The probability of the difference between the pre- and post-intervention scores being due to chance is less than 5% (1 in 20).
(d) This would increase the chance of making a Type II error. This happens when we make it more difficult to reject chance as an explanation for the results. By adopting a 0.01 significance level instead of a 0.05 level we must be 99% confident that chance has not caused the change in behaviour rather than 95% confident with a 0.05 level.

De-individuation p.164–165

One for you to try: The state of de-individuation is aroused when individuals join crowds. Zimbardo believed that being in a large group gave people a 'cloak of anonymity' that diminished any personal consequences for their actions.
Tyson mentions that members of the Sharpeville Six were members of a 'mob' during the protest march, so according to de-individuation theory this would have led to a feeling of diminished responsibility for any individual actions.
De-individuation also means that social norms inhibiting 'uncivilised' behaviour and concerns about being easily identifiable are removed. Being anonymous in a crowd leads to a reduction of inner restraints and an increase in behaviours that are usually inhibited. The accused in the trial were part of a protest march (and therefore largely unidentifiable) so these inhibitions would have been removed. As individuals it is unlikely that they would have considered murdering

the deputy mayor, but without inner restraints this became more likely.

Research methods:
(a) There will be a difference in the extent to which warriors who change their appearance and those who do not kill, torture, or mutilate their victims.
(b) At $p<0.05$, for a two-tailed test, and with one degree of freedom, the tabled value of chi-squared is 3.84. Since the calculated value (9.67) is bigger than the tabled value, the null hypothesis can be rejected at the $p<0.05$ level.
(c) Warriors who change their appearance are significantly more likely than warriors who do not change their appearance to engage in high levels of killing, torture, and mutilation.

Institutional aggression in prisons p.166–167

One for you to try: One 'very good reason' is that if most violence occurs in overheated, noisy and overcrowded environments, then decreasing these factors should reduce aggression. This is what Wilson (2010) did at HMP Woodhill and found a large reduction in assaults on prison staff and other inmates. These findings suggest that situational variables are at least one cause of prison violence, and can be successfully applied to reduce prison violence.

Research methods: (a) Strength – This method provides in-depth insights into the dispositional explanation of institutional aggression that might be overlooked by other methods. Limitation – it is difficult to generalise from specific members of violent gangs to all violent individuals in prison. The unique experiences of one individual may not apply to others.
(b) In an unstructured interview, the interviewer has some initial fairly open questions, and the conversation between interviewer and interviewee develops depending on the answers given. Unstructured interviews allow researchers to obtain more detailed information and deeper insights into individuals' feelings, thoughts and experiences.
(c) How do you think your experiences with your gang shaped your behaviour while you were in prison?
(d) An ethical issue is invasion of privacy because researchers used video material showing prisoners' interactions with other inmates and prison staff. Although inmates and staff would expect to be observed given the nature of the prison environment, the researchers should still take steps to keep all information gained from these recordings as confidential as possible, including removing names and, if possible, blurring faces and disguising voices.

Media influences on aggression p.168–169

One for you to try: This activity relates to Przybylski *et al.*'s (2014) research. They found that aggressive behaviour may be due to the player's frustration and failure during a game, rather than the violent storyline. Apparently, 'Super Hexagon' (iOS, 2013) is one of the hardest games ever, the aim simply being to survive for as long as possible. It could be that the brother playing this game is finding it difficult to master, and that this is leading to frustration and aggression.

Research methods: (a) Students who played the violent video game responded much more aggressively than those who played the nonviolent video game on all three dependent variables (thoughts, feelings and actions) did.
(b) Mann-Whitney U test
(c) An independent groups design has been used, and a difference is being looked for. Additionally, the data are at least at the ordinal level.

Explanations of media influences p.170–171

One for you to try: The study appears to offer support for desensitisation theory. It could be argued that playing violent games desensitised the players to the violent images, and this is reflected in the smaller brain response as compared with those who played the nonviolent game. The study was originally done by Engelhardt *et al.* (2011). They found that participants showed a reduction in the P3 component of the event-related brain potential to violent images, and that this is evidence of a neural marker which can at least partially account for the causal link between violent game exposure and desensitisation.

Research methods: One ethical issue that arises with this method is that participants are led to believe that they are delivering electric shocks to another participant. Thus, the method uses deception. One way in which this issue can be dealt with is by debriefing participants after the study is over. They should be told about the deception that was used and why it was necessary to use it.

Chapter 10 Forensic psychology
Offender profiling: The top-down approach p.172–173

One for you to try: (a) Luke could identify behavioural categories that would match each group's profile, for example organised offenders move the body away from the crime scene; disorganised offenders tend to leave evidence like blood or semen. He could then read the transcripts and tally the different behaviours, and see how they match the two different profiles, or whether some contain behaviours from both types of profile.
(b) The criminals may not be honest, or may not remember details correctly because of the passage of time or mental illness or drug or alcohol use at the time of the crime, whereas the court and police reports were written at the time of the crime's investigation so may be more accurate.

Research methods: (a) Both groups rated the profile as highly accurate (4 = neutral on a 7-point Likert scale), and there was no difference between the mean accuracy ratings. However, there was a greater standard deviation in scores in Group B, so there was more variation in scores of accuracy of the fabricated offender, showing that police had more varied opinions about the accuracy in this group.
(b) The police were not able to match the genuine offender any better than the fabricated one, despite differences in their characteristics, so these profiles may not be very useful for identifying an offender.
(c) As the median is 6 it suggests that the bulk of the scores are high but that a few extreme low scores skew the mean (5.3) and result in a negative skewed distribution.

Offender profiling: The bottom-up approach p.174–175

One for you to try: Saga and Henrik could use Geographic profiling by making a CGT map to see where the offender was most likely to live in the Malmö or Copenhagen region, based on the crime sites; this would narrow down search areas. They could look up research findings about similar serial murders where bodies were staged, to see if there were useful themes that could help them narrow down suspects. They would also be taking into consideration that the murderer may have had some experience of police techniques and was leaving deliberate clues or misleading evidence.

Research methods: (a) 6
(b) Validity increases the more crime sites are available for analysis. Validity is poor when there are few crime sites.
(c) A commuter commits crimes at a different location from their residence; this model assumes that they live within the area that the crimes were committed.

Biological explanations of offending behaviour: A historical approach p.176–177

One for you to try: Atavistic means throwback to ancestral type, ape-like. Lombroso identified

peculiarities of ears, nose, jaw, chin, arms etc. Dracula's massive eyebrows, bushy hair, protruding lips, coarse, broad hands and hairy palms are ape-like qualities. The aquiline face was characteristic of murderers, according to Lombroso. Overall, the description is atavistic as it implies that a murderous person must have the appearance of a lower primate, and the description of Dracula contains some of these features.

Research methods: (a) Strengths: large sample size; objective measurements of physical features; Limitations: no control or comparison group; only studied males
(b) He attempted to use empirical observations to collect data and studied actual criminals.
(c) His conclusions were based on assumptions which were ethnocentric (certain physical characteristics being less evolved) and androcentric (women being less evolved). He also ignored the possibility of free will, that people may decide to commit crimes based on cognitive reasoning.

Biological explanations of offending behaviour: Genetic and neural p.178–179

One for you to try: Faulty MAOA gene leads to low serotonin and occurred in 28 Dutch men studied by Brunner; combination with faulty CDH13 gene found in Finnish offenders makes it hard to resist violence. However, Caspi showed that the interaction with childhood maltreatment was important. The gene alone does not determine violent behaviour. In adoption studies, 80% of boys with biological parents who were criminals did not become criminals themselves. He may have inherited genes such as MAOA or CDH13 variants, but even if he has, this does not mean he will become a murderer. Childhood experiences are also important. Alan has not been brought up with his father so has not received social influences from him. As Alan has not suffered maltreatment as a child he would be unlikely to become a criminal despite his genes.

Research methods: 1. (a) There are genetic factors in delinquency, as the concordance rate for MZ is higher and they have identical DNA whereas DZ only have 50% the same DNA. However, there are other factors involved too as the concordance rate for MZ twins is not 100%.
(b) MZ twins may be treated more similarly because they look the same, and will always be the same sex, so there is greater environmental similarity for MZ twins too.
(c) Early studies classified twins by appearance, so some may have been wrongly classified; DZ twins may look extremely similar. Now it is possible to use DNA testing so mistakes can't be made.

2. (a) If children spend some time with their biological parents, they might experience abuse, neglect or social learning (environmental influences) from them. This means that the similarities with biological parents are not just due to heredity.
(b) Families may have similarities in culture, education, ethnicity, religious beliefs etc.; this means that shared environmental factors make it more difficult to separate out biological and environmental influences.
(c) Children may be traumatised by breaking an attachment to the birth mother, or they may have been neglected and have attachment disorders which mean they find it difficult to form healthy relationships with their adopted parents.

Psychological explanations of offending behaviour: Eysenck's theory p.180–181

One for you to try: Luca probably scores high on extraversion, as he loves partying and is the class clown, and he gets bored easily, so seeks external stimulation like climbing things. He is high on neuroticism, as he feels low and anxious when he is alone. He is also high on psychoticism, as he is rude to the teacher and doesn't seem to care what people think. Extraverts

become involved in dangerous risk-taking behaviour, which Luca is starting to do. Neurotics are unstable and can overreact, which Luca does by being stroppy to the teacher. All three traits seem to be leading him into anti-social behaviour.

Research methods: (a) The same participants take the same test after an interval of time, such as a week later. The two sets of results are compared by correlation. High correlation means good reliability.
(b) Some items may need to be removed or rewritten to make them less ambiguous.
(c) The scores match those from a previously validated scale.
(d) The correlation between scores from both scales was high, so the new scale is measuring the same traits as the original one.
(e) Face validity. The items on the scale should be considered to see whether they are obviously related to the traits of extraversion, neuroticism and psychoticism.
(f) The questions are forced-choice so there is no possibility of answering 'sometimes', which may be a more valid answer as people behave differently in different situations. There may be social desirability effects where people answer as they think is socially acceptable rather than being honest about their negative behaviours, so they are not truthful.

Psychological explanations of offending behaviour: Cognitive p.182–183

One for you to try: (a) (i) His wife needs it so he should steal it as long as he thought he wouldn't get caught.
(ii) He is doing the right thing to help his wife, she would expect it from him. It is difficult though, because he would be breaking the law.
(iii) Saving his wife's life is more important than the chemist making money from the drug, so Heinz is justified in stealing it.
(b) The scenarios are imaginary, and people may behave differently in real life. The participants were young males who would not have experienced marriage or life-threatening illness so could not imagine how they would respond. The sample is all male so cannot be generalised to females, whose moral principles may be different.

Research methods: 1. Colby, A., Kohlberg, L., Gibbs, J., and Lieberman, M. (1983). A longitudinal study of moral judgement. *Monographs of the Society for Research in Child Development, 48*, nos 1-2.

2. Kennedy, H.G. and Grubin, D.H. (1992). Patterns of denial in sex offenders. *Psychological Medicine, 22* (01), 191-6.

Psychological explanations of offending behaviour: Differential association p.184–185

One for you to try: Differential association theory proposes that offending behaviour is learned from other people, particularly peers and the local community. Lauren is hanging out with girls who have been excluded from school, so Lauren is learning norms, attitudes to crime, and methods from them through observation and direct reinforcement. According to Sutherland, the frequency, length and personal meaning of social associations determine their degree of influence; Lauren is spending a lot of time with these girls and she didn't have friends in the area before, so they are important to her at a vulnerable time after her parents' divorce and the house move.

Research methods: (a) How many cigarettes do you smoke in a week?
(b) Describe your reasons for smoking or for vaping.
(c) You are being asked to take part in a study about smoking and vaping habits of sixth form students. If you choose to take part, you will be given a short questionnaire to complete, which should take you about 10 minutes. Your answers will be anonymous

and confidential so please be as honest as you can in your answers. You may withdraw at any time during this study, and we will give you a code so that you may withdraw your answers at a later date if you wish. If you have any questions, please ask me. If you are happy to take part, please sign below.

Signed:………………………

Date……………………

Psychological explanations of offending behaviour: Psychodynamic p.186–187

One for you to try: In Freud's theory, a child with strict parents internalises the parents' morality and develops a harsh superego, which leads to guilt and anxiety. These feelings could be relieved by acting out criminal activity and being punished for it, as the person feels they deserve punishment anyway. They could also try to relieve their guilt by being harsh to their children, hoping to instil a strong moral compass in their children. This could explain why the fathers didn't show much warmth or affection to their children.

Research methods: (a) Opportunity sampling. May not represent other offenders, and the young people may not have had a choice about participating.
(b) This could lead to researcher bias: the observations which led to his diagnosis may have been biased due to Bowlby knowing which of the young people were thieves and which were controls.
(c) Their memories may not have been accurate as it was a relatively long time ago. They may also have been responding to what they thought Bowlby wanted to hear, i.e. displaying demand characteristics.

Dealing with offending behaviour: Custodial sentencing and recidivism p.188–189

One for you to try: Custodial sentencing can worsen depression and there are high rates of self-harm and suicide in prison. Brigitte is vulnerable to depression already and imprisonment may make it worse for her. Children with a parent in prison are affected financially and psychologically. Brigitte has a young baby and imprisoning her is likely to separate her from her baby, which will cause anxiety for both of them, and possibly long-term damage to the baby. Other types of sentencing such as community service can be more effective for non-violent and first-time offenders. Brigitte needs support rather than punishment, and a community sentence could be more effective.

Research methods: (a) $0.48 \times 3,948 = 1,895$
(b) $100 - 81 = 19\%$
(c) Almost twice the percentage of women as men had psychotic symptoms, and more than twice the percentage of women had attempted suicide than men, which is a sign of depression. Also women were twice as likely to have experienced abuse which is likely to lead to psychological problems.

Dealing with offending behaviour: Behaviour modification in custody p.190–191

One for you to try: It needs to be carefully planned. Mrs Cole should decide what the key aims are, then agree with staff and student representatives what hierarchy of behaviours and rewards the staff will use. All the students must be aware of the new system, and what tokens they will get for each behaviour and what rewards will be available. The rewards should be extra treats, not essential items like lunch as this would be unethical. All the staff must be trained so they remain consistent. This would be expected to improve pro-social behaviour and reduce anti-social behaviour of students as long as the reinforcements continue consistently and the rewards are things the students' value. Token economy can improve behaviour short-term and improve life in the institution for staff and students.

Research methods: (a) IV = before and after token system, DV = number of behaviours in each category
(b) The boys in one cottage were not included in the token system, and were used as a control – this was a naturally occurring group and they were not randomly allocated.
(c) So reliability could be calculated by comparing their tallies of behaviours for each boy, and to make sure all behaviours were observed.
(d) Train the supervisors better, or make sure they are not trying to carry out other tasks at the same time as recording observations, such as dealing with behavioural issues.
(e) The supervisors were busy doing other things, and became less consistent in monitoring behaviour and issuing tokens, so the token economy system became less effective and got dropped.
(f) Operant conditioning requires a schedule of reinforcement, otherwise the stimulus-response link is extinguished. The boys will no longer have this when they are released, they would have different environments and some of the behaviours, like walking in a straight line, would no longer be relevant. However, young offenders did maintain some learning in Cohen and Filipcjak's study, and reoffending rates were decreased, so Hobbs and Holt's participants may have some generalisation of learned behaviours like following rules.

Dealing with offending behaviour: Anger management p.192–193

One for you to try: Stress inoculation therapy is a CBT model, three stages: cognitive preparation, skill acquisition, application training. Aims are: cognitive restructuring, regulation of arousal, behavioural strategies. Dexter should be offered SIT. It is important that he agree to this and is willing to change, as readiness to change reduces dropout and improves the success of the treatment. He will learn about anger generally and analyse his own patterns of anger and triggers, for example going to clubs and bars. He will acquire skills to regulate his emotional and physiological state of anger in those situations, such as breathing and relaxation, and alternative strategies like walking out of the bar when he is feeling angry, or talking in a calm voice. He will then practise these skills with other group members in role play, who will give him feedback about how he's coming over, then he will try them in real-world situations.
Hopefully he now has better self-awareness and control, and some useful strategies to stop him getting angry.

Research methods: (a) $S = 2$
(b) Yes. $N = 16$, critical value of $S = 4$ at $p < 0.05$. Calculated value is less than critical value so it is significant, and in the expected direction.
(c) They are young people who have shown some willingness to change, as they have signed up for the course. They are otherwise similar, living in the same environment etc.
(d) The calculated value of S for the control group is 6, $N = 14$, Critical value ($p < 0.05$) $S = 3$, so this decrease in anger is not significant. The control group shows that the change is due to the anger management course, not some other changes that are going on at the secure training centre, as the group who completed the programme decreased their anger ratings but the control group did not have a significant decrease.
(e) The self-report measure is not very objective, and may be affected by demand characteristics; the young people may want to be helpful and say that they are less angry than they were, the 'hello—goodbye' effect. Or an improvement in anger ratings may get them other benefits like early release.

Dealing with offending behaviour: Restorative justice programmes p.194–195

One for you to try: Purpose: rehabilitation of offenders, atonement for wrongdoing, victim having a voice and understanding the offender's reasons for offending. It could benefit Craig by hearing Nick's distress about losing his brother, which will reduce the chance of him committing a similar crime in the future. He also had the chance to express his remorse and say sorry. Nick was helped to understand that Craig realised he had made a mistake, and that Craig deserved a second chance in life.

Research methods: (a) 90%
(b) 45%
(c) 20
(d) 6,941

Chapter 11 Addiction
Describing addiction p.196–197

One for you to try: Elaine is clearly showing withdrawal symptoms because she starts to feel nauseous and anxious when the effect off the caffeine wears off. Furthermore, she is also demonstrating tolerance because she now needs more coffee in order to feel the same effect and stay awake, which could be the result of metabolic tolerance.

Research methods: (a) Nominal (b) Ordinal (c) Interval (d) Ordinal

Risk factors: Genetics, stress and personality p.198–199

One for you to try: First, it is possible that Chris has a genetic vulnerability to smoking. It could be that Chris has inherited a dopamine receptor gene (as both of his parent's smoke) which causes him to suffer from abnormally low levels of dopamine and the smoking activates the dopamine receptors in the brain creating strong feelings of euphoria. Secondly, it could also be that Chris is using smoking to deal with his stressful job as the smoking may make him feel better or help him to forget the stress.

Research methods: (a) Mean score for Group A 67.9; Mean score for Group B 19.8.

(b) The mean is the most appropriate measure because it takes into account all of the scores for Group A and Group B. As there are no outliers, the data will not be distorted, which is why this measure is the most appropriate.

(c)
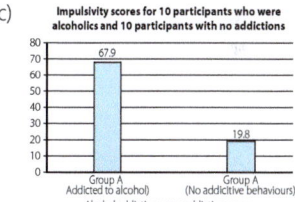
Impulsivity scores for 10 participants who were alcoholics and 10 participants with no addictions

Risk factors: Family influences and peers p.200–201

One for you to try: Tola is being indirectly influenced by peers and a desire to fit in with a popular group at school. Social identity theory could explain why Tola smokes, as she wants to be socially accepted with the 'ingroup' (who smoke) and therefore adopts their behaviour.
Furthermore, the lack of parental influence may also contribute to Tola's addiction. Stattin and Kerr (2000) suggest that a lack of parental monitoring may result from adolescents disclosing too much information about their substance abuse. Therefore, her parents' inability to deal with this information may cause them to stop monitoring Tola which therefore contributes to her addiction.

Research methods: (a) This is an opportunity sample.
(b) One limitation is that the sample is restricted to those people available at the time. These may not be representative of all types of gamblers.
(c) A strength of using qualitative data is that it allows researchers to collect much richer data about causes, motivations, family background etc. of gamblers (i.e. their 'gambling story') than would be possible with

quantitative data.
(d) Reith, G. and Dobbie, F. (2011). Beginning gambling: The role of social networks and environment. *Addiction Research and Theory*, 19 (6), 483-493.

Explanations for nicotine addiction: Brain neurochemistry p.202–203

One for you to try: Nicotine becomes addictive because it activates the reward pathways of the brain. When nicotine attaches to neurons in the ventral tegmental area (VTA), it triggers release of dopamine. When Paige began smoking cigarettes, this would have caused an increase of dopamine in her brain's reward system, something she would have found pleasurable. The brain gradually develops a nicotine-dependent state. This means that the smoker suffers withdrawal symptoms if they try to stop smoking. Paige finds it surprisingly hard to give up smoking when she meets Ian, suggesting that her brain is in a nicotine-dependent state and without a cigarette she experiences withdrawal symptoms.

Research methods: (a) Related *t* test. This is because researchers are testing for a difference in glutamate levels in smokers and non-smokers. As participants in the two groups were matched for age and general health, this meant that a related *t* test was more appropriate than an independent *t* test.
(b) Pearson's *r*. This is because researchers are testing for a correlation between glutamate levels and number of cigarettes smoked. The two variables (glutamate levels and number of cigarettes smoked) are measured using an interval level of measurement.
(c) This indicates that higher glutamate levels are found when a low number of cigarettes have been smoked over the previous 30 days and lower glutamate levels are found when a high number of cigarettes have been smoked.

Explanations for nicotine addiction: Learning theory p.204–205

One for you to try: There are two key answers here. Firstly, Nico associates leaving his work building with smoking (a smoking-related cue) and the rewarding effects of smoking, which therefore contributes to his urge. Furthermore, he also finds that the urges are stronger when he has a stressful day and therefore he is craving the negative reinforcement (removal of the stress) which he is used to experiencing through smoking.

Research methods: (a) They would have used a volunteer sample. A limitation of this type of sampling technique is that individuals who volunteer for research studies may be different from those who do not. For example, they may be better motivated than those who do not volunteer, and this could affect the likelihood of them responding positively to treatment.
(b) It is important because this allows a researcher's peers to consider whether the well-being of the research participants is being met and that the study conforms to the ethical guidelines set by professional bodies such as the BPS.
(c) Those participants who continued to the end of their treatment may well have been experiencing some positive effects of treatment and those who withdrew may not have experienced any positive effects of treatment. This would bias the results and make conclusions based on the remaining participants invalid.

Explanations for gambling addiction: Learning theory p.206-207

One for you to try: Pathological gamblers often report having a 'big win' early in their gambling career. They continue to gamble because of a desire to repeat that early 'peak experience' (Aasved, 2003).
When Sally plays her first Euro she immediately wins 10 Euros. She wins 20 Euros on her second play. She keeps playing, desperate to repeat the euphoria of her early wins.
With a partial reinforcement schedule, wins follow some bets, but not all. This means that gambling

behaviours are much slower to extinguish because of the uncertainty of reinforcement. This would explain why Sally continues to play (even without winning) until she las lost 100 Euros.

Research methods: (a) A case study is a detailed study of a single individual, institution or event.
(b) Strength – This method provides in-depth insights into a specific behaviour that might be overlooked by other methods. Limitation – it is difficult to generalise from specific cases to a wider population. The unique experiences of one individual may not apply to others.
(c) David's gambling behaviour was initially positively reinforced by winning money (operant conditioning), but this was eventually replaced by a classically conditioned association between gambling (NS) and the lights and sounds (UCS) that led to excitement (UCR).

Explanation for gambling addiction: Cognitive theory p.208–209

One for you to try: Matt is displaying the 'near-miss' bias. Near misses occur when an unsuccessful outcome is close to a win. Because Matt has come close to winning on a few occasions, he believes he is not losing but 'nearly winning', and this spurs him on. He is also displaying the 'gamblers' fallacy', the belief that runs of losses will be balanced out by wins. For example, he states that he is 'statistically' bound to win big soon.

Research methods: (a) Regular fruit machine gamblers show more evidence of cognitive biases when gambling than non-regular fruit machine gamblers.
(b) A quasi-experimental independent groups design is where the independent variable occurs naturally rather than being manipulated by the researcher. In this study, gamblers have already developed their patterns of gambling behaviour, rather than being randomly allocated to these different groups by the researcher.
(c) A limitation is that the design cannot control all possible differences between the two groups of gamblers. For example, the group that play fruit machines regularly may be less well-educated or more likely to be unemployed compared to the group that does not gamble regularly.
(d) Volunteers may be different in some important way compared to those who do not volunteer. As a result, a volunteer sample may not be truly representative of the target population.

Reducing addiction: Drug therapy p.210–211

One for you to try: Drug treatments such as Bupropion reduce craving for tobacco and help with withdrawal symptoms. Bupropion works by inhibiting re-uptake of the neurotransmitter dopamine. Drugs known as opioid antagonists block opioid receptors in the body,. This prevents the individual experiencing the rewarding response they associate with smoking. Nicotine replacement therapy works by gradually releasing nicotine into the bloodstream at lower levels than in a cigarette and without the harmful chemicals found in cigarette smoke. This helps the individual control their cravings for a cigarette.
Both types of treatment have been shown to be effective for smoking addiction. In a meta-analysis of 150 trials, NRT was found to be effective in helping people kick their nicotine habit, and 70% more effective than a placebo. Because opioid antagonists stop the brain from releasing dopamine, these could cause some patients to lose pleasure in other areas of life while they are on the drug.

Research methods: (a) (i) Double blind in the context of this study would mean that neither the patients or the researchers assessing them would be aware whether they had received the nicotine or the placebo.
(ii) If participants know they had received the placebo they may be more likely to report withdrawal effects. If researchers are aware of whether a participant is in the NRT or placebo group they may be more likely to judge ambiguous reports in a way that would be expected of

participants in that group.
(b) (i) Because they would not be receiving the benefits of NRT so would be less motivated to continue.
(ii) If attrition rates are higher for the placebo group compared to the NRT group, this means that the sample that is left no longer resembles the original sample. This means any results cannot be generalised back to the population from which the original sample was taken.

Reducing addiction: Behavioural interventions p.212–213

One for you to try: Aversion therapy works to eliminate an undesirable behaviour by associating it with an unpleasant sensation. Through the process of classical conditioning, Tim's gambling on horse races would be associated with an unpleasant stimulus. During aversion therapy, the individual is asked to engage in the behaviour while at the same time being exposed to something unpleasant such as a drug that makes them nauseous. Tim could be given a drug that makes him feel nauseous at the same time as being allowed to check form and place bets. Because gambling is no longer enjoyable he will avoid it in the future.

Research methods: (a) 450 (b) 13/20 (c) 67 (d) (i) 43.8 (ii) 101.26 (iii) 7.129 (e) 8.5, 8.53

Reducing addiction: Cognitive behavioural therapy p.214–215

One for you to try: Gareth may not be aware of the cognitive biases on which he bases his decisions when gambling. The therapist can educate him about biases such as the gamblers' fallacy and that gambling outcomes are determined by chance, not skill. After Gareth begins to think differently about his gambling, he can be encouraged to practise these changes in his daily life. For example, he may be asked to visit a casino and refrain from betting. He can be prevented from lapsing into gambling again by learning to identify and avoid the risky situations that might trigger feelings or thoughts that lead him to gamble again.

Research methods:

(a)
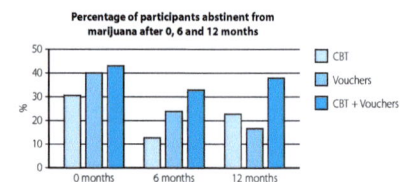

(b) At all three time points, CBT plus vouchers is more effective at ensuring abstinence from marijuana than CBT or vouchers alone. Although the use of vouchers is initially more effective than CBT at reducing marijuana use, its long-term effectiveness is less than that of CBT.
(c) It was important to randomly assign participants to different treatment groups to avoid any systematic bias. For example, without this, different types of marijuana user might have been assigned different treatment types, biasing any outcome.

The theory of planned behaviour p.216–217

One for you to try: Gamblers are more likely to hold a favourable attitude if they believe that behaviour will lead to positive outcomes. Radha could change Gareth's attitude toward gambling by showing him case studies of people who have lost their friends and families because of their gambling habit.
Subjective norms reflect what significant others feel is the right thing to do, as well as what others are actually doing. Radha could collect information about how many of his peers gamble and how they feel about gambling. She could then make Gareth aware of how negatively his peers think and feel about gambling. An individual with higher perceived behavioural control is likely to persevere for longer when trying to give up their addictive behaviour. Gareth may believe he is incapable of stopping gambling because he has failed before but Radha can focus on when he has resisted the

urge to gamble to show he does have control over his behaviour.

Research methods: (a) Publication bias refers to the tendency of journals to publish mainly those studies that have demonstrated a positive effect. This can give a biased overview of research in a particular area, by ignoring studies where no effect has been found. This also means that researchers no longer submit studies where no significant effect has been found, knowing that they will not be published (the file-drawer effect).
(b) This means that any conclusions drawn might be invalid because self-reports may not be completely accurate. For example, participants may report behaviour that they think the researcher is looking for (demand characteristics) or behaviour that they think the researcher will approve of (social desirability bias).
(c) Addiction places a significant burden on the UK economy in terms of medical treatment provided through the NHS and social security payments to people who cannot work or lose jobs as a result of their addictive behaviour. By understanding the role played by, for example, attitude and social norms, positive steps can be taken to manipulate these and reduce addictive behaviour and consequently the economic burden on the rest of society.

Prochaska's six-stage model of behaviour change p.218–219

One for you to try: (i) Respondent A: Preparation, (ii) Respondent B: Termination, (iii) Respondent C: Precontemplation, (iv) Respondent D: Action

Research methods: (a) Thematic analysis is a way of grouping qualitative responses of participants into a number of identifiable themes. A strength is its flexibility as categories don't need to be set up in advance, meaning that it can more easily discover 'unknown' themes from the data.
(b) Qualitative, because respondents' data is in terms of words that describe their current experiences in trying to give up smoking.
(c) The majority of people attending a smoking cessation clinic might be more motivated to give up smoking. As a result, this group may not be sufficiently representative of all smokers who are trying to give up the habit, which limits the validity of any conclusions drawn from this study.
(d) Confidentiality. The researcher could use participant numbers rather than names and ensure that no personal information is taken that might link an individual to their data. This data should be kept in a password protected file on a locked computer.